LYDIA AS A RHETORICAL CONSTRUCT IN ACTS

EMORY STUDIES IN EARLY CHRISTIANITY

Vernon K. Robbins, General Editor
David B. Gowler, General Editor
Bart B. Bruehler, Associate Editor
Robert H. von Thaden Jr., Associate Editor
Richard S. Ascough
Juan Hernández Jr.
Susan E. Hylen
Brigitte Kahl
Mikeal C. Parsons
Christopher C. Rowland
Russell B. Sisson
Elaine M. Wainwright

Number 18

LYDIA AS A RHETORICAL CONSTRUCT IN ACTS

Alexandra Gruca-Macaulay

SBL PRESS

SBL PRESS

Atlanta

Copyright © 2016 by SBL Press

Publication of this volume was made possible by the generous support of the Pierce Program in Religion of Oxford College of Emory University.

The editors of this volume express their sincere gratitude to David E. Orton and Deo Publishing for publication of this series 2009–2013.

All rights reserved. No part of this work may be reproduced or transmitted in any form or by any means, electronic or mechanical, including photocopying and recording, or by means of any information storage or retrieval system, except as may be expressly permitted by the 1976 Copyright Act or in writing from the publisher. Requests for permission should be addressed in writing to the Rights and Permissions Office, SBL Press, 825 Houston Mill Road, Atlanta, GA 30329 USA.

Library of Congress Cataloging-in-Publication Data

Names: Gruca-Macaulay, Alexandra, author.
Title: Lydia as a rhetorical construct in Acts / by Alexandra Gruca-Macaulay.
Description: Atlanta : SBL Press, 2016. | Series: Society of Biblical Literature Emory studies in early Christianity ; Number 18 | Includes bibliographical references and index.
Identifiers: LCCN 2016012121 (print) | LCCN 2016014138 (ebook) | ISBN 9781628371376 (pbk. : alk. paper) | ISBN 9780884141600 (hardcover : alk. paper) | ISBN 9780884141594 (e-book)
Subjects: LCSH: Bible. Acts, XVI—Socio-rhetorical criticism. | Lydia (Biblical figure)
Classification: LCC BS2625.52 .G78 2016 (print) | LCC BS2625.52 (ebook) | DDC 226.6/06—dc23
LC record available at http://lccn.loc.gov/2016012121

Cover design is an adaptation by Bernard Madden of Rick A. Robbins, Mixed Media (19" x 24" pen and ink on paper, 1981). Cover design used by permission of Deo Publishing.

Printed on acid-free paper.

CONTENTS

Acknowledgments vii
Abbreviations ix

Introduction 1

1. History of Interpretation 9
    1.1. History of Interpretation of the Lydia Passages   9
    1.2. Conclusion: History of Interpretation   30

2. Method 33
    2.1. Choice of Sociorhetorical Interpretation to Address the
          Role of Lydia in Acts 16   33
    2.2. Conclusion: Method   63

3. Inner Textual Analysis 65
    3.1. Repetitive Texture and Pattern   67
    3.2. Progressive Texture and Pattern   71
    3.3. Rhetorical Boundaries Texture and Pattern: Refined
          Delimitation   76
    3.4. Narrational and Sensory-Aesthetic Texture and Pattern   80
    3.5. Argumentative Texture   92
    3.6. Conclusion: Inner Textual Analysis   113

4. Intertextural Analysis 115
    4.1. Introduction to Intertextural Analysis   115
    4.2. Lydia: Topoi of Lydian Physiognomy   117
    4.3. Paul's Vision of the Macedonian Man: Military Topoi   162
    4.4. Social Power in Roman Philippi   179

4.5. Topoi of Prison	188
4.6. Conclusion: Intertextural Analysis	197

5. Ideological Texture...201
    5.1. Introduction to Ideological Texture   201
    5.2. The Παρακαλέω of the Macedonian Man: Blending Military Frames   211
    5.3. The Παρακαλέω of Lydia: Discerning a "Worshiper of God"   216
    5.4. The Implicit Παρακαλέω of the Slave Woman   239
    5.5. Paul's Implicit Παρακαλέω in Prison: Bringing to Right-Sightedness by Staying in Faith   247
    5.6. The Inverted Παρακαλέω of the Magistrates: Separating Apart   252
    5.7. Paul's Παρακαλέω to the Assembly at Lydia's: Mutual Recognition   259
    5.8. Conclusion: Ideological Texture   266

Conclusion 269

Bibliography..281
Ancient Sources Index..301
Modern Authors Index...313
Subject Index...317

Acknowledgments

Inside our minds, we create pictures and construct stories in order to make sense of the events, people, and places that we encounter in ancient texts. This book is about a female figure, Lydia of Thyatira, and the difference between the pictures of her that have been evoked through the history of scholarship and those that would have unfolded within the imaginations of the first audiences of Acts. I have sought to show how the Philippi episode in Acts 16 is structured rhetorically, thereby allowing us to perceive its rhetorical force.

    I could not have made my way into this new rhetorical landscape without the remarkable support of my advisor and mentor, L. Gregory Bloomquist. Greg's sharing of his unparalleled expertise in the analytics of sociorhetorical interpretation, his questions, challenges, and astute insights, provided me with the analytical mooring that pulled me back from what, on many occasions, could have been an untethered drift in a sea of research. Greg has been a gracious teacher in the truest sense of these terms, and I will always be deeply grateful for his academic acuity and generosity.

    I am thankful to Normand Bonneau and Christian Dionne, for their ongoing engagement with my project, for their encouragement not to lose sight of the forest for the trees, and for their faith that a forest ultimately would come into view. I am also appreciative of the support of many faculty at Saint Paul University and wish especially to recognize Andrea Spatafora, James Pambrun, and the late Kevin Coyle. Thank you as well to my cherished colleagues at Saint Paul; our talks and discussions were immensely helpful in bringing this project into articulate form.

    I am especially indebted to Vernon K. Robbins, the founder of sociorhetorical interpretation, for welcoming me into the Society of Biblical Literature's Rhetoric of Religious Antiquity group: a group of sociorhetorical scholars devoted to the development of their work through regular collegia meetings. Our lively discussions over the years have nurtured my understanding of sociorhetorical interpretation and opened the possibility for this current incremental contribution to its ongoing development. I am especially grateful to Vernon for bringing new questions to this project and for the benefit of his astute editorial eye in helping to bring this book to publication.

The skilled people of SBL Press have been wonderful, and I owe everyone there a debt of gratitude. This project was supported through the Social Sciences and Humanities Council of Canada, and I will always appreciate their generous support. Also, I am highly appreciative of the generous support of the Pierce Program in Religion of Oxford College of Emory University, which made possible the publication of this volume.

There are so many others who played key roles in supporting me from this project's beginning to its end, and I remember and treasure each and every kindness. Finally, I cannot find adequate words to express my gratitude for the remarkable support I received from my husband, Doug, our son, Chris, and daughter, Alanna. This book is dedicated to them.

Abbreviations

Primary Sources

1 Tars.	Dio Chrysostom, *Tarsica Prior*
3 Philip.	Demosthenes, *Philippica iii*
Acts Paul	Acts of Paul and Thecla
Ad Act.	Hugo Grotius, *Ad Acta apostolorum*
Ages.	Plutarch, *Agesilaus*; Xenophon, *Agesilaus*
Aen.	Virgil, *Aeneid*
Ag. Ap.	Josephus, *Against Apion*
Alex. fort.	Plutarch, *De Alexandri magni fortuna aut virtute*
Amic.	Cicero, *De amicitia*
Anab.	Arrian, *Anabasis*
Anon. Physiogn.	Anonymous, *De Physiognomonia Liber*
Ant.	Josephus, *Jewish Antiquities*
Arat.	Plutarch, *Aratus*
Arch.	Virtruvius, *On Architecture*
Art.	Plutarch, *Artaxerxes*
Bacch.	Euripides, *Bacchae*
Bell. civ.	Appian, *Bella civilia*
Ben.	Seneca, *De beneficiis*
Carm.	Horace, *Carmina*
Cat. Min.	Plutarch, *Cato Minor*
Cels.	Origen, *Contra Celsus*
Char.	Theophrastus, *Characters*
Contempl. Life	Philo, *On the Contemplative Life*
Cyr.	Xenophon, *Cyropaedia*
Decl.	Choricius of Gaza, *Preliminary Talks and Declamations*
Deipn.	Athenaeus, *Deipnosophists*
Dem.	Plutarch, *Demosthenes*
Demetr.	Plutarch, *Demetrius*

Embassy	Philo, *On the Embassy to Gaius*
Ep.	Seneca, *Epistulae morales*
Ep. hist. Phil.	Justinus, *Epitome historiarum Philippicarum*
Epict. diss.	Arrian, *Epicteti dissertiationes*
Epid.	Hippocrates, *Epidemics*
Epig.	Martial, *Epigrams*
Ep. Cyr.	John Chrysostom, *Epistula ad Cyriacum*
Eq.	Aristophanes, *Equites*
Eq. mag.	Xenophon, *De equitum magistro*
Exp. Ps.	John Chrysostom, *Expositiones in Psalmos*
Flaccus	Philo, *Against Flaccus*
Frag.	Various authors, *Fragmenta*
Geogr.	Strabo, *Geography*
Glor. Ath.	Plutarch, *De gloria Atheniensium*
Gorg.	Plato, *Gorgias*
Gos. Thom.	Gospel of Thomas
Hell.	Xenophon, *Hellenica*
Her. mal.	Plutarch, *De Herodoti malignitate*
Hist.	Herodotus, *Histories*; Polybius, *The Histories*
Hist. eccl.	Eusebius, *Historia ecclesiastica*
Hom. 1 Cor.	John Chrysostom, *Homiliae in epistulam i ad Corinthios*
Hom. Act.	John Chrysostom, *Homiliae in Acta apostolorum*
Hom. Matt.	John Chrysostom, *Homiliae in Matthaeum*
Il.	Homer, *Illiad*
In Act.	John Calvin, *In Acta Apostolorum*
Inst.	Quintilian, *Institutio Oratoria*
Iph. taur.	Euripides, *Iphigenia taurica*
J.W.	Josephus, *Jewish War*
Joseph	Philo, *On the Life of Joseph*
Jul.	Suetonius, *Divus Julius*
Lap.	Theophrastus, *De Lapidibus*
Leg.	Plato, *Leges*
Life	Josephus, *The Life*
Lives	Plutarch, *Parallel Lives*
Luc.	Plutarch, *Lucullus*
Mech.	Aristotle, *Mechanica*
Med.	Euripides, *Medea*
Mem.	Xenophon, *Memorabilia*

ABBREVIATIONS

Metam.	Ovid, *Metamorphoses*
Mos.	Artapanus, *Moses*; Philo, *On the Life of Moses*
Mulier. virt.	Plutarch, *Mulierum virtutes*
Nat.	Pliny the Elder, *Naturalis historia*
Nat. d.	Cicero, *De natura decorum*
Oec.	Xenophon, *Oeconomicus*
Off.	Cicero, *De officiis*
Per.	Plutarch, *Pericles*
Phoc.	Plutarch, *Phocion*
Physiogn.	Polemo, *Physiognomy*
Poet.	Aristotle, *Poetics*
Pomp.	Plutarch, *Pompeuis*
Prae. ger. rei publ.	Plutarch, *Praecepta gerendae rei publicae*
Praep. ev.	Eusebius, *Praeparatio evangelica*
Progymn.	*Progymnasmata*
Prot. Jas.	Protevangelium of James
Praed.	Augustine, *De Praedestinatione Sanctorum*
P.W.	Thucydides, *History of the Peloponnesian War*
Pyth.	Pindar, *Pythian Odes*
Quaest. rom.	Plutarch, *Questiones romanae et graecae*
Ran.	Aristophanes, *Ranae*
Reg. imp. apophth.	Plutarch, *Regum et imperatorum apophthegmata*
Rerum nat.	Lucretius, *De rerum natura*
Rhet.	Aristotle, *Rhetoric*
Sat.	Juvenal, *Satire*
Sept.	Aeschylus, *Septum contra Thebes*
Sert.	Plutarch, *Sertorius*
Sib. Or.	Sibylline Oracles
Str.	Polyaenus of Macedonia, *Strategems of War*
Strom.	Clement of Alexandria, *Stromateis*
Sync.	Aelius Theon, *On Syncrisis*
Them.	Plutarch, *Themistocles*
Top.	Cicero, *Topica*
Tox.	Lucian, *Toxaris*
Verr.	Cicero, *In Verrum*
Vit. Apoll.	Philostratus, *Vita Apollonii*
Vit. X orat.	Plutarch, *Vitae decem oratorum*

Secondary Sources

AB	Anchor Bible
AcBib	Academia Biblica
AJP	*American Journal of Philology*
AJSR	*Association for Jewish Studies Review*
AmER	*American Economic Review*
ANTC	Abingdon New Testament Commentaries
AOS	American Oriental Series
Argu	*Argumentation*
ASP	American Studies in Papyrology
BDAG	Danker, Frederick W., Walter Bauer, William F. Arndt, and F. Wilbur Gingrich. *Greek-English Lexicon of the New Testament and Other Early Christian Literature*. 3rd ed. Chicago: University of Chicago Press, 2000.
BGBE	Beiträge zur Geschichte der biblischen Exegese
BibInt	Biblical Interpretation Series
BJS	Brown Judaic Studies
BMCR	*Bryn Mawr Classical Review*
BNP	*Brill's New Pauly: Encyclopaedia of the Ancient World*. 22 vols. Edited by Hubert Cancik. Leiden: Brill, 2002–2011.
BTB	*Biblical Theology Bulletin*
BZ	*Biblische Zeitschrift*
BZNW	Beihefte zur Zeitschrift für die neutestamentliche Wissenschaft und die Kunde der älteren Kirche
CalC	Calvin's Commentaries
CCS	Cambridge Classical Studies
CibR	*Ciba Review*
CJ	*Classical Journal*
ClAnt	*Classical Antiquity*
ClQ	*Classical Quarterly*
ConBNT	Coniectanea Biblica: New Testament Series
CP	*Classical Philology*
CRS	Classics in Religious Studies
ESEC	Emory Studies in Early Christianity
Ebib	Études bibliques
EHST	Europäische Hochschulschriften. Series 23: Theologie
FC	The Fathers of the Church: A New Translation

FCNTECW	Feminist Companion to the New Testament and Early Christian Writings
frag.	fragment
HR	*History of Religions*
HSem	*Horae semiticae*
Int	*Interpretation*
JBL	*Journal of Biblical Literature*
JESHO	*Journal of the Economic and Social History of the Orient*
JNES	*Journal of Near Eastern Studies*
JSJSup	Supplements to Journal for the Study of Judaism
JSNT	*Journal for the Study of the New Testament*
JSNTSup	Journal for the Study of the New Testament Supplement Series
JSOTSup	Journal for the Study of the Old Testament Supplement Series
KJV	King James Version
Latomus	Latomus Revue d'Études Latines
LCL	Loeb Classical Library
LNTS	Library of New Testament Studies
LSJ	Liddell, Henry George, Robert Scott, and Henry Stuart Jones. *A Greek-English Lexicon*. 9th ed. with revised supplement. Oxford: Clarendon, 1996.
LXX	Septuagint
MM	Moulton, James H., and George Milligan. *The Vocabulary of the Greek Testament*. 1930. Repr. Peabody, MA: Hendrickson, 1997.
NA	*Novum Testamentum Graece*, Nestle-Aland
NewDocs	Horsley, G. H. R. *New Documents Illustrating Early Christianity*. North Ryde, NSW: The Ancient History Documentary Research Centre, Macquarie University, 1981–.
NewY	*New Yorker*
NPNF[1]	*Nicene and Post-Nicene Fathers*, Series 1
NRTh	*La Nouvelle Revue Théologique*
NTMo	New Testament Monographs
OCSJC	Oeuvres Complètes de Saint Jean Chrysostome
ODCW	*Oxford Dictionary of the Classical World*. Edited by John Roberts. Oxford Reference Online. Oxford: Oxford University Press, 2007.

OECS	Oxford Early Christian Studies
OTP	*Old Testament Pseudepigrapha*. 2 vols. Edited by James H. Charlesworth. New York: Doubleday, 1983–1985.
PG	Patrologia Graeca
Phil	*Philologus*
PhRh	*Philosophy and Rhetoric*
PRSt	*Perspectives in Religious Studies*
RGRW	Religions in the Graeco-Roman World
RhetR	*Rhetoric Review*
RRA	Rhetoric of Religious Antiquity
SAC	Studies in Antiquity and Christianity
SBL	Society of Biblical Literature
SBLDS	Society of Biblical Literature Dissertation Series
SE	Studia Evangelica
SNTSMS	Society for New Testament Studies Monograph Series
SP	Sacra Pagina
StBibLit	Studies in Biblical Literature
STDJ	Studies on the Texts of the Desert of Judah
SymS	Symposium Series
TAPA	*Transactions of the American Philological Association*
TAPS	Transactions of the American Philosophical Society
TBAW	Tübinger Beiträge Zur Altertumswissenschaft
TDNT	*Theological Dictionary of the New Testament*. 10 vols. Edited by Gerhard Kittel and Gerhard Friedrich. Translated by Geoffrey W. Bromiley. Grand Rapids: Eerdmans, 1964–1976.
Thf	*Theoforum*
TLG	*Thesaurus Linguae Graecae: Canon of Greek Authors and Works*. 3rd ed. Edited by Luci Berkowitz and Karl A. Squitier. New York: Oxford University Press, 1990.
TPAPA	*Transactions and Proceedings of the American Philological Association*
UBS	*The Greek New Testament*, United Bible Societies
VC	*Vigiliae Christianae*
WBC	Word Biblical Commentary
WGRW	Writings from the Greco-Roman World
WUNT	Wissenschaftliche Untersuchungen zum Neuen Testament

Introduction

The hostess, the purple-selling "well-to-do textile merchant," "the 'most illustrious convert of Philippi,'" and "representative of feminine propriety" has become the prevailing image of Lydia of Thyatira of Acts 16:14–15, 40, in contemporary biblical scholarship.[1] So understood, Lydia's role in the narrative of the Pauline group's visit to Philippi has almost universally been reduced to that of a supplier of material resources, a role that is either praised as a model of generous hospitality or critiqued as another example of "Luke's" having exclusively restricted the role of women to that of resource suppliers.[2] More recently, it has been suggested that Lydia's high status was deployed as a rhetorical tool by the author in order to promote an agenda of Christian propaganda.[3] Although there is nothing inherently problematic with advocating for generous giving, nor with critiques of ecclesial ideologies that restrict women from developing the fullness of their competency, nor again with colonizing agendas, anchoring these interpretations in scholarship's image of Lydia takes up a profile formed by

---

1. Wayne A. Meeks, "The Image of the Androgyne: Some Uses of a Symbol in Earliest Christianity," HR 13 (1974): 198; David Lertis Matson, *Household Conversion Narratives in Acts: Pattern and Interpretation*, JSNTSup 123 (Sheffield: Sheffield Academic, 1996), 136; quoting Robert T. O'Toole, *The Unity of Luke's Theology: An Analysis of Luke-Acts* (Wilmington, DE: Glazier, 1984), 124; Jeffrey L. Staley, "Changing Woman: Toward a Postcolonial Postfeminist Interpretation of Acts 16:6–40," in *A Feminist Companion to the Acts of the Apostles*, ed. Amy-Jill Levine and Marianne Blickenstaff, FCNTECW 9 (Cleveland: Pilgrim, 2004), 186.

2. Halvor Moxnes, "Patron-Client Relations and the New Community in Luke-Acts," in *The Social World of Luke-Acts: Models for Interpretation*, ed. Jerome H. Neyrey (Peabody, MA: Hendrickson, 1991), 241–68; Gail R. O'Day, "Acts," in *Women's Bible Commentary*, ed. Carol A. Newsom and Sharon H. Ringe, 2nd ed. (Louisville: Westminster John Knox, 1998), 394–402.

3. Shelly Matthews, *First Converts: Rich Pagan Women and the Rhetoric of Mission in Early Judaism and Christianity*, Contraversions: Jews and Other Differences (Stanford, CA: Stanford University Press, 2001).

the history of interpretation rather than reflecting the implications of an image that would have been seen in the minds of first-century Mediterranean audiences.

Just as significantly, the contemporary image of Lydia seems to leave scholarship at a loss as to why the author would have introduced this figure into the narrative of Philippi in the first place. The following quote aptly sums up the current state of scholarship on Lydia:

> The story of the conversion of Lydia and her household is a brief story (primarily vv. 13–15) that has not attracted much scholarly attention. It is hard to find any remarks in the literature of scholarship concerning the function of this story in Luke-Acts. Even Haenchen fails to comment on what Luke was trying to do with this story.[4]

The presentation of Lydia in Acts 16 does not seem to contribute much to the overall development of the Philippi episode. For example, Richard Hillier observed the curiosity that Arator, an early commentator on Acts, omitted any mention of Lydia's baptism, this despite his interest in baptisms in Acts. Offering a rationale as to why that may have been the case, Hillier suggests:

> His reasons for doing so can only be surmised. Lydia occurs only briefly in the narrative of Acts and is of little interest for Arator: she is not of the significance of, say, Cornelius, nor does her name provide him with an excuse for a digression in which to exercise his ingenuity.[5]

In turn, a narrative-critical approach, which is especially attuned to the flow of narrative unity, hits an obstacle when it attempts to ascribe purpose to Lydia's role in the overall structure of the narrative. Literary

---

4. Robert Allen Black, "The Conversion Stories in the Acts of the Apostles: A Study of Their Forms and Functions" (PhD diss., Emory University, Atlanta, 1985), 166–67; Matson, *Household Conversion*, 136, 149. Black's suggestions regarding the function of Lydia are twofold: "The story of Lydia's conversion functions primarily as the story of the first convert in Macedonia. It marks the beginning of an important new geographical step in the Christian mission"; and, "Another function of Lydia's story is to give an example of the conversion of a woman of some standing" (Black, "Conversion Stories," 169). For Matson's suggestions see §1.2. More recently, a monograph dedicated to Lydia has been published by Richard Ascough, see §1.1.5.

5. Richard Hillier, *Arator on the Acts of the Apostles: A Baptismal Commentary*, OECS (Oxford: Clarendon, 1993), 23.

critic Luke Timothy Johnson writes: "The entire episode with Lydia and the women can be seen as a narrative interlude."[6] Yet while biblical narrative might contain rhetorical digressions that contribute to a text's rhetorical impact, it is difficult to find occasions of narrative "pauses" as intended by Johnson.[7] Rather, biblical prose is marked by its economy of narration to such an extent that literary theories have been constructed around it.[8] Although the Lydia passages may indeed function as a pause between narrative events, the uncommon nature of such a biblical literary structure invites us to consider other possibilities. Two important clues that help to point the direction to further investigation are offered by Robert Tannehill's analysis of the narrative structure of Acts. Tannehill observes, first, that the "references to Lydia and her household form a frame around the rest of the episode," and second, that Lydia forms a literary bridge between the place-of-prayer context that introduces her and the ensuing reference to a place of prayer that introduces the slave woman with the Python spirit.[9] These two narrative structural attributes, framing and bridging, invite us to explore further the possible interplay between the Lydia passages and the broader Philippian episode. Yet the lack of a defined causal connection between the episode introducing Lydia and that of the slave woman has limited the ability of a narrative-literary approach to suggest how the two bridged episodes might be linked within the narrative's logical structure. Such unanswered questions call for an approach that can bring new questions to the role played by the figure of Lydia in the narrative.

A plotline-based literary-historical approach to the text has not yielded much insight into what the author of Acts may have intended to bring to the narrative by introducing Lydia and portraying her as a Lydian purple-seller. Yet, as Tannehill's insights suggest, even the surface-level structure of the text signals that the author did have something in mind. A first step leading toward a possible new direction of inquiry involves taking the

---

6. Luke Timothy Johnson, *The Acts of the Apostles*, SP 5 (Collegeville, MN: Liturgical Press, 1992), 293.

7. For the rhetorical role of digressions, see Peter S. Perry, *The Rhetoric of Digressions: Revelation 7:1–17 and 10:1–11:13 and Ancient Communication* (Tübingen: Mohr Siebeck, 2009).

8. E.g., Erich Auerbach, *Mimesis: The Representation of Reality in Western Literature*, trans. Willard R. Trask (Princeton: Princeton University Press, 1968).

9. Robert C. Tannehill, *The Acts of the Apostles*, vol. 2 of *The Narrative Unity of Luke-Acts: A Literary Interpretation* (Minneapolis: Fortress, 1990), 196–97.

author's communicative culture into consideration. For texts written in a rhetorical communicative milieu, as was Acts, rhetorical structure was an important component in meaning-making. When, in his now legendary presidential address, James Muilenburg called the academy to rhetorical criticism, he stressed that

> a major concern of the rhetorical critic is to recognize the structure of a composition and to discern the configuration of its component parts, to delineate the warp and woof out of which the literary fabric is woven.[10]

In the case of Lydia, it is highly significant that, as Tannehill observed, the Philippi visit both opens and closes with Lydia (Acts 16:14–15, 40). Moreover, the opening and closing "Lydia passages" share common lexica with each other as well as other passages in the Philippi episode.[11] In other words, the Lydia verses point to an *inclusio* at work, a framing device that does not simply delimit boundaries but also imbues meaning to the discourse found within its limits.[12] We would expect, therefore, the frame to be somehow in dialogue with the narrative situated within.

While the enigmatic role of the Lydia passages presents an interesting interpretive puzzle, given Lydia's prominent opening positioning within a narrative context of high anticipation ("immediately we sought to go on into Macedonia, concluding that God had called us," Acts 16:10), the question of the function of these passages has possible ideological implications as well. The Pauline group's crossing to Macedonia has typically been understood as the launch of a new phase of the Pauline mission. Moreover, this new initiative is understood by the disciples as a response to a divine commission. If the encounter with Lydia is a point of departure for this apparently divinely sanctioned new phase of the Pauline mission, then the function of the Lydia passages warrants a closer investigation in order to more fully discern the ideological perspective represented by the Philippi episode.

Although ideological implications for the passages have been suggested, such as that Lydia "the illustrious first convert on European soil"

---

10. James Muilenburg, "Form Criticism and Beyond," *JBL* 88 (1969): 10 (the presidential address delivered at the Annual Meeting of the Society of Biblical Literature on 18 December 1968, at the University of California, Berkeley).

11. See "Progressive Texture and Pattern," §3.2 below.

12. For *inclusio*, see Muilenburg, "Form Criticism and Beyond," 9–10.

evidences the triumphant spread of Christianity or that Lydia functions apologetically to demonstrate the superiority of the Pauline religion[13] and/or that through her presumed status, she helps to raise the public perception of the mission, the ideological perspective that might result from the interplay of Acts 16:14–15, 40, and the surrounding text has rarely been investigated. The few attempts at connecting Lydia with the events that follow continue to be constrained by the influence of prior constructions of the personage of Lydia.[14] As a result of the pervasive influence of the history of interpretation on Lydia's portrayal, such attempts at joining the Lydia passages to the broader narrative are built on data that limit our ability to discern the rhetorically active points of connection between Lydia and other key elements of the Philippi visit and the rhetorical fabric of Luke-Acts generally.

As a rhetorical figure, Lydia would both influence and be influenced by the ideology of the surrounding text of Acts 16, as well as the approach throughout Luke-Acts to people who are somehow like Lydia. In order to explore the rhetorical function of Lydia in the narrative, this investigation seeks to expand the data field and to ask questions of the Lydia passages that engage fully with the complex network of topoi evoked by Lydia. Sociorhetorical interpretation (SRI) is ideally suited to this task: it programmatically explores the rhetorical movement of a text informed by social, cultural, economic, religious, political, and literary elements that shape and configure this movement. As a result of SRI's focus on the multitextured nature of a text's rhetorical discourse, the questions brought to the Lydia passages can be expanded to explore the rhetorical function of Lydia within the context of Acts 16:9–40 specifically and Luke-Acts generally.[15]

As I entered this project with special interests in the interpretive-analytical strategies of SRI, I found myself drawn to Lydia "the businesswoman." She seemed to call to me from the pages of Acts, a kindred sister through occupational affinity, although removed through time and space.

---

13. Dennis R. MacDonald, "Lydia and Her Sisters as Lukan Fictions," in Levine and Blickenstaff, *Feminist Companion to the Acts of the Apostles*, 105–10.

14. For example, Staley, "Changing Woman," is able to reanimate the dynamic between Lydia and the slave woman only through recourse to contemporary literature, despite astutely recognizing that Philippi functions as some form of "borderland."

15. For the unit's delimitation, see "Rhetorical Boundaries Texture and Pattern," §3.3 below.

I read voraciously on the topic of Greco-Roman voluntary associations and *collegia*, on theories of ancient economic trade, and on the purple-dyeing guilds of Thyatira. Armed with knowledge of ancient economics, I presented my first paper on the role of Lydia at a conference on rhetorics at the University of Redlands, California, chaired by James D. Hester and J. David Hester.[16] The polite verdict: at best a marginally interesting sociohistorical investigation but without any rhetorical-critically derived insight. I had not yet managed to discover the entryway into a rhetorical analysis of the role of Lydia.

My early inability to move from the sociohistorical into the rhetorical stemmed from two main impediments: I was insufficiently self-aware of the way in which the history of interpretation of Lydia was guiding my choice and perception of the elements associated with her, and I had not come to appreciate that topoi are formed dynamically and, moreover, that it is this very *dynamis* of their formation that animates the rhetorics of a passage. I was confident of, however, that Lydia's prominence in the opening and closure of the Philippi narrative was strategically intentional, as was the symbolism of her name.

An entryway into the Lydia puzzle came to me one day from Professor L. Gregory Bloomquist, who is at the forefront of sociorhetorical interpretation's understanding of the key function of the topos in rhetoric. Responding to my frustration over the enigma of Lydia's name, he suggested I look to see what *Der Neue Pauly* had to say about Lydian ethnography. There it was: within a distinguished tome of German historical scholarship lay the doorway to Lydia's rhetorically constructed Lydian profile, waiting for a sociorhetorical-sensitive lens to perceive its import.[17] Throughout this project, a postcard of the University of Redlands pinned up in front of my computer monitor has reminded me to keep to the task of rhetorical criticism. More specifically, as a sociorhetorical critic, I have had to examine my own presumptions and ideological perspective in order to become aware of my relation to the history of interpretation.[18] It has

---

16. Alexandra Gruca-Macaulay, "Disrupting the *Polis*: Greco-Roman Voluntary Associations and the Conversion of Lydia of Thyatira in Acts 16:14–15, 40" (paper presented at Rhetorics of Social Formation conference, University of Redlands, CA, 20 January 2007).

17. Hans Kaletsch, "Lydia," *BNP*.

18. "Socio-rhetorical criticism calls for interpretive practices that include minute attention to the ideologies that guide interpreters' selection, analysis and interpreta-

been a transformative experience in ways that I could not have foreseen in those early days of searching for "Lydia the businesswoman."

While it may seem that the prevailing image of Lydia has always been with us, in chapter 1 ("History of Interpretation"), we will watch this image take shape through the history of scholarship as influential commentators gradually introduced and blended new topoi into Lydia's portrayal. Curiously, from the fourth century to the twentieth, we also will see one topos, that of the "courtesan," resurface time and again in comments on Lydia only to be swiftly subsumed by an image of noble Lydia. After observing the milestones of Lydia's image making, I move in chapter 2 ("Method") to my choice of analytics, sociorhetorical interpretation, and explain how this systematic topos-based approach will help us to uncover the image of Lydia situated in first-century antiquity and the role she performs in the rhetorical development of the passage. In this chapter, I also discuss how Greco-Roman physiognomy, the cultural-social logic of stereotypes and conventions, is crucial to uncovering the topoi that shaped the personage of Lydia.

In chapter 3 ("Inner Textural Analysis"), I seek to remove the prevailing assumptions about the meaning of Acts 16 and take a fresh look at the inner lexical, argumentative, narrational, and sensory-aesthetic dynamics of the text. Then, in chapter 4 ("Intertextural Analysis"), I will examine the historical, cultural, social, economic, and religious constituents of the narrative's key topoi that were used rhetorically by Luke. In chapter 5 ("Ideological Texture"), I will link my findings of inner textural analysis with the, by now, culturally contextualized topoi discussed in intertextural analysis to suggest how Luke developed the rhetorical movement of this passage and how this movement fits within Luke-Acts. I will conclude in chapter 6 with observations on the rhetorical force of Lydia's portrayal in Acts 16, as well as implications of my analysis for the future study of Luke-Acts.

---

tion of data" (Vernon K. Robbins, *The Tapestry of Early Christian Discourse: Rhetoric, Society and Ideology* [New York: Routledge, 1996], 201; see Robbins, *Exploring the Texture of Texts: A Guide to Socio-rhetorical Interpretation* [Valley Forge, PA: Trinity Press International, 1996], 4).

1
History of Interpretation

1.1. History of Interpretation of the Lydia Passages

Today's image of Lydia as a pious, resource-sharing, wealthy patroness of the Pauline mission is so ubiquitous that it might seem that even the earliest audiences would have pictured "Lydia the hostess" when hearing the text of Acts 16.[1] Yet, a survey of the history of interpretation will evidence signs that key elements of Lydia's profile have been suppressed in subsequent commentary, while at the same time others have been reconfigured. This book will argue that such shifts in Lydia's portrayal gradually reshaped the first-century profile of Lydia of Acts 16 to the point that the Lydia of the history of interpretation clashes dramatically with the personage who would have naturally been prompted in the minds of Acts' first audiences.[2] Support for this claim will unfold principally through the

---

1. The focus of this book is on investigating how the rhetorical role of Lydia of Thyatira contributes to the overall development of the message of the rhetorical unit, Acts 16:9–40 (for the rhetorical unit's boundaries, see §3.3 below), and therefore the concern of this chapter is with the history of interpretation of the figure of Lydia. For the history of interpretation of episodes that fall outside of the Lydia passages but that are within the rhetorical unit, the reader is directed to John B. Faulkenberry Miller, *Convinced That God Had Called Us: Dreams, Visions and the Perception of God's Will in Luke-Acts*, BibInt 85 (Leiden: Brill, 2007), 65–90, for a survey of criticism of Paul's dream-vision at Troas; William Sanger Campbell, *The "We" Passages in the Acts of the Apostles: The Narrator as Narrative Character*, StBibLit 14 (Atlanta: Society of Biblical Literature, 2007), 1–12, regarding the shift of narrative voice to first-person plural in Acts 16:10; and to John B. Weaver, *Plots of Epiphany: Prison-Escape in Acts of the Apostles*, BZNW 131 (New York: de Gruyter, 2004), 11–22, for scholarship's approaches to Paul and Silas's "prison escape."

2. Initial arguments for the "reimaging" function of the history of interpretation were presented in Alexandra Gruca-Macaulay, "Reading 'Lydia' in Acts 16: A Figure

ensuing intertextural and ideological phases of analysis. First, a number of representative works will be surveyed in order to highlight how the history of interpretation produced the template for today's discussions of Lydia.

1.1.1. Patristic

As Ward Gasque observed in his survey of the history of interpretation of Acts, "very little information has come down to us concerning the study of the Book of Acts during the fifteen centuries prior to the reformation."[3] Even less did early commentators show interest in Lydia. However, during this period five commentaries on Acts signaled the possibility of an underlying issue with Lydia and the women by the river.

In the late fourth century, John Chrysostom's portrayal of Lydia launched a key trajectory of interpretation. In only one work does Chrysostom call Lydia by her name; in nine others he refers instead to a "purple-seller" or "purple-selling woman."[4] Chrysostom casts the "purple-seller" as a "lowly" or "humble" woman on account of her profession who, despite her lowly occupation, displays an inner nature that is "philosophic" and full of "wisdom":

---

in Rhetoric or a Rhetorical Figure?" (paper presented at the Annual Meeting of the Society of Biblical Literature, San Diego, CA, 21 November 2007).

3. W. Ward Gasque, *A History of the Interpretation of the Acts of the Apostles* (Tübingen: Mohr Siebeck, 1975; repr., Eugene, OR: Wipf & Stock, 2000), 7.

4. Chrysostom refers to Lydia by name in *Hom. Act.* 36 (twice in reference to her house, i.e., "house of Lydia"). Chrysostom refers to the "purple-seller," "purple-selling woman," "seller of purple" in *Hom. Act.* 35, 36 (Bareille); *Ep. Cyr.* 125; *Hom. 1 Cor.* 15, 14 (Bareille); *Hom. Matt.* 73; *Ex. Ps.* 113 (Bareille); *Homiliae in epistulam ad Philippenses*. *Epistulae ad Olympiadem* uses the plural "female sellers of purple." Augustine (354–430 CE) also referred to Lydia only as "that seller of purple" in his argument on predestination. He wrote: "This gift of heavenly grace had descended to that seller of purple for whom, as Scripture says in the Acts of the Apostles, 'The Lord opened her heart, and she gave heed [*intendebat*] unto the things which were said by Paul; for she was so called that she might believe. Because God does what He will in the hearts of men, either by assistance or by judgment; so that, even through their means may be fulfilled what His hand and counsel have predestined to be done" (*Praed.* 41 [Holmes and Wallis]). Augustine's characterization of Lydia's heart as a passive receptor both of divine intervention and Paul's teaching will be further developed under Hugo Grotius, as discussed below.

Look again at the lack of arrogance [of the Pauline group]. A lowly/humble woman, as is evident from her trade/craft, but look at the philosophic [heart] of her [ὅρα τὸ φιλόσοφον αὐτῆς].... Furthermore, look at her insight, how she importunes/shames the apostles, how full of humility her phrase [Acts 16:15b] is, how full of wisdom. (*Hom. Act.* 35 [*NPNF*[1] 11:219, modified])[5]

Chrysostom elaborates on the specific quality of this "philosophic" inner heart:

And in the apostles' time also both men and women were together. Because the men were men, and the women women, but now altogether the contrary; the women have urged themselves into the habits of courtesans, but the men are in no better state than frantic horses. Had you not heard, that the men and women were gathered together in the upper room, and that congregation was worthy of the heavens? And very reasonably. For then women were philosophically [φιλοσοφίαν ἤσκουν] formed, and the men in dignity and moderation [σεμνότητα καὶ σωφροσύνην]. Hear, for instance, the seller of purple saying, "If you have judged me worthy of the Lord, come in, and abide with me." (*Hom. Matt.* 73 [*NPNF*[1] 10:443, modified])[6]

In the homily, Chrysostom raises the topos of courtesans and presents Lydia as its paradigmatic antithesis. Chrysostom argues that while women of the apostolic age practiced φιλοσοφία—when "men were men and women were women"—in contrast, the degenerate women of Chrysostom's time have abandoned themselves to the customs of courtesans, and the men have assumed the nature of wild beasts. In this argument, the feminine nature of φιλοσοφία stands in direct opposition to the practices of

---

5. Ὅρα τὸ ἄτυφον πάλιν. Γυνὴ καὶ ταπεινὴ αὕτη, καὶ δῆλον ἀπὸ τῆς τέχνης· ἀλλ' ὅρα τὸ φιλόσοφον αὐτῆς ... εἶτα βλέτε σύνεσιν, πῶς δυσωπεῖ τοὺς ἀποστόλος, πόσης ταπεινότητος γέμει τὰ ῥήματα, πόσης σοφίας. Unless otherwise indicated, all translations of ancient sources are my own.

6. Καὶ ἐπὶ τῶν ἀποστόλων δὲ ὁμοῦ καὶ ἄνδρες καὶ γυναῖκες ἦσαν. Καὶ γὰρ οἱ ἄνδρες, ἄνδρες ἦσαν, καὶ αἱ γυναῖκες, γυναῖκες· νῦν δὲ πᾶν τοὐναντίον, αἱ μὲν γυναῖκες εἰς τὰ τῶν ἑταιρίδων ἑαυτὰς ἐξώθησαν ἤθη· οἱ δὲ ἄνδρες ἵππων μαινομένων οὐδὲν ἄμεινον διάκεινται. Οὐκ ἠκούσατε, ὅτι ἦσαν συνηγμένοι ἄνδρες καὶ γυναῖκες ἐν τῷ ὑπερῴῳ, καὶ τῶν οὐρανῶν ἐκεῖνος ὁ σύλλογος ἄξιος ἦν; Καὶ μάλα εἰκότως. Πολλὴν γὰρ καὶ γυναῖκες τότε φιλοσοφίαν ἤσκουν, καὶ ἄνδρες σεμνότητα καὶ σωφροσύνην. Ἀκούσατε γοῦν τῆς πορφυροπώλιδος λεγούσης· Εἰ κεκρίκατέ με ἀξίαν τῷ Κυρίῳ, εἰσελθόντες μείνατε παρ' ἐμοί.

courtesans and, accordingly, infers socially normative feminine modesty and moral rectitude.[7] Lydia's words demonstrate her "philosophic" attribute: chaste modesty.

In this way, Chrysostom presents the "modest purple-seller" as a biblical example of feminine propriety. Although Lydia may be a purple-seller and therefore is "lowly" in terms of status, she is not base in terms of moral character. After Chrysostom's treatment, the audience is assured that if the Pauline disciples were to stay in the home of a female purple-seller, a home without evident male presence, it would be a proper and modest home, headed by a humble and virtuous woman.

In addition to shaping the "purple-seller" into a model of feminine virtue, Chrysostom also introduced another element that has endured in interpretations of Lydia: resource sharing suggested by an offer of hospitality. Chrysostom writes:

> And throughout the world all houses were open to them [the disciples], and they who offered them took coming as a favour, and they came to them as to friends and kindred. For so they came to the woman who was a seller of purple [πορφυροπώλιδα], and she, like a handmaid, set before them what she had. And to the keeper of the prison; and he opened to them all his house. (*Hom. 1 Cor.* 15.14 [Parker])[8]

Despite the fact that the text of Acts is silent on Lydia having set anything before the disciples, Chrysostom groups the jailer's meal sharing with Lydia's offer. Inferentially, Lydia becomes a modest meal provider under Chrysostom's hand. Explicitly, in *Hom. Act.* 36, Chrysostom refers to Lydia as a "hostess" (ξενοδόχον), launching the prevailing trajectory of interpretation of Lydia.

In contrast, three pre-Reformation commentaries on Acts—Ephrem (306–373 CE), Arator (sixth century CE), and Bede (672/673–735 CE)—simply bypass Lydia and move directly from Paul's vision of the Mace-

---

7. To illustrate the modesty of the women of days gone by, Chrysostom cites the words of "the purple-seller" of Acts 16:15 and modifies them by replacing πιστός with ἄξιος so that "if you have judged me faithful/loyal, to the Lord" is reconfigured into the social language of honor/shame: "if you have judged me worthy of the Lord."

8. Καὶ γὰρ αἱ κατὰ τὴν οἰκουμένην αὐτοῖς οἰκίαι ἦσαν ἀνεῳγμέναι πᾶσαι, καὶ χάριν εἶχον οἱ παρέχοντες, καὶ ὡς πρὸς φίλους καὶ συγγενεῖς ἤρχοντο. Καὶ γὰρ πρὸς τὴν πορφυροπώλιδα ἦλθον, καὶ ἐκείνη καθάπερ θεραπαινὶς τὰ ἑαυτῆς προῦθηκε· καὶ πρὸς τὸν δεσμοφύλακα, κἀκεῖνος τὴν οἰκίαν αὐτοῖς ἀνέῳξεν ἅπασαν.

donian man to Paul's encounter with the slave woman with the Python spirit; in addition, Isho'dad of Merv (ca. 850 CE) skips from Timothy's circumcision to the slave woman, omitting the Macedonian man as well as Lydia.[9] Although it is certainly possible to adduce from these omissions that the writers simply found Lydia inconsequential to their discussion, Arator and Bede do comment obliquely within the very sections where discussion about Lydia would rightfully be located. The nature of these comments, discussed in ideological texture, point to the presence of an issue far greater than the omissions might first indicate.[10]

1.1.2. Reformation

When we turn to the material on Acts from the Reformation, we find that Chrysostom's characterization of Lydia's feminine modesty begins to take on a more targeted profile of feminine Jewish religious piety. Also, Lydia's occupation, which under Chrysostom simply suggested "humble modesty," becomes a growing point of interest. In addition, the Reformation commentators show an increasing focus on Lydia's place of origin, her name, and the possible connection between these.

For example, John Calvin's commentary on Acts (1554 CE) introduced two elements related to Lydia: reference to the women by the river as a Jewish ritual gathering and situating the geographic location of her city of origin, Thyatira, within Lydia. In addition, much of Calvin's remarks related to the role played by Lydia's heart in the narrative, an aspect of Lydia's portrayal that has all but disappeared from subsequent discussion, yet one that further analysis will show is key to the rhetorical development of the text.

Calvin suggested that the mention of the Sabbath suggests that "Luke is speaking about Jews" and moreover that, since the author "commends

---

9. For these lacunae, see Ephrem, "The Commentary of Ephrem on Acts," trans. Frederick C. Conybeare, in *The Text of Acts*, ed. James Hardy Ropes, vol. 3 of *The Acts of the Apostles*, part 1 of *The Beginnings of Christianity*, ed. F. J. Foakes Jackson and Kirsopp Lake (London: Macmillan, 1926), 429–31; Arator, *Arator's On the Acts of the Apostles (De Actibus Apostolorum)*, ed. Richard J. Schrader, trans. Joseph L. Roberts and John F. Makowski, CRS 6 (Atlanta: Scholars Press, 1987), 68–70; Bede, *The Venerable Bede: Commentary on the Acts of the Apostles*, trans. and ed. Lawrence T. Martin, Cistercian Studies (Kalamazoo, MI: Cistercian, 1989), 136; Isho'dad of Merv, *The Commentaries of Isho'dad of Merv, Bishop of Hadatha (c. 850 A.D.) in Syriac and English*, trans. Margaret Dunlop Gibson, HSem 10 (Cambridge: Cambridge University Press, 1913), 4:26.

10. For Arator's and Venerable Bede's comments, see §5.3.1 below.

the piety of Lydia, she must have been a Jewess" (John Calvin, *In Act.* 16.13 [Fraser, CalC]). Furthermore, Calvin conforms the text's presentation of a gathering of women into a more conventional synagogue configuration by assuming the presence of men:

> Since it is likely to me that prayer was shared by men and women in that place, I think that Luke made no mention of men, because either they were unwilling to listen, or they got no benefit out of what they heard. (*In Act.* 16.13 [Fraser, CalC])

Whereas John Chrysostom had referred to Lydia through her occupational epithet, Calvin does not refer to her purple-selling at all and shows no compunction about using the name Lydia. In his remarks on Acts 16:14, he points out a key detail—"Geographers teach that *Thyatira* is a city of Lydia"—but makes no comment on the correlation between Lydia's name and ethnic origin. Instead, much of Calvin's discussion deals with the role played by Lydia's heart:

> By the word *heart* Scripture sometimes means the mind, as when Moses says (Deut. 29.4), "until now the Lord has not given you a heart to understand." So also in this verse Luke means not only that Lydia was moved by the inspiration of the Holy Spirit to embrace the Gospel with a feeling of the heart, but that her mind was illuminated to understand.... If the mind of Lydia had not been opened, the preaching of Paul would have been mere words (*literalis*); yet God inspires her not only with mere revelations but with reverence for His Word, so that the voice of a man, which otherwise would have vanished into thin air, penetrates a mind that has received the gift of heavenly light (*In Act.*16.15 [Fraser, CalC]; brackets and emphasis original)

Introduced as a pious Jewish woman, Lydia is also profiled by Calvin as someone who has been endowed with a capacity that allows her to engage cognitively with Paul's teaching. While the Jewish element will be retained in later commentary, the presentation of Lydia as one who receives the intellectual capacity to comprehend Paul's teaching on a par with the most perspicacious disciples will all but disappear.

In his influential 1644 commentary on Acts, Hugo Grotius made abundant use of patristic sources, including the works of Chrysostom.[11]

---

11. Henning Graf Reventlow, "Humanistic Exegesis: The Famous Hugo Grotius,"

According to Henning Graf Reventlow, Grotius was fully versed in Greek and Latin literature and considered one of his most important tasks "to be the explanation of the historical background of [biblical] names and events that are mentioned," using a wide range of Greek and Latin sources, including Herodotus.[12] Whereas Chrysostom avoided using the name Lydia, Grotius, in his commentary on Acts 16:14, made explicit the link already suggested by Calvin's comment on Thyatira's Lydian location:

> *named Lydia*. It is said that the name is derived from her birth place [*Ita dicta à solo natali*]: for Thyatira is in Lydia wrote Stephanus. The women of Lydia were noble by the weaving of garments. (Hugo Grotius, *Ad Act*.16.14)[13]

The added gloss—"the women of Lydia were noble by the weaving of garments"—introduced an unstated premise that Lydia, the Lydian woman, was a noble weaver. Although weaving was indisputably a common female domestic pursuit, Acts itself does not characterize Lydia in terms of weaving or indeed any form of textile production. In fact, as we shall see, the uncommon designation πορφυρόπωλις squarely situates her in the realm of sellers and the marketplace, rather than the looms of domestic space. Moreover, there is no literary evidence of any kind to support a portrayal of Lydian women as illustrious weavers.[14] Nonetheless, Grotius's is an enduring image: in 1992 Ivoni Richter Reimer claimed that Lydian women were "celebrated in poetry for their textile work and dyeing."[15] The three cited supporting sources are less than definitive: (1) Homer's *Iliad* (4.141) has ivory cheek-pieces for horses dyed scarlet by Lydian women; (2) Clau-

---

in *Creative Biblical Exegesis: Christian and Jewish Hermeneutics through the Centuries*, ed. Henning Graf Reventlow and Benjamin Uffenheimer, JSOTSup 59 (Sheffield: JSOT Press, 1988), 176.

12. Ibid., 179–81.

13. Hugo Grotius, "*Ad Acta Apostolorum*," in *Hugo Grotius Opera Omnia Theologica: Faksimile-Neudruck der Ausgabe Amsterdam 1679* (1679; repr., Stuttgart-Bad Cannstatt: Frommann, 1972), 579–668.

14. There is some ancient support for presenting the people of Lydia as dyers but not for depicting Lydian women as noble weavers, Pliny writes: "The Egyptians invented weaving; the Lydians of Sardis the art of dyeing wool" (*Nat.* 7.57 [Rackham et al., LCL]).

15. Ivoni Richter Reimer, *Women in the Acts of the Apostles: A Feminist Liberation Perspective*, trans. Linda M. Maloney (Minneapolis: Fortress, 1992), 139 n. 161.

dian's *Rape of Proserpine* (1.275) again refers to the ivory-dyeing Lydian women; and (3) Valerius Flaccus's sexually suggestive reference in the *Argonautica* (4.369) to a "Lydian bride who bespeckles her 'web' or 'warp' [*tela*] with flecks of purple."

Grotius's conjecture is, however, not surprising. In the seventeenth century, the prevailing image of the ideal woman was deeply rooted in the trope of the ideal wife of Prov 31, who "puts her hands to the distaff and ... spindle" (31:19). Indeed, the essence of feminine high moral character, which since classical times had been located metaphorically in the distaff and spindle, by the Renaissance had developed into a commonplace, prolifically recurring in the literature and personal correspondence of the day. Not only was the "distaff and spindle or needle" an emblem of feminine virtuosity, but also, importantly, this trope was particularly incompatible with typical symbols of masculine intellectual pursuits. When Dutch scholar Anna Maria van Schurman argued for access to education for women in a letter written to André Rivet, coincidentally, also a correspondent of Hugo Grotius's, she decried the view that "pulling the needle and distaff is an ample enough school for women."[16] The Jesuit Pierre Le Moyne argued that women are indeed capable of "true philosophy," as long as they do not convert their "needles and distaffs" into "astrolabes and spheres," that is, the tools of navigators, geographers, and astronomers. Rather, female minds are illuminated with the philosophy of "decency in manners" and "stability in life."[17]

By recasting Lydia as a woman of the loom, Grotius also recharted Calvin's suggestion that the opening of Lydia's heart involved her cognitive faculties as active participants in a divine-human collaboration:

> "The Lord opened her heart": "'God opened,' by her permitting to be opened, but not by an opening in her own way, as it appears in Rev. 3.20. So, 'to be drawn' is said of one who willingly follows the drawer. So 'to be given' of what is received." (Hugo Grotius, *Ad Act.* 16.15)[18]

---

16. Anna Maria van Schurman, *Whether a Christian Woman Should Be Educated and Other Writings from Her Intellectual Circle*, ed. and trans. Joyce L. Irwin, The Other Voice in Early Modern Europe (Chicago: University of Chicago Press, 1998), 43–44.

17. Pierre Le Moyne, *The Gallery of Heroick Women*, trans. John Paulet Winchester (London: R. Norton for Henry Seile, 1652), 73–77.

18. Translation courtesy of L. Gregory Bloomquist.

1. HISTORY OF INTERPRETATION

The Lord's opening of Lydia's heart in Acts 16 is thus contextualized by Grotius as Lydia's suppliant willingness "to be drawn by God so that she might receive what is given." Following Grotius, moderns were left with a Lydian woman as a gender-appropriate, virtuous, passive receptor of Paul's teaching. Lydia was framed by an entire network of images connected to seventeenth-century notions of femininity. Chrysostom had begun with presenting a "purple-seller" as a model of feminine modesty; Grotius completed the picture by drawing this modesty into an ethnographic profile of Lydia as a seventeenth-century weaver.

1.1.3. Modern Historical-Critical

With Heinrich Meyer's commentary on Acts (1835), we move to modern commentary.[19] During this period, Lydia's occupation will become increasingly linked with epigraphic evidence of Thyatiran dyers. At the same time, Lydia's elevated moral profile will develop into socioeconomic high status.

Chrysostom's and Grotius's characterizations of Lydia's feminine virtue remained operative in Meyer's account, but with the advent of the historical-critical lens of his time, Meyer implicitly reshaped Lydia's occupation by overmapping it with archaeological data related to a different purple-related profession. Whereas Grotius linked Thyatira both with Lydia's name and with weaving in general, Meyer attempted to divorce the name from its corresponding Lydian location and instead shifted the focus to Thyatira as a center of cloth dyeing, thereby converting Lydia's occupation of "purple-seller" into "dyer":

> Πορφυρόπωλις: ἡ τὰ πορφυρά, fabrics and clothes dyed purple, πωλοῦσα. The dyeing of purple was actively carried on, especially in Lydia, to which *Thyatira* belonged, and an inscription found at Thyatira particularly mentions the guild of dyers of that place.[20]

In his comments on the use of παραβιάζομαι to describe Lydia's urging of the disciples (Acts 16:15), Meyer also converted Grotius's presentation of Lydia's heart into a demonstration of the intensity of Lydia's

---

19. Heinrich August Wilhelm Meyer, *Critical and Exegetical Handbook to the Acts of the Apostles*, ed. William P. Dickson, trans. Paton J. Gloag, 4th ed., Meyer Commentary Series (New York: Funk & Wagnalls, 1883).

20. Ibid., 311.

gratitude. Lydia is not a forceful woman, but rather an extremely grateful one. In casting παραβιάζομαι as an expression of gratitude, Meyer also removed any suggestion of resistance to the offer on the part of the disciples. The narrative no longer leaves off with Lydia's unratified invitation, but instead the audience can assume that the Pauline group went on to stay with Lydia before the narrative moves on to the episode with the slave woman with a Python spirit: "That Paul and his companions accepted this pressing invitation of Lydia, and chose her house for their abode, Luke leaves the reader to infer from καὶ παρεβιάσατο ἡμᾶς."[21] With Meyer, Lydia now becomes increasingly associated with Thyatira's dyeing industry.[22]

Some years later, Eugène Jacquier (1926) continued the exploration of Lydia's name and concluded that it was intentionally ethnic, but to create a contrast with other Lydias of the day he wrote:

> Λυδία: this woman was from the city of Thyatira, in Lydia. We can conclude that she had received her name from her country of origin, as was the case for other women, Λυχίη, Μιλησία, Ῥοδία, Φρυγία. Names, such as these, derived from their countries of origin were taken mainly by courtesans, slaves, or freed slaves. It can therefore be concluded that Lydia was a freed slave, perhaps Jewish from birth. But the name of Lydia is frequently encountered as a name of courtesans in the Roman poets, Horace, *Odes*, 1.8, 1; 13, 1; 25, 8; 3, 9, 6; Martial, *Epigr.* 11.21.—Zahn had conjectured that Paul hadn't named Lydia alongside Euodia and Syntyche in his letter to the Philippians, 4:2, because Λυδία was not a given name, but rather a nickname: the Lydian.[23]

---

21. Ibid., 312.

22. Meyer also raised a tangential trajectory of interpretation that used the baptism of Lydia's household as a point of departure for doctrinal debates about infant baptism. Meyer rightfully observes: "Of what members her family consisted, cannot be determined" (ibid., 311).

23. "Λυδία: cette femme était de la ville de Thyatires, en Lydie. On en a conclu qu'elle avait reçu son nom de son pays d'origine comme ce fut le cas pour d'autres femmes, Λυχίη, Μιλησία, Ῥοδία, Φρυγία. Ces noms tirés du nom de leur pays étaient portés surtout par des hétaïres, des esclaves ou des affranchies. Il faudrait donc conclure que Lydia était une esclave affranchie, peut-être juive de naissance. Mais ce nom de Lydia se rencontre fréquemment chez les Romains comme nom de courtisanes, Horace, *Odes*, 1.8, 1; 13, 1; 25, 8; 3, 9, 6; Martial, *Epigr.* 11.21.—Zahn conjecture que Paul ne nomme pas Lydia dans son épître aux Philippiens, à côté de Evodie et de Syn-

In this manner, Lydia of Thyatira gains some distance from the potential tarnish found in the Lydias of literature, who were all courtesans. Jacquier's work strikingly made clear how the formed image of Lydia of Thyatira's propriety rendered impossible any connection with the courtesans and prostitutes who command the same name.

Jacquier also associates Thyatira with purple-dyeing and then takes an inferential step that will be found in most future interpretations of Lydia: "Lydia must have possessed considerable capital to have traded in such expensive wares."[24] In other words, because a seller of a good such as purple would need considerable capital to keep up an inventory of an expensive good, Lydia was wealthy, including as a householder having servants.[25] Lydia the woman of means was clearly taking shape, as was a growing focus on her economic status. Jacquier concluded: "It is probable that Lydia, whose wealth permitted her certain liberties, contributed a good part of her goods. She was one of those Christian women who supported Christian propaganda and by which Christianity was propagated."[26] Lydia, still honorable, takes on the role of a hospitable financier economically enabling the expansion of the Christian church.

The historical-critical trajectory for Lydia the prominent, wealthy noblewoman reaches its apex with the 1956 authoritative commentary on Acts by Ernest Haenchen. Haenchen also begins with the issue of Lydia's name but immediately curtails any speculation about a connection between Lydia and the Lydias of literature by invoking Lydia's honor: "[The personal name Lydia] is frequently found in Horace, e.g. Odes 1.8, 13, 25. Since there courtesans are meant, but Lydia here is an honourable woman, Zahn conjectures that she was called 'the Lydian' to distinguish her from

---

tiche, 4, 2, parce que Λυδία n'était pas son nom, mais un surnom: la Lydienne" (Eugène Jacquier, *Les Actes Des Apôtres*, Ebib [Paris: Gabalda, 1926], 489).

24. "Lydia devait posséder un capital considérable pour faire le commerce de ces marchandises de prix élevé" (ibid.).

25. Ibid. Jean-Pierre Sterck-Degueldre extrapolates Lydia's access to capital even further by suggesting the possible need for transport animals, carts, tools, etc. (*Eine Frau namens Lydia: Zu Geschichte und Komposition in Apostelgeschichte 16, 11–15.40*, WUNT 2/176 [Tübingen: Mohr Siebeck, 2004], 237).

26. "Il est probable que Lydia, à laquelle son état de fortune permettait des libéralités, contribua pour une bonne part à ces dons. Elle fut une de ces femmes chrétiennes qui aidèrent la propagande du christianisme et dont la race s'est propagée" (Jacquier, *Actes*, 491).

other merchants of purple."²⁷ Haenchen effectively closed down any future speculation that Horace's Lydias may have been closer to what Luke had in mind.²⁸ Haenchen also placed a finer point on Jacquier's claim of Lydia's economic status. Whereas Jacquier made a pragmatic argument for Lydia's wealth, arguing for access to capital, Haenchen subtly shifts the argument. Instead of capital, purple's symbolism as a luxury good is brought to the fore and concurrently so too are the implied purchasers of purple goods— "rich people": "Purple goods were a markedly luxury item for rich people; Lydia will have been wealthy herself."²⁹ Lydia increasingly becomes associated with wealth and now too with high status by means of her relation to other wealthy people.

Haenchen also shows how the wealth and its materials are put at Paul's disposal. Haenchen suggests that prior to Lydia's offer to the Pauline group, the disciples "had probably up to this time lived in an inn at their own expense,"³⁰ and he concludes:

---

27. Ernst Haenchen, *The Acts of the Apostles: A Commentary*, trans. Bernard Noble and Gerald Shinn, rev. Robert McL. Wilson, 14th ed. (Göttingen: Vandenhoeck & Ruprecht, 1965; repr., Oxford: Blackwell, 1971), 494 n. 8.

28. Haenchen omits Horace, *Ode* 3.9. The Roman poet Martial too wrote an ode to Lydia, see p. 126 below. Although he does not give credence to it, Haenchen continues on with Ernest Renan's proposal that Lydia was actually married to Paul. Renan suggested that Lydia became Paul's wife: "The absolute purity of Christian morals precluded any suspicion. Although, perhaps it is not too bold to suggest that it is Lydia whom Paul calls 'my dear spouse' in his letter to the Philippians. This expression would be, if one wishes, a simple metaphor. Is it, however, absolutely impossible that Paul had engaged with this sister in a more intimate union? We cannot confirm this. The one certain thing is that Paul did not bring this sister with him on his voyages. Notwithstanding, an entire branch of ecclesial tradition claimed that he was married." ("La pureté absolue des mœurs chrétiennes écartait tout soupçon. Peut-être, d'ailleurs, n'est-il pas trop hardi de supposer que c'est Lydie que Paul, dans son épître aux Philippiens appelle 'ma chère épouse.' Cette expression sera, si l'on veut; une simple métaphore. Est-il cependant absolument impossible que Paul ait contracté avec cette sœur une union plus intime? On ne saurait l'affirmer. La seule chose qui soit sûre, c'est que Paul ne menait pas avec lui de sœur dans ses voyages. Toute une branche de la tradition ecclésiastique a prétendu, nonobstant cela, qu'il était marié" [Ernest Renan, *Saint Paul*, Histoire des Origines du Christianisme 3 (Paris: Michel Lévy Frères, 1869), 148–49]). Renan's speculation about Paul and Lydia rests in part on Clement of Alexandria's claim that the "yokefellow" (γνήσιε σύζυγε) addressed by Paul in Phil 4:3 is a metaphor for "spouse" (Clement of Alexandria, *Strom.* 3.53.1–3).

29. Haenchen, *Acts*, 494.

30. Ibid., 495 n. 3.

In Thyatira, a centre for the manufacture of purple dye which lies southeast of Pergamum in Asia Minor in the Lydian district, she has grown up as a pagan child. Now she lives here as a well-to-do lady known as "Lydia" or "the Lydian." She has joined the small Jewish congregation as a listener. Now she dares to cross over into the new community and lets herself be baptized. Her "house," relatives and slaves, follows her. Her faith is linked with action. She will not tolerate that the missionaries should stay in just any quarters. They must move to her house, and living there they now assemble the brethren who are gradually won.[31]

Haenchen's work thus completed the historical-critical construction of the image of Lydia as a high-standing, wife-like woman whose principal role in Philippi would be to provide material resources to the Pauline mission. This image has pervaded most of the subsequent historical-critical discourse on Lydia.

1.1.4. Feminist Approaches

When feminist biblical criticism emerged, it began to ask new questions of how the history of interpretation had presented female figures. Yet despite the advent of a new critical lens, the figure of Lydia remained an unyielding construct. Lydia, now commonly represented as a "businesswoman," retained the essential attributes developed by historical criticism.

For example, in *The Women's Bible Commentary*, Gail O' Day writes:

Lydia is a businesswoman who sells purple cloth, which was a luxury item for the wealthy (cf. Luke 16:9). Her business therefore put her in contact with the elite of Philippi. Her offer of her home as a missionary center and the information that she was the head of her household (16:15) suggests that Lydia is wealthy herself. Once again Luke draws attention to a wealthy woman who acts as benefactor to a growing Christian community. Lydia embodies Luke's ideal of women's contribution to the church: to provide housing and economic resources.[32]

---

31. Ibid., 499.
32. O'Day, "Acts," 400.

A new turn, however, is created by finding fault with the author of Acts precisely for this presentation, which is critiqued for limiting the role of women to that of providing economic resources.[33]

In contrast, Reimer's liberationist approach to Lydia retained historical criticism's focus on Lydia's status but inverted it in order to reframe Lydia as a nonelite, hard-working woman involved in cloth production and especially purple-dyeing.[34] In her extensive discussion on types of purple dyes and dyeing processes, Reimer drew attention to the wide variety of purples available in antiquity and to the widespread use of purple, even by slaves. For Reimer, however, this spectrum of grades of purple, and of clientele for its products, did not in the end lead her to conclude that Lydia's income and status were indeterminate, but rather to invert the argument raised by Haenchen and his predecessors:

> The common notion that Lydia's house was very large and that her business had "brought her a substantial fortune," that is, that she had enjoyed "economic success," is unpersuasive for two reasons: On the one hand, at that time there was no large-scale textile production. On the other hand, it cannot be demonstrated that people who worked in the production and sale of purple goods ever played an important economic role in Philippi; there is only one *purpuraia(ii)* inscription at Philippi. From what has been said thus far, we are more inclined to conclude that Lydia's work was a subsistence occupation for herself and her house.[35]

Nevertheless, the pull of historical-critical scholarship's portrayal of Lydia's economic success remained strong even for Reimer. Whereas most commentators extrapolated Lydia's presumed economic comfort into high social status, Reimer rightfully distinguished between economic and social measures of worth. Yet in so doing, Reimer subtly shifted her argument to suggest that while Lydia may have enjoyed a level of financial comfort, she would have been devoid of social status from an elite vantage point. In this way, Reimer retained an echo of the history of interpretation's view

---

33. For another similar example, see Clarice J. Martin, "The Acts of the Apostles," in *Searching the Scriptures*, ed. Elisabeth Schüssler Fiorenza (New York: Crossroad, 1993), 784.

34. Ivoni Richter Reimer, "Lydia and Her House," in *Women in the Acts of the Apostles: A Feminist Liberation Perspective*, trans. Linda M. Maloney (Minneapolis: Fortress Press, 1992), 71–149.

35. Ibid., 112.

1. HISTORY OF INTERPRETATION 23

of Lydia as enjoying economic advantage but repositioned her argument concerning Lydia's status in the social rather than economic sphere:

> Craftspeople and small merchants were also part of the *plebs urbana*. Even when they had a "better" economic status (in comparison, say, to beggars), so that they even employed a few slaves or freed people, they were socially despised by the upper classes. In the eyes of the upper class their economic position was insignificant.[36]

Having astutely raised the historic reality of a wide variety of types of purple being produced and sold in antiquity, Reimer does not move to the logical conclusion that it is not possible to form an opinion on Lydia's economic status; instead, through a liberationist lens, she reframes Lydia as a socially oppressed textile worker whose offer of hospitality to the disciples enacts a form of resistance to Roman imperial rule.[37] Though Reimer's arguments had little impact on the mainstream presentation of Lydia as a woman of means, they did destabilize the argument on which future interpreters could present high-income, high-status Lydia.

Shelly Matthews, in the monograph *First Converts*, argued that Lydia's high status was used by the author of Acts to help legitimize the new Christian movement.[38] Matthews acknowledged Reimer's portrayal of Lydia's low status; however, she did not find it convincing since, according to Matthews, the author of Acts employed "the conversion of prominent women" as a rhetorical strategy "in support of a propagandistic agenda."[39] Implicitly for Matthews, the image of historical criticism's high-standing Lydia provided the point of departure for her argument regarding the author's rhetorical strategy.

The findings of Reimer and others that the status of female purple workers and purple sellers would likely be found at the lower end of the social scale did not alter Matthews's claim that Lydia was a tool of propaganda, but rather served to narrow the audience for Acts. Matthews argued:

---

36. Ibid.
37. Ibid., 114.
38. Shelly Matthews, *First Converts: Rich Pagan Women and the Rhetoric of Mission in Early Judaism and Christianity*, Contraversions: Jews and Other Differences (Stanford, CA: Stanford University Press, 2001).
39. Ibid., 75, 87.

The audience for whom Luke writes is more appropriately identified as a group of people with some wealth and education into which persons of low status with wealth were also included. Such an audience would view a character involved in trade, who has also achieved a measure of respectability, as mirroring their own social and economic aspirations. Lydia's status markers—a dealer in purple who is also a householder—thus positions her at least among the ranks of this "quasi-elite" class.[40]

In this manner, Lydia retains a high-status profile but within a smaller sphere of influence.

Matthews suggested that new cults, such as the one introduced by Dionysus, frequently "drew on the topos of high-standing women as one means of mediating between their adherents and the larger culture."[41] Citing long-acknowledged similarities between Euripides's *Bacchae* and Acts 16, Matthews argued that the author of Acts used Lydia toward a similar propagandistic goal.[42] In the end, Matthews presented the prevailing image of Lydia: "Lydia is a well-to-do Christian convert and patroness of Paul, who extends hospitality to the missionaries in her house." Matthews concluded with a critique of Lydia's "portrayal only as a convert accommodating Paul and his mission, and not as a Christian missionary/leader in her own right."[43] Although Matthews did acknowledge a "symbolic richness" in Lydia's name, she did not delve into this symbolism but instead considered the name's symbolism a sign that she is a "character created by Luke."[44] The character of Lydia, concluded Matthews, is a rhetorical device intended to bolster the perceived status of early Christianity.

1.1.5. Most Recent Interpretations

Though utilizing the name "sociorhetorical," Ben Witherington's interpretation simply confirms most of the insights derived from historical criticism.[45] Returning to the question of Lydia's name that had long vexed past interpreters, Witherington claims:

---

40. Ibid., 88.
41. Ibid., 72.
42. Ibid., 73.
43. Ibid., 94.
44. Ibid., 93.
45. Ben Witherington III, *The Acts of the Apostles: A Socio-rhetorical Commentary* (Grand Rapids: Eerdmans, 1998).

While it is possible that the Greek means "the Lydian woman," there is now clear evidence for Lydia as a proper name (e.g. Julia Lydia from Sardis), and that is the most natural way to read the Greek here—she was named Lydia.[46]

Missing the paradox of his warrant regarding Lydia's name, since Sardis was interchangeable with Lydia and first-century audiences would therefore naturally have understood "Julia Lydia from Sardis" as "Julia Lydia from Lydia,"[47] Witherington carries on:

> That she is mentioned by name may be quite significant. Roman women were normally called by their family's cognomen, not by a personal name or nickname. That Lydia is called by her personal name suggests she is of Greek extraction, and it probably also indicates she is a person of some status, since it was normal in such a Greco-Roman setting *not* to mention women by personal name in public unless they were either notable or notorious.[48]

Lest any reader turn to the possibility of "notorious," Witherington immediately asserts that Lydia's occupation situated her in the "notable" category by speculating on a connection between Lydia's occupation and a conjured imperial monopoly on purple. Witherington argues:

> The term πορφυρόπωλις refers to someone who is a seller of purple cloth. It is clear enough from the reference to Lydia's house and household that she should not be seen as someone of servile status, and the term πορφυρόπωλις also suggests the opposite. There is evidence that dealing in this color was an imperial monopoly, though it may date from later than this period, in fact those involved in this trade were members of "Caesar's household." This would not be patricians but the elite among the freedmen and freedwomen (and some slaves) who were in the imperial service.... She is clearly being portrayed here as a person of some social importance and means, and as we have already seen Luke has an interest in recording the conversion of this kind of folk perhaps because they were of a similar station to Luke's audience.[49]

---

46. Ibid., 491.
47. See pp. 120–21 below.
48. Witherington, *Acts of the Apostles*, 492.
49. Ibid., 492.

At this point, Witherington's use of purported historical data signals an ideological agenda rather than a historically grounded argument, since, while certain emperors had occasionally attempted to limit the broader public's access to purple with limited degrees of success, there did not exist an imperial monopoly in purple cloth or dye in antiquity.[50] Nonetheless, Witherington found recourse in earlier speculation that had linked Lydia to the imperial household. In *NewDocs*, G. H. R. Horsley had mused:

> One further tantalizing question may be raised here. *AE* 800 reports a fragmentary inscription from Miletos: [... Τιβ]ερίου [Κ]λαυδίου Νέρω[νος] Καίσαρος ἐπάνω τῶν πορφυρῶν. The importance of this brief wording is that it shows that the imperial monopoly on purple goes back at least to Nero.[51] The person whose name is lost must have been a slave or freedman, whose function is described in Greek by the equivalent of the Latin *a purpuris*. The implication flowing from this is that those involved in the purple trade—who appear to be of freed status, as noted above—are members of the *familia Caesaris*. If this imperial monopoly were initiated prior to Nero—by Claudius, perhaps, since he is often claimed to be the great innovator in centralized administration?—we might just be able to identify Lydia more exactly, as being a member of

---

50. "As early as the Fourth Century B.C., and continuing through the Hellenistic period and the Roman Empire, there existed many industries engaged in producing inexpensive substitutes that simulated all sorts of costly products for individuals desiring to imitate the status symbols of richer strata of the population.... It was these imitation purples that made possible the widespread arrogation by middle and lower classes of the elite color everywhere. Thus, despite incipient efforts in the First Century A.D. to restrict some uses of purple for official purposes, the Second Century would appear to be the period when the general use of purple, both the most expensive qualities and the various substitutes, was at its highest intensity in the ancient world" (Meyer Reinhold, *History of Purple as a Status Symbol in Antiquity*, Latomus 116 [Brussels: Latomus, 1970], 53–54; see also 58).

51. Horsley's recourse to any form of "imperial monopoly" seems to be derived from an implied link between Eusebius's account of a eunuch being granted charge over a purple-dye works at Tyre (*Hist. eccl.* 7.32.4) and an inscription that reads: φῖσε μνῆμα μαρμάρινον Καθηκουμένων, διαφέρον Θεοκτίστου κογχυλοπλυτοῦ τοῦ εἰεροτάτου βαρίου. Both this and the "Nero" inscription can be understood any number of ways including an honorific acknowledgment of a patron; Eusebius speaks of a dye works not a dye monopoly. See G. H. R. Horsley, "The Purple Trade, and the Status of Lydia of Thyatira," *NewDocs* 2:26.

"Caesar's household."... It must be emphasized, however, that this particular suggestion about Lydia is no more than an intriguing possibility.[52]

But, in the next issue of *NewDocs*, Horsley qualified his prior comments about the connection between Lydia and Caesar:

> The account of the purple-trade in *New Docs 1977*, 3, does not raise the possibility that the purple in which Lydia dealt was not the Tyrian murex but a less expensive dye from the roots of the madder plant (*Rubia*), the so-called "Turkey Red," whose use has a very long history in Western Anatolia.... Shifts of perspective here could affect our conception of Lydia's social status. If in fact her trade was separate from the imperial monopoly in the expensive marine dye, it does not support the attractive suggestion that she was a freedwoman of the imperial household. The possibility is of course not excluded (cf. Phil. 4.22).[53]

Horsley's view, therefore, is that discussion about Lydia's purple trade needs to consider the possibility that Lydia's purple may well have been sourced from a less-expensive dye. For Witherington, however, neither a historical lack of evidence supporting any imperial monopoly on purple nor Horsley's retraction had any impact on his framing Lydia as a socially "appropriate" convert to the Christian mission. As Haenchen had earlier curtailed any suggestion of courtesan-Lydias with his authoritative warrant that "Lydia here is an honourable woman," so too did Witherington with his claim that Lydia's name signaled that she was a "notable" woman of the highest status. Moreover, not only did Lydia enjoy high social status, but also: "It was money and social status that procured women or men important roles in such religious settings, and it is no accident that higher-status women played important roles in early Christianity as well, in this case providing a venue for the church to meet and be nurtured."[54] Lydia remains a woman of substantial financial means. Her role in the narrative is to show paradigmatically how "Luke connects spiritual dispositions to the disposition of possessions."[55] Ultimately, under Witherington's treat-

---

52. Ibid., 2:28.
53. G. H. R. Horsley, "Lydia and the Purple Trade," *NewDocs* 3:53–54.
54. Witherington, *Acts of the Apostles*, 492–93.
55. Ibid., 493, quoting Luke Timothy Johnson, *The Acts of the Apostles*, SP 5 (Collegeville, MN: Liturgical Press, 1992), 297.

ment, Lydia is the "right" kind of convert who has the financial wherewithal to provide the right kind of home for the expanding church.[56]

Both the degree to which the history of interpretation has etched Lydia's profile into the imaginations of interpreters and the limitations of historical criticism to tackle questions raised by the presentation in Acts of Lydia have come to full expression in Richard Ascough's recent monograph on Lydia.[57] Ascough's point of departure for his investigation of Lydia is the historical-critical a priori conclusion: "Luke is portraying Lydia as a woman of means who owns her own house."[58] Despite Acts not providing any information about the size, physical makeup, economic or social status of Lydia's household, nor narrating any mention of the Pauline group eating at Lydia's, Ascough goes on imaginatively to lay out a dining room and seating plan—complete with a pictograph—for the meals that Lydia would have served Paul in her ample home:

> In the case of Lydia, we can again extrapolate from the typical to suggest that as their host she would have entertained Paul and his companions in the proper fashion by having her slaves prepare a triclinium and her cook prepare a meal.... The meal would have been tailored to reflect the honor of the guest, while bringing praise and honor to the host. It would certainly have included leafy vegetables and bread, along with *garum* (the ubiquitous highly salted fish sauce of the Roman diet), and perhaps fish or meat if Paul was considered a particularly honored guest. The food would have been accompanied by wine, diluted appropriately with water. The cook might have been cautioned against preparing stuffed dormice—a frequent delicacy—since the most common stuffing involved pork. The final course would have involved dried and fresh fruits and perhaps some pastries.[59]

These types of detailed descriptions clearly bring "Lydia the hostess" before the reader's eyes; however, they also preclude any form of critical engagement with them.

---

56. Witherington, *Acts of the Apostles*, 499; Ben Witherington III, *Women in the Earliest Churches*, SNTSMS 59 (Cambridge: Cambridge University Press, 1988), 149.

57. Richard S. Ascough, *Lydia: Paul's Cosmopolitan Hostess*, Paul's Social Network (Collegeville, MN: Liturgical Press, 2009). Similarly, Sterck-Degueldre, *Frau namens Lydia*.

58. Ascough, *Lydia*, 32.

59. Ibid., 48–50.

1. HISTORY OF INTERPRETATION

Historical-critical claims, which in some cases are incompatible regarding Lydia's status, are simply blended and quickly followed by a detailed rehearsal of types of purple, its uses, its sources, including the historically speculative "imperial monopoly":

> The manufacture and trade of purple dye and purple goods was a well-organized and important industry during the Roman Empire, and it is within this scope of occupations that Acts 16:14 locates Lydia by noting that she was a "purple dealer" (*porphyropōlis*). The trade of purple dye became an imperial monopoly, controlled by various emperors over time, perhaps from as early as the time of Claudius. If Lydia dealt with true purple she would have been under imperial control and may even have been a member of "the emperor's household" (Phil 4:22). The slaves and freed persons that belonged to the imperial household were probably the most mobile group in Roman society, and thus it would have been no surprise to find one of them in Philippi. Against this suggestion, however, is the existence of the manufacture of cheaper quality (non-imperial) purple in Thyatira and the use of the name Lydia for freeborn women (as opposed to it being a slave name meaning "the Lydian"). Thus, a direct connection cannot be assumed between Lydia of Acts and the household of Caesar.[60]

Following his discussion of the varied sources of, and uses for, purple, Ascough summarizes: "Again, we find in the social world of Paul's day evidence for the type of person Lydia would have been—an independent woman working in the trade of a luxury good and supporting others, perhaps even being a benefactor to an elective social formation through her income."[61] While questions regarding Lydia's religious background and economic and social status continue to produce incompatible assertions, what does remain fixed in Ascough's descriptive details is moneyed Lydia—the product of the history of interpretation. Ascough writes: "In the end, I imagine Lydia as a Romanized immigrant living in Philippi, well-off, but not elite, involved in ritual piety and expressing all the typical patterns of householder hospitality one would expect in antiquity."[62] In spite of his use of social-scientific modeling, Ascough does not raise questions such as how it is that in a highly gendered honor-shame society,

---

60. Ibid., 76.
61. Ibid., 80.
62. Ibid., 99.

an "un-manned" female of indeterminate status could publicly "press" a group of men to come into her home, or, if Lydia might have been engaged in the widespread use of inexpensive low-quality purples, how she could be seen as a woman of financial means.[63]

1.2. Conclusion: History of Interpretation

The contemporary image of Lydia was launched when Chrysostom featured the "purple-seller" of Acts 16 as a model of modesty and feminine propriety. Within the social honor codes of the ancient world, gendered moral qualities such as modesty would have conferred elevated status to a woman. Grotius's recasting of Lydia as a weaver solidified her gender-appropriate status but also opened the way for future connections between Lydia and textile production. The historical-critical period moved Lydia into the realm of the purple-dyeing industry, while it retained her feminine honor. Purple's symbolic elite status linked with Lydia's elevated feminine status led sociohistorical critics to shade Lydia's purple with wealth. What began with Chrysostom as gender-appropriate, morally derived status transformed over the centuries into socioeconomic status. Moreover, Chrysostom's casting of Lydia as a hostess has worked alongside the developing image of a woman of means to create today's profile of a generous "patroness."

Any number of critics' comments could be cited to illustrate how the prevailing image of Lydia almost exclusively focuses on her perceived economic means and restricts her role to providing resources to the Pauline mission.

> As a God-fearer loosely connected to the synagogue, her conversion represents the winning of one on the margins of Judaism to the messianic community centered in the house. As a Gentile of some status and economic means, she represents the type of convert that creates jealousy on the part of "the Jews." By offering her house to Paul, she uses her resources to advance the mission, resulting in the separation of the community from the synagogue. As the first convert on European soil, Lydia provides a proper example of the use of wealth by foreshadowing the conversion of other prominent women.[64]

---

63. Ibid.
64. Matson, *Household Conversion*, 150.

In such interpretations, the financially endowed Lydia is moved by the Spirit to finance the church's expansion in her well-appointed home. Increasingly, feminist interpretations have critiqued Lydia's limited economically sourced role but have understood this role to have been advanced through the interests of the author of Acts. The image itself, with the possible exception of Reimer's work, has not, since the historical-critical period, been in question.

Against this solidly entrenched, authoritatively warranted figure, argumentative inconsistencies are swiftly overlooked and questions that should be raised remain invisible, outside of the interpretive reach of commentators. Yet throughout the history of interpretation, there have been consistent signs that on the other side of the coin lies an alternate image of Lydia. For example, the possible implications of Lydia's name, remarked on and swiftly overwritten by a number of authorities, bear closer examination. Unearthing this alternate image, the image most closely shared by the first audiences of Acts, will be the objective of this book.

2
Method

2.1. Choice of Sociorhetorical Interpretation to Address the Role of Lydia in Acts 16

The goal of this book is to bring sociorhetorically framed questions to the figure of Lydia in Acts 16. By narrating Lydia as the first point of contact with an important new step in the disciples' mission, Acts 16 emphasizes that Lydia is of interest to the author. In addition, the author focuses heightened attention on Lydia by opening and closing the Philippi episode with Lydia (Acts 16:14–15, 40), by detailing God's explicit interest in Lydia's heart, and by according Lydia a narrative speaking voice. Given these indicators of Lydia's narrative prominence, it is necessary to reexamine the prevalent scholarly suggestions concerning the Lydia episode. These include the suggestion that the Lydia episode plays no role other than being an "interlude" in a seemingly isolated passage and the conclusion that Lydia enjoys high status and wealth despite an absence in the narrative of any clear indication of these attributes. Such inconsistencies raise questions about the suggestion that Lydia is introduced as a figure solely to showcase appropriate status and wealth sharing. Perhaps of greater importance, though, is the need to explore further the tantalizing enigma of the role of Lydia's name. A full rhetorical analysis of the material here seems to require dealing with these several matters. Sociorhetorical interpretation is ideally suited to bring new light to bear on the Lydia texts of Acts 16.

2.1.1. Rhetoric and the Rhetorical Communicative Culture of the First-Century Mediterranean Environment

Sociorhetorical interpretation (SRI), a multidisciplinary approach to the rhetorical analysis of texts, conceived and inaugurated by Vernon K.

Robbins,[1] arguably is the contemporary interpretive approach most sensitive to the rhetorical communicative culture from within which the New Testament texts were created. Robbins has rightfully contended that nineteenth- and twentieth-century biblical interpretation was shaped by inherent assumptions about scribal communicative culture, that is, communication that is sourced in scribal reproduction and recitation. After these assumptions produced textual criticism, the skills of textual criticism were transported first to source criticism and then to form criticism. These procedures of analysis and interpretation are biased toward New Testament compositions as reproductions of preceding texts or events, even when the final form of a writing is interpreted through strategies of redaction criticism. This "reproductive" view of New Testament texts gained further momentum as photocopying technology advanced beyond the printing press in the dominant print culture of the twentieth and twenty-first centuries. The result, according to Robbins, has been a "failure to recognize the pervasiveness of rhetorical culture throughout Mediterranean society during the Hellenistic period."[2]

In contrast to the scribal view of culture, in a rhetorical culture "oral and written speech interact closely with one another."[3] While rhetorical culture may suggest to most people rhetorical oration and specifically the types of speeches orators delivered in the traditional rhetorical venues of the courtroom (judicial), political assembly (deliberative), or civil ceremony (epideictic), Robbins recognized that by the first century a rhetorical culture implied a fusion between oral and written communication. This fusion was materially illustrated within the education system of the time through the *progymnasmata*, handbooks of written rhetorical exercises taught and practiced in grammar schools.[4]

The *progymnasmata* trained students to write "traditional materials ... persuasively" as a means of teaching students how to redeploy the

---

1. Vernon K. Robbins, *Exploring the Texture of Texts*; Robbins, *Tapestry of Early Christian Discourse*.

2. Vernon K. Robbins, "Writing as a Rhetorical Act in Plutarch and the Gospels," in *Persuasive Artistry: Studies in New Testament Rhetoric in Honor of George A. Kennedy*, ed. Duane F. Watson (Sheffield: JSOT Press, 1991), 144.

3. Ibid., 145.

4. For examples see George A. Kennedy, trans., *Progymnasmata: Greek Textbooks of Prose Composition and Rhetoric*, WGRW 10 (Atlanta: Society of Biblical Literature, 2003); Craig A. Gibson, *Libanius's* Progymnasmata: *Model Exercises in Greek Prose Composition and Rhetoric*, WGRW 27 (Atlanta: Society of Biblical Literature, 2008).

material toward new persuasive ends. In this way, a student was taught to move "away from verbatim reproduction of an oral or written text" and instead shift the materials into a reconfigured argument.[5] An important implication from Robbins's insights into the rhetorical culture of the *progymnasmata* is that the building blocks of rhetoric came not only from the common topics of elite civic oratory but also from popular anecdotes, stories, and oral traditions imbued in cultural memory.

The most comprehensive articulation to date of the constitutive characteristics of writing produced within a classically influenced rhetorical communicative culture is found in Chaïm Perelman and Lucie Olbrechts-Tyteca's *The New Rhetoric*.[6] Using the insights of *The New Rhetoric*, it is possible to identify four key assumptions that undergirded writing within a rhetorical culture in texts such as those found in the New Testament:

1. Broadly, the goal of rhetorical argumentation is "to create or increase the adherence of minds to the theses presented for their assent."[7]
2. Rhetorical texts respond to a perceived exigence within an author's environment.[8] As a result, rhetorical argumentation is oriented toward human decision-making, and as Perelman and Olbrechts-Tyteca claim, it is "oriented towards the future, it sets out to bring about some action or to prepare for it by acting, by discursive methods, on the minds of the hearers."[9]

---

5. Robbins, "Writing as a Rhetorical Act," 145–47.

6. Chaïm Perelman and Lucie Olbrechts-Tyteca, *The New Rhetoric: A Treatise on Argumentation*, trans. John Wilkinson and Purcell Weaver (Notre Dame: University of Notre Dame Press, 1969).

7. Ibid., 45.

8. For a discussion of "rhetorical situation" and exigence, see Lloyd F. Bitzer, "The Rhetorical Situation," *PhRh* 1 (1968): 1–14; Keith Grant-Davie, "Rhetorical Situations and Their Constituents," *RhetR* 15 (1997): 264–79.

9. Perelman and Olbrechts-Tyteca, *New Rhetoric*, 47. "Tournée vers l'avenir, elle se propose de provoquer une action ou d'y préparer, en agissant par des moyens discursifs sur l'esprit des auditeurs" (Perelman and Olbrechts-Tyteca, *Traité de l'Argumentation: La Nouvelle Rhétorique*, 5th ed. [Brussels: Éditions de l'Université de Bruxelles, 1958], 62). "L'esprit" was translated as "mind," but the sense conveyed by the biblical heart, i.e., the seat of the inner human encompassing thought, emotions, and volition, would be closer to Perelman and Olbrechts-Tyteca's intent: "Rhetoric gives first place to the

3. In contrast to the type of argumentation found in mathematical logical proofs that rely on the "rational self-evidence" of their premises, rhetorical argumentation relies on social logic:

> If judgments of reality are to provide an indisputable object of common understanding, the terms they contain must be free of all ambiguity, either because it is possible to know their true meaning, or because a unanimously accepted convention does away with all controversy on the subject. These two possibilities, which are respectively the approaches of realism and nominalism in the linguistic field, are both untenable, as they regard language either as a reflection of reality or as an arbitrary creation of an individual, and forget an essential element, the social aspect of language, which is an instrument of communication and influence on others.
>
> All language is the language of community, be this a community bound by biological ties, or by the practice of a common discipline or technique. The terms used, their meanings, by definition, can only be understood in the context of the habits, ways of thought, methods, external circumstances, and traditions known to the users of those terms.[10]

4. Although at times rhetorical figures have become associated in the popular imagination with stylistic embellishment, such as certain cases of alliteration, when used in argumentation that is intended to function rhetorically (i.e., to influence human decision-making), figures can be considered "rhetorical" to the extent that they contribute to a change of perspective in the audience: "Forms which seem at first to be used in an unusual manner may come to appear normal if their use is justified by the speech taken as a whole. We consider a figure to be *argumentative*, if it brings about a change of perspective, and its use seems normal in relation to this new situation."[11]

The following succinct summary of Perelman and Olbrechts-Tyteca's presentation of the function and means of rhetoric essentially summarizes this project's understanding of rhetoric:

---

influence which a speech has on the entire personality of the hearers" (Perelman and Olbrechts-Tyteca, *New Rhetoric*, 54).

10. Perelman and Olbrechts-Tyteca, *New Rhetoric*, 513.

11. Ibid., 169.

The speaker gains adherence of any audience by attempting to transfer existing adherence from premises that the audience presumably already accepts to conclusions drawn from those premises. Furthermore, the speaker wins adherence by creating "presence" for the main premise of the proposition. Presence, or foregrounding, is created using the topics. The different types of argument create "liaisons"—not necessarily [formal] logical connections—between premises and conclusions.[12]

From Perelman and Olbrechts-Tyteca's insights into rhetorical communicative culture, it is possible to identify a number of key attributes of rhetorical texts that can help guide a rhetorically oriented approach to analysis:

1. At all times, rhetoric is culturally and socially contextualized, and therefore the premises of a rhetorical argument are located in the communion of conventions and values shared between the rhetor and his or her audience.
2. Through what Perelman and Olbrechts-Tyteca term "presence," rhetoric consciously foregrounds the topoi it has chosen to employ and develop in argumentation.
3. The argument moves toward its conclusion through linkages ("liaisons") argumentatively developed (deductively and/or inductively) between the salient topics.

2.1.2. Sociorhetorical Interpretation as a Means of Identifying Rhetorical Topoi and Their Rhetorical Role in the Text

Ancient writings present two major obstacles to their contemporary rhetorical interpretation. The first is that modern interpreters are removed not only by history from their texts but also removed by cultural and social norms, conventions, and practices. The gap of history is normally recognized, such that significant attention and resources have been dedicated for at least the past two centuries to researching the historical background of ancient texts of various eras and genres. Interpreters are not as readily self-aware, however, of the concurrent distance in social and cultural norms that also separate a text from its interpretation. As a result,

---

12. "Chaïm Perelman," in *The Rhetorical Tradition: Readings from Classical Times to the Present*, ed. Patricia Bizzell and Bruce Herzberg, 2nd ed. (New York: St. Martin's, 2001), 1373–74.

interpretations may be able to represent a relatively accurate image of a historical environment, providing details such as architecture, geography, or political conflicts, but at the same time either introduce social and cultural anachronisms or overlook key elements altogether.

A second, and far more potentially damaging, obstacle to the rhetorical interpretation of earlier writings is a lack of awareness of how topoi have been reconfigured and reshaped by centuries of past interpretations. Particularly problematic is the way in which reimaged elements may have triggered imaginative elaborations and thereby seeded new topoi into interpretive discourse. If these subsequent topoi reappeared with sufficient frequency, they may have eventually entrenched themselves under the guise of the rhetoric of the subject text. This book argues that the topoi associated with Lydia have indeed been reconfigured over the course of the reception history of Acts, together with other topoi in the rhetorical unit, such that key aspects of the rhetoric of the text have been either expurgated or radically recast.

SRI seeks to redress both obstacles, that of social, cultural, and historical distance and that of the recalibration of the topoi of a text in the history of its interpretation. SRI redresses the distance and the recalibration by focusing on the constitutive role of a topos—its dynamic quality of bringing forth a "constellation of networks of meaning"[13]—rather than representing a discrete value. In rhetorical discourse, a portion of any given constellation of elements associated with a topos exhibit themselves "on the page" through their presence in a strategic semantic cluster, but a portion of their constellation must also be located "off the page" in an audience's "long-term schematic knowledge."[14] For rhetorician Carolyn Miller, an essential attribute of a topos is that it is found at "a point in semantic space that is particularly rich in connectivity to other significant or highly connected points."[15] The two axes of connectivity—liaisons

---

13. L. Gregory Bloomquist, "Paul's Inclusive Language: The Ideological Texture of Romans 1," in *Fabrics of Discourse: Essays in Honor of Vernon K. Robbins*, ed. David B. Gowler, L. Gregory Bloomquist, and Duane F. Watson (Harrisburg, PA: Trinity Press International, 2003), 174.

14. Gilles Fauconnier and Mark Turner, *The Way We Think: Conceptual Blending and the Mind's Hidden Complexities* (New York: Basic Books, 2002), 40.

15. Carolyn R. Miller, "The Aristotelian Topos: Hunting for Novelty," in *Rereading Aristotle's Rhetoric*, ed. Alan G. Gross and Arthur E. Walzer (Carbondale: Southern Illinois University Press, 2000), 142.

between textual elements and mental elaborations—become more visible to an interpreter when social, cultural, political, economic, sacred, and historical details inform the understanding of elements located in the text. Once the interpreter identifies a text's topoi, that interpreter is equipped to investigate the ideological texture of the text, that is, to examine how the author of the text has used these topoi argumentatively in order to advance his or her message.

Recognized as "one of the foremost practitioners of socio-rhetorical criticism as developed in the many writings of Vernon Robbins,"[16] L. Gregory Bloomquist has continued to refine and extend the application of SRI, initially conceived as textural analysis, into a topos-centered analytic. The interpreter, in investigating a text's inner and intertextures, is led to discover the prominent topoi of interest evidenced by the text itself and the social and cultural environment that gives shape and meaning to the topoi. The goal of SRI is not merely to identify the topoi that are operative in the text, however, but ultimately to investigate how those topoi have been deployed by the author to advance his or her communicative objective.

A topos, it should be clarified, is not entirely synonymous with a modern understanding of "topic," since a rhetorical communicative culture understood topoi as predictable clusters of elements where the linkages, the connectivity between elements, are the salient feature that shape and determine the topos. Out of a vast resource pool of social and cultural topics, certain elements, when joined together in the discourse, take on the distinctive shape of a topos. For this reason, topoi are both formed interactively and function interactively. As we shall see, a significant example of this dynamic nature of a topos will be illustrated by the way the color purple becomes part of a distinctive topos when it is linked to Lydia's ethnic and occupational profile.

Predicated on "the Aristotelian notion that a *topos* is," in the words of Miller, "a place to which an arguer (or problem solver or thinker) may mentally go to find arguments,"[17] Bloomquist defined topoi as follows:

---

16. James D. Hester, "Rhetorics in and for the New Millennium," in *Rhetorics in the New Millennium: Promise and Fulfillment*, ed. James D. Hester and J. David Hester, SAC (New York: T&T Clark, 2010), 13.

17. Miller, "Aristotelian Topos," 130–46, as referenced by Bloomquist, "Paul's Inclusive Language," 174.

> *Topoi* ... can be understood as those landmarks on the mental geography of thought, which themselves evoke a constellation of networks of meanings as a result of social, cultural, or ideological use—and the argumentative embedding of these *topoi* in the presentation of the argument(s) of the text.[18]

SRI's primary goal is to seek out topoi and examine how they are "argumentatively embedded" in the rhetorical argumentation of the text. The key components of this investigative process—inner, inter-, and ideological textural analyses—will be discussed in the following sections.

2.1.3. The World of the Text: Inner Textural Analysis

Inner textural analysis involves a thorough investigation of the lexically derived patterns, narrational elements, and argumentative structure of the text. This first programmatic step of analysis is the foundation and point of departure for SRI. The challenge of inner textural analysis is for an interpreter to suspend all of his or her presumptions about "what the text is about" and instead allow the text itself to show its topics of concern to the interpreter in the form of lexical indicators, narrative characters, forms of action, temporal and spatial settings, and so on. Robbins writes: "This is a stage of analysis prior to the analysis of 'meanings,' that is, prior to 'real interpretation' of the text."[19]

Inner textural analysis investigates at least five textures: (1) repetitive texture and pattern; (2) progressive texture and pattern; (3) rhetorical boundaries texture and pattern; (4) narrational and sensory-aesthetic texture and pattern; and (5) argumentative texture and pattern.[20] Inner

---

18. Bloomquist, "Paul's Inclusive Language," 174.
19. Robbins, *Exploring the Texture of Texts*, 7.
20. Following Bloomquist, this project treats sensory-aesthetic texture and pattern as a component of narrational texture and pattern; see L. Gregory Bloomquist, "The Rhetoric of Suffering in Paul's Letter to the Philippians: Socio-rhetorical Reflections and Further Thoughts on a Post-colonial Contribution to the Discussion," *Thf* 35 (2004): 203; Bloomquist, "First-Century Models of Bodily Healing and Their Socio-rhetorical Transformation in Some NT Traditions" (paper presented at the Rhetorics of Healing Conference, Claremont Graduate University, Claremont, CA, 24 January 2002), 3.

2. METHOD

textural analysis establishes a blueprint of a text's rhetorical framework. I will discuss each of these inner textural components in turn.

Repetitive texture and pattern examines the text for repeated lexical and "grammatical, syntactical, verbal, or topical phenomena."[21] Repetitive elements are the first signal to possible topoi that function rhetorically in the text. For example, in the analysis of repetitive texture, we will discover a number of repetitive distinguishing features of Acts 16:9–40, such as an abundance of prefixed ἔρχομαι terms, pervasive instances of the plural form, and varied uses of terms often associated with the sacred.

I will also look for repetition in the analysis of progressive texture. Whereas in repetitive texture I simply aggregate repetitive elements, in progressive texture I begin to look for clusters of elements that are found repetitively, as well as any progressions or sequences that seem to unfold along the repetitive elements. In progressive texture, I will look closely at progressive or sequential patterns and begin to notice how repetitive elements are structured in the text. Progressive textural analysis will be the first indicator of the rhetorical structure of the text. For example, the analysis of progressive texture will show that the repetitive term παρακαλέω is found in the unit's first and final verse and participates in a major progressive pattern.

Within narrative, we need to be aware of an additional form of progression, called "qualitative progression" by Kenneth Burke. In qualitative progression, "the presence of one quality prepares us for the introduction of another."[22] Robbins's description of the Gospel of Mark's account of Jesus's crucifixion provides a good example of qualitative progression:

> The next scene (15:33–39) begins with another reference to time. It took three hours for the door to close on any hope for Jesus' release. During this time, Jesus' speech stopped, his body was beaten and mocked, and his body was led off to be hung on a cross.... At the end of this time period, according to the narrator, the universe itself responded. The response was not a flash of light, a roar of thunder, a miraculous release of the body from the cross, and a glorious ascent of the body into heaven. Rather, the light that the earth gives forth during the day to give life to the world suddenly became darkness. In other words, the universe itself became passive, much as Jesus' body became passive during the scene

---

21. Robbins, *Exploring the Texture of Texts*, 8.
22. Kenneth Burke, "Lexicon Rhetoricae," in *Counter-Statement*, 2nd ed. (Berkeley: University of California Press, 1968), 125.

with Pilate. Not only did all people forsake him, but the universe itself—with God as its inward center of emotion, thought, and will—withdrew into passivity. And the universe remained in this passive state for three hours, the same length of time as the opening series of events and the same length of time during which Jesus' body hung on the cross in ridicule and shame.[23]

As Robbins connects the passivity of Jesus's body, beginning with his silence, followed by his crucifixion to the withdrawal of the earth into darkness, then with Jesus's death scene and the earth's darkness framed by the three-hour time frame, a key feature of qualitative progression is foregrounded: "We are put in a state of mind which another state of mind can appropriately follow."[24]

The distinguishing feature of qualitative progression is that it functions through amplification and aggregation. Qualitative progression can amplify an element's presence such as in the preceding example of the cumulative effect of the role of silence in the events surrounding Jesus's crucifixion. But also, qualitative progression can help to develop a new understanding of a notion. In such a role, qualitative progression works with progressive texture to develop and expand the meaning of certain repetitive elements in the text. However, unlike repetitive and progressive textures, which are concerned with repeated lexically centered patterns, the emphasis in qualitative progression is not as directly on the lexica (although it can include these) as on any narrative element, which repeats and progresses throughout the discourse. One of the examples used by Robbins to illustrate qualitative progression is when "new attributes and new titles emerge in the portrayal of Jesus."[25] While these may or may not be lexically repetitive, their aggregation helps to develop an understanding of the text's unfolding of Jesus's identity.

In inner textual analysis, we also establish the initial boundaries for the unit, loosely corresponding to what Robbins calls "opening-middle-closing texture and pattern."[26] In the case of a narrative, this might correspond to the opening, middle, and closing of a story's plot or the opening, middle, and closing of a speech given by a narrative character. However,

---

23. Robbins, *Exploring the Texture of Texts*, 33.
24. Burke, "Lexicon Rhetoricae," 125.
25. Robbins, *Exploring the Texture of Texts*, 23.
26. Ibid., 19–21.

rhetorical units are not necessarily the same as episodic story units, nor bounded by a narrated speech. For example, the story of the wasteful steward (Luke 16:1–8a) is a story component that leads to the rhetorical message "You cannot serve God and mammon" (Luke 16:13). In similar manner, while Stephen's speech in Acts is limited by Acts 7:2–53, the rhetorical unit goes beyond the speech boundaries (Acts 7:51), for no sooner does Stephen indict the "stiff-necked people, uncircumcised in heart and ears" in his speech than does his audience "stop their ears" (Acts 7:57) as they rush to stone the speaker. Thus the rhetorical message moves beyond the speech unit. Rhetorical units are determined by rhetorical, rather than narrative-driven, criteria.

Rhetorical units can only truly be established from the findings of repetitive and progressive textural analyses. However, somewhat circuitously, these analyses cannot be commenced without some type of initial boundaries. Therefore, in the analysis, the Philippi visit (Acts 16:11–40) acts as a proxy for the rhetorical unit proper until I complete the repetitive and progressive analyses. Once I investigate the repetitive and progressive textures, it is then possible to look for shifts in clusters of elements and changes in progressive sequences around the borders of the proxy unit, so that, ultimately, the temporary boundaries can be slightly modified to encompass the final rhetorical unit of Acts 16:9–40.

This analysis of narrational, repetitive, and progressive textures will participate in what is essentially an exercise in "presence." Presence, to paraphrase Perelman and Olbrechts-Tyteca, is created by selecting and presenting certain elements as important and pertinent to the discussion.[27] From a large field of potential elements, the author foregrounds those of concern to the argument and attempts to make these "present to the consciousness" of the audience. Repetitive and progressive analyses mainly seek to bring to the interpreter's consciousness those elements and patterns that the author made prominent in structuring the discourse.

Narrational texture brings out a text's prominent narrative elements including characters and their actions, spatial and temporal settings, and events. As originally formulated, narrational texture was primarily focused on voices in the narrative, perhaps showing the abiding influence of oratory on rhetorical criticism.[28] However, as Robbins also recognized, not

---

27. Perelman and Olbrechts-Tyteca, *New Rhetoric*, 116.
28. "Narrational texture resides in voices (often not identified with a specific

only speaking voices but also the wider range of bodily actions and who (or what) is performing them contributes to rhetorical development. For this reason, he introduced sensory-aesthetic texture, which in *Exploring the Texture of Texts* was a distinct component of inner texture, but which since has been assimilated into narrational texture in Bloomquist's recent work and will be in this analysis as well.[29]

Sensory-aesthetic texture is based on Bernard de Géradon's tripartite model of the body as it was later appropriated in Bruce Malina's cultural-anthropological approach to the New Testament. In his 1958 work, de Géradon contended that the Bible portrays the human as an acting subject composed of three integrated loci of activity: thought, speech, and action-motion. According to de Géradon, biblical anthropology sees the human being primarily as an agent of vital activity who acts on, and reacts to, his or her environment. As a result, "a human being is endowed with a heart for thinking, a mouth for speaking and hands and feet for acting and moving."[30] The Bible rarely describes human organs and limbs statically but rather as dynamic acting agents. So, we see a hand introduced because it acts, a mouth because it speaks, and a heart because it thinks and perceives. In addition to bringing an anthropological awareness to biblical interpretation, de Géradon's model helped to sharpen the focus on the ways that biblical actors engage with their environment and situations by broadening the notion of action to include speech, thought, and perception.

Malina further developed de Géradon's initial categories into a model composed of three body zones: (1) the zone of emotion-fused thought, which includes "eyes, heart, eyelids, pupils ... : to see, ... understand, think, ... choose, feel [and so on].... In [North American] culture, this zone would cover the areas we refer to as intellect, will, judgment, conscience, personality thrust ... affection, and so on"; (2) the zone of self-

---

character) through which the words in texts speak" (Robbins, *Exploring the Texture of Texts*, 15).

29. Ibid., 29–36.

30. "L'homme est doté d'un coeur pour penser, d'une bouche pour parler, de mains et de pieds pour agir et se mouvoir" (Bernard de Géradon, "L'Homme à l'Image de Dieu," *NRTh* 80 [1958]: 683). The role of de Géradon's model in sociorhetorical analysis was presented in Alexandra Gruca-Macaulay, "De Géradon's Body-Zone Model and Greco-Roman Physiognomy: The Role of Socio-culturally Encoded Bodily Actions in Socio-rhetorical Analysis" (paper presented at the Annual Meeting of the Society of Biblical Literature, San Francisco, CA, 21 November 2011).

expressive speech, which includes "mouth, tongue, lips, throat, teeth, jaws … : to speak, hear, say, call, question" and so on, where "this zone would cover the area we refer to as self-revelation through speech"; and (3) the zone of purposeful action, which includes "hands, feet, arms, fingers, legs … in our culture this zone would cover … all external activity."[31]

Since much is conveyed in the biblical narrative through bodies and how they act, narrational texture is interested in who acts and how they act, including actions of self-expression such as speaking, inner acts of thinking, perceiving and feeling, and the physical actions of external body parts. The agent who acts, the part of the body involved in the action, and the body zone of the action all contribute to the rhetoric of the text. For example, later analysis will contend that the Pauline group's act of sitting down with the women by the river (Acts 16:13) is rhetorically significant and that emotion-fused acts of interpreting, supposing, and concluding move the plot forward. Narrational texture identifies the foregrounded acting agents through actions, body zones, and spatial and temporal settings.

2.1.3.1. Argumentative Texture and Pattern

Argumentative texture forms the final phase of inner textural analysis, and like the other textures it is concerned with "presence" rather than the fully developed rhetorical argument. As noted above, rhetorical argumentation relies on social logic, and until the relevant elements of this logic are discovered in intertextual analysis, it will be possible to examine only the surface-level argumentative structure of the text rather than its full argumentative force.[32] But even here, we can note that a rhetorical argument functions

---

31. Bruce J. Malina, *The New Testament World: Insights from Cultural Anthropology*, 3rd rev. and expanded ed. (Louisville: Westminster John Knox, 2001), 69.

32. As an example of the embedded nature of social logic in argumentation, consider the following popular riddle that circulated in the early 1970s: "A man and his son are driving in a car one day, when they get into a fatal accident. The man is killed instantly. The boy is knocked unconscious, but he is still alive. He is rushed to hospital, and will need immediate surgery. The doctor enters the emergency room, looks at the boy, and says, 'I can't operate on this boy, he is my son.' How can this be?" ("I Can't Operate on This Boy; He Is My Son," *Everything2.com*, http://tinyurl.com/SBL4818a). The riddle seemed insoluble to most of us at the time it first circulated, yet my own children had no difficulty providing the answer that the doctor was the boy's mother. The riddle functions on the assumption that the mental image of "doctor" would be

through either deductive or inductive argumentation, and it is delivered through either the explicit words of the text (rhetology) or through cognitive linkages formed through those mental images that have been evoked by the text (rhetography). Often, rhetorical arguments integrate both methods of argumentation and means of delivery.

2.1.3.1.1. Modes of Rhetorical Argumentation: Deductive and Inductive

Deductive rhetorical argumentation bears some similarity to formal argumentation, where the underlying assumptions could be accepted as scientifically self-evident by any rational human: "Formal reasoning results from a process of simplification which is possible only under special conditions, within isolated and limited systems. But, since there are formal proofs of recognized validity, quasi-logical arguments derive their persuasive strength from their similarity with these well-established modes of reasoning."[33] For Aristotle, a formal rhetorical reasoning structure was best illustrated through the enthymeme (*Rhet.* 1356b8). Aristotle suggested that the enthymeme be considered the rhetorical equivalent of a syllogism involving an argument with a premise, which requires the audience to fill in implicit elements or premises from its social knowledge, and a conclusion. He gives as one example: "There is no one of men who is free. For he is a slave of money or of chance" (*Rhet.* 1394b1–2 [Kennedy]). An example of deductive rhetorical argumentation from Luke 16:13 is the claim (similar to Aristotle's):

> Premise: "No servant can serve two masters";
> Rationale: "For either he will hate the one and love the other, or he will be devoted to the one and despise the other."
> Conclusion: "You cannot serve God and mammon."

The argumentative mode is deductive in Luke, because it argues through mutual exclusivity: what is "false" cannot at the same time be considered "true." Nevertheless, Perelman and Olbrechts-Tyteca maintain that, by its very nature, rhetoric lies outside of the closed system of formal logic.

---

male. With today's changed social reality regarding women in medicine, the riddle's inner logic, while unchanged at the structural level, has been dramatically changed to the point whereby the riddle's argumentation can no longer function effectively for many contemporary North American hearers.

33. Perelman and Olbrechts-Tyteca, *New Rhetoric*, 193.

Inductive rhetorical argumentation draws inferences through linkages other than those found in quasi-logical argumentation. Aristotle associates rhetorical induction with argumentation through "paradigm," which essentially means arguing by illustration or example (*Rhet.* 1356b10). Aristotle suggests two forms of paradigm: examples from history or fables (the dividing line between these was not strictly drawn in practice). Each of these could be used to suggest an analogous relationship between the paradigm and the premise on which a rhetor was seeking assent on.[34]

Moreover, "historical example" and "fable" encompass a broad range of data that can also include social wisdom or common sense. Analogy through common sense undergirds Aristotle's mention of Socratic sayings as a form of induction:

> Socratic sayings are an instance of comparison: for example, if someone were to say that officials should not be chosen by lot (for that would be as if someone were to choose athletes randomly—not those able to compete, but those on whom the lot fell); or [as if] choosing by lot any one of the sailors to act as pilot rather than the one who knew how. (*Rhet.* 1393b4 [Kennedy])

As such, Aristotle's understanding of inductive argumentation is a subset of the type of inductive argumentation that Perelman and Olbrechts-Tyteca characterize as "arguments based on the structure of the real":[35]

> Whereas quasi-logical arguments lay claim to a certain validity owing to their rational appearance, which derives from their more-or-less close relation with certain logical or mathematical formulae, the arguments based on the structure of reality make use of this structure to establish solidarity between accepted judgments and others which one wishes to promote.[36]

---

34. The rhetorical concept of argumentation through induction cannot be conflated with scientific induction, as D. W. Hamlyn points out: "[Aristotelian induction] has nothing very much in common with what has come in modern times to be called 'ampliative induction'—generalizing from observed instances; rather it is a form of argument from analogy, in the sense that the other party to the debate is got to see the analogy between cases and that analogy is used to get a further conclusion" (D. W. Hamlyn, "Aristotelian *Epagogue*," *Phronesis* 21 [1976]: 168).

35. Perelman and Olbrechts-Tyteca, *New Rhetoric*, 228.

36. Ibid., 261. Perelman and Olbrechts-Tyteca emphasize that arguments based on the structure of reality do not necessarily reflect objective reality: "What we are

An example of inductive argumentation can be found in Acts 19:2–5, when Paul confronts a group of disciples in Ephesus about their baptism:

> And he said to them, "Did you receive the Holy Spirit when you believed?" And they said, "No, we have never even heard that there is a Holy Spirit." And he said, "Into what then were you baptized?" They said, "Into John's baptism." And Paul said, "John baptized with the baptism of repentance, telling the people to believe in the one who was to come after him, that is, Jesus." On hearing this, they were baptized in the name of the Lord Jesus.

Paul uses an "ends and means" inductive argument that argues that John's baptism was a means intended to facilitate the "end" of baptism "in the name of Jesus Christ."[37] Spotting the inductive nature of Paul's argumentation helps to prevent inaccurate readings that might unwittingly recast the inductive argument into a deductive attempt at discrediting John's baptism as "false" in contrast with Paul's "true" baptism. By understanding the method of argumentation, an interpreter is guided to an author's argumentative goals.

2.1.3.1.2. Narrative Plotline Logical Progression

In *Exploring the Texture of Texts*, Robbins suggests a form of narrative progression, "logical progression" (called "syllogistic progression" by Burke), that through narrative form supports an inductive argument.[38] Logical progression functions through the causal links that move a narrative's plot along. When Burke defines syllogistic progression as a "perfectly conducted argument, advancing step by step," he does not intend the structure of formal logic but rather the inner logic of a plot's development.

Burke describes syllogistic progression as when "the arrows of our desires are turned in a certain direction, and the plot follows the direction of the arrows."[39] In narrative, this plot direction forms along what Perelman and Olbrechts-Tyteca call "the causal link," and although called "syllogistic" by Burke and "logical" by Robbins, argumentatively this type of

---

interested in here is not an objective description of reality, but the manner in which opinions concerning it are presented. These can, moreover, be treated as facts, truths, or presumptions" (262).

37. For "ends and means" in argumentation, see ibid., 270–78.
38. Robbins, *Exploring the Texture of Texts*, 23.
39. Burke, "Lexicon Rhetoricae," 124.

2. METHOD

progression is a form of inductive argumentation that develops sequential relations between events. Perelman and Olbrechts-Tyteca suggest three types of argumentation through the causal link:

1. Argumentation tending to attach two given successive events to each other by means of a causal link.
2. Argumentation tending to reveal the existence of a cause that could have determined a given event.
3. Argumentation tending to show the effect which must result from a given event.[40]

Logical progression permits new events to reverse expectation raised by prior causal linkages. However, the "logical" component of the logical progression requires that any reversals cannot appear to result purely from chance or random events but rather from the plot's design. In *Poetics* (1452a21–29), Aristotle cites plot reversals as one of the key features of plot, but these reversals must occur either through "necessity or probability." Aristotle stresses that events that occur "contrary to expectation" still need to be narrated in a way that they seem not to occur by chance but rather "on account of one another" (1452a1–10). The more sophisticated type of plot, according to Aristotle, will demonstrate reversal in combination with "recognition," that is, when there is a change "from ignorance to knowledge" that coincides with, or is the cause of, the realignment of a plot's arrows to an opposite direction (1452a30–32). When, for example, Peter, in his new theological understanding, baptizes gentiles for the first time in Acts 10:48, reversing his presumptions of what categorizes people as clean or unclean, the event linkages of the preceding plot lead to the "rightness of the conclusion."[41] From an analytical perspective, logical progression is helpful in locating reversals that point to particularly intense areas of rhetorical interest.

2.1.3.1.3. Means of Rhetorical Argumentation: Rhetology and Rhetography
Aristotle seemed to recognize that both deductive and inductive methods of argumentation can be delivered explicitly through words, or by

---

40. Perelman and Olbrechts-Tyteca, *New Rhetoric*, 263.
41. "In so far as the audience, from its acquaintance with the premises, feels the rightness of the conclusion, the work is formal" (i.e., displays the form of syllogistic progression). Burke, "Lexicon Rhetoricae," 124.

argumentation that functions "through the rhetoric": "Some rhetorical utterances are paradigmatic, some enthymematic, and similarly, some orators are paradigmatic, some enthymematic" (*Rhet.* 1356b10 [Kennedy]). In SRI, this difference in the "delivery platforms" of rhetoric is termed rhetology and rhetography.

Despite debates about the exact definitional difference between rhetology and rhetography in the Rhetoric of Religious Antiquity (RRA) working group, there is a common understanding that rhetorical argumentation has two different, although frequently interlinked, means of delivery: surface-level words (*logos*) and cognitive mental images evoked by the words (*graphē*) and their argumentative configuration.[42] Accordingly, it seems that Aristotle, as well as the RRA discussions around rhetology and rhetography, intends to distinguish between mode and manner of argumentation. For that reason, the term *rhetology* will be understood in this project as "conveying rhetorical argumentation primarily by the explicit words of the text," while *rhetography* will be understood as "conveying rhetorical argumentation primarily through cognitive mental images evoked by the words of the text."[43]

In many cases, deductive argumentation, which tends to resemble the statements of formal logic, is delivered primarily by rhetology, and inductive argumentation is delivered by rhetography. However, the deductive and inductive argumentative modes are not synonymous with the rhetological and rhetographical means, or platforms, of delivery of the modes. For example, although the mode of argumentation that expresses the means of John's baptism as an end to baptism in Jesus (Acts 19:2–5) is inductive,[44] its platform for delivery is rhetological; the argument comes to the audience directly from the words of the text.

---

42. *Graphē* intends the visual depiction of some concept, i.e., graphic. Its meaning originated in the visual depiction of words through writing. Because of the "pictorial" nature of the graphic, the notion of rhetography, which intends argumentation through cognitive mental imagery, has at times been confused with descriptive elements of texts that "paint a picture" in the mind of the audience. Descriptive prose can play a rhetorical role but should not be confused with rhetography.

43. These definitions affirm Bloomquist's understanding that a topos can also be found explicitly articulated by the words (topology) or in a mental elaboration evoked by the words (topography). See L. Gregory Bloomquist, "Rhetoric, Culture, and Ideology: Socio-rhetorical Analysis in the Reading of New Testament Texts," in Hester and Hester, *Rhetorics in the New Millennium*, 137.

44. Acts 19:2–5 also employs an "argument of direction" in which one stage—

Another example, Luke 21:1–4, shows how a deductive argument is conveyed first by rhetography and then explicitly articulated by rhetology: "He looked up and saw the rich putting their gifts into the treasury; and he saw a poor widow put in two copper coins. And he said, 'Truly I tell you, this poor widow has put in more than all of them; for they all contributed out of their abundance, but she out of her poverty put in all the living that she had'" (Luke 21:1–4). The argument uses "the idea of measure, which underlies arguments by comparison"[45] together with "argumentation by sacrifice"[46] in order to recast the notion of "worth." Whereas conventional wisdom would ascribe higher value to the higher nominal value of the gifts of the rich, the text inverts the scales of value by substituting degree of sacrifice for nominal value. The significant personal sacrifice involved in the widow's gift (essentially all of her livelihood) results in her gift being affirmed as the one of higher worth in comparison with the (aggregated!) gifts of the rich.

To some members of the audience, the deductive argument might have been adequately conveyed rhetographically by Luke 21:1–2 alone, by its having evoked a mental picture of the gifts of the rich and another of the widow's coins and by evoking a mental scale that would "weigh" these gifts alongside each other on a scale of personal sacrifice. The rhetographical delivery of the argument is then reiterated rhetologically in Luke 21:3, through the explicit words "this poor widow has put in more than all of them." In reality, rhetorical arguments, including the examples cited above, are delivered through a blend of rhetology and rhetography. Nonetheless, distinguishing between modes and manner of argumentation helps to bring the argumentative texture into sharper relief. Most especially, since the argumentative force of rhetography depends on cognitive mental images, spotting rhetographical argumentation can help to bring this argumentation to light.

2.1.4. The World "around" the Text: Intertextural Analysis

To the extent that inner textural analysis helps an interpreter become aware of rhetorical elements, it also calls for the next step of interpretation: a

---

John's baptism—is to lead to the next stage—baptism in Jesus. For "argument of direction," see Perelman and Olbrechts-Tyteca, *New Rhetoric*, 281–83.

45. Ibid., 242.
46. Ibid., 248.

socially and culturally informed investigation of these elements and how they would have been perceived in the first-century "thought-world of Mediterranean culture."[47] After all, rhetoric is predicated on such shared and common social and cultural textures. Intertexture examines the social, cultural, oral-scribal, historical, and sacred textures of the world around the text.[48] As Bloomquist notes, the world of the text

> intersects a larger world, a world that, through historical reconstruction we can know. This world has its own social and cultural features, some of which can be known historically or deduced through models. Part of the goal of SR is to provide a configuration of the world around the text, partly on the basis of social phenomena (what humans do) and partly on the basis of cultural phenomena (what humans do or did in the local culture whence the text has come to us). SR then proceeds to ask how the text and its world intersects this social and cultural world, that is, what social and cultural realities figure in the text.[49]

Social texture involves the use of social topics, like the role of virtue in Roman society; cultural texture involves the use of culturally-specific topics, such as the way Greeks and Romans used Lydian ethnography to speak of Lydians as luxury-loving and effeminate; historical intertexture provides historical background, whether in the material world, such as locations of ancient synagogues, or in events such as Alexander the Great's conquests; oral-scribal texture involves recitations, reconfigurations, and allusions to other written and material texts, such as the common elements between Euripides's *Bacchae*, and the Philippi episode of Acts 16;[50] sacred texture involves topics concerning deities, spiritual beings, symbolically derived notions such as holiness, as well as religious

---

47. Robbins, *Exploring the Texture of Texts*, 30.
48. Excellent descriptions of the components of intertexture are available elsewhere, and there is no need to rehearse these in detail. See Bloomquist, "Rhetoric, Culture and Ideology," 118–23; Bloomquist, "Rhetoric of Suffering," 203–5; Robbins, *Exploring the Texture of Texts*, 40–94; Robbins, *Tapestry of Early Christian Discourse*, 96–191.
49. Bloomquist, "First-Century Models," 5.
50. Oral-scribal texture would be what many associate with "intertexture." This project follows Bloomquist in using the term *intertextural* rather than *intertextual* so as not to confuse oral-scribal texture with the full intertextural enterprise; see Bloomquist, "Rhetoric, Culture and Ideology," 123 n. 34.

communities such as the role of the enigmatic "place of prayer" (Acts 16:13, 16) in the rhetorical unit.

The goal of intertexture is to investigate those intertextual elements that either contribute to or form the text's rhetorical topoi as they would have been used and heard in a first-century environment. Thus the intertextural enterprise is not concerned with "painting a picture" of the first-century world but rather, under the guidance of inner textural results, delving into the world that gave rise to the text in order to flesh out that world's topoi as they relate to the rhetorical unit under study. Bloomquist writes:

> In terms of its intertexture, ... the text is a rhetorical subset of social, cultural, oral-scribal, historical, and sacred possibilities drawn from that world, rather than some artificially exhaustive representation of the real world of the author's day (as historical-critical study used to argue) or even a faithful one (as positivistic approaches to historical-critical study still argue).[51]

Intertexture looks to see which social, cultural, oral-scribal, historical, and sacred elements the author invoked in constructing the text's rhetorical argument. As remarked in the discussion of topoi above, topoi are constituted by liaisons of elements found in the text as well as in the long-term schematic knowledge of the audience. As a result of this interplay of linkages, intertextual analysis performs its role by unearthing the relevant intertextual elements based on the points of connectivity among a unit's elements, both those explicitly found in the text and those implicitly evoked by the text.

2.1.5. The Role of Physiognomy in Intertextual Analysis

Physiognomy is an especially important facet of social and cultural texture in my interpretation of the Philippi episode. Ancient authors drew on commonly held social and cultural identity stereotypes that were based on a person's physical appearance, ethnicity, gender, occupation, and/or social status. These stereotypes were given "scientific" credence through the study of "physiognomy," or "the study of the relation of the features of a [person] to his [or her] inner character,"[52] which held that

---

51. Bloomquist, "Rhetoric, Culture and Ideology," 122–23.
52. Elizabeth C. Evans, "Physiognomics in the Ancient World," *TAPS* 59.5 (1969): 5.

a person's character could be inferred on the basis of his or her physical appearance. For example, from Hippocrates comes the following physiognomic characterization:

> Those with ruddy complexion, flat nose, large eyes, are good.
> If the head is large and the eyes small, if they are stammerers, they are quick to anger.
> Those with large head, large dark eyes, thick, blunt nose, are good.
> Those with small head, thin neck, narrow chest, are equable. (Hippocrates, *Epid.* 2.5.1; 2.6.1 [Jones et al., LCL])[53]

Character stereotyping, however, was not confined to a person's physique, for other external attributes also contributed to stereotyped classifications of a person's character. Any external marker of a person, whether physical or social, could regularly supply a "ready-made" topos of conventional character traits. Stereotypes based on gender, occupation, status, and ethnicity were highly pervasive. While some stereotypes operated in narrower cultural locations, others functioned transculturally throughout the first-century Mediterranean environment of antiquity.

Ethnography, or "rhetorical profiling,"[54] constituted a major element of characterization in a variety of literatures and was the source of the broader enterprise of physiognomy. One of the earliest examples of the explicit connections between a people's geographic environment and their inherent nature is found in *Airs, Waters, Places*, traditionally ascribed to Hippocrates.[55] As Benjamin Isaac explains, this treatise introduced the notion of "bipolarity between Europe and Asia":[56]

---

53. As quoted in Mladen Popović, *Reading the Human Body: Physiognomics and Astrology in the Dead Sea Scrolls and Hellenistic-Early Roman Period Judaism*, STDJ 67 (Leiden: Brill, 2007), 91.

54. An apt descriptor for ethnography suggested by L. Gregory Bloomquist, "Rhetorical Profiling," conversation with the author, Ottawa, 2007. For a similar form of rhetorical profiling based on affinity to a philosophical school, see L. Gregory Bloomquist, "The Epicurean Tag in Plutarch: Implications for New Testament Study" (paper presented at the Eastern International Region Meeting of the American Academy of Religion, UQAM. Montreal, Quebec, March 1994).

55. See Benjamin Isaac, *The Invention of Racism in Classical Antiquity* (Princeton: Princeton University Press, 2004), 60–69.

56. Ibid., 61.

2. METHOD

"For everything in Asia is far more beautiful and grows to far greater size; the region is more cultured than the other, the character of the inhabitants is more tractable and gentle. The cause of this is the moderate climate, because it lies further east in the middle between the risings of the sun, and farther away from the cold." The best part of it has good water, is not too hot or too dry. Food is plentiful. "People are well nourished, of very fine physique and very tall, and hardly differ from each other in shape or length.... Courage, tenacity, energy and will-power could not develop under such natural conditions ... either among the locals or among the immigrants, but pleasure must dominate."[57]

A proliferation of other examples attest to the pervasiveness of ethnographic characterizations. For instance, Plato asserts:

> Some districts are naturally superior to others for the breeding of men of a good or bad type.... Some districts are ill-conditioned or well-conditioned owing to a variety of winds or to sunshine ... others owing simply to the produce of the soil, which offers produce either good or bad for their bodies, and equally able to effect similar results in their souls as well. (Plato, *Leg.* 5.747d–e [Lamb et al., LCL])

A similar sentiment is echoed by Cicero:

> It may be observed that the inhabitants of those countries in which the air is pure and rarefied have keener wits and greater powers of understanding than persons who live in a dense and heavy climate; moreover the substance employed as food is also believed to have some influence on mental acuteness. (Cicero, *Nat. d.* 2.16.42 [Rackham, LCL])

The argumentative undercurrent that structured physiognomic logic held that geography determined a people's character, as well as contributed to a people's distinguishing physical characteristics that would then signal their inner character.[58]

Of particular interest for the current analysis was the inculcated concept of "environmental determinism," which implicitly held that "entire nations are believed to have common characteristics determined wholly

---

57. Ibid., 62; quotations are from Hippocrates, *Airs, Waters, Places* 12.
58. E.g., "Those living in the north are brave and stiff-haired, and those in the south are cowardly and have soft hair." Isaac, *Invention of Racism*, 151; quoting *Anon. Physiogn.* 806b (André).

by factors outside themselves, which are, by implication, unchangeable."[59] What we rightly call "racism" was standard practice of making sense of others in the first-century world. As Elizabeth Evans reminded us, "We do it—so did the Greeks and Romans, but they made an organized science of it."[60]

While handbooks of physiognomy were written as a form of scientific/medical manuals, Malina and Jerome Neyrey contend that the broader practice of "thinking in stereotypes" characterizes all group-oriented societies that "[made] sense of other people by assessing them 'sociologically' rather than 'psychologically.'"[61] In the first-century Mediterranean world, the self-understanding of the human being was not located in the modern Western concept of individualism, but rather in a group orientation that Malina calls "collectivism." A collectivist personality, Malina writes, "is essentially a group-embedded and group-oriented person (some call such a person 'collectively-oriented'). Such a group-embedded, collectivistic personality is one who simply needs another continually in order to know who he or she really is."[62] One impact of the highly normative structure of group identity was that actions of the human body reflected on the social body within which it was embedded. For this reason, the initial observations related to sensory-aesthetic texture in inner textural analysis "take on flesh" when examined in light of the social-cultural encoding of bodies and their actions.

While physiognomy is clearly a form of racism and, when made explicit, is understood today primarily within such a paradigm, the role physiognomy performed in the ancient world was far more nuanced. Maud Gleason, in particular, has recognized that a person's ability to assess character played a crucial role in his or her future success and that this imperative for discernment played an important role in motivating physiognomic thinking. Gleason writes:

> To follow the thought-patterns of the physiognomist is to enter the forest of eyes that made up what we lightly call today "the face-to-face society" of the ancient Mediterranean city. This was a world in which the

---

59. Isaac, *Invention of Racism*, 163–64.
60. Elizabeth C. Evans, "Physiognomics in the Roman Empire," *CJ* 45 (1950): 277.
61. Bruce J. Malina and Jerome H. Neyrey, *Portraits of Paul: An Archaeology of Ancient Personality* (Louisville: Westminster John Knox, 1996), 169.
62. Malina, *New Testament World*, 62.

scrutiny of faces was not an idle pastime but an essential survival skill. In this world, the practice of divination, in many forms and at various levels of formality, was a ubiquitous reflex in response to uncertainty. Everyone who had to choose a son-in-law or a traveling companion, deposit valuables before a journey, buy slaves, or make a business loan became perforce an amateur physiognomist: he made risky inferences from human surfaces to human depths.[63]

Ancient audiences, almost assuredly, would have been acutely attuned to any physiognomic markers of identity displayed by narrative characters. By definition, in physiognomic profiling a person's external label infers character, and this presumed correlation between the external and the internal often found its way into rhetorical argumentation. As Evans observes, "As a quasi-science [physiognomy] always bore a close relationship to the science of medicine; as an art, to the practice of rhetoric."[64]

One example of physiognomic thinking provided by Evans gives an excellent example of how an author could assume a physiognomic appraisal system in his or her audience. Evans profiles Xenophon's personified depiction of the antithetical figures of Virtue and Vice. Xenophon writes: "And there appeared two women of great stature making toward him. The one was fair to see and of high bearing; … her limbs were adorned with purity, her eyes with modesty; sober was her figure.… The other was plump and soft with high feeding.… Open-eyed was she" (Xenophon, *Mem.* 2.1.22 [Marchant et al., LCL]).[65] While Vice's plump figure signals a sumptuous lifestyle, her "open eyes," as Evans remarks, are a sign of her shamelessness.[66]

One of the key cultural determinants of status in first-century Mediterranean antiquity functioned through the social system of honor and shame. A predominantly male value, honor "is a claim to worth *and* the social acknowledgement of that worth"[67] that "expresses one's public standing."[68] The complementary feminine value of "shame" referred to the

---

63. Maud W. Gleason, *Making Men: Sophists and Self-Presentation in Ancient Rome* (Princeton: Princeton University Press, 1995), 55.
64. Evans, "Physiognomics in the Roman Empire," 5.
65. Quoted in Evans, "Physiognomics in the Ancient World," 46.
66. Ibid., 46.
67. Malina, *New Testament World*, 30.
68. Jerome H. Neyrey, "Loss of Wealth, Loss of Family, Loss of Honor: The Cultural Context of the Original Makarisms in Q," in *The Social World of the New Testa-*

first-century understanding that a woman's role was to protect the honor of the male within which she was socially embedded; that is, her concern was for the reputation of her male-defined kinship group. The honor/shame social system was bodily engendered in ancient Mediterranean culture, as Malina explains:

> Male honor is symboled in the testicles and covers typically male behavior, running from the ethically neutral to the ethically valued: manliness, courage (the willingness to challenge and affront another male), authority, defense of the family's honor, concern for prestige, and social eminence—all this is honorable behavior for the male. Female shame, on the other hand, is symboled in the maidenhead and likewise covers a range running from the ethically neutral to the ethically valued: feelings of sensitivity of "shame" to reveal nakedness, modesty, shyness, blushing, timidity, restraint, sexual exclusiveness—all this is positive shame for the female and makes her honorable.[69]

An understanding of the honor/shame value system thereby informs the "open-eyed" physiognomic characterization of Vice as "shameless" wherein "a shameless person ... is one who does not recognize the rules of human interaction."[70] As Evans's study of physiognomy in the ancient world demonstrated, the works of ancient authors, "representing such diverse literary forms as epic, elegy and lyric, history and biography, drama, philosophy, satire and fiction," displayed a "physiognomic consciousness" that served "to illumine the effects of physiognomic thinking upon the art of characterization."[71]

An understanding of first-century physiognomic thinking will lead us to ask questions of the figure of Lydia that have not been asked before. As intertextual analysis will show, each of the descriptors in Lydia's profile—gender, ethnicity, occupation, and "worshiper of God"— would have evoked particular images from within the social logic of physiognomy. Therefore, an appreciation for the role of physiognomy in rhetoric will

---

ment: Insights and Models, ed. Jerome H. Neyrey and Eric C. Stewart (Peabody, MA: Hendrickson, 2008), 88.

69. Malina, *New Testament World*, 49.

70. Ibid.

71. Evans, "Physiognomics in the Ancient World," 6; See Isaac, *Invention of Racism*, 151.

2. METHOD

lead us to search for those intertextural elements that are most relevant to investigating the role and function of Lydia in Acts 16.

2.1.6. The Conceptual Movement of the Text: Ideological Textural Analysis

Inner and intertextural analyses bring to light those historically, socially, and culturally contextualized topoi that play a role in a given text's rhetorical discourse. These earlier phases of the sociorhetorical project seek to uncover the topics of interest to the author, as well as the sociocultural understanding of these topics shared between author and audience. They comprise the text and the world around the text. As Bloomquist has recently contended, these, in a sense, remain "descriptive" phases of analysis that provide a comprehensive look at the text and its environment but still leave short an understanding of the rhetorical force of the work. Moving an analysis from the "socio-" to that of truly *rhetorical* ultimately requires that an interpreter investigate how and for what purpose the author has deployed the topoi. This, therefore, becomes the concern in analyzing the ideological texture of the text: discovering the conceptual movement of the text in relation to the conceptual movement of the hearer/reader.[72]

"Ideology" is understood variously, and it needs to be clarified how this book understands the relationship of ideology to ideological texture. Perhaps the fullest investigation of the role of ideology in SRI has been undertaken by Bloomquist in a number of recent works.[73] While ideology is at times "associated pejoratively with distortion,"[74] Bloomquist's approach, also adopted in this project, understands ideology to refer not

---

72. Bloomquist, "Rhetoric, Culture and Ideology," 123–24; Bloomquist, "Paul's Inclusive Language," 172–76.

73. See Bloomquist, "Paul's Inclusive Language"; Bloomquist, "Rhetoric, Culture and Ideology"; Bloomquist, "The Role of the Audience in the Determination of Argumentation: The Gospel of Luke and the Acts of the Apostles," in *Rhetorical Argumentation in Biblical Texts: Essays from the Lund 2000 Conference*, ed. Anders Eriksson, Thomas H. Olbricht, and Walter Übelacker, ESEC 8 (Harrisburg, PA: Trinity Press International, 2002), 157–73; Bloomquist, "The Role of Argumentation in the Miracle Stories of Luke-Acts: Towards a Fuller Identification of Miracle Discourse for Use in Socio-rhetorical Analysis," in *Miracle Discourse in the Argumentation of the New Testament*, ed. Duane F. Watson (Atlanta: Society of Biblical Literature, 2012), 85–124.

74. Bloomquist, "Paul's Inclusive Language," 174.

to a rhetoric of guile, but rather, more analytically, to the manner by which the text attempts to reconfigure a localized cultural understanding.

The rhetorically focused enterprise of ideological texture, however, does not deal with static cultural positions, but rather, as Bloomquist has expressed, "that 'movement' by which peoples and cultures and forms of people in culture change from one way of being or looking at the world to another."[75] Ideological textural analysis "discerns the text's attempt to move an audience to new static positions in which people find themselves, or the text's putative movement in which people are reconfirmed in a place which they have not left."[76] The aim of ideological texture is to display how a moment of "culture in movement" is captured by the text through its rhetorical deployment of topoi. More specifically, Bloomquist has suggested that "ideological texture deals with what authors do with preexisting *topoi*: alter, confirm, nuance, reshape, etc. Rhetorically, authors employ them in ways that reconfigure them (changing them from a static identity to another) or what is done with them (changing how they have been employed or could otherwise be used in argumentation to that point)."[77] While topoi can sometimes be confirmed or strengthened in rhetorical discourse, what analysis of ideological texture often discerns is an author's attempts to transform conventional topoi.[78]

Bloomquist's insights into how topoi function argumentatively have led him to suggest that some of the recent findings of cognitive science, particularly as formulated by Gilles Fauconnier and Mark Turner, can inform ideological textural analysis.[79] Fauconnier and Turner explain how cognitive linguistic modeling displays the way in which forms, such as stereotypes and conventions, "prompt largely unconscious and unnoticed constructions of the imagination" used by humans in their process of finding meaning.[80] These convention-triggered constructions of the imagination draw on "mental spaces," defined as

---

75. Bloomquist, "Role of the Audience," 166.
76. Bloomquist, "Paul's Inclusive Language," 172. He notes that "what the analysis of ideological texture should enable us to get at is how rhetors seek to move audiences away from or in variance to or even to confirm existing cultural practices." Bloomquist, "Rhetoric, Culture and Ideology," 124.
77. Bloomquist, "Paul's Inclusive Language," 175.
78. Bloomquist, "Rhetoric, Culture and Ideology," 139–40.
79. L. Gregory Bloomquist, "Rhetography and *Topoi*" (e-mail correspondence with the Rhetoric of Religious Antiquity Context group, 6 September 2007).
80. Fauconnier and Turner, *Way We Think*, 11.

2. METHOD

small conceptual packets constructed as we think and talk, for purposes of local understanding and action. They are very partial assemblies containing elements, structured by frames and cognitive models.... Spaces have elements and, often, relations between them. When these elements and relations are organized as a package that we already know about, we say that a mental space is *framed* and we call that organization a "frame." So, for example, a mental space in which Julie purchases coffee at Peet's coffee shop has individual elements that are framed by *commercial transaction*, as well as by the subframe—highly important for Julie—of *buying coffee at Peet's*.[81]

As Bloomquist astutely recognized, the formation and function of mental spaces closely resembles an SRI understanding of topoi, which in essence are "rhetorical packets" recruited by a rhetor for communication.[82]

An essential feature of a topos, as Bloomquist's work has underscored, is its ability to evoke "a constellation of networks of meanings as a result of social, cultural, or ideological use."[83] A topos automatically incorporates a network of conventional associations, the configuration of which depends in part on how the topos is "framed," where a "frame" structures the topoi gathered within it.[84] Fauconnier and Turner explain that an event such as "buying a cup of coffee" might be framed as a "commercial transaction," or alternatively, "taking a break from work, going to a public place for entertainment, or adherence to a daily routine."[85] The basis for the connectivity between elements and topoi, usually situated in the argumentative structure, determines the appropriate frame, and, by corollary, a frame arises from interelemental linkages.[86]

---

81. Ibid., 102.
82. Bloomquist, "Rhetography and *Topoi*."
83. Bloomquist, "Paul's Inclusive Language," 174.
84. Fauconnier and Turner define "frame" as "long-term schematic knowledge" (*Way We Think*, 40). Since Fauconnier and Turner's interest is human cognition, they also define a second type of frame that reflects personal experience relating to "long-term specific knowledge ... such as the memory of the time you climbed Mount Rainier in 2001" (40). Rhetoric, by definition, is a communal enterprise and is mainly concerned with the first type of frame, that of "long-term schematic knowledge," which incorporates social and cultural knowledge shared by a community.
85. Ibid., 103.
86. "An organizing frame provides a topology for the space it organizes; that is, it provides a set of organizing relations among the elements in the space" (ibid., 123).

Cognitive science suggests that meaning develops from blends of mental spaces, where the blend produces a new space that does not simply replicate the input spaces but instead imaginatively produces an "emergent structure." Mental spaces blend within different configurations of "integration networks" in which common elements connect with each other as the blends are formed. An emergent structure results in a "new construal of the situation."[87] As an example of an integration network, Fauconnier and Turner imagine a scenario where competition between two corporate executives is described in terms of a boxing match: "We say that one CEO landed a blow but the other one recovered, one of them tripped and the other took advantage, one of them knocked the other out cold. This construal of the situation builds up a conceptual integration network."[88] Any audience reading such an account of the competition between two executives would not read the account literally and imagine that two executives actually stepped into a boxing ring. Instead, a situation of competition between these two competitors is framed as a boxing match that blends a competitive business dynamic with the form of sporting competition that takes place within a boxing ring. The resulting blend does not duplicate a boxing ring proper; rather the emergent blend has the executives boxing for dominance in an economic environment that has been transposed into a boxing ring. The example here is banal and reflects the type of communication that is regularly found in daily life; however, the process of developing a "new construal of situation" is closely related to how ideological texture attempts to move an audience from one static position to a new way of looking at the world. In this manner, ideological textural analysis embarks on a form of culturally localized "cognitive rhetorical analysis."[89]

As a topos-centered analytic, SRI is concerned not only with the topoi found in a text's original environment but also with how those topoi have been appropriated and reconfigured by a text's reception history. SRI "calls for interpretive practices that include minute attention to the ideologies that guide interpreters' selection, analysis and interpretation of data."[90] As cognitive sociologist Eviatar Zerubavel's work has demonstrated: "Not

---

87. Ibid., 227.
88. Ibid., 126.
89. The descriptor "cognitive rhetorical analysis" is ascribed to the work of Seana Coulson in ibid., 221.
90. Robbins, *Tapestry of Early Christian Discourse*, 201.

only does our social environment affect how we perceive the world; it also helps determine what actually 'enters' our minds in the first place."[91]

The topoi that are prominent in contemporary discussions of Lydia have been incrementally shaped by the ideological frameworks of interpreters over the ages, as the history of interpretation of the Lydia passages suggests and further analysis will demonstrate. For example, despite the fact that Lydia is identified as a seller of purple, and *not* a producer of cloth, from Grotius on to today discussions about Lydia have tended to focus on the production of purple cloth. The ideological bent toward purple cloth began with a topos of weaving as a metonym for feminine propriety, developed into historical-critical descriptions of cloth production, dyeing, and guilds in Thyatira and then blended with contemporary feminist concerns into the current image of Lydia: a businesswoman of the textile industry who hosts the Pauline group. Within this blend, the element of propriety, pointedly introduced through Chrysostom's work, remained a crucial influence that framed the image of "Lydia the hostess."

Not only has ideology reshaped interpreters' perceptions of Lydia, but it has also largely removed from view crucial elements, such as the rhetorical role of Lydia's name, except where this has had value in confirming the ideological a priori. As a result, significant topoi that would have been self-evident to a first-century audience have disappeared entirely, while others have been overmapped onto the text and continue to redirect exegetical inquiry. One of the foundational goals in this ideological texture will be to uncover those topoi that animate the rhetorical development of the text but that have been erased through the history of interpretation and also to raise to awareness how others have been inserted and have thereby redirected the ideological goals of the author of Acts.

2.2. Conclusion: Method

SRI will bring a new set of questions to the figure of Lydia, questions that either have not been asked at all, or at least not systematically, by other methodological approaches. Although only three verses in the rhetorical unit are directly related to Lydia, SRI will investigate whether Lydia

---

91. Eviatar Zerubavel, *Social Mindscapes: An Invitation to Cognitive Sociology* (Cambridge: Harvard University Press, 1997), 35. The implications of Zerubavel's work on SRI were proposed by Bloomquist to the RRA group at the 2006 RRA summer session, Ottawa, Canada.

participates in any repetitive or progressive patterns beyond these verses. Argumentative and then ideological texture will probe into the curious placement of Lydia at the beginning and ending of the events at Philippi. Intertextural analysis will investigate the yet unexplored physiognomic questions raised by the correlation between Lydia's name and ethnic origin. By bringing these and other questions to the role of Lydia in Acts 16 within a programmatic analytical approach, it will become possible for us to see whether the author's portrayal of Lydia does indeed point to a "culture in movement."

3
Inner Textural Analysis

Most exegetical analyses of biblical texts begin with delimiting the boundaries of the text under investigation. Recognizing both the need for and the problems of delimitation in rhetorical analysis, Muilenburg writes:

> The delimitation of the passage is essential if we are to learn how its major motif, usually stated at the beginning, is resolved. The latter point is of special importance because no rhetorical feature is more conspicuous and frequent among the poets and narrators of ancient Israel [and antiquity] than the proclivity to bring the successive predications to their culmination. One must admit that the problem is not always simple because within a single literary unit we may have and often do have several points of climax. But to construe each of these as conclusion to the poem [or rhetorical unit] is to disregard its structure, to resolve it into fragments, and to obscure the relation of the successive strophes to each other. This mistaken procedure has been followed by many scholars, with unfortunate consequences.[1]

However, as George Kennedy admits, defining rhetorical units can be difficult, particularly in "longer works which are not immediately evident self-contained units."[2]

While critics tend to delimit passages from the perspective of narrative "episodes," a rhetorical unit often unfolds its argumentation by way of a number of paratactically positioned episodes.[3] It is possible for a rhetorical

---

1. Muilenburg, "Form Criticism and Beyond," 9.
2. George A. Kennedy, *New Testament Interpretation through Rhetorical Criticism* (Chapel Hill: University of North Carolina Press, 1984), 34.
3. Many interpretations of Acts use the visit to Philippi as the delimiting criterion, thereby locating the interpretive unit at Acts 16:11–40: Robert C. Tannehill, *Acts of the Apostles*, 196; Mikeal C. Parsons, *Acts*, Paideia Commentaries on the New Testa-

unit and a narrative unit to overlap, but they are not necessarily equivalent, and what distinguishes these has rarely been discussed. It is therefore not surprising that little has been offered in terms of concrete criteria that can help to delimit a rhetorical unit within a broader narrative. Kennedy's suggestion that delimitation requires an experimental approach "by seeking signs of opening and closure"[4] falls short of establishing clear boundary-distinguishing guidelines, since rhetorical units do not necessarily follow the "opening/closing" principles of a narrative plot-centered focus.[5]

Given the challenges presented by delimitation, it may first be helpful to identify the defining characteristics of a rhetorical unit and then to suggest criteria for identifying its boundaries. Insofar as the purpose of rhetoric is to "create or increase the adherence of minds to the theses presented for their assent,"[6] a rhetorical unit may be considered any closely knit pattern of topoi brought together for the purpose of creating or increasing this adherence. While this definition of a rhetorical unit may be helpful in distinguishing between a narrative story and rhetorical unit, at the same time it introduces a number of new challenges to the problem of delimitation. One immediate challenge to establishing the boundaries of a rhetorical unit is that a text's rhetorical topoi are not known in advance of the analysis, inasmuch as one of the principal objectives of SRI is identifying the topoi that are rhetorically employed. Another challenge is that the proposition of an argument, that which constitutes the "theses presented for their assent," are seldom explicitly articulated in a narrative text, especially where inductive, rhetographical argumentation often predominates. Another obstacle to distinguishing the limits of any rhetori-

---

ment (Grand Rapids: Baker Academic, 2008), 229; Bruce J. Malina and John J. Pilch, *Social-Science Commentary on the Book of Acts* (Minneapolis: Fortress, 2008), 115; Haenchen, *Acts of the Apostles*, 492; Joseph A. Fitzmyer, *The Acts of the Apostles: A New Translation with Introduction and Commentary*, AB 31 (New York: Doubleday, 1998), 581. Charles Talbert is one exception to the trend that treats Acts 16:6–40 as one unit composed of the commission (16:6–10) and visit to Philippi (16:11–40): Charles H. Talbert, *Reading Acts: A Literary and Theological Commentary on the Acts of the Apostles*, Reading the New Testament (New York: Crossroad, 1997), 146.

4. Kennedy, *New Testament Interpretation*, 34.

5. Robbins's suggestion that "opening-middle-closing texture resides in the nature of the beginning, body, and conclusion of a section of discourse" implicitly also assumes either a narrative episode or a rhetorical speech (*Exploring the Texture of Texts*, 19).

6. Perelman and Olbrechts-Tyteca, *New Rhetoric*, 45.

cal unit in biblical narrative is that biblical texts typically employ transitions that bridge one rhetorical unit to the next. These transitional verses, which continue to use lexica and topics found in the main rhetorical unit, blur the boundary markers between the end of one rhetorical unit and the beginning of another.

In this project, prior to the execution of inner textual analysis, I assumed a narratively situated episodic unit as a point of departure for analysis; however, since the rhetorical unit's boundaries might not necessarily be identical with those suggested by the story's narrative, in the repetitive and progressive textual analyses, I looked beyond these initial parameters in order to locate more clearly the rhetorical unit's boundaries. Once I identified clusters of repetitive textual patterns, words, sequences, and initial topics, it was then possible to refine the delimitation exercise along rhetorically defined boundaries. In this manner, delimitation followed two steps: one prior to and the second following the repetitive and progressive textual analyses. The refined postanalysis step of delimitation will be presented following repetitive and progressive textual analyses, which in their presentation will reflect only the final rhetorical unit: Acts 16:9–40.

Inner textual analysis identifies which textual elements and topics are of primary concern to the author of the rhetorical unit in question (Acts 16:9–40) and then investigates how these operate within the text's argumentative structure. The two initial textures of inner textual analysis, repetitive and progressive, are concerned with flagging recurrent elements and examining how these progress through the unit. Narrational textual analysis contributes to the repetitive/progressive analyses by investigating which elements are given narrative prominence and observing how they are contextualized within the narrative. In the final portion of inner textual analysis, argumentative texture, I will examine how the textual-level argumentative framework of the unit connects the elements and shapes their rhetorical function. Together these textures allow for a comprehensive investigation of what elements the text itself proffers as rhetorically significant.

3.1. Repetitive Texture and Pattern

In repetitive textual analysis, I will look for lexica, grammatical and syntactical formations, and lexically identifiable topics that recur in the rhetorical unit. This stage of analysis is concerned with identifying any repeated elements, including even seemingly inconsequential ones, so as not to overlook those that may be rhetorically significant. Along with locating repeated elements, repetitive textural analysis seeks out patterns and groupings of these.

An initial scan of the rhetorical unit shows that Paul continues to figure prominently in this second portion of Acts, and not surprisingly, his name is the most frequently occurring noun in this unit (Acts 16:9, 14, 17, 18, 19, 25, 28, 29, 36, 37).[7] What is less expected, however, is that the narrative voice moves into the first-person plural in Acts 16:10, beginning the first of four "we-sections" in Acts and thereby, at times, assimilating Paul within a Pauline "we-group."[8] While the uncommon first-person plural narrative voice is an important repetitive element, a closer examination of this unit shows that the plural form generally, and as it refers to groups of people particularly, is one of the distinguishing features of this passage. For example, while κύριος occurs 107 times in Acts, only in this rhetorical unit is it found in the plural (Acts 16:16, 19, 30; in the singular, 16:14, 15, 31, 32). Indeed, the plural form pervades this passage, identifying a wide variety of possible groupings of people—based on gender, ethnicity, occupation, and/or religious affiliation.[9]

This unit is also marked by forms of speech such as proclamation, command, and preaching, which are demonstrated by αγγελ-derived verbs and nouns (Acts 16:10, 17, 18, 21, 23, 24, 36, 38). The speech acts of this passage are distinguished by a recurrent direct-discourse form,[10] which at times result from individuals speaking but can also involve several people

---

7. Repeated names of other secular characters are Silas (Acts 16:19, 25, 29) and Lydia (Acts 16:14, 40).

8. The "we-sections" in Acts: Acts 16:10–17; 20:5–15; 21:1–18; 27:1–29; 28:1–16.

9. Αἱ γυναῖκες (Acts 16:13), οἱ ἄνθρωποι (16:17, 20, 35, 37), οἱ Ἰουδαῖοι (16:20), οἱ ἄρχοντες (16:19)/οἱ στρατηγοί (16:20, 22, 35, 36, 38), οἱ Ῥωμαῖοι (16:21, 37, 38), οἱ δέσμιοι (16:25, 27), οἱ ῥαβδοῦχοι (16:35, 38; *hapax legomena*), and οἱ ἀδελφοί (16:40). Also an implicit "us [Macedonians]" in the Macedonian man's plea, "help us by coming over to Macedonia" (Acts 16:9). The pervasive use of the plural in this unit also includes the somewhat unusual reference to Sabbath in the plural: τῇ τε ἡμέρᾳ τῶν σαββάτων (Acts 16:13). According to Mikeal C. Parsons and Martin M. Culy, "There does not appear to be any difference in meaning between the plural ([Acts 13:14] also at 16:13; Luke 4:16) and the singular (Luke 13:14, 16; 14:5) form of σάββατον in this construction" (*Acts: A Handbook on the Greek Text* [Waco, TX: Baylor University Press, 2003], 251).

10. Introduced by λέγω/εἶπον: Acts 16:9, 15, 17, 18, 20, 28, 31, 35; φημί: 16:30, 37.

speaking as one.[11] Whereas it might be expected that Paul, as the prominent figure of this narrative, would speak most frequently, he speaks alone only in three instances. The range and number of speaking voices that are found, including two females, is rare. In addition to the numerous speaking voices, another feature of the direct discourse is the use of the imperative mood (Acts 16:9, 15, 31, 35, 36, 37), which last occurred in Acts 15:13[12] and is not seen again until Acts 18:9.[13]

This passage also contains a number of requests or orders to come or go, and its characters (mostly Paul or members of the Pauline group) come, go, and/or are dragged into and expelled out of locations. As will be discussed in progressive texture below, the verb παρακαλέω (Acts 16:9, 15, 39, 40) forms a repetitive backbone to this unit as it appears with characters who plead with Paul and the disciples either to come[14] or, in the case of the magistrates, to leave (16:39).

Together with requests to come and go, recurrent acts of going to places and coming out of them[15] are displayed by an abundance of ἔρχομαι-prefixed verbs (Acts 16:10, 13 [x2], 15, 18 [x2], 19, 36, 37, 39 [x2], 40 [x3]). Found repetitively as well are verbs associated with bringing forward, seizing, and casting out such as ἀγω-, λαμβάνω-, and βάλλω-prefixed verbs as Paul and other disciples are brought in and out of a variety of spaces through the force of others.[16]

Functioning repetitively is the term ὁράω (Acts 16:9, 10, 19, 27, 40), which both opens and closes the rhetorical unit. As will be discussed in progressive texture, the term's use varies as it refers to different perceptive

---

11. Macedonian man: Acts 16:9; Lydia: 16:15; slave woman: 16:17; Paul: 16:18, 28, 37; Paul and Silas: 16:31; slave owners 16:20–21; jailer: 16:30, 36; lictors: 16:35.

12. Excluding the "farewell"/ἔρρωσθε sign-off to the Jerusalem letter in 15:29. This imperative is excluded, because it is classified as a "stereotypical imperative": "Sometimes the imperative is used in a stereotyped manner in which it has suppressed its original injunctive force. The imperative is reduced to an exclamation. This occurs especially in greetings" (Daniel B. Wallace, *Greek Grammar: Beyond the Basics; An Exegetical Syntax of the New Testament with Scripture, Subject, and Greek Word Indexes* [Grand Rapids: Zondervan, 1996], 493).

13. When again a vision appears to Paul (next and final occurrence of ὅραμα after Acts 16:9).

14. Macedonian man: Acts 16:9; Lydia: 16:15.

15. Ἔξω: Acts 16:13, 30.

16. Ἀγω- (Acts 16:11, 20, 30, 34, 37, 39), λαμβάνω- (16:19, 24, 33), and βάλλω- (16:23, 24, 37 [2x]).

functions. Perceptivity also plays a repetitive role in displays of "concluding/supposing" in this unit, including συμβιβάζω (Acts 16:10)—an interpretation that catalyzes the ensuing events—and νομίζω (16:13, 27).

Not only is the πόλις (Acts 16:11, 12 [x2], 14, 20, 39) a repetitive element, but it also functions as a referent for situating the location of key events in this unit. The women by the river are encountered outside of Philippi's gates (v. 13); and Paul and Silas are dragged by the slave owners into the heart of the city to its public square,[17] interned in its prison (v. 23), and asked by its authorities to leave (v. 39), with the departure out of Philippi closing the unit. While the "city" is an important repetitive term, somewhat paradoxically, so too is house and household.[18] Overlapping both πόλις and οἶκος/οἰκία is Philippi's prison, which figures prominently in this passage, represented by a host of lexica referring both to the people associated with the prison system—magistrates, lictors, jailer, prisoners—and the prison itself.[19] At the same time, embedded within the prison compound are repeated occurrences of house and household as the jailer and his household are baptized and receive Paul and Silas into his house. Both the events occurring outside of the city and those inside are introduced within the context of the Pauline group's going to a place of prayer.[20]

A number of lexica typically associated with sacred elements repeat in this passage. However, as I will discuss further, their meanings frequently vary or are ambiguous. Already mentioned in this category are κύριος, Ἰησοῦς, πνεῦμα, and θεός.[21] In fact, this rhetorical unit is characterized by both ambiguous and multivalent meanings for terms that typically would be understood in Luke-Acts as referring to sacred elements and/or pertaining to the Jewish-Christian God. These terms are highly repetitive in the passage, are often altered into a variety of word forms, or display the related rhetorical practice of *traductio*, which "comprises the repetition of only apparently equivalent word-forms with quite different meanings."[22]

---

17. Ἀγορά, 16:19.

18. Οἶκος/οἰκία (Acts 16: 15 [x2], 31, 32, 34; πανοικεί, 16:34, *hapax legomenon*).

19. Magistrates (οἱ ἄρχοντες: Acts 16:19/οἱ στρατηγοί: 16:20, 22, 35, 36, 38), lictors (οἱ ῥαβδοῦχοι: 16:35, 38), jailer (ὁ δεσμοφύλαξ: 16:23, 27, 36), prisoners (οἱ δέσμιοι: 16:25, 27), as well as the prison itself (ἡ φυλακή: 16:23, 24, 27, 37, 40).

20. Προσευχή: Acts 16:13, 16.

21. Κύριος (Acts 16:14, 15, 16, 19, 30, 31, 32); Ἰησοῦς (16:18, 31); πνεῦμα (16:16, 18); and θεός (16:10, 14, 17, 25, 34).

22. Heinrich Lausberg, *Handbook of Literary Rhetoric: A Foundation for Literary*

Conclusion: Repetitive Texture and Pattern. The initial survey of this rhetorical unit's repetitive patterns illuminates a number of textual landmarks that warrant deeper exploration. The uncommon shift of the narrative voice into the first-person plural in Acts 16:10 participates in a pattern of groups and groupings of people found throughout this passage. People's actions in this unit are characterized by three functions: (1) speaking, with a number of individuals engaging in direct discourse, including two juxtaposed female figures, as well as speech in general, both direct and indirect, which includes several occurrences of requests to the Pauline group to either come or to go; (2) acts of coming and going, as well as being physically forced into or out of various locations; and (3) seeing/perceiving, including repetitive cases of characters being motivated to act on the basis of what they "conclude" or "suppose." The city, prison, house/household, and "place of prayer" are key locative terms that occur repetitively in this passage. A number of terms that typically refer to divine or sacred figures in the New Testament repeat here, with varying meanings.

3.2. Progressive Texture and Pattern

Although an exercise in locating textual repetitive elements may suggest an interest in similarity and likeness, as Perelman and Olbrechts-Tyteca point out, repetition "really aim[s] at suggesting distinctions."[23] In contrast to reiterating sameness, within a rhetorical unit each repetitive element interacts with other repetitive elements in order to help develop and intensify the rhetorical meaning of a text. Progressive repetition is a component of a building process that rhetorically moves the audience along: "The verbal linking of clauses by means of a repetition of terms suggests an increase of intensity. Repetition gives a feeling of presence, but it does more than this. As Quintilian says, 'Before passing to a new point, [it] dwells on those which precede.'"[24] Therefore, one rhetorical function of progressive repetition is an intensification and development of the meaning of repeated elements. Another function of progressive texture, which is more pertinent to this stage of the analysis, is described by Robbins as

---

Study, ed. R. Dean Anderson, trans. David E. Orton, foreword by George A. Kennedy (Leiden: Brill, 1973), 295, par. 658.

23. Perelman and Olbrechts-Tyteca, *New Rhetoric*, 175.
24. Ibid., 504, using wording in the LCL translation.

demonstrating "stepping stones to other phenomena in the text."[25] While repetitive texture is concerned with identifying initial markers of a text's rhetorical landscape, progressive texture begins to unveil how, and where, those markers may, in some way, connect with each other. A primary objective of progressive texture is to display possible rhetorical linkages emanating from repetitive elements.

A text such as Luke-Acts, which is characterized not only by repeated lexica but also by parallelism generally, offers the potential to discover virtually endless sequential possibilities. In order to narrow these choices to those constructive for analysis, I used the following selective criteria in my analysis:

1. The sequence of repetitive elements progresses through a wide range of the rhetorical unit: it is not narrowly localized.
2. The sequence manifests progression rather than being solely repetitive.
3. Yet at the same time the sequence builds on a platform of repetition.
4. The sequence displays clusters of repetitive elements.

One term in particular—παρακαλέω—functions as a rhetorical pegboard for a key progressive sequence in this passage.[26] The term παρακαλέω spans the rhetorical unit, frames both Lydia's and the Macedonian man's direct discourse, and denotes the Pauline group's final act at Lydia's prior to leaving Philippi. Through the patterns that synthesize around παρακαλέω, a number of key rhetorical elements emerge. In Acts 16:9, 15, παρακαλέω frames two requests to come. In verse 9, Paul is asked by a Macedonian man to cross over into Macedonia in a vision, and in verse 15 Paul and his coworkers are asked by Lydia to come into her home. Acts 16:39 reverses the context for παρακαλέω from summoning

---

25. Robbins, *Exploring the Texture of Texts*, 10.
26. Acts 16:9: Καὶ ὅραμα διὰ [τῆς] νυκτὸς τῷ Παύλῳ ὤφθη, ἀνὴρ Μακεδών τις ἦν ἑστὼς καὶ παρακαλῶν αὐτὸν καὶ λέγων· διαβὰς εἰς Μακεδονίαν βοήθησον ἡμῖν. Acts 16:15: ὡς δὲ ἐβαπτίσθη καὶ ὁ οἶκος αὐτῆς, παρεκάλεσεν λέγουσα· εἰ κεκρίκατέ με πιστὴν τῷ κυρίῳ εἶναι, εἰσελθόντες εἰς τὸν οἶκόν μου μένετε· καὶ παρεβιάσατο ἡμᾶς. Acts 16:39: καὶ ἐλθόντες παρεκάλεσαν αὐτοὺς καὶ ἐξαγαγόντες ἠρώτων ἀπελθεῖν ἀπὸ τῆς πόλεως. Acts 16:40: ἐξελθόντες δὲ ἀπὸ τῆς φυλακῆς εἰσῆλθον πρὸς τὴν Λυδίαν καὶ ἰδόντες παρεκάλεσαν τοὺς ἀδελφοὺς καὶ ἐξῆλθαν.

to expelling as the magistrates (as representatives of a Roman πόλις) seek Paul and Silas's cooperation in leaving the city.[27]

Although the final occurrence of παρακαλέω in Acts 16:40 occurs in a phrase that echoes the syntax of 16:39,[28] the meaning and context of its occurrence in 16:40 shifts considerably. For the first time in Acts 16:40, Paul (and his group) becomes the acting subject delivering its effects. For the first time as well, παρακαλέω is not associated with a request to come or to depart, but rather with some form of encouragement.

Lydia's "παρακαλέω request" to the Pauline group is expressed conditionally: "If you have judged me to be faithful [πιστήν] to the Lord."[29] The adjective πιστός occurs only four times in Acts, with the penultimate instance occurring in Acts 16:1 (one of the rhetorical unit's transitional verses) and the final in 16:15. The repetitive aspect of πιστός is emphasized by the subsequent occurrences of the verbal form πιστεύω in Acts 16:31, 34. In Acts 16:15, Lydia asks the Pauline group to assess the quality of her "faithfulness to the Lord"[30] in a conditional request, whereas in 16:31 the jailer is exhorted with the verbal πιστεύω to "believe in the Lord Jesus"[31] in response to the question, "What must I do to be saved?" (Acts 16:30). This sequence, clustered around a grammatical alteration from the adjective πιστός in Acts 16:15 to the verb πιστεύω in 16:31, 34, is embedded in another broader progressive sequence that displays a rhetorical connection between Lydia and the jailer. The repetitive connection between Lydia and the jailer is most evident in the term οἶκος, which in this passage involves either Lydia (Acts 16:15 [x2], as well as implicitly in 16:40) or the jailer (Acts 16:31, 34),[32] where the meaning of the οἶκος terms vacillates

---

27. The meaning of παρακαλέω in Acts 16:39 should probably be read according to Fitzmyer's translation as "to placate." Fitzmyer, *Acts of the Apostles*, 582. Also supported by Danker: "in several places παρ. appears to mean simply treat someone in an inviting or congenial manner, someth. like our 'be open to the other, have an open door' ... Ac 16:39 (the officials are conciliatory, but 'apologize to' may be overinterpretation)" (BDAG, s.v. παρακαλέω).

28. Acts 16:39: καὶ ἐλθόντες παρεκάλεσαν αὐτούς. Acts 16:40: καὶ ἰδόντες παρεκάλεσαν τοὺς ἀδελφούς.

29. εἰ κεκρίκατέ με πιστὴν τῷ κυρίῳ εἶναι (Acts 16:15).

30. πιστὴν τῷ κυρίῳ.

31. Πίστευσον ἐπὶ τὸν κύριον Ἰησοῦν.

32. As well as the modified word-form, οἰκία (16:32) and the adverb πανοικεί (16:34).

between "household" and "house."³³ Along with the recurrent use of οἶκος, other repetitive elements clustered in these verses display their progressive nature. Just as in Acts 16:13, where Paul and his group spoke (λαλέω) to the women who were gathered by the river outside, in Acts 16:32 Paul and Silas speak to a gathering,³⁴ also in an outdoor setting. In each case, the listening audience is not clearly defined; however, both cases involve Paul and others speaking to a group where one particular member of the group (i.e., Lydia, jailer) participates in direct discourse and is baptized. The description of the jailer's baptism in Acts 16:33 closely follows the language of Acts 16:15a, except that an explicit reference to the jailer's οἶκος is absent, replaced by "and all of his."³⁵ A progressive subunit is also displayed from baptism in Acts 16:15 to washing in 16:33a to baptism in 16:33b, where both βαπτίζω and λούω can mean wash, cleanse, or purify. The οἶκος-centered progression ends with a notable absence of οἶκος where, in 16:40b, the Pauline group goes to Lydia's but without explicit reference to her οἶκος;³⁶ rather, those at Lydia's are identified with the familial ἀδελφός.

Lydia is also connected lexically to the female slave with the Python spirit, as both have their direct discourse introduced by the feminine participle λέγουσα (Acts 16:15, 17), a lexical connection that is emphasized by its occurring only in these two instances in Acts. These two cases of λέγουσα are located in a progressive sequence connected to the terms προσευχή/προσεύχομαι where, looking for a place of prayer, the Pauline group encounters a woman who listens to them (Acts 16:13–15), immediately followed by the Pauline group's going to a place of prayer and being encountered by a woman who yells after them (16:16–17), followed by Paul and Silas praying and singing hymns in prison while prisoners listen on (16:25).

---

33. Acts 16:15: ὡς δὲ ἐβαπτίσθη καὶ ὁ οἶκος αὐτῆς, παρεκάλεσεν λέγουσα· εἰ κεκρίκατέ με πιστὴν τῷ κυρίῳ εἶναι, εἰσελθόντες εἰς τὸν οἶκόν μου μένετε· καὶ παρεβιάσατο ἡμᾶς. Acts 16:31: οἱ δὲ εἶπαν· πίστευσον ἐπὶ τὸν κύριον Ἰησοῦν καὶ σωθήσῃ σὺ καὶ ὁ οἶκός σου. Acts 16:32: καὶ ἐλάλησαν αὐτῷ τὸν λόγον τοῦ κυρίου σὺν πᾶσιν τοῖς ἐν τῇ οἰκίᾳ αὐτοῦ. Acts 16:33: καὶ παραλαβὼν αὐτοὺς ἐν ἐκείνῃ τῇ ὥρᾳ τῆς νυκτὸς ἔλουσεν ἀπὸ τῶν πληγῶν, καὶ ἐβαπτίσθη αὐτὸς καὶ οἱ αὐτοῦ πάντες παραχρῆμα. Acts 16:34: ἀναγαγών τε αὐτοὺς εἰς τὸν οἶκον παρέθηκεν τράπεζαν καὶ ἠγαλλιάσατο πανοικεὶ πεπιστευκὼς τῷ θεῷ. Acts 16:40: ἐξελθόντες δὲ ἀπὸ τῆς φυλακῆς εἰσῆλθον πρὸς τὴν Λυδίαν καὶ ἰδόντες παρεκάλεσαν τοὺς ἀδελφοὺς καὶ ἐξῆλθαν.

34. Composed of the jailer and "all who were in his house."

35. Οἱ αὐτοῦ πάντες.

36. Εἰσῆλθον πρὸς τὴν Λυδίαν.

The mission to Macedonia is catalyzed by a group interpretation—"concluding that God had summoned us"—of a vision seen by Paul (Acts 16:9-10). This inaugural interpretation participates in a pattern where key events are repeatedly motivated by the perceptive emotion-fused quality of sight intermingling with the interpretive functions of concluding/supposing.[37] The quality of sight is stressed in Acts 16:9-10 by a concentration of two occurrences of ὁράω, together with two of ὅραμα, followed by the interpretive function of συμβιβάζω. Later, an assumption regarding the location of a place of prayer precipitates the Pauline group's encounter with the women by the river (16:13);[38] the "sight" of the loss of hope of gain motivates the slave owners to prosecute Paul and Silas (16:19); the sight of open prison doors leads the jailer to suppose that the prisoners had escaped, motivating a suicide attempt (16:27); and the final act of παρακαλέω in this passage is precipitated by the sight of those gathered at Lydia's (16:40).

Conclusion: Progressive Texture and Pattern. The primary purpose of this progressive textual analysis was to identify key linkages between recurrent elements of the text. The use of παρακαλέω appears to indicate a number of features connecting Lydia to the Macedonian man. Both of these individuals are described in terms of their ethnic identity, both participate

---

37. Acts 16:9: Καὶ ὅραμα διὰ [τῆς] νυκτὸς τῷ Παύλῳ ὤφθη. Acts 16:10: ὡς δὲ τὸ ὅραμα εἶδεν, εὐθέως ἐζητήσαμεν ἐξελθεῖν εἰς Μακεδονίαν συμβιβάζοντες ὅτι προσκέκληται ἡμᾶς ὁ θεὸς εὐαγγελίσασθαι αὐτούς. Acts 16:13: τῇ τε ἡμέρᾳ τῶν σαββάτων ἐξήλθομεν ἔξω τῆς πύλης παρὰ ποταμὸν οὗ ἐνομίζομεν προσευχὴν εἶναι. Acts 16:19: ἰδόντες δὲ οἱ κύριοι αὐτῆς ὅτι ἐξῆλθεν ἡ ἐλπὶς τῆς ἐργασίας αὐτῶν, ἐπιλαβόμενοι τὸν Παῦλον καὶ τὸν Σιλᾶν εἵλκυσαν εἰς τὴν ἀγορὰν ἐπὶ τοὺς ἄρχοντας. Acts 16:27: ἔξυπνος δὲ γενόμενος ὁ δεσμοφύλαξ καὶ ἰδὼν ἀνεῳγμένας τὰς θύρας τῆς φυλακῆς, σπασάμενος [τὴν] μάχαιραν ἤμελλεν ἑαυτὸν ἀναιρεῖν νομίζων ἐκπεφευγέναι τοὺς δεσμίους. Acts 16:40: εἰσῆλθον πρὸς τὴν Λυδίαν καὶ ἰδόντες παρεκάλεσαν τοὺς ἀδελφοὺς καὶ ἐξῆλθαν.

38. While the UBS/NA reading of ἐνομίζομεν προσευχὴν εἶναι is supported by three major witnesses, A², C, and Ψ, there is a great deal of diversity supporting other readings. Of issue for this analysis are readings of the passive impersonal form ἐνομίζετο προσευχὴν εἶναι, which in the KJV has been translated as "where prayer was wont to be made," that is, "it was the custom for there to be prayer" (Parsons and Culy, *Acts*, 312). This analysis favors the reading of "we supposed/assumed," since this is the context for νομίζω in all other occurrences in Luke-Acts and the Bible in general; Acts 17:2 employs εἴωθα to convey "custom" (also Luke 4:16); and "supposing" is consistent with a progressive pattern that begins with the group's "concluding" in Acts 16:10 and that continues on throughout the passage.

in direct discourse, and both request Paul's (or the Pauline group's) presence. Lydia is also connected progressively to the jailer through the term οἶκος, where both are members of a larger "listening group" who hear Paul's words, both participate in direct discourse with Paul that introduces the quality of πιστός/πιστεύω, both are baptized together with their households, and both receive Paul and other disciples in their homes. Other progressions overmap the rhetoric of the overall unit. These include requests to come or to go, together with forcible confining or expelling, in which not only the Pauline group, the Macedonian man, Lydia and the jailer participate, but so too do the slave woman with the Python spirit, her owners, the crowd, magistrates, and lictors.

3.3. Rhetorical Boundaries Texture and Pattern: Refined Delimitation

By locating the clusters and patterns of repetitive terms in this passage, it became possible for us to further delimit the Philippi episode in order to reflect its rhetorical boundaries. Although the initial interpretive unit was chosen on the basis of a geographically located narrative episode, the findings from the repetitive and progressive textural analyses guided delimitation toward a sharper rhetorical focus. This project's primary concern lies in examining the rhetorical role of the figure of Lydia, and therefore the relevant rhetorical unit for the analysis is the one operative for the Lydia passages. Direct reference to Lydia is limited to three verses: Acts 16:14–15, 40, but 16:13, which opens the Lydia episode, could arguably be included in the Lydia passages. From a narrational perspective, the story moves on and away from Lydia after Acts 16:15, and it would appear that Acts 16:13–15 functions as a micro unit at best. As such, these three verses, at most four (if Acts 16:13 be included), cannot credibly function as a rhetorical unit on their own. According to Kennedy:

> In rhetorical criticism it is important that the rhetorical unit chosen have some magnitude. It has to have within itself a discernible beginning and ending, connected by some action or argument. Five or six verses probably constitute the minimum text which can be subjected to rhetorical criticism as a distinct unit, but most will be longer, extending for the better part of a chapter or for several chapters.[39]

---

39. Kennedy, *New Testament Interpretation*, 35.

Since clearly the Lydia passages are not directly connected beyond themselves through "some action," the question becomes whether other patterns might exist that could suggest that the Lydia passages are somehow rhetorically linked to a larger span of verses.

It is also clear that the Lydia verses do not argumentatively provide a proposition that is then argued deductively through the verses that follow. Yet, as will be discussed in argumentative texture, Lydia's conditional request to the Pauline group in Acts 16:15 is argumentatively structured, and since it implicitly contains the interrogative form, it implies an argumentative opening that seeks an answer of some type. At the same time, since the immediately following narrative leaves Lydia's request unanswered and instead moves to the episode of the slave woman with the Python spirit, the potentially argumentative opening of Acts 16:15 most certainly does not continue with either a deductively argued development or a logical plot progression.

We can see strong repetitive connections between the first two verses, referring to Lydia (Acts 16:14–15), and the final one (16:40): the name Lydia is repeated, as are key repetitive verbs εἰσέρχομαι and παρακαλέω; moreover, where 16:15 ends with Lydia's urging the Pauline group to come to her house, in 16:40 they do go to Lydia's. While on the basis of repetition a case could be made for linkages between Acts 16:14–15 and 16:40, from the perspective of defining a rhetorical unit, the question remains whether the Lydia passages participate in textual patterns beyond themselves into surrounding text.

When we examine the text surrounding Acts 16:14–15, we immediately see one evident connection: Lydia's direct discourse, introduced by the participle λέγουσα, is followed by the direct discourse of another female, namely, the slave woman with the Python spirit, whose speech is introduced by the same participle in Acts 16:17. These two occasions constitute the only two occurrences of λέγουσα in Acts.[40] Moreover, the two encounters between the Pauline group and the speaking women occur in the context of the group's intention to find a "place of prayer"; the noun προσευχή occurs only in Acts 16:13, 16. In addition, the quality of profit-taking is present both with Lydia, who is a seller of purple (Acts 16:14),

---

40. The only other female character who speaks directly in Acts is Sapphira in Acts 5:8, whose speech is introduced by εἶπεν.

as well as with the slave woman's owners, since they receive "much profit" from the mantic's activities (16:16).

A close examination of the text reveals a second set of lexical connections, this time between Lydia and the jailer. Another important repetitive term—οἶκος/οἰκία—clusters with these two characters (Acts 16: 15 [x2], 31, 32, 34; πανοικεί: 16:34) as Lydia and the jailer each listen to Paul's preaching and are baptized along with their households. Repetitive connections are therefore present with Lydia, the female slave, the slave owners, and the jailer. A few verses back, another set of lexical connections comes to view between Lydia and the Macedonian man. Both, through the verb παρακαλέω, beseech Paul (or the Pauline group) to "come," using direct discourse that is introduced with the participle λέγων/λέγουσα and that includes the imperative form.

We might also consider one additional set of possible lexical linkages between the Lydia passages and Acts 16:1–5, a section of text that is typically associated with the distribution of the report from the Jerusalem conference.[41] Acts 16:1 is the first direct reference to a woman (Timothy's mother) since 13:50, and this woman is identified as a "believer" by the adjective πιστός,[42] the same quality on which Lydia will seek favorable judgment in 16:15. Moreover, Acts 16:3 uses the term λαμβάνω as Paul "takes" Timothy to be circumcised, thereby resonating with a pattern described in detail in the narrational and argumentative textures involving the taking, forcing, leading, and violating of bodies, a pattern, as will be observed below, that seems to escalate after Lydia's "prevailing" upon them.[43] Moreover, Acts 16:4 introduces the term φυλάσσω, here meaning "observe" but having the primary meaning of "watch, guard" and phonetically resonating with the upcoming highly repetitive use of φυλακή (Acts 16:23, 24, 27, 37, 40) in the course of Paul and Silas's imprisonment, as well as κρίνω, a significant term in Lydia's request in 16:15.[44] Finally,

---

41. See Parsons, *Acts*, 222–23.
42. This adjective occurs only four times in Acts, two of which are in Acts 16.
43. Παραβιάζομαι (16:15).
44. Εἰ κεκρίκατέ με πιστὴν τῷ κυρίῳ εἶναι. The closest prior occurrence of φυλάσσω is in Acts 12:4 and next in 21:24; and prior to the φυλακή cluster in Acts 16, its closest occurrence is in Acts 12:17 and next in 22:4. The closest prior occurrence of κρίνω is Acts 15:19 and next in Acts 17:31. The differing meanings of terms found in Acts 16:1–5 and the Philippi text (such as φυλάσσω and κρίνω) is of less concern due to the rhetorical practice of *distinctio*.

Acts 16:5 summarizes on a global basis what happens locally in Acts 16:40: the strengthening in faith of believers. Whereas Acts 16:5 uses the term στερεόω to denote the act of strengthening, Acts 16:40 uses the key progressive term παρακαλέω.[45]

On the basis of lexical patterns, then, a good case could be made for including Acts 16:1–5 in the rhetorical unit that includes the Lydia passages. However, there are key differences. One is the absence of the direct discourse that characterizes the Philippi passages, particularly that of demands/requests. More importantly, Acts 16:1–5 is part of a different narrative story situated in a different environment and therefore cannot be joined narratively with the Philippi unit. At the same time, given the presence of lexical patterns between the two units, it does appear to be connected in some manner to the rhetoric of the main unit. The most likely explanation is that Acts 16:1–5 functions as a transitional device that is outside the main rhetorical unit yet still contributes to the rhetoric of the unit. Bruce Longenecker, in his work on transitional devices, emphasizes that their rhetorical role has frequently been undervalued: "A well-constructed transition oils the machinery of rhetorical persuasion, indicating that a new line of thought is beginning and occasionally giving some indication as to the content of the new topic and how it relates to what has gone previously. Transitional units often play a critical role in the process of interpreting a text."[46]

Another transition appears to be evident in Acts 17:1–4, where the pattern of Paul going to a place of prayer/synagogue on the Sabbath[47] and teaching and proclaiming repeats. In addition, where the term διανοίγω denotes the Lord's "opening" of Lydia's heart to Paul's words in Acts 16:15, in Acts 17:3 it refers to Paul's "explaining" the crux of his message. In 17:4, the participle form of σέβω acts as a qualifier of Greeks, while in 16:14 it qualifies Lydia through the epithet σεβομένη τὸν θεόν; moreover, 17:4 includes another reference to women. As the Thessalonica episode progresses, other features also correspond to events at Philippi, including an attacking "mob of the marketplace" (Acts 16:22; 17:5), similar-sounding

---

45. In Acts 14:22, ἐπιστηρίζω (strengthen) is used with παρακαλέω in a similar context.

46. Bruce W. Longenecker, *Rhetoric at the Boundaries: The Art and Theology of the New Testament Chain-Link Transitions* (Waco, TX: Baylor University Press, 2005), 2–3.

47. Σάββατον in the plural in both 16:13; 17:2.

accusations in front of city authorities (Acts 16:20–21; 17:6), the prominent featuring of a resident's house (Acts 17:5),[48] and a quick departure to a new locale (Acts 16:40; 17:10). In fact, the overall similarities between the two episodes suggest that the Thessalonica episode, rather than functioning as a transition, works alongside with the Philippi episode as each informs the other rhetorically.

Conclusion: Rhetorical Boundaries Texture and Pattern. Given that the primary focus in this analysis is on the rhetorical figure of Lydia, the key patterns outlined above suggest that "Lydia's" main rhetorical unit opens with the plea of the Macedonian man in Acts 16:9 and closes with the group's visit to Lydia's in Acts 16:40. This main rhetorical unit is shaped rhetorically by the "opening" transitional verses of Acts 16:1–5 as well as the following Thessalonica episode in Acts 17:1–10a. The rhetorical unit coincides with the major part of the geographically derived unit (Acts 16:11–40), but also includes 16:9–10 because of the commencement of the παρακαλέω progression found there. Moreover, this rhetorical unit is rhetorically informed by the transitional verses of Acts 16:1–5 and the paradigmatically juxtaposed Thessalonica episode of Acts 17:1–10a. Whereas oral-scribal intertextural elements found in other sections of Luke-Acts also inform this main rhetorical unit, the proximity of Acts 16:1–5 and Acts 17:1–10a places them within an immediate field of influence.

The main rhetorical unit of Acts 16:9–40 incorporates both the geographically based narrative unit in which the Lydia passages reside and the more evident repetitive patterns and sequences that link the Lydia passages to the surrounding discourse. As such, the process of delimitation provides an encouraging sign that the Lydia passages, rather than being peripheral to the Philippi episode, instead are somehow integrated into the unit's rhetorical structure.

3.4. Narrational and Sensory-Aesthetic Texture and Pattern

Through the story's telling, the repetitive and progressive elements discussed above become narratively contextualized. Moreover, as the narrative unfolds, certain aspects of these elements gain prominence or, as I noted in chapter 2, "Method," their presence is developed. Narrational

---

48. See οἶκος/οἰκία above.

texture and pattern will help to contextualize the recurrent elements within the narrative and to situate narratively prominent elements.

The rhetorical unit begins with Paul's dream-vision in Troas: a Macedonian man pleads with Paul to help "us" by coming over to Macedonia. The we-group subsequently interprets this plea as a call from God to preach the gospel (Acts 16:9–10). Three characters are featured here: the Macedonian man, Paul, and the we-group.[49] Although the previous two verses recounted the movements of the Pauline group in the third-person plural form, the vision of Acts 16:9 explicitly involves an interaction between two individuals (manifested within a visionary experience) and specifically between two human males (a "Macedonian man" [ἀνὴρ Μακεδών] and Paul). By assigning an ethnic designation to the Macedonian man, the text stresses his earthly, rather than heavenly, character.[50] Moreover, the Macedonian man is associated with a larger earthly group since his plea of help is not solely for himself but rather on behalf of "us."[51] In fact, surprisingly absent, given the dream-vision event, is any spiritual-being element in the dream-vision itself.

Immediately following the vision, the narration reverts to describing not just Paul but also the broader Pauline group when the narrative voice switches to first-person plural narration in Acts 16:10.[52] Although this is not the first occurrence of first-person plural narration, previous instances were embedded in discourse, such as when the crowd at Pentecost questions,

---

49. The term "character" in narrational texture refers to those plot elements that are represented by human characteristics including human activities of thought, self-expression, and motion and action, as guided by Mieke Bal's definition: "A character is the effect that occurs when an actor is endowed with distinctive human characteristics." Mieke Bal, *Narratology: Introduction to the Theory of Narrative*, trans. Christine van Boheemen (Toronto: University of Toronto Press, 1985), 115. The process of "characterization," or filling in a fuller representation of a character's distinguishing characteristics, is not a concern of narrational texture. Elements that may be considered as contributing to characterization will be identified in the argumentative, intertextural, and ideological texture analyses. Through the we-group's act of interpretation, "God" enters as a possible fourth character. Although here God is rhetographically formed: the character of God is "seen" in the minds of the members of the we-group as a conclusion of an interpretative act.

50. In contrast, see the appearance of two men dressed in dazzling clothes who appear to the women at the empty tomb in Luke 24:4.

51. Διαβὰς εἰς Μακεδονίαν βοήθησον ἡμῖν.

52. As observed in repetitive texture above, this initiates the first of the we-sections: Acts 16:10–17; 20:5–15; 21:1–18; 27:1–29; 28:1–16.

"How is it that we hear [ἀκούομεν], each of us, in our own native language?" (Acts 2:8) or when Peter and John together answer the temple authorities "for we cannot keep from speaking about what we have seen and heard" (4:20). In Acts 16:10–17, the we-group character does not just speak in the first-person plural; it also narrates events and actions in which it participates as the story unfolds.[53] Other than Paul, the text does not specify who else constitutes the we-group in Acts 16:10–17, nor, in fact, whether it is the same "we" members who are consistently represented.

The first person to speak in this passage is the Macedonian man, although his speech is "heard" by Paul through a vision. Although the Macedonian speaks, his words are not heard by Paul's ears (i.e., within the zone of self-expressive speech), but rather through the emotion-fused act of "seeing."[54] Paul's visual reception of the Macedonian's message is emphasized by ὅραμα (Acts 16:9–10) and by the verb ὁράω (Acts 16:9; εἶδον [16:10]). When the we-group interprets Paul's vision as a call from God, they are immediately motivated into action for the journey into Macedonia. In this way, the motivating impetus for crossing from Asia into Europe remains located in the zone of emotion-fused thought, except that it is a

---

53. Historical-critical interpretations have treated the we-passages as some form of first-person account whether derived from "author-as-eyewitness" or "source-as-eyewitness" (Campbell, *"We" Passages in the Acts of the Apostles*, 87). More recently, narrative critics have suggested reader-response-based readings of the use of the first-person plural. One recent example is Campbell's suggestion that the we-character takes over from Barnabas as a trustworthy character who validates Paul's credibility and authority for the reader (see ibid.). Offering a literary-critical perspective on the we-passages, Robbins has observed that ancient narratives often shifted to the first-person plural in accounts of sea voyages and battles. Vernon K. Robbins, "By Land and by Sea: The We-Passages and Ancient Sea Voyages," in *Perspectives on Luke-Acts*, ed. Charles H. Talbert, PRSt, Special Studies Series 5 (Edinburgh: T&T Clark, 1978), 215–42; Robbins's theory has been critiqued by interpreters who have questioned how applicable first-person sea-voyage accounts may be to the Acts we-passages, which often take place on "land." There are, however, compelling reasons for continuing to investigate Robbins's theory, not the least of which is the metaphorical use of "ship" in ancient literature, such as the "ship of state." See Vernon K. Robbins, *Sea Voyages and Beyond: Emerging Strategies in Socio-rhetorical Interpretation*, ed. Vernon K. Robbins, David B. Gowler, and Robert von Thaden Jr., ESEC 14 (Dorset, UK: Deo, 2010), 82–113.

54. The triadic body-zone model composed of emotion-fused thought, self-expressive speech, and purposeful action was discussed in chapter 2: "Method."

group rather than an individual who forms a judgment on the meaning of the vision.⁵⁵

Following the vision, the we-group immediately sets off for Philippi, with their swift passage marking a stark contrast to the restricted travel of the previous few verses.⁵⁶ They reach Philippi through its port city of Neapolis and stay there "some days."⁵⁷ The narrative locates the city of Philippi by the phrase ἥτις ἐστὶν πρώτη[ς] μερίδος τῆς Μακεδονίας πόλις, κολωνία (Acts 16:12). Some translations, including the NRSV, understand πρῶτος as "leading": "and from there to Philippi, which is the leading city of the district of Macedonia, and a Roman colony."⁵⁸ The mention of the group's coming to Neapolis before Philippi is not troubling since it was not uncommon to refer to a city and its port interchangeably.⁵⁹ However, since "first" is the most common meaning of πρῶτος in Acts, the text may well intend its more basic meaning of "first," as in the initial city of arrival. Regardless of what was intended by "first," the text does explicitly position Philippi as a colony in relation to Macedonia and as a πόλις. The narrative does not describe what the group did during the early part of their stay in Philippi; it merely informs the reader that the group arrived and stayed some days.

When the Philippi episode proper does commence, narration begins with the we-group leaving Philippi's gates and looking for a "place of

---

55. Note that in a list of the eight most common New Testament verbs dealing with perception/communication: δοκέω, ἐρωτάω (Acts 16:39), κελεύω (16:22), κρίνω (16:15), λέγω (16:9, 15, 17–18, 20, 28, 31, 35), νομίζω (16:13, 27), παραγγέλλω (16:18, 23), and παρακαλέω (16:9, 15, 39, 40), seven are found between Acts 16:9–40. See Wallace, *Greek Grammar*, 604.

56. "They went through the region of Phrygia and Galatia, having been forbidden by the Holy Spirit to speak the word in Asia. When they had come opposite Mysia, they attempted to go into Bithynia, but the Spirit of Jesus did not allow them" (Acts 16:6–7).

57. Διατρίβοντες ἡμέρας τινάς: Acts 16:12.

58. The difficulty in translating the intended meaning of πρώτη "led the UBS committee to take the drastic step of positing a conjectural reading (πρώτης μερίδος τῆς Μακεδονίας πόλις: 'a city of the first district of Macedonia') that is supported by only three late Latin manuscripts." Parsons and Culy, *Acts*, 311.

59. For example, Demosthenes warns of the potential danger of Philip's attacking Athens in terms of its port, "not even if he [Philip] comes into Attica itself and to the Peiraeus will he admit this" (*3 Philip.* 10), where Peiraeus was the port of Athens (see Aristotle, *On Rhetoric* [Kennedy], 281 n. 40). Acts 13:4 has Paul and Barnabas leaving Antioch through its port, Seleucia.

prayer" on a temporally sacred day, namely, Sabbath. Outside Philippi, by the river, the we-group encounters another group, a group of gathered women. The we-group sits down and begins speaking to the women (Acts 16:13); however, the narrative does not specify what the nature of the women's gathering was. Once again the emotion-fused act of "inferring" or "supposing" propels the plot forward. In Troas, it was the interpretation of Paul's dream that compelled the group to embark on their sea crossing, and now it was a supposition that a "place of prayer" would be located outside of Philippi.

Strikingly, while the we-group is here because of the appearance of a Macedonian male in Acts 16:9, the first group to whom the we-group speaks in Macedonia is female. One woman of the group, Lydia, stands out. She is profiled in Acts 16:14–15, contributing to the trend of narrating individuals concurrently within a broader group context to which they belong: the Macedonian man and "us," Paul and the we-group, and now Lydia and the women. Lydia is described as a purple seller from the city of Thyatira who is σεβομένη τὸν θεόν, or "one worshiping God" (Acts 16:14). Not only is Lydia named, but the fact that three descriptors are attributed to her also suggests some form of deliberate focus on this character.

As Lydia listens to the we-group's preaching, her heart is opened by the Lord so that she may listen attentively to Paul. This opening of Lydia's heart constitutes the sole event of explicit divinely initiated action in this rhetorical unit (Acts 16:14). Although self-expressive speech seems prominent in Acts 16:13–14, the emphasis remains within the zone of emotion-fused thought. The divine enhancement of Lydia's listening is profiled, yet no discourse, either direct or indirect, is narrated. Neither do actions or movement distract from emotion-fused thought until Lydia is baptized.

When Lydia and her household are baptized—an event that is narratively presented as almost an incidental backdrop to what follows (suggested by the temporal conjunction ὡς)—she emphatically asks the we-group to come to her home to stay if they evaluate her as being "faithful" to the Lord.[60] She then "prevails" (παραβιάζομαι) upon the group, presumably to accept her offer. Neither Paul nor the we-group have yet spoken through direct speech in the rhetorical unit,[61] but both the Macedonian man and

---

60. "If you have judged me to be faithful to the Lord, come and stay at my home" (Acts 16:15).

61. Paradoxically, despite the narration of their interpretation of Paul's dream as a divine call to proclaim.

Lydia have, in one manner or another, called Paul to themselves through the verb παρακαλέω, and both have used the imperative in their requests. At this point in the narrative, only Lydia has displayed both emotion-fused thought and self-expressive speech, emphasized by divine initiative in the former and the use of λέγω in the latter.

Despite the narrative's having raised an expectation of a response to Lydia's forceful request in Acts 16:15, it does not provide one; rather, a new paratactic episode commences in Acts 16:16, once again opening en route to the place of prayer, except that this time the group appears certain of its intended destination in contrast to the "supposing" of Acts 16:13. Also, in contrast to Acts 16:13, this time the group is encountered by,[62] rather than itself encountering, a woman (Acts 16:16). This woman, a slave, is described as being endowed with the "spirit of Python," and her mantic proclamations through this spirit bring "much profit" to her owners. Over the course of many days, the slave woman follows Paul and his group around, crying out, "These men are slaves of the Most High God, who proclaim to you a way of salvation" (Acts 16:17). Once again, a character other than a member of the Pauline group speaks directly, and the slave woman's direct discourse is preceded, as was the case with Lydia's, by λέγουσα. Moreover, while emotion-fused thought was paired with Lydia's speech, here it is the slave woman's purposeful action of following the group around that pairs with her speech.

The slave woman's actions continue for many days until Paul, "highly disturbed" (διαπονέομαι), turns and commands the spirit, "In the name of Jesus Christ to come out of her."[63] The Python spirit acquiesces to Paul's command and comes out "that very hour" (Acts 16:18). Paul's charge to the spirit is the first instance of his direct speech in this unit, although Paul speaks by the "name of Jesus Christ" and the direct discourse is addressed to a spirit. The narrative does not explain what caused Paul to address or expel the spirit. Since the slave woman had been following the we-group and calling out her proclamation for "many days," her activity did not present enough of an immediate problem to provoke an earlier response from Paul. If the content of the slave woman's proclamation

---

62. Ὑπαντῆσαι ἡμῖν.

63. The only other time that διαπονέομαι occurs in the New Testament is in Acts 4:2, when the priests, captain of the temple (called a στρατηγός [Acts 4:1] as are Philippi's magistrates [Acts 16:35, 36, 38]), and the Sadducees are all "greatly disturbed" by Peter and John's teaching about Jesus and the resurrection and try to silence them.

clearly contravened the Pauline group's theological understanding, then it would not likely have been tolerated over many days. Yet it was, leaving the provocation leading to Paul's unannounced action unexplained.

Unlike other cases of exorcisms in Luke-Acts, the narrative does not describe the aftereffect of the expulsion of the Python spirit on the slave woman, who drops out of the narrative; rather, the narrative turns to the effect of the spirit's expulsion on her owners (κύριοι). The narrational dramatization of the slave woman is through her direct speech; in contrast, the narrational presentation of Paul's turning to the spirit, and not to the woman, makes it clear that, for Paul, it is the Python spirit who speaks through the medium of the woman.[64]

Moreover, the slave woman's intermediary function is stressed by the narrative's silence on the "exorcism's" effect on her and instead its detailing of the aftereffect, not on her but on her owners. The owners' first response is in the zone of emotion-fused thought; they "see" that their hope of profit left with the Python spirit. There is no descriptive narration of the slave woman's being healed or restored.[65] Luke gives the motivation for the slave owners' reaction narratively by writing that, when they perceive their loss of profit, the slave woman's owners purposefully seize Paul and Silas and drag them into the public square before Philippi's leaders (Acts 16:19). The slave owners react immediately and forcefully; in contrast, Paul and Silas's dragged bodies are presented passively.

Once in front of the magistrates, the slave owners present their charge against Paul and Silas: "These men are disturbing our city; they are Jews and were advocating customs that are not lawful for us as Romans to adopt or observe" (Acts 16:20–21). While the charge itself is ambiguous in presenting a clear, punishable offense, it does contribute to the narrative portrayal of the slave woman's owners since they characterize themselves as Romans, continuing the narrative trend of joining characters to a larger social body. Moreover, they also characterize Philippi as a Roman city, bolstering its earlier κολωνία designation. In their charge, the slave owners characterize Paul and Silas as Jews who are promoting "unlawful" customs and practices among Philippi's inhabitants.

---

64. See the demons who speak to Jesus through the "Gerasene demoniac" in Luke 8:28–31.

65. Supporting Tannehill's claim that "the exorcism in 16:16–18 is not the main focus of attention" (*Acts of the Apostles*, 197).

The crowd, and then the magistrates, respond immediately by attacking Paul and Silas, and the magistrates order Paul and Silas stripped and beaten with rods, after which they order them to be imprisoned and securely guarded by the jailer (Acts 16:22–23). The jailer receives his charge from the magistrates and accordingly imprisons Paul and Silas in the innermost prison and fastens their feet in stocks (Acts 16:24). The purposeful action of the slave owners remains forceful, moving into explicit and extreme violence as their quest for vengeance is joined by the crowd and magistrates. The jailer contributes to the physical abuse of Paul and Silas by fastening their beaten bodies in stocks, a purposeful act that, as will be discussed in intertextural analysis, caused significant pain and suffering to prisoners. Once again, Paul and Silas's bodies are recipients of the violent action of others.

During the night, Paul and Silas pray and sing hymns while the prisoners listen, becoming the second group, following the women by the river, to be depicted as listeners to Paul and his disciples (Acts 16:25). Whereas Paul spoke to the listeners at the river and to the Python spirit (vv. 13, 18), he now prays and sings hymns to God. In this manner, Paul's participation in divine communication continues to be emphasized. The section began with a vision being interpreted as a divine commission; it was followed by speech and divinely enabled listening at the river; this was followed by the command to the Python spirit in the name of Jesus Christ; and now Paul prays and sings hymns to God. This realm of divine communication is punctuated by these receptive audiences: the women at the river, the Python spirit, and the prisoners.

While Paul and Silas pray, the earth becomes the source of purposeful action, as a violent earthquake severely shakes the foundations of the prison and springs open the prison doors as well as the prisoners' fetters and chains (Acts 16:26). The jailer awakes and, seeing the prison doors wide open, readies to kill himself by the sword since he concludes that the prisoners must have escaped. Just as he draws his sword, Paul calls out in a great voice (ἐφώνησεν μεγάλῃ φωνῇ, "do not harm yourself, for we are all here": Acts 16:27–28). While the role of recurrent stories of divinely initiated earthquakes assisting prison releases will be discussed in intertextural analysis, in narrational analysis, the significant factor is that the narrative does not detail any form of divine collusion in the release of fetters. Just as Paul's Troas vision was of a human man, now here too events regularly associated with the divine realm are portrayed without the narrative presence of the divine.

The jailer is ready to commit suicide when he sees the open doors; the narrative provides the motive: seeing the doors open, he has concluded that the prisoners have escaped (Acts 16:27). Why this conclusion might lead him to take such a drastic step will be discussed in intertextural analysis, but here again a narrative pattern is supported, namely, that of conclusions or suppositions that motivate actions that move the plot forward. The strength and rigidity of the jailer's assumption are emphasized by his calling for lights (Acts 16:29), highlighting that it was dark (it is shortly after midnight) and implying that, although his ability to see is limited by the darkness, the very sight of open doors was enough to compel him immediately to try to kill himself.

For the first time in the narrative, Paul speaks to a human in direct discourse, as he shouts out his and the prisoners' presence. The jailer prostrates himself in front of Paul and Silas, brings them outside, and addressing them as κύριοι—the term that previously had referred to the slave owners—asks, "what must I do to be saved?" to which Paul and Silas reply, "Believe [or have faith in] the Lord Jesus and you will be saved, you and your household." They then proceed to speak "the word of the Lord" to the jailer and all who are in his house.[66]

Paul and Silas's bodies continue to be the recipients of the purposeful action of others, but now, in a reversal, their bodies receive healing and nurturing action rather than being subjected to violent, destructive action. The jailer takes Paul and Silas, washes their wounds, and is baptized along with "all of his." He then takes them into his home and sets out food for them, as "he and his entire household rejoiced that he had believed in God" (Acts 16:33–34).

As was the case with Lydia, the jailer's baptism is narrated in terms of its reception, where the narrative states that Lydia and the jailer each receives baptism, but the "baptizing action" of those administering the baptism is not narrated. In the case of the jailer, the depiction of his receiving baptism juxtaposes with the narration of his purposeful action of bathing Paul and Silas's wounds. Also, as was the case with Lydia, members of their respective households receive baptism along with them. The symbiotic relationship between an individual and a group is once again emphasized when the jailer and his household rejoice, because *he* had believed in God.

---

66. Which may have included the other prisoners: Acts 16:30–32.

At the outset of the next scene, self-expressive speech is conveyed through intermediaries. In the morning, the magistrates dispatch the lictors to the prison, to instruct the jailer to release Paul and Silas.[67] The jailer then conveys this message to Paul and Silas, ending with "therefore come out now and go in peace" (Acts 16:36). Rather than leaving prison, however, Paul responds with a countercharge and a challenge in the longest passage of direct discourse in the rhetorical unit (Acts 16:37). His message is again mediated in reverse via the lictors to the magistrates, who respond in fear at the news that Paul and Silas are Roman citizens.

Motivated by emotion-fused fear, the magistrates do come themselves to the prison, try to conciliate with Paul and Silas,[68] and then take them out of prison and ask them to leave Philippi (Acts 16:38–39). Here, too, implicitly the plot was propelled by a supposition (in this case, incorrect) that Paul and Silas were "Jews" but not "Romans." A significant portion of plot development in the rhetorical unit is motivated by emotion-fused suppositions.

Despite being asked to leave by Philippi's leaders, Paul and Silas instead go to the place of Lydia and in so doing confirm their response to Lydia's offer to come to her house (Acts 16:15). However, in contrast to the disciples' stay with the jailer, the visit to Lydia's home is absent the types of purposeful acts that would be associated with hosting, such as the setting out of a meal, and instead is framed by emotion-fused thought. As Paul and Silas see (ἰδόντες) the assembly there,[69] they also encourage them (παρεκάλεσαν τοὺς ἀδελφούς: Acts 16:40). Consistent with the narrative emphasis on Lydia's heart in verse 14, the entire visit to Lydia's home is framed by emotion-fused thought. Moreover, in each of the two narrated encounters between the Pauline group and the two assemblies that feature Lydia, the groups come together within a frame of missionary activity. What the disciples initiate with the women by the river they strengthen with their final visit to Lydia's house. Following their "stay" at Lydia's, the disciples leave Philippi.

Conclusion: Narrational and Sensory-Aesthetic Texture and Pattern. This analysis of narrational texture has contributed to the findings of repetitive and progressive textural analyses by contextualizing some of the

---

67. "Let those men go" (Acts 16:35).
68. Παρεκάλεσαν αὐτούς.
69. Which now includes men, as can be inferred from the masculine ἀδελφούς.

repetitive and progressive elements within the rhetorical unit's narrative presentation of them. In the analysis of repetitive texture, I observed that the plural form, and more specifically designations of groups of people, is a feature of this unit. We can see in narrational texture that characters are often presented as groups, and significantly, groups speak as one: the we-group to the women by the river; the slave owners to the people of Philippi; Paul and Silas to the jailer and those gathered in the prison compound; the magistrates to the lictors, the lictors to the jailer, and the lictors to the magistrates; the magistrates to Paul and Silas; and the Pauline group to those assembled at Lydia's. Moreover, characters often speak on behalf of others, including human beings on behalf of spiritual beings: the Macedonian man calls on behalf of "us"; the slave woman vocalizes the words of the Python spirit; Paul casts the Python spirit out in the name of Jesus Christ; the slave owners accuse Paul and Silas on behalf of "us Romans"; Paul calls to the jailer on behalf of all the prisoners and then countercharges the magistrates on his and Silas's behalf; Paul and Silas speak "the word of the Lord" to the prison assembly; the jailer relays the message of the magistrates that had been delivered by the lictors to Paul and Silas, and then Paul's message is relayed in reverse through the same parties. The author of Acts also uses direct speech to foreground a particular member(s) of a group: the Macedonian man, Lydia, the slave woman, Paul, the slave owners, the jailer, and the magistrates.

The analysis of narrational texture has also revealed that the author has helped to focus attention particularly on three characters by nature of their uncommon presentation: the first appearance of a we-group narrational voice, Lydia, and the slave woman—the latter two juxtaposed women who both speak through direct discourse.[70] Overall, the analysis of narrational texture suggests that the author uses self-expressive speech strategically in order to characterize groups and to highlight their representatives.

Although self-expressive speech plays a strategic role in the rhetorical unit, this analysis of narrational texture provides grounds for suggesting that the author's principal rhetorical interest is situated within the body zone of emotion-fused thought. More specifically, the plot develops mainly as a consequence of narrative characters forming suppositions or judgments of enigmatic situations and then acting in response to their

---

70. The only other two women with direct discourse in one unit in Luke-Acts are Mary and Elizabeth (Luke 1:42–55).

interpretations. Some of the clearest examples are the we-group interpreting the call of the Macedonian man in Paul's vision as a call from God; the men of Philippi assuming that Paul and Silas are outsiders and not Roman citizens; and the jailer assuming that the prisoners had escaped. Other less self-evident examples, such as the we-group sitting down and preaching to the women by the river and Paul's discerning a problematic situation associated with the slave woman with the Python spirit, are arguably the more salient rhetorically. Moreover, the sole case of explicit divine initiative in this unit is that of God's acting within Lydia's heart, where the heart is the center of emotion-fused thought. In addition, the fact that the content of Paul's speech to the women is not narrated, nor, directly, the impact of God's action on Lydia, further suggests that acts of emotion-fused thought rather than self-expressive speech are the most rhetorically salient here.

This analysis of narrational texture has also revealed a striking contrast between the authoritative voice accorded to Paul through self-expressive acts, such as vocally casting out the Python spirit, calling the jailer to salvation, and challenging the magistrates, with that of Paul's purposeful actions, which are either purposeful/passive, such as sitting down with women, or completely passive, to the extent of being physically subject to the violent purposeful actions of other men. In fact, one could make a case for suggesting that violent acts against Paul (and Silas) escalate after Lydia's forceful offer, which culminates with a word most closely associated with severe violence: παραβιάζομαι (Acts 16:15). The author presents a clear dichotomy between the authority of Paul's (and whatever group he is narratively embedded in) self-expressive speech and that of the purposeful acts of the disciples' bodies.

Given that this repetitive and progressive textural analyses revealed a concentration of terms associated with "to come" or "to go," most notably ἔρχομαι-prefixed terms, and the παρακαλέω progression, it is not surprising that we see a great deal of coming and going, as well as human beings coming together and separating apart in the analysis of narrational texture. The we-group is called to Macedonia by a Macedonian representative, it crosses over to Philippi, then it leaves the city in search of a place of prayer where it joins with the gathered women; Lydia asks the we-group to join with her in her home; the we-group is joined by the slave woman and is then dragged to Philippi's marketplace by her owners after Paul sends the Python spirit away; Paul and Silas are taken into prison, call the jailer to themselves, and then are led out of their cell into the jailer's home, after which they leave prison; the magistrates ask Paul and Silas to leave Philippi; the disciples go to Lydia's and join with the believers who had gathered there; and finally, the Pauline group leaves Philippi. We see a remarkable amount of movement in the unit composed of groups entering and leaving, or being brought into or out of spaces, and in tandem, groups of people joining together and also separating apart.

Paradoxically, given all the entering and leaving, with the exception of Philippi's prison, we have seen that the classification of spaces performs an enigmatic role in the rhetorical unit. From the outset, spaces are not clearly classified. For example, a man of Macedonia calls Paul to Macedonia, yet the narrative situates Philippi as a Roman colony; the disciples initially spend some time in Philippi, but the narrator does not disclose where; within a sacred temporal setting of Sabbath, the disciples search for a synagogue, yet encounter a gathering of women; once again, on the way to a place of prayer the disciples do not seemingly reach one yet in prison partake in worship; while at the jailer's house the disciples technically remain in the prison compound yet are portrayed as guests; finally, no information is given about Lydia's house or household. However, whereas the assembled space where Lydia is first encountered is characterized by gender, that is, gathered women against the backdrop of the sacred space of Sabbath, the space associated with Lydia at the episode's closing is defined by the union between Paul and Silas with the "brother and sister" members of the Christ-movement. Within the movement of coming and going, the groups and spaces associated with the Macedonian man, Lydia, the slave woman, and the jailer undergo unexpected transformations through their encounters with the Pauline group.

3.5. Argumentative Texture

As noted in chapter 2, the fullness of a text's argumentative and rhetorical impact cannot be displayed until relevant social, cultural, historical, and oral-scribal intertextural elements can be incorporated into the analysis. Accordingly, in the analysis of argumentative texture, I will be concerned only with displaying how the text is structured argumentatively at the textual level. I will also highlight those elements that are linked argumentatively.

With the contrast between Paul's cryptic vision and the immediacy of its apprehension by the Pauline group, we see the first signs that Luke predominantly employs inductive, rhetographical argumentation in the rhetorical unit. At Troas during the night, Paul receives a vision of a Macedonian man (ἀνὴρ Μακεδών) who beseeches him to "help us by crossing over to Macedonia" (Acts 16:9). The text enigmatically does not explain who the man is or what identifies him as a Macedonian, nor is there any indication as to what type of "help" (βοηθέω) is being solicited.⁷¹ Yet despite the puzzling nature of the vision, it nonetheless catalyzes the we-group into immediate action, impelling them to go to Macedonia, since the disciples infer that the vision is a divine call to announce "good news" (εὐαγγελίζομαι: Acts 16:10) to "them."

While the vision functions as a temporal precondition to the Pauline group's reaction,⁷² the text does not explain how the we-group learned of the vision,⁷³ nor how it came to interpret the vision, for the vision does not come with an interpretive guide as did other visions referring to human characters in Acts.⁷⁴ At the same time, the text stresses the clarity of the vision for the group by the immediacy of their response to the vision (Acts 16:10).

Although the vision is interpreted as a call from God, it is notably absent of any markers of divine elements or spiritual beings. Instead, the vision features a human male, identified through his earthly, ethnic Macedonian origin. Other than two prior Spirit interventions (Acts 16:6, 7) that

---

71. Fitzmyer claims that "Paul recognizes the figure as Macedonian from what he says," but given that the man is identified as Macedonian before he speaks and that Philippi is then characterized as "Roman" more than "Macedonian" where a Lydian is the first one to be baptized, the premise that "us" is what defines the man as Macedonian is not ironclad (Fitzmyer, *Acts of the Apostles*, 579). Others have speculated that it was the Macedonian's clothing that identified him as such despite the text's complete absence of any such descriptive detail. See Haenchen, *Acts of the Apostles*, 488 nn. 1, 3.

72. "When he had seen the vision" (Acts 16:10), where the temporal conjunction ὡς δέ could probably be better understood as "after" rather than "when."

73. The Western text fills in this gap: "*When therefore he had risen up, he related to us the vision*, and we perceived that *the Lord* had called us to preach the gospel to *those who were in Macedonia*," observes Metzger: "The purpose of the banal addition is clear enough: the reviser wanted to make sure that the reader will understand how it was that Paul's companions knew what he had seen in the vision—Paul told them!" (Bruce M. Metzger, *A Textual Commentary on the Greek New Testament: A Companion Volume to the United Bible Societies' Greek New Testament [Fourth Revised Edition]*, 2nd ed. [Stuttgart: Deutsche Bibelgesellschaft, 1994], 392, emphasis original).

74. Previously, for example, God had sent a vision of Ananias to the sightless Saul so that Saul could consequently recognize that Ananias had been divinely sent (Acts 9:11–12, 17). Similarly, Peter was told by the Spirit to go with Cornelius's three servants, because they, too, had been sent by God (10:19–20). Yet Paul's vision in Troas seems limited to the Macedonian man's plea.

might suggest, through qualitative progression, a subsequent divine origin to the vision, nothing in Paul's vision itself represents divine presence.[75] Luke inductively fuses the Macedonian man's call[76] with the we-group's interpretation of it as a call from God,[77] in part through a lexical connection between παρακαλέω and προσκαλέω.

The vision and its interpretation initiate a logical plot progression. The interpretation of the vision catalyzes the group's crossing into Macedonia and accordingly provides an inaugurating motive that supplies the cause for the plot's opening movement. Not only does the plot gain its forward movement from the vision's interpretation, but also an escalating sense of immediacy is triggered by the vision's source being attributed to divine communication. Through qualitative progression, the narrative supports the growing sense that the we-group was responding to an urgent divine call by describing a swift sea crossing to Philippi (Acts 16:11–12a), in contrast with earlier, restricted land-crossing attempts (Acts 16:6–7). In addition, the positioning of Philippi as a "first," together with its being cast as a Roman colony, also contributed to a growing sense of the journey's importance. The "arrows of desire,"[78] triggered by these early elements of qualitative progression that undergird the "causal" logical plot progression, develop an expectation of an upcoming significant missionary encounter involving the Pauline group and the people of Macedonia.

In Acts 16:12b, however, the plot's intense movement encounters a curious step. In stark contrast with the immediately preceding fast-paced urgency of the we-group's move to Macedonia, the disciples, upon reaching their intended destination, at first simply "remained [διατρίβοντες] in the city for some days."[79] When plot development does resume in Acts 16:13, its direction further departs from that inferred by its early plot progression. The temporal setting of the Sabbath, together with the group's

---

75. John Faulkenberry Miller has also remarked on the absence of explicit divine elements in the vision: "Luke employs dream-visions frequently in his narrative, and characters are sometimes required to interpret these visionary encounters. Nevertheless, it is important that this dream-vision lacks a divine agent and invites interpretation" (*Convinced That God Had Called Us*, 97).

76. Παρακαλέω: Acts 16:9.

77. Προσκαλέω: 16:10.

78. See p. 48.

79. The term διατρίβω literally means to "rub away" with a sense of "rubbing away time" and here means to remain or stay but without any apparent activity or purpose attached to this period, like Peter's stay with Simon the Tanner in Acts 9:43–10:23.

searching for a place of prayer, raises an audience expectation that the group is about to come upon a synagogue.[80] However, in Acts 16:13, rather than encountering another typical synagogue gathering, the Pauline group instead finds an assembly of women. When Lydia is introduced in Acts 16:14, it becomes increasingly clear that the plot's progression has truly diverted from its presumed course. Beverly Gaventa recalls Calvin's observation of the "delicious incongruity" presented by the situation, since, although the vision of the Macedonian man's plea in Acts 16:9 "creates the expectation that the whole of Macedonia awaits Paul and his colleagues[,] they encounter no men … but a group of women, and the one woman who is converted is not Macedonian."[81]

We can see that by introducing the women by the river and Lydia, the author upsets two sets of expectations: one based on plot progression and the second based on the mental image of a synagogue. In the first instance, the women are clearly not the Macedonian men that the plot's narrative had led the audience to expect, and in the second, through their female gender, they clash dramatically with a traditional Jewish synagogue setting. Yet, inasmuch as the gathering of women presents a highly ambiguous setting, the we-group and God respond to them as if there were no ambiguity present. The we-group encounters the women and, following a narratively banal καί conjunction, reacts by sitting down with the women and speaking to them. In turn, God performs the only explicit solely directed divine action in the unit through the act of opening Lydia's heart to understand Paul's words. By portraying the we-group and God as seeing something in the women and Lydia other than what the audience has been led to expect, the narrator suggests to us that the author

---

80. The opening phrase, τῇ ἡμέρᾳ τῶν σαββάτων, uses the relatively uncommon plural form to refer to one Sabbath day. "Sabbath" is designated by σαββάτων two other times in Luke-Acts, each time within a synagogue context: when Jesus reads the Isaiah scroll in the synagogue in Nazareth (Luke 4:16) and in Antioch (Acts 13:14) when the Pauline group enters the synagogue and, similarly to Acts 16:13, sits down with the people gathered there.

81. Beverly Roberts Gaventa, *The Acts of the Apostles*, ANTC (Nashville: Abingdon, 2003), 236. Calvin wrote, "Having entered the principal city they find nobody there to whom to give their services. Therefore they are forced to go out into the open country, to speak in an unfrequented and out-of-the-way spot. There they cannot meet with even a single man, to listen to their teaching. They only obtain one woman as a disciple for Christ, and a foreigner at that" (Calvin, *Acts of the Apostles 14–28*, 71).

deliberately uses elements of ambiguity in order to begin to develop a rhetographical, inductive argument.

The narrator does not explicitly describe the aftereffects of Lydia's heart being opened. Instead, we can infer that since Lydia was already listening to the disciples (ἤκουεν), God's intervention facilitated a different form of listening that privileged Lydia's cognitive, intellectual, and moral center over her ears. However, despite this narratively featured divine action, we can see narrative gaps continue to accumulate. As in the ὡς δέ conjunction of Acts 16:10, where Paul's vision was a precondition to the group's decision to cross to Macedonia, so too Lydia's baptism is preceded by a ὡς δέ conjunction in Acts 16:15 and appears as a precondition to her twofold request of having her faithfulness to the Lord positively evaluated and the Pauline group come to her home. Once again, though, while the ὡς δέ ostensibly marks a logical plot progression, in reality it highlights the presence of a gap: the connection between Lydia's heart being opened and her baptism is unclear since the baptism event is not described, and the role it might play between Lydia's listening and her request to Paul is not explained.

As was the case with the Macedonian man, Lydia's request in Acts 16:15 is introduced through παρακαλέω and involves an emphatic request to come. However, whereas the Macedonian gives a reason, albeit an enigmatic one, as to why he is calling Paul ("help us"), Lydia's request does not furnish the reason for the invitation (Paul's group had already been staying in Philippi). Rather, the request functions as the consequent of a first-class conditional phrase.[82] The antecedent ("if you have judged me to be faithful to the Lord," Acts 16:15) begins with εἰ introducing a first-class condition where the argumentation is premised on an assumption of truth for argument's sake and expresses the sentiment, "*if—and let us assume that this is true for the sake of argument—then....*"[83] Paraphrasing Daniel Wallace's

---

82. The argumentative basis for Lydia's offer is described in Wallace's discussion of conditional sentences: "The second relation the protasis can have to the apodosis is that of ground, or evidence, to inference. Here the speaker infers something (the apodosis) from some evidence. That is, he makes an induction about the *implications* that a piece of evidence suggests to him. For example, 'If she has a ring on her left hand, then she's married.' Notice that the protasis is not the *cause* of the apodosis. In fact, it is just the opposite: 'If she gets married, she will wear a ring on her left hand.' Thus, often though not always, the ground-inference condition will semantically be the *converse* of the cause-effect condition." Wallace, *Greek Grammar*, 683 (emphasis original).

83. Ibid., 690, emphasis original.

formula, Lydia's request might be expressed argumentatively as follows: "If you have judged me to be faithful to the Lord, and let us assume that you have, then come into my house and stay."

For Haenchen, the connection between Lydia's baptism and being judged faithful to the Lord was so strong that he considered Lydia's conditional request simply a case of "politeness" since "Lydia is already recognized as a Christian through her baptism."[84] However, the text itself suggests that the outcome of Lydia's request is much less self-evident than Haenchen admits. The conditional offer raises the question of whether the past assessment of Lydia's faithfulness, as demonstrated by her baptism, still continues and, moreover, as suggested by the nature of the request (come to my house and stay), is expected to remain valid in the future.[85]

The conditional nature of Lydia's offer is further emphasized by the narrative contrast between the we-group's immediate response to the Macedonian man's request with the narrative absence of a response to Lydia's request. When the narration of Lydia's offer ends with "and she prevailed upon/urged/constrained [παρεβιάσατο] us" (Acts 16:15), it underscores the fact that the offer, with its preceding condition, remains unanswered. The narrative then heightens the uncertainty over the we-group's response when Lydia's story line is dropped; instead, the narrator switches to the slave woman episode, followed by the rhetorical unit's sole "hosting" scenario, which takes place not at Lydia's but rather at the Philippian jailer's. When the narrative does rejoin Lydia in Acts 16:40, Paul enters her home, sees and encourages the believers gathered there, and then leaves Philippi. This apparent acceptance of her offer is deferred until virtually the entire Philippi episode had been played out, leaving the outcome of the request in abeyance until the end of the rhetorical unit. The absence of an immediate answer is argumentatively significant, for the author would not have raised the unusual setting by the river, profiled God's action in Lydia's heart, and framed Lydia's offer within a forceful request for an evaluation of her faithfulness only to move abruptly on to another episode. In fact, I will later argue that Luke uses Lydia's request to have her faith evaluated

---

84. Haenchen, *Acts of the Apostles*, 495.
85. The conditional part of Lydia's request can be distinguished from other conditional requests such as Jesus's poignant plea in Luke 22:42 ("Father, if you are willing [εἰ βούλει], remove this cup from me; yet, not my will but yours be done"), where βούλομαι appears in the indicative present and carries no presumption that "removing the cup" had already been willed by God.

in order to launch a rhetographical argument that unfolds the nature and meaning of "faith in the Lord" throughout the remainder of the rhetorical unit. Lydia's request amplifies a developing qualitative progression that ties requests to come with the need for discernment.

Following Lydia's request, a progressive sequence begins a new subunit in Acts 16:16 that relies on comparison and contrast for its argumentative impact. As was the case when the women by the river were encountered, once again the we-group is en route to a place of prayer, has its preaching featured, and meets up with a woman who speaks through direct discourse (Acts 16:16–17).[86] Again, progressive differences give the text its rhetorical direction.

The group proceeds to a place of prayer (Acts 16:16), without any apparent show of uncertainty as to its location (see Acts 16:13). The disciples do not here encounter anyone; rather, they are encountered *by* a woman (παιδίσκην ... ὑπαντῆσαι ἡμῖν: 16:16).[87] In contrast with Lydia's listening, this woman proclaims. Whereas Lydia's capacity to understand the essence of the disciples' preaching requires divine intervention, the slave woman's announcement seems to display this essence: "who proclaim to you a way of salvation" (Acts 16:17). The Pauline group and their mission are publicly and vocally announced in the streets of Philippi for "many days" by the slave woman (Acts 16:18). In the progression from the riverside encounter to that of being encountered by the slave woman, the we-group shifts from being strangers to being publicly recognized. On the surface, it seems that the missionary activities inaugurated by the disciples with the women by the river and Lydia have continued to develop and spread into the streets of Philippi.

As the earlier discussion of physiognomy has detailed, in the first century a person's identity was closely related to the group(s) others perceived that person as belonging to. When the slave woman repeatedly and publicly proclaimed the essence of the Pauline group's identity and mission while moving through Philippi's streets together with them, it would have suggested to the people of Philippi that the we-group and the Python

---

86. "As we were going to the place of prayer, we were met by a slave girl who had a spirit of divination and brought her owners much gain by soothsaying. She followed Paul and us, crying, 'These men are servants of the Most High God, who proclaim to you a way of salvation'" (Acts 16:16–17).

87. Παιδίσκην functions as "the accusative subject of the infinitive [ὑπαντῆσαι]" (Parsons and Culy, *Acts*, 314).

group were somehow allied. Acknowledged as men of the "Most High God" (Acts 16:17), the mission of the we-group appears to have been aided by the energetic support of the Python group.

When Paul eventually sends the Python spirit away in Acts 16:18, the motive for his reaction is enigmatic. Rhetorically, the absence of explicit argumentative rationale allows us to suggest again the presence of another argumentative gap.[88] At times overlooked, the fact that the slave woman proceeded with her proclamation for "many days" implies that a problematic aspect to her behavior was not immediately apparent. As the vision of the Macedonian needed interpretation and as Lydia's faithfulness required evaluation, so too do Paul's actions vis-à-vis the slave woman's. If the content of the slave woman's proclamation were inherently offensive to the missionary enterprise, then the spirit would undoubtedly have been swiftly silenced; yet it was allowed to proclaim for "many days" (Acts 16:18).[89] The lack of explicit rationale for Paul's actions has led commentators to offer a number of possible suggestions of their own.[90] Some take

---

88. Both the term for becoming greatly disturbed, διαπονέομαι, as well as for turning, ἐπιστρέφω, and attendant-circumstance participles (διαπονηθείς/ἐπιστρέψας) function as "something of a prerequisite" to the finite verb "to speak," λέγω/εἶπον, in the phrase "Paul, very much annoyed, turned and said" (Acts 16:18). Parsons and Culy classify these two participles as attendant circumstance: "Given the fact that conjoined participles must share the same function, διαπονηθείς cannot be causal since it is conjoined to ἐπιστρέψας, which is clearly not causal" (*Acts*, 315). "The [attendant circumstance] participle is something of a prerequisite before the action of the main verb can occur" (Wallace, *Greek Grammar*, 643).

89. The tolerance for this proclamation contrasts with the immediate correction of the Lycaonians' misperception of Paul and Barnabas's divinity in Acts 14:14–15.

90. Some think that the continuous noise from the proclamations was the problem: "So why does Paul exorcise the spirit? Nowhere in this story is the 'Python spirit' labeled unclean or evil or demonic. This fact sets the scene apart from other exorcism stories to which this one has been compared, especially Luke 8:26–39. Here her incessant mantic activity, not the misleading nature of her message, so annoys Paul that he exorcises the spirit to get a little peace and quiet" (Parsons, *Acts*, 231; see Haenchen, *Acts of the Apostles*, 495). While a desire for "peace and quiet" may certainly be a possibility for Paul's reaction, the text suggests that this would not have been a primary factor leading to the exorcism. It is likely that Paul would have spoken to the woman or her owners if all he wished for was quiet rather than challenging the spirit directly. More significantly, when Paul and Silas are consequently beaten and imprisoned, they remain quite vocal themselves, singing hymns and praying in the middle of the night despite their undoubtedly being severely physically exhausted at that point. There is

into account the effect of the exorcism and suggest that financial profit-taking from the slave woman's mantic activities was the reason for Paul's distress.[91] This is plausible, given the motive for the slave owners' retaliation against Paul and Silas. Moreover, as will be discussed in intertextural analysis, the mantic industry was notorious for profit-taking. However, the gain of the slave woman's owners is not expressed explicitly in monetary terms, since ἐργασία (Acts 16:16, 19) does not necessarily mean strictly financial gain, although the slave woman does clearly bring some form of great benefit to her owners. We can see that Luke argumentatively juxtaposes two profit-seekers: Lydia the seller of purple cloth and the purveyors of mantic activities, the slave woman's owners. In this manner, Luke's progressive sequence that first linked two women by *synkrisis*, Lydia and the slave woman, extends and elaborates the synkratic movement to reach beyond the slave woman and enjoin the slave owners in a comparison with Lydia through their common element of profit-taking.[92]

In contrast with Paul's delayed reaction to the Python's proclamations, the slave owners immediately perceive and react to the spirit's departure.[93] The slave owners clearly attribute their perceived loss of gain to Paul's exorcism.[94] Through the slave owners' violent reaction of seizing Paul and Silas and dragging them to the public square, Luke rhetographically depicts the rupture of any possible perceived alliance between themselves and the we-group.

If previously the we-group and the Python group may have seemed somehow associated with each other, the slave owners' charge against Paul and Silas clearly separates them into an oppositional "us against them"

---

little in the text to suggest that a desire for peace and quiet was the motivating factor for the exorcism.

91. "What is clearly distressing to Luke/Paul is that the girl's owners ... were profiting financially from her soothsaying (v. 16)" (Malina and Pilch, *Social-Science Commentary*, 118).

92. *Synkrisis* is defined on p. 102 below.

93. "But when her owners saw that their hope of gain was gone, they seized Paul and Silas and dragged them into the public square before the rulers" (Acts 16:19).

94. "Luke's sense of humour appears in his choice of ἐξῆλθεν here [Acts 16:19] after its use in ver. 18; their 'hope of profit' was in fact the expelled spirit itself" (F. F. Bruce, *The Acts of the Apostles: The Greek Text with Introduction and Commentary*, 2nd ed. [London: Tyndale, 1951], 316).

argumentative stance.⁹⁵ The slave owners identify Paul and Silas as "Jews," and, much as the audience is not told how the man in Paul's vision is identified as Macedonian, so here too what distinguishes Paul and Silas as Jews to the slave owners is unknown. The slave owners' suggestion that Paul and Silas are Jews does not seem to be based on Philippi's deep-rooted experience with a Jewish community, and therefore the term "Jew" likely functions argumentatively as simply a designation of "foreigner" and, thereby, "outsider."⁹⁶ While the charge against Paul and Silas functions as a stock charge against a foreign cult, it is argumentatively significant that prior to Paul's expulsion of the Python spirit, any foreign "cultlike" activities that the disciples may have manifested were not only unproblematic for the Philippians but instead were supported by the mantic enterprise of the locally powerful slave owners. As a result, in the case of the charges against Paul and Silas, historical questions over whether either Christianity or Judaism was sanctioned by the Romans as a legitimate religion are irrelevant to the argumentative point of the text. Rather, the cause of the separation between Paul and Silas and the slave owners is the author's argumentative concern, conveyed rhetographically.

Much as Luke signaled the connection between the departure of the Python spirit and the departure of the slave owners' hope of profit by the repetitive use of ἐξῆλθεν (Acts 16:18–19), so too the connection between the slave woman's announcement of the content of the disciples' proclamation and the slave owners' condemnation of this content is signaled by the repetitive use of καταγγέλλουσιν (Acts 16:17, 21). Where the slave woman calls out that "these men … proclaim [καταγγέλλουσιν] to you a way of salvation" (Acts 16:17), the slave woman's owners charge that "these men … proclaim [καταγγέλλουσιν] customs which it is not lawful for us Romans to accept or practice" (16:20–21). Through Luke's use of irony, the slave owners represent the customs of "us Romans" as being antithetical to "a way of salvation." Moreover, it is loss of profit that triggers the charge against Paul and Silas, and therefore one can suggest that a way of

---

95. "These men are disturbing our city; they are Jews and are advocating customs that are not lawful for us as Romans to adopt or observe" (Acts 16:20–21).

96. Since the source of the slave woman's proclamation was Paul's preaching and since this preaching normally referred in some manner to (Jewish) Scripture (as will explicitly be the case in the upcoming Thessalonica episode [Acts 17:2]), this may have been sufficient to relate Paul and Silas to Judaism, but as the speech in Athens demonstrates this was not necessarily the case.

salvation is placed in opposition with the hope of a materially profitable alliance with members of the Christ movement.[97]

In focusing on the argumentative flow of this passage, we can see that a complex argumentative link has been developed rhetographically through the means of *synkrisis* between profit-seeking Lydia and the profit-seeking slave owners by way of a sequential bridge provided by the slave woman. Argumentatively structured comparisons of like with like developed in rhetorical schools into formal exercises of comparison, or *synkrisis*. Synkrisis, "language setting the better or worse side by side" (Aelius Theon, *Sync.* 10.112),[98] became one of the formal rhetorical exercises used in the program of early rhetorical education (*progymnasmata*). When dealing with persons, *synkrisis* used combinations of encomium (positive appraisal of a person's actions)[99] or invective (negative appraisal) to compare the deeds of two people.[100] Plutarch's *Parallel Lives* is an example of an extended work modeled on *synkrisis* as it pairs off Greeks with Romans in order to demonstrate "what the ancient world had accomplished in the world of action."[101]

As conceived by Aelius Theon, the earliest writer of *progymnasmata*, *synkrisis* functioned through disanalogy by drawing differences into

---

97. This line of argument concerning profit and divine mediation is consistent with that of other cases in Acts such as Simon's attempt to purchase the power of the Holy Spirit and the rioting Ephesian silversmiths (Acts 8:8–24; 19:23–40).

98. Kennedy, *Progymnasmata*, 52.

99. "*Praise* [*epainos*] is speech that makes clear the great virtue [of the subject praised].... *Encomium*, in contrast, is concerned with deeds.... The deeds are signs of the person's habitual character" (Aristotle, *Rhetoric* 1.9.1367b.33 [Kennedy; emphasis and brackets in translation]).

100. "The exercise in comparison (*synkrisis*) naturally follows the exercise(s) in encomium and invective (Nicolaus 60), as it takes the form of a double encomium, double invective, or a combination of encomium and invective (Aphthonius 31; cf. [Hermogenes] 18; Nicolaus 59–60)" (Craig A. Gibson, *Libanius's* Progymnasmata: *Model Exercises in Greek Prose Composition and Rhetoric*, WGRW 27 [Atlanta: Society of Biblical Literature, 2008], 321, brackets in original).

101. Bernadotte Perrin, introduction to *Plutarch's Lives: Theseus and Romulus; Lycurgus and Numa; Solon and Pulicola*, trans. Bernadotte Perrin, LCL (Cambridge: Harvard University Press, 1914), xiii. In another work, Plutarch also argues for the benefit of comparing like with like in order to better profile a person's character: "Is it not possible to learn better the similarity and the difference between the virtues of men and of women from any other source than by putting lives and actions beside actions?" (Plutarch, *Mulier. virt.* 243B–C [Perrin et al., LCL]).

prominence by comparing seeming like with like:[102] "First, let it be specified that syncrises are not comparisons of things having a great difference between them; for someone wondering whether Achilles or Thersites was braver would be laughable. Comparison should be of likes and where we are in doubt which should be preferred because of no evident superiority of one to the other" (Aelius Theon, *Sync*. 10.112–113).[103] At this point in the narrative, we do not yet have an answer to the question of whether Lydia ultimately will come through the *synkrisis* with the slave owners as "better or worse" than the slave owners. We know that her implicit request to be assessed as "faithful to the Lord" has not, as yet, been explicitly ratified by the narrative. What is clear, however, is that being faithful to profit can be incompatible with being faithful to the Lord. From this examination of the argumentative texture of this passage, I can suggest that Lydia and the slave woman/owners are comparative figures intended toward a rhetorical goal. Later intertextural analysis will add critical information that will then be applied to a comprehensive interpretation of the role of this *synkrisis* in the discussion of ideological texture.

Although the slave owners see that the Python spirit has acceded to Paul's authority, the slave owners' hostile reaction to Paul and Silas displays remarkable hubris. By seizing and dragging Paul and Silas into the public square (ἀγορά), the slave owners show unquestioning faith in their own perceived superior authority. With the ready and violent reaction of both the mob and the magistrates, it is clear that the self-confidence of the slave owners, who in the text are referred to as κύριοι, is not unfounded.[104] As soon as the slave owners issue their charge, the mob and then the magistrates join in the attack without even a thought of hearing a defense from Paul and Silas. The anger of the slave owners is sufficient to mobilize the entire city of Philippi. In contrast, when a similar situation erupts in Ephesus, the town clerk calms the crowd and insists on due process (Acts 19:35–41). In Philippi, however, due process, as Paul will later point out, is not remotely considered. The slave owners appear rightly confident in their local power. As a result, the magistrates charge Philippi's jailer to keep

---

102. For disanalogy see p. 203.
103. Kennedy, *Progymnasmata*, 52–53.
104. "The crowd joined in attacking them; and the magistrates tore the garments off them and gave orders to beat them with rods. And when they had inflicted many blows upon them, they threw them into prison, charging the jailer to keep them safely" (Acts 16:22–23).

Paul and Silas securely. The jailer, whose mandate is given by the adverb ἀσφαλῶς (Acts 16:23), enacts this order literally as he secures (ἀσφαλίζω: 16:24) Paul and Silas in stocks in the innermost cell.

In prison, qualitative progression develops ironic rhetographical argumentation. Although on two previous occasions Paul had been making his way to a place of prayer (Acts 16:13, 16), it is here in Philippi's prison that he is most explicitly described as praying, including singing hymns (Acts 16:25) and soon after expounding on "the word of the Lord" to those gathered in the prison compound (Acts 16:32). Second, as noted above, the Pauline group had not made any local (Macedonian) acquaintances who could bring them to a place of prayer when they first set out in Acts 16:13. Now, in dramatic fashion, they are dragged to and cast into the depths of Macedonian earth by Philippian locals.

Qualitatively relating previous events, the rhetorical unit that began with a night vision reaches a dramatic moment through another event that occurs in the middle of the night. As Paul and Silas pray and sing hymns to God (Acts 16:25), prayers that are heard by the prisoners, their prayers are interrupted by a powerful earthquake, which releases all chains and fetters and opens the prison's doors (Acts 16:26). The earthquake may have been divinely initiated; however, no explicit signs of divine presence make an appearance. Instead, a jailer calls for lights and leads the prisoners out of the cell but still within the prison compound. Moreover, while the Philippi earthquake is often classified as another example of a miraculous "prison-escape" scene like those involving the apostles and Peter, it more rightfully should be categorized as a miraculous "prison-stay" scene. Argumentatively, if indeed there has been divine intervention, its objective does not appear to be Paul and Silas's escape, but rather the creation of circumstances that will make possible the salvation of the jailer.

The acts of surmising, concluding, or discerning have recurrently signaled key events in the rhetorical unit, and following the earthquake, a pivotal case of "concluding" leads to a salvific outcome. When the jailer wakes up and sees the prison doors ajar after the earthquake, he immediately prepares to take his life since he presumes that the prisoners have escaped (Acts 16:27). The jailer's assumption is so certain in his own mind that, despite not being able to see the prisoners (only later does he call for lights), and despite not having checked and verified his assumption, the jailer draws his sword and prepares to commit suicide. In reciprocal fashion, Paul also concludes that the jailer will have presumed their escape, and despite not seeing the jailer, he calls out to him in a loud voice and orders him not to harm himself (Acts 16:28). The jailer's virtual certainty over the prisoners' escape, emphasized by his assumption that his life is for all intents and purposes already over, rhetographically underlines the strikingly unexpected nature of a prisoner's act of staying in prison when escape has been enabled.

Once again, argumentation functions primarily through rhetography as Paul and Silas's act of staying in prison leads to their being affirmed as the ones whom the slave woman had proclaimed. Although the Python spirit had recognized the disciples as "slaves of the Most High God who proclaim … a way of salvation," the slave owners had attempted to displace this identity by publicly humiliating, physically violating, and incarcerating Paul and Silas. The disciples' seeming impotence would have appeared incongruous with their designated identity, much as the crucified Jesus drew ridicule for seemingly not having the power to save himself and thereby demonstrate his divine agency (Luke 23:35–39). Paradoxically, however, by not saving themselves through escaping, Paul and Silas are recognized as divine mediators by the jailer.

As observed in the analysis of repetitive texture, the term κύριος is found in its plural form in Acts only in this rhetorical unit, where it twice refers to the slave owners (Acts 16:16, 19) and then in 16:30 is used by the jailer to address Paul and Silas. When the jailer, trembling with fear, prostrates himself and addresses Paul and Silas as κύριοι, his use of the vocative emphasizes how he has reconceived the prisoners, whom he had witnessed being dominated by the Philippian power brokers and by himself personally, as persons of some authority. The juxtaposition of the slave owners with Paul and Silas is argumentatively emphasized by the repeated use of the term κύριοι, referring first to the former and then to the latter. This shift of referent for the term κύριοι signals the beginnings of a corresponding shift of the jailer's allegiance. The text has been careful to note that the jailer had been ordered by the magistrates to keep Paul and Silas securely and that he had both received and implemented this charge (Acts 16:23–24). However, following Paul's call to the jailer after the earthquake, the jailer leads Paul and Silas out of their cell (Acts 16:30), signaling a loosening of commitment to the magistrates' orders with a corresponding shift toward Paul and Silas.

The jailer's trembling question to Paul and Silas, "What must I do [in order] to be saved?" has often been understood theologically, but within the context of the narrative it can suggest alternate meanings. As noted by Malina, "'salvation' meant rescue from a difficult situation; it was not a specifically God-oriented word."¹⁰⁵ The ambiguous use of σωθῶ in Acts 16:30 may refer to the jailer's immediate difficult situation of not knowing what to do with prisoners who could still attempt to escape, where the threat of their escape had already proven itself to be a life-or-death matter for the jailer.¹⁰⁶ The jailer's life hangs in the balance of the prisoners' hands, and his question to them, which uses the causal conjunction ἵνα, literally asks what he must do in order to secure his rescue from a critical predicament.

Paul and Silas's response to the jailer, "Believe in the Lord Jesus and you will be saved, you and your household" (Acts 16:31), together with their following-on by speaking the "word of the Lord" to the jailer and his household (16:32), expands on a number of this passage's qualitative progressions. One of these continues to build on the irony of the slave owners' charge. Paul and Silas do exactly what the slave woman had proclaimed them to be doing: they proclaim a way of salvation. Moreover, by remaining imprisoned and by declaring themselves as subject to their Lord, that is, Jesus, they position themselves as "slaves/servants of the Most High God." The charge against Paul and Silas had them "disrupting" Philippi by preaching impermissible customs that Romans were not allowed to receive or practice. Qualitatively the text shows that "a way of salvation" is advanced by Paul and Silas in stark contrast to the vengeance enacted by the other κύριοι, despite the fact that these prisoners have both grounds and opportunity for extracting vengeance from the jailer.¹⁰⁷ However, by advancing "a way of salvation," they do in fact disrupt the internal workings of Philippi's power structure, for by showing the jailer a way of salvation, Paul and Silas disrupt Philippi's violence-centered justice system.

Affirming the slave owners' charges, the jailer does receive Paul and Silas' proclamation (Acts 16:32) and then puts this proclamation into practice as he turns from functioning as an instrument of brutality to healer and nurturer by washing their wounds and setting food before them in his home (Acts 16:33–34). He both receives and enacts their proclamation, thereby ironically participating in exactly the sort of "illegitimate"

---

105. Malina, *New Testament World*, 94.

106. In similar manner, the imperative of guards to keep their prisoners secure is emphasized when, after almost losing their lives at sea, the priority of the shipwrecked soldiers is to "kill the prisoners" so that none can escape (Acts 27:42).

107. The physical brutality implicit in their situation will be discussed in intertextual analysis.

activity promoted by the disciples. The jailer's turnaround, although dramatic, remains ambiguous and is perhaps best understood as a potentiality of "conversion" rather than definitive realization. The jailer does not actually release Paul and Silas, since, although they are taken from their cell to the jailer's house, they remain within the prison compound. (The text is silent on the fate of the other prisoners who had stayed.)[108] On one level, the jailer continues to remain obedient to the charge that he had received from his superiors, that is, to keep Paul and Silas secure. Yet by according Paul and Silas authority, listening to their preaching, and tending to their needs, the jailer significantly alters his role.

The jailer is baptized after he washes Paul and Silas's wounds (Acts 16:33). Once again, an explicitly human action seems to be profiled alongside a similar principle that is associated with the sacred realm. The jailer needs to call for lights in prison so that he can literally see that he has been saved from his presumed fate, and then he bathes the prisoners before he himself is "bathed" through baptism. In bathing the prisoners' wounds, the jailer demonstrably shifts away from the force-driven agenda of the slave owners and magistrates. At daybreak, the magistrates will send the lictors with a message of release to the prisoners (Acts 16:35). The Philippian rulers' continued focus on coercively driving Paul and Silas out of Philippi is emphasized by their conveying their message of release by the very rod-bearers who had hours earlier flogged Paul and Silas.[109] The jailer, by taking Paul and Silas out of their cell, cleaning their wounds, and then feeding them, undermines his superiors' agenda of brutalizing Paul and Silas into leaving.

Progressive textural analysis suggested close lexical linkages between the jailer and Lydia, and inductive argumentation begins to develop a

---

108. That they remain within the prison compound is stressed by the lictors bringing permission for their release in the morning (Acts 16:35).

109. Bruce is correct in suggesting that the beating, imprisonment, and release had been motivated by a desire to expel the disciples coercively: "They [the magistrates] probably considered that Paul and Silas had been taught a sufficient lesson by the stripes and the night in prison. They had exercised the police-right of *coercitio*" (*Acts of the Apostles*, 322). Certain Western witnesses offer a contrived explanation for the message of release: "In order to explain the sudden change of attitude on the part of the magistrates, who now entreat the apostles to leave, D syr^{hmg} Cassiodorus and Ephraem read ... ('But when it was day the magistrates *assembled together in the market place, and recollecting the earthquake that had taken place, they were afraid; and sent the police, saying ...*')" (Metzger, *Textual Commentary*, 398).

fuller connection between these two figures. As mentioned, not only are both the jailer and Lydia baptized but so too are their households. Both the jailer and Lydia listen to Paul's preaching. Lydia invites Paul into her home. The jailer brings Paul into his. Each of their respective episodes is preceded by the Pauline group's making its way to a place of prayer. The close proximity between the baptisms of the jailer, Lydia, and their respective households, along with their "episodes" sharing common lexical elements, tentatively suggests a deliberate connection between the two figures.

One of the lexical points of repetitive connection between Lydia and the jailer is πιστός/πιστεύω, which takes on particular significance given Lydia's conditional "hanging question"—"if you have judged me to be faithful [πιστήν] to the Lord" (Acts 16:15)—that remains textually unanswered yet reverberates qualitatively with Paul and Silas's answer to the jailer: "believe [πίστευσον] in the Lord Jesus" (Acts 16:31). Readings of the verb πιστεύω, noun πίστις, and adjective πιστός tend to be assimilated into centuries of Christian interpretation, which understand words related to "faith" as referring to belief in Jesus as the Christ. Moreover, Paul and Silas's specific words to the jailer do in fact refer to "the Lord Jesus," who brings salvation (σῴζω Acts 16:31). That their words refer to the Christian kerygma is indisputable; however, there are two reasons to suggest that perhaps other meanings of πιστεύω and its variants are simultaneously deployed for rhetorical ends by the author.

One factor is the repeated examples of what appears to be deliberate fluidity between sacred and secular terms and settings in this unit. The second factor involves the context for the jailer's shift from subordinating himself to the authority of the disciples rather than the magistrates. While Luke presented Lydia's request to the disciples within the social model of hospitality and thereby rhetographically evoked the qualities of trustworthiness and fidelity that were found in the meaning of the term πιστός, he simultaneously evoked the notion of salvific faith implied by the use of this term through Paul and Silas's response to the jailer (Acts 16:31).

It was already noted above that the jailer's leading Paul and Silas out of their cell and into his home, along with his care of them, almost certainly would have constituted an act of insubordination given that his superiors had directly charged him to keep Paul and Silas secure. When the jailer, thinking the prisoners have escaped, immediately moves to kill himself, his drastic action makes a fine point on the fact that he was unconditionally expected to fulfill his job as jailer. Yet upon hearing Paul's voice, the jailer becomes a disloyal and unreliable jailer. He does not remain faithful to his role or to his superiors. Moreover, by "accepting and practicing" the customs advocated by Paul and Silas, the jailer, from the perspective of the slave owners' charges, was also unfaithful to the rules of Roman custom. Thus the jailer's quality of πιστός, understood as fidelity to his masters, begins to dissolve while, concurrently, he begins to develop faith in Paul and Silas and, through them, in their God.

An analogous relationship develops, thereby, between "belief in the Lord Jesus" and "trust in Paul and Silas," as Paul and Silas's staying shows them as "faithful servants" to God by being trustworthy prisoners for the jailer and thereby saving his earthly life and opening the possibility of his immortality in the future. Luke inductively demonstrates that by trusting Paul and Silas as men, the jailer becomes open to trusting what they have to say about their divinity. When Paul and Silas stay in prison a second time (Acts 16:37), despite being granted the means for release (this time by the authority of the magistrates: 16:35), the jailer sees that his trust has not been misplaced. The author continues to develop an inductive argument by illustrating Paul and Silas's steadfast faith though their courage. The extent of this courage displays itself in full when they challenge the magistrates by way of the lictors, the men who most likely administered Paul and Silas's flogging.[110] Throughout this ongoing interplay among faithfulness, fidelity, and trustworthiness in prison, Lydia's call for evaluation, "if you have judged me to be faithful to the Lord, come to my house and stay" (Acts 16:15), remains an unfulfilled conditional offer.

Strikingly, in a unit marked by inductive, rhetographical argumentation, the only two cases of truly rhetological, deductive argumentation occur within a forensic context. In the first instance, the slave owners charge Paul and Silas with disturbing the city by trying to persuade the people of Philippi to accept and practice customs that are not permissible to Romans (16:20–21). In the second, Paul countercharges the magistrates with having transgressed Roman custom and law by beating and incarcerating Roman citizens without due legal process. The two rhetological arguments form a charge and countercharge and evoke forensic, courtroom discourse.[111] However, while the charges themselves are rhetological, their

---

110. "But Paul said to them [the lictors], 'They have beaten us publicly, uncondemned, men who are Roman citizens, and have thrown us into prison; and do they now cast us out secretly? No! let them come themselves and take us out'" (Acts 16:37).

111. The fact that it was the slave owners who made the initial charge against Paul and Silas and now Paul countercharges the magistrates and not the slave owners only

effect is rhetographical. Whereas the goal of the magistrates' maltreatment of Paul and Silas was to frighten them out of Philippi, in yet another ironic twist to this unit's plot, upon learning that Paul and Silas are Romans, it is the magistrates who end up afraid. The only characters that are contextualized in terms of "fear" by the unit's end are the magistrates, and their fear stems from their knowledge that they have acted against Roman custom in denying Paul and Silas due judicial process. Ironically, in accepting and acting on the words of the κύριοι (i.e., slave owners), the magistrates become the ones who both receive and implement customs that are not lawful for Romans. The fear of the magistrates is not depicted in isolation but instead rhetographically contrasts with the courage that Paul and Silas manifest by "staying."

With the magistrates' final request to Paul and Silas to leave Philippi, the progressive/repetitive term παρακαλέω is used once more. As noted previously, while παρακαλέω is at times translated as "apologized" in Acts 16:39, its meaning lies closer to "placate." Progression often functions rhetorically through *distinctio*, where tension is created between the normal or customary meaning of a word and another particular emphasis of that word's meaning highlighted by means of its repetition. Moreover, this semantic tension between a customary meaning and the meaning emphasized in the particular discourse can either reinforce or disrupt the word's customary meaning.[112] The positive emphasis on, or alternative negation of, the meaning of παρακαλέω and its iterations in the rhetorical unit is rhetorically significant. The Macedonian man's and Lydia's requests to Paul to come are consistent with the customary meaning of παρακαλέω, of calling someone to oneself.[113] However, although the magistrates attempt to placate or conciliate with Paul and Silas, they do so in order to make them more cooperative to their request to leave. Rather than calling Paul and Silas to themselves, as would be suggested by the normative use of

---

serves to emphasize inductively the close-knit social alliance between the slave owners and the magistrates.

112. "The semantic tension between normal meaning and the full emphatic meaning can be used positively (by the normal word being reinforced semantically in the emphasis) or negatively (when the normal word in the emphasis is denied its full meaning)" (Lausberg, *Handbook of Literary Rhetoric*, 296, par. 660).

113. While the term παρακαλέω can have varied meanings including "to call to one's side, urge, entreat, encourage, or conciliate" (BDAG, s.v. παρακαλέω), "we begin by noting that the manifold linguistic use of [παρακαλέω] ... goes back to the sense of 'to call someone to oneself'" (Otto Schmitz, "Παρακαλέω," *TDNT* 5:774).

παρακαλέω, in the case of the magistrates the contrasting context for παρακαλέω is found in their desire to expel Paul and Silas from Philippi (Acts 16:39). This reversal of the normal meaning of παρακαλέω suggests that Luke uses *distinctio* strategically within a rhetorical progression. The rhetorical impact of this crucial progression will be explored more comprehensively in ideological texture.

After being asked by the magistrates to leave Philippi, Paul and Silas instead "stay" by visiting Lydia's (Acts 16:40), and in so doing they literally fulfill Lydia's request from Acts 16:15. The author leads us to an argumentative inference that Lydia is assessed as being faithful to God by the Pauline group since, as requested, they do go into her home and "stay" (lexically emphasized by the repetition of εἰσέρχομαι in 16:15, 40).[114] However, in keeping with the numerous gaps found throughout the narrative, the narrator does not account for the basis on which Lydia is ultimately judged as being faithful. Nor does the narrative describe, or even explicitly mention, a house, nor the profile of those who were gathered at Lydia's, beyond the masculine form of ἀδελφός pointing to at least one man in the assembly and the term itself inferring believers. At Lydia's, Paul and Silas "see" the gathered believers and encourage (παρακαλέω) the assembly (Acts 16:40). This final occurrence in the παρακαλέω progression works closely with both the quality of "fidelity" or "faithfulness," as well as with courage and salvific faith. What constitutes salvific fidelity (πίστις) is revealed as an argumentative topos of significant concern to the author.

Conclusion: Argumentative Texture. This analysis of argumentative texture suggests that the author of Acts structures the rhetoric of Acts 16:9–40 primarily through inductive, rhetographical argumentation that makes deliberate use of ambiguity and argumentative gaps in the text. We can further suggest that these gaps, ambiguous situations, and events function to reenforce those emotion-fused acts of interpretation and discernment that are used by the author to develop the narrative's plot and concurrently to develop the argumentative texture of the text. For although argumentative gaps might disrupt argumentative logic and thereby fragment argumentative flow, when used strategically they can also trigger inductive connections that help an audience resolve the gaps and ambiguity.

---

114. Technically, the consequent "come into my house and stay" has fulfilled the condition of the antecedent "if you have judged me to be faithful to the Lord" (Acts 16:15).

The earlier analysis of progressive texture provides grounds for suggesting that, despite or rather as a result of narrative and argumentative gaps in the text, the author leads the audience to make inductive connections throughout the narrative. When we progressively link the Macedonian man's call and Lydia's offer to the disciples, together with the progressive relationship between the we-group's interpretation of Paul's vision as a response of the delivery of "good news" to the Macedonians with Lydia's heart being divinely enabled to "listen" to Paul's preaching of the good news, we can suggest that Luke inductively overmaps the Macedonian man and his group with Lydia and the women. Going forward in the narrative, the author blends Lydia's rhetorical profile with the Macedonian's for rhetorical effect.

The Macedonian man requested "help" from the Pauline group, and they had understood that preaching the good news would deliver this help. After Lydia becomes the recipient of the good news, she responds by another request to the Pauline group to evaluate her faith in God and to come to her house and stay. Inductively, this new request extends and elaborates the Macedonian man's. But, concurrently, Lydia's offer is expressed conditionally, and this condition that Lydia's fidelity to God needs first to be affirmed waits for a response throughout the remainder of the narrative. The author follows Lydia's request to the disciples with a series of narrative events that elaborate the meaning of fidelity to/faith in God. These illustrative examples, such as Paul and Silas's decision to stay in prison, rhetographically develop the criteria for how Lydia's faith is to be evaluated. Through a complex inductive relationship between the Macedonian man and Lydia, the author argues that it is only through a positive affirmation of Lydia's faith that the "Macedonians" can receive their "help."

Although it has been possible to discern an argumentative texture to the rhetorical unit, much of the analysis here has raised new and puzzling questions. For example, the argumentative structure allows us to claim that the author has deliberately connected Lydia with the Macedonian man. Furthermore, we have discovered that Lydia the purple seller and the profit-motivated slave owners are linked argumentatively through *synkrisis* by way of a sequential link between two women: Lydia and the Python-spirit woman. Therefore, we can suggest that a complex argumentative structure undergirds the rhetorical unit. Since Lydia blends with the Macedonian man rhetographically, the Macedonian man also, somehow, will participate in the synkratic argument. The bases for these argumentative connections seem incomprehensible at this point. For that reason, the next two phases of analysis, intertexture and ideological texture, are critical. The rhetorical flow and unity of the text can become clear only after we discover, and relate back to the argumentative structure of the text, those intertextural elements and topoi that would have been automatically and naturally evoked in the minds of the audience.

3.6. Conclusion: Inner Textural Analysis

This analysis of inner texture has allowed us to situate narrative characters, events, and settings within a textually based blueprint of the argumentative structure of the text. I can conclude, on the basis of the repetitive, progressive, narrational, and argumentative textural analyses, that the author uses groups and their representatives, such as the Macedonian man and his people, Lydia and the women, Paul and the we-group, within a pattern of calls between them, as evidenced by the παρακαλέω progression, in order to rhetorically define the ambiguously termed sacred-social space of "place of prayer." Although much of the narrative events unfold as a consequence of the we-group's search for a place of prayer, the narrator never explicitly presents any one space, or group of people, as constituting a traditional Jewish prayer house. Instead, highly ambiguous situations and argumentative gaps contribute to the author's argument that a place of prayer, and its representative group, need to be discerned based on a set of rhetorically presented evaluative criteria. Moreover, by inaugurating the rhetorical unit by the we-group's interpretation of Paul's vision as a call from God to deliver good news, the author inductively asserts that a place of prayer is a space that mediates the delivery of God's good news.

As suggested in the above analysis of argumentative texture, through Lydia's offer to the Pauline group, the author fuses Lydia's call with that of the Macedonian man's in order to elaborate argumentatively the implications of the call. We saw that the major part of Luke's argumentative objective is triggered through Lydia's conditional offer, which calls on the disciples to affirm that she is faithful to God. Within the series of ensuing paratactic episodes, Luke uses *synkrisis* rhetographically to illustrate what faith to God is and is not and thereby defines the boundaries for an assembly of those who would be evaluated as "faithful" to God. Intertextural analysis will reveal the topoi that shape Lydia's rhetorical profile, and with this knowledge the impact of the *synkrisis* between Lydia and the slave owners will become more evident. Once we reach ideological texture, I will argue that Luke uses *synkrisis* in order to isolate the particular qualities of fidelity/faith that will serve to substitute traditional criteria that would have governed culturally normative assessments of who belongs to, and thereby constitutes, a salvific house of prayer.

4
Intertextural Analysis

4.1. Introduction to Intertextural Analysis

Through working with SRI in the time following its initial conception, Robbins and other scholars have developed it into a topos-centered analytic.[1] This gradual adoption of the topos as the focus of SRI analysis has shifted SRI away from treating intertextural analysis as a catalog of discrete, delineated textures such as "historical" or "cultural" and toward an investigation of those salient elements (which could include historical and cultural among others) that drew together to elicit a rhetorical topos. A key feature of a topos is its dynamism that is manifested through the way that a topos both interconnects elements and connects to other clusters of elements. A topos is itself a constellation of elements, but it also takes on its life as a topos by its being situated within a network of elements.[2] As a result of this defining feature of dynamic interconnectivity, one topos might draw on several, at times overlapping, textures. For example, we will see that the social identity of the Philippian slave owners and magistrates as "Romans" takes on its rhetorical relevance within the culturally located physiognomic profile of a Roman masculine ideal. Thus an aspect of social intertexture—a Roman social identity—is relevant to us because of its physiognomic cultural portrayal.

While analytically fruitful, a topos-centered approach presents a set of challenges. One challenge comes from the variable nature of a topos.

---

1. As originally conceived, intertextural analysis systematically worked through the various textures of intertexture (oral-scribal, social, cultural, and historical) and then followed these with three related textures: social and cultural, ideological, and sacred. See Robbins, *Exploring the Texture of Texts*, 40–94, 120–31.

2. See L. Gregory Bloomquist, "Paul's Inclusive Language," 174.

The ancients recognized that a topos can mean "subject matter indicator," and it can also mean "scheme of argument."[3] Moreover, as Robbins's work with "rhetorolects" has demonstrated, rhetoric can also employ localized rhetorical discourse modes, which operate through groupings of topoi embedded within argumentation.[4] Such is the case with a form of discourse, here named as "Lydian touchstone *synkrisis*," which performs a key rhetographical argumentative role in the text, yet is better situated in our discussion of ideological texture. For that reason, discussion of Lydia touchstone *synkrisis* will follow in chapter 5.

A more fundamental challenge to presenting effectively the intertexture of topoi stems from the function of a topos. A topos is a component of rhetorical discourse; therefore, its most basic function is argumentative. However, intertextural analysis does not truly take on its rhetorical shape until the findings of intertexture are integrated with ideological texture. Therefore, at times it is difficult to present intertexture within an argumentative flow. The problem of how to present intertexture coherently is only compounded when a text is marked by rhetographical argumentation, which by its very nature operates from a mental elaboration that goes beyond the words found on the pages of the text. As a result, until the illumination of ideological texture, certain intertextural topics might leave a reader scratching her or his head as to why they are being discussed, since they do not appear to be suggested by the words of the text. The rhetographical role of Lydian touchstone *synkrisis* makes for an illustrative example. Undoubtedly, SRI interpreters will find a better solution to the challenge of presenting intertextural data than this current project has managed to do. In the meantime, I will investigate intertexture through the framework of topoi in the following sections. In such a framework, oral-scribal, social, cultural, sacred, and historical elements will be discussed when, and only if, they might benefit our understanding of relevant topoi and how they are used argumentatively.

First, I will explore how Lydia's social identity as a Lydian woman evokes a strong cultural characterization and how the sociocultural symbolic meaning ascribed to Lydia's ethnic identity joins with "purple," as well as to "seller," to develop a clearly defined character frame. As a result

---

3. Sara Rubinelli, "The Ancient Argumentative Game: Τόποι and *Loci* in Action," *Argu* 20 (2006): 253–72.

4. See Vernon K. Robbins, *The Invention of Christian Discourse*, RRA 1 (Dorset, UK: Deo, 2009).

of this investigation, we will understand how it is possible to suggest that Lydia's socioreligious descriptive attribute, worshiper of God, clashes with the other elements of her identity. Further, it will become apparent just how incongruent a fit the Sabbath setting of "place of prayer" is with Lydia's profile. Second, I will look at which social and cultural codes were relevant to the social model of hospitality in the particular case of Lydia's offer to the disciples. Third, I will examine how Paul's vision introduces a network of military elements. The vision evokes a cultural understanding of the vision itself, the social identity of the Macedonian man and the cultural echoes it evokes, the literary-historical contextualization of what the man says, and the cultural understanding of the historical-geographic setting for the vision. Fourth, I will show that, when the slave owners frame their accusation as an affront to Roman custom, they invoke physiognomic Roman social identity as a well as the social code of honor. Within such a competition for honor, Philippi's penal system and its network of social alliances play vital roles. Fifth, I will examine how Paul and Silas's imprisonment evokes other stories of miraculous prison escapes. Sixth, Paul and Silas's imprisonment raises the prison topos to prominence, which involves the historical conditions of first-century prisons, the cultural depiction of the social role of jailers, and the social role of punishment. Together these, as well as several tangential intertextural elements, will inform our ability to understand the topoi that shape the rhetorical development of the text and consequently to perceive how they function in the ideological texture of the text.

4.2. Lydia: Topoi of Lydian Physiognomy

After Sapphira (Acts 5:8), the second female narrative character who speaks directly in Acts is Lydia (Acts 16:14–15). Not only does Lydia speak, but she is also endowed with a string of descriptors that rhetorically focus a spotlight on her character. Moreover, Lydia's request to the Pauline group in Acts 16:15 continues the unit's παρακαλέω progression that had been commenced by the Macedonian man calling the Pauline group to Macedonia. We shall see that Lydia's descriptive profile shapes the rhetorical impact of what she says and also influences the progressive rhetorical development of the passage.

4.2.1. Lydia's Indeterminate Social Status

The primary focus of modern scholarship's attention to Lydia has been the question of her social status. Discussions around Lydia's socioeconomic status have been fueled primarily by her occupation of "purple seller," πορφυρόπωλις (Acts 16:14), by drawing inferences from the color's presumed high status, for purple was highly valued in antiquity. Indeed, by the first century, the desire for purple as a status symbol spawned an industry devoted to sham purples whose lower cost was accessible to lower classes.[5] While these ersatz purples might also generate a profit, the text offers no clues as to what Lydia actually sold (dye, cosmetic, cloth?), what its quality may have been (genuine Tyrian sea purple, or one of its copiously varied imitations?), and what level of profit, if any, it generated. As a result of historical evidence for the variety of purples being produced in the first century, along with the lack of textual indicators that might help us to gauge the profitability of Lydia's trade, it is not possible to situate Lydia on an economic-status scale from her occupation of purple seller.

Similarly, Lydia's status as a reputed "householder" has developed in scholarship without the benefit of any description of what the configuration of her house may have been. There is no indication of who constituted her household; neither is there any indication of how many or how few constituted the Pauline group she invited, nor who formed the ἀδελφοί in her house (Acts 16:40). Although the apostle Peter's mother-in-law served many in her house (Luke 4:38–40), Peter has not been characterized by commentary as a wealthy householder but rather a "poor fisherman."[6] In

---

5. Reinhold, *History of Purple as a Status Symbol in Antiquity*, 53. The Stockholm Papyrus (third century CE) lists "no fewer than 70 recipes for dyers, most of them concerning the production of sham purples," many of which were passed on from earlier times. Wolfgang Born, "Purple in Classical Antiquity," *CibR* 4 (1937): 113. The Stockholm Papyrus is considered a continuation of the earlier Leiden Papyrus, an alchemist's manual, which primarily suggested ways in which gold and silver could be replicated from base stones.

6. Similarly, in Ovid's *Metamorphoses*, divine guests Zeus and Hermes are hosted in the home of a very poor aged couple—Philemon and Baucis—who together constitute the whole "household": "But pious old Baucis and Philemon, of equal age, were in that cottage wedded in their youth, and in that cottage had grown old together; there they made their poverty light by owning it, and by bearing it in a contended spirit. It was of no use to ask for masters or for servants in that house; they two were the whole household, together they served and ruled" (*Met.* 8.631–636 [Miller, LCL]).

the case of Lydia, the inferred high status associated with purple's symbolism has shaded a similar wealthy characterization of her household. But, put simply, there is no evidence in the text of the extent or lack of status that Lydia's purple would have accorded. Not only is Lydia's economic status indeterminate, but more significantly, despite being a principal concern of modern scholarship, the question of Lydia's social status is not where the author of Acts' interest has been engaged.[7]

Rather, what is of fundamental concern and interest is Lydia's ethnographic profile. Historically, Thyatira had been located in the ancient kingdom of Lydia.[8] As a result, most commentators have observed the

---

7. Social status or wealth may be incidental or secondary in descriptions of a person or character. A woman of indisputably high status was Roman Philippi's namesake, Augustus's daughter Julia Augusta, yet it was not her status that made her a subject of interest to several authors but rather her various purported adulteries. Seneca writes: "The emperor Augustus banished his daughter and made public the scandals of his House. She had received lovers in droves [*admissos gregatim adulteros*]. She had roamed the city in nocturnal revels, choosing for her pleasures the Forum, and the very Rostrum from which her father had proposed his adultery law. Turning from adultery to prostitution, she had stationed herself at the statue of Marsyas, seeking gratification of every kind in the arms of casual lovers" (*Ben.* 6.1–2), as quoted in Richard A. Bauman, *Women and Politics in Ancient Rome* (New York: Routledge, 1992), 113. Interest in Julia Augusta's purported promiscuity endured: Macrobius (ca. 400 CE) compiled a collection of anecdotes about her, including the following: "When people expressed surprise that her children looked like Agrippa [her husband], she replied, 'I only take a passenger on board when I have a full cargo'" (2.5.9) (quoted in Bauman, *Women and Politics*, 110).

8. Thyatira was considered a Lydian city and is designated as such by the sixth-century geographic lexicographer Stephanus of Byzantium (Θυάτειρα, πόλις Λυδίας); in addition, its name is "native Lydian" (Colin J. Hemer, "Thyatira," in *The Letters to the Seven Churches of Asia in Their Local Setting*, JSNTSup 11 [Sheffield: Sheffield Academic, 1986], 107). Although Thyatira had been located in Lydia, overall ancient writing was far more concerned with ethnography than geography. See Robert M. Grant, "Early Christian Geography," *VC* 46 (1992): 105–11, esp. 105–6. Geographer Strabo's writings generally demonstrate how geographic boundaries, and the ethnicities contained within them, could be fluid; as a sample: "Sardeis is a great city, and, though of later date than the Trojan times, is nevertheless old, and has a strong citadel. It was the royal city of the Lydians, whom the poet calls Meïonians; and later writers call them Maeonians, some identifying them with the Lydians and others representing them as different, but it is better to call them the same people" (*Geogr.* 13.4.5 [Jones, LCL]). "The parts situated next to this region towards the south as far as the Taurus are so inwoven with one another that the Phrygian and the Carian and the Lydian parts, as also those of the Mysians, since they merge into one another, are hard to distinguish"

coincidence of Lydia's name with her place of origin (Acts 16:14).[9] From this confluence between Lydia's name and her ethnicity, some have suggested that Lydia's name conveys a symbolic meaning.[10] Here again, however, investigations into the meaning of the connection between Lydia's name and ethnicity have remained distracted by the issue of Lydia's status, generating questions such as whether the name of Lydia suggested a slave, a former slave, or a person of high status. Questions over whether Lydia would have been a slave or free woman stem, in part, from Strabo's remarks that slaves often bore the names of their nations of origin (*Geogr.* 7.3.12 [Jones, LCL]) and by the support of epigraphic evidence.[11] More recent discussions of Lydia's name have added new epigraphic evidence from the first or second century of two women of high status (denoted by the name Julia) whose names contained Lydia—Julia Lydia Laterane of Ephesus and Julia Lydia of Sardis—to counter any suggestions that the self-evidently "high-status Lydia" might have been a slave.[12] Predictably, these discussions around Lydia's name have continued to revolve around the "straw man" debate over Lydia's social status, missing the significance of her most important feature, that her Lydian ethnicity is accentuated by her name of Lydia.

A more pertinent feature common to both "higher-status Lydias" named above is that, in addition to the elite name of Julia, their names point to their ethnic heritage. Ephesus was settled as a "Greek-Lydian hybrid city,"[13] and Sardis, the historical storehouse of the renowned Lydian

---

(*Geogr.* 13.4.12 [Jones, LCL]). And again, we see Strabo write, "On the road to Sardeis, one comes to Thyateira, on the left-hand side ... which by some is called the farthermost city of the Mysians" (*Geogr.* 13.4.4 [Jones, LCL]. As we will see in the discussion below, in the case of Lydia of Thyatira, her name of Lydia mapped Thyatira into Lydian ethnography.

9. For example, "Λυδία lit., 'the Lydian woman' (Thyatira was in Lydia). Perhaps she had another personal name" (F. F. Bruce, *Acts of the Apostles*, 314).

10. Matthews, *First Converts*, 93.

11. "For 'Lydia' suggests a servile status, many slaves being accorded a name which reflected their geographical origin (e.g. Thratta, Phryx). The index to *CIL* VI attests only one Lydia, who appears from her son's name to be a slave.... Further, closely related names ... are possessed (where status can be determined) by either slaves or *liberti/libertae*" (Horsley, "Purple Trade," 2:27).

12. G. H. R. Horsley, "Addenda to *New Docs 1976–1979, New Docs 1977*, note 3," *NewDocs* 5:139.

13. Peter Scherrer, "Ephesus," *BNP*.

treasury, was virtually interchangeable with Lydia.[14] Therefore, whether slave or high status, epigraphic evidence suggests that women carrying the name of Lydia did so in reference to their Lydian ethnic backgrounds.[15]

In any event, whatever may have been the historical background of other Lydias, the text of Acts 16 squarely presents Lydia as a Lydian woman and, by correlating her name with her origin, profiles her Lydian ethnicity as her most prominent descriptive element. Naming characters by their key characteristics was not an uncommon practice for the author of Luke-Acts, as attested by Peter (πέτρος, "rock"); Barnabas, whose name means "son of encouragement" (Acts 4:36); and Eutychus the "fortunate one" (Acts 20:9); nor was it foreign to ancient authors generally. In fact, one of Aristotle's cataloged common topics (topoi) includes a type of punning device where the meaning of a proper name corresponds to the name itself. For example, "As Herodicus said to Thrasymachus, 'You are always *thrasymakhos* ["bold in fight"] and to Polus, 'You are always a *polus* ["a colt"], and of Dracon the lawgiver that his laws were not those of a human being but of a *drakon* ["snake"]; for they were harsh" (*Rhet.* 1400b29 [Kennedy]).[16] Rhetorically, such plays on names, belonging to the broader category of *antonomasia*,[17] drew attention to a particular characteristic of

---

14. An example of the ready connection between Sardis and Lydia is found in a portion of the dialogue between Dionysus and Pentheus in Euripides's *Bacchae*, where in response to Pentheus's query "tell me who your family is" Dionysus responds by first naming his place of origin, "Dionysus: I suppose you are familiar with flowery Tmolus. / Pentheus: I know of it; it surrounds the city of Sardis. / Dionysus: I am from there, and Lydia is my fatherland." (*Bacch.* 461–463 [Buckley]).

15. A survey of *A Lexicon of Greek Personal Names* yields only one case where the name of Lydia is attested outside of Asia Minor, in the third–fifth century CE in Sicily. There is also a case of Λυδιας from 170–175 CE in Athens. P. M. Fraser, E. Matthews, and the British Academy, eds., *A Lexicon of Greek Personal Names*, 5 vols. (Oxford: Clarendon, 1987–2013). Not only is this personal name of Lydia attested only in coastal Asia Minor prior to the first century, but it is also rarely attested in general. Compare, for example, 5 cases of Lydia, with 131 examples of the feminine name Ἄμμιον in coastal Asia Minor. See Alcorac Alonso Déniz, review of *Coastal Asia Minor: Pontos to Ionia*, vol. 5A of *A Lexicon of Greek Personal Names*, ed. T. Corsten, BMCR, http://bmcr.brynmawr.edu/2011/2011-01-11.html.

16. Brackets in the translation.

17. An *antonomasia* is a "kind of a *synecdoche* which consists of using a common name for a proper name, or a proper name for a common name," where a *synecdoche* uses a characteristic aspect of an object to designate it, such as "'the sail' for the ship and 'mortals' for men" (Perelman and Olbrechts-Tyteca, *New Rhetoric*, 174, 336).

the named person. Much as an epithet or title "results from the visible selection of a quality which is emphasized,"[18] the *antonomasia* "qualifies," that is, describes, someone "in a manner that helps the argument."[19]

From within a first-century collective understanding of personality, an important reference point for determining a person's identity was place of origin, and, second to family background, that place was arguably a key determinant of who a person was understood to be.[20] As studies of physiognomy have shown, these ethnic identity markers were commonly employed in order to "rhetorically profile" a person's character. The connection between Lydia's name and ethnic Lydian origin has been subsumed by discussions concerning the question of her status, missing the critical question of interest generated by this correlation, that is, the ethnographic profile generated by Lydia the Lydian woman.

4.2.2. Topos of Ethnography of Lydian Women

Inasmuch as Lydia of Thyatira's social status and wealth has been a red herring for interpreters, there nonetheless resides an important rhetorical link between wealth and Lydians. The ancient Lydian nation and wealth were interchangeable; gold dust was said to have run in its river Pactolus from Mount Tmolus, and its treasury in Sardis was considered the world's richest. The wealth of Lydian king Croesus—the "richest man in the world"—was both legendary and proverbial. Authors throughout the ages referred to it, with the simile "rich as Croesus" still enjoying contemporary currency (e.g., Theocritus, *Idylls* 8.53–54; 10.32). The name Croesus developed into an eponym for "wealthy." The Lydian kingdom's legendary wealth was one reason Lydians and Lydia held such a wide and lingering fascination for authors. Three times the phrase "Lydians rich in gold" recurs in the Sibylline Oracles (Sib. Or. 3.170; 5.287, 292). In defending his integrity as one who is immune to bribery and gifts of patronage, Apollonius of Tyana metonymically asserts: "I have no need of Lydia and all

---

18. Ibid., 126; Lausberg, *Handbook of Literary Rhetoric*, 305.

19. Perelman and Olbrechts-Tyteca, *New Rhetoric*, 174; Lausberg, *Handbook of Literary Rhetoric*, 264–66.

20. Consistent with this emphasis on ethnography, the man in Paul's vision is explicitly identified as Macedonian, the Lord first introduces Paul to Ananias as "a man of Tarsus" (Acts 9:11), and Paul identifies himself as coming from "Tarsus in Cilicia" (Acts 21:39; 22:3).

of the Pactolus [τὸ γὰρ δεῖσθαι μηδενὸς ἐμοὶ Λυδία καὶ τὸ Πακτωλοῦ πᾶν]" (Philostratus, *Vit. Apoll.* 8.34 [Jones et al., LCL]). Thus by his imperviousness to the allure of "Lydia," Apollonius argues, he considers himself morally "rich."[21] As the following discussion will show, this Lydian wealth was regularly used in literature to evoke a topos of degenerate luxury.

We can see this linkage between Lydian wealth and degeneracy appear in Herodotus's "geographic-historical" description of Lydia. But also, in Herodotus's work we can see how the Lydian topos, imbued with an element of "wealth," became a versatile topos in discourse that shaded degeneracy from within cultural sexual-moral codes. This intertwining of legendary Lydian wealth with immoral living found its most pervasive expression in moral codes associated with female sexuality.

Herodotus begins by stating that Lydia bears little to distinguish it from other countries other than the gold dust that runs from Mount Tmolus. After the gold reference, Herodotus immediately follows with a description of King Croesus's father's tomb (Alyattes). In what follows, however, Herodotus focuses attention not on the appearance of the tomb but rather on its sponsors. Herodotus claims: "It was built by the men of the market [οἱ ἀγοραῖοι ἄνθρωποι] and the artificers [οἱ χειρώνακτες] and the prostitutes [αἱ ἐνεργαζόμεναι παιδίσκαι]" (*Hist.* 1.93 [Godley, LCL]). Moreover, while a tomb is intended as a monument of remembrance to honor the deceased, it is the prostitutes who instead are memorialized in Herodotus's account: "There remained till my time five corner-stones set on the top of the tomb, and on these was graven the record of the work done by each kind: and measurement showed that the prostitutes' share of the work was the greatest" (1.93 [Godley, LCL]).

---

21. The Lydian river Pactolus is also used by Dio Chrysostom in his *First Tarsic*, devoted to warning the Tarsians that they have succumbed to luxury's degenerative influences and therefore, if left unchecked, will suffer the same fate as other nations who had fallen to luxury. Chrysostom argues that the Tarsians have deluded themselves into thinking they are naturally blessed because of their fortuitous geographical location, which includes a river, since access to luxury leads not to blessing but to ruin. Invoking Lydia's famous Pactolus, Chrysostom writes: "Welcome the man who will point out to you some of your faults, and will first of all, if he can, enable you to think, because such things as I have named do not make you blessed, not even if the mighty Nile itself should flow through your city … not even if Pactolus, appearing here, should bear to you its gold, not grain by grain, as they say it used to do for the Lydians in days gone by, but in a mass like mud" (Dio Chrysostom, *1 Tars.* 23 [Cohoon and Crosby, LCL]).

The prostitutes are introduced by the term ἐνεργάζομαι, and together with other market people such as the traders and artisans, the "working girls" are contextualized within the sphere of the marketplace, not the bedroom. Herodotus continues his focus on the Lydian prostitutes by progressively moving from the remarkable tomb to another noteworthy feature: "All the daughters of the common people of Lydia ply the trade of prostitutes [αἱ θυγατέρες πορνεύονται]" (*Hist.* 1.93 [Godley, LCL]). This they do, according to Herodotus, in order to earn their dowries. Dowries are not provided by the wealth of the fathers but rather through the sexual trade of the daughters. Moreover, inferential logic suggests that since all "maidens" prostitute themselves, all Lydian husbands have former prostitutes as wives. Through his "geohistorical" account, Herodotus deftly frames an inductive argument that infers that the very nucleus of its society, Lydian kinship, was developed through prostitution.

In this third reference to prostitutes, Herodotus links the more common term for prostitution, πορνεύω, to the sponsors of Alyattes's tomb. Within a few verses, Herodotus repeats, "The customs of the Lydians are like those of the Greeks, save that they make prostitutes of their female children [θήλεα τέκνα καταπορνεύουσι]" (*Hist.* 1.94 [Godley, LCL]). He immediately follows with a claim that Lydians were the first to coin gold and silver currency and the first retail sellers (κάπηλοι). In this manner, a unit beginning with a reference to Lydia's gold-flowing river, the ostensible source of Lydia's wealth, ends with a reference to huckstering and gold as a medium of exchange. By framing his account with a gold reference *inclusio*, Herodotus's focus on Lydian prostitutes suggests that the prostitute topos functions to characterize Lydia's wealth. The "working girls" link lexically to trading and selling through πορνεύω—a term etymologically closely connected with selling.[22] In Herodotus's telling, social exchange in the wealthiest society in the world was constituted by prostitution.[23]

As Lydia in Acts is a Lydian woman, we will look carefully at how ancient authors depicted the women of Lydia. Two early stories, one from

---

22. See note 71.

23. Leslie Kurke has argued that the figure of a prostitute was used metaphorically in critiques of civic systems of economic exchange. See Leslie Kurke, *Coins, Bodies, Games and Gold: The Politics of Meaning in Archaic Greece* (Princeton: Princeton University Press, 1999); Kurke, "Pindar and the Prostitutes, or Reading Ancient 'Pornography,'" in *Constructions of the Classical Body*, The Body, in Theory: Histories of Cultural Materialism (Ann Arbor: University of Michigan Press, 1999), 101–25.

Herodotus and the other from Nicolaus of Damascus, point us to a broader sociocultural peculiarity regarding the portrayal of Lydian women. In Herodotus's version of the story, Persian King Darius sits in the Lydian city of Sardis and sees a Paeonian woman walking by while plying her distaff (Herodotus, *Hist.* 5.12–14), and in a similar version, Lydian King Alyattes sees a Thracian woman walking by, also engaged in gender-appropriate spinning and carrying of water (Nicolaus of Damascus, *Frag.* 71). In each version, the king is said to be amazed at the sight of a woman engaged in gender-appropriate purposeful activity, since it contrasts markedly with the lifestyle of his own native women.

While the sight of a woman arousing a man's response is an age-old story line, a key element seems somewhat off-kilter in these two renditions. In contrast, for example, to Rachel (Gen 29:9–18) or Bathsheba (2 Sam 11:2–4) arousing sexual desire in the men—Jacob or David—who happened to see them, the sight of the Western women aroused a desire in Kings Darius and Alyattes for their gender-appropriate industrious activity, evidently absent in Lydian women. Central to the two vignettes is the amazement-inducing gender-appropriate industriousness of the Western women, displayed by spinning wool and fetching water, in contrast to that of the Eastern, in the second account pointedly Lydian, women.[24] In fact, a survey of literature ranging from the classical period into antiquity yields a recurring, and virtually uniform, stereotype of Lydian women that drew on a prostitute topos and formed the background to Herodotus's and Nicolaus of Damascus's stories, as well as to Herodotus's account of Alyattes's tomb.

Testimony to the enduring quality of the Lydian prostitute trajectory can be found in Strabo's recitation of Herodotus's claim regarding the sponsors of Alyattes's tomb along with an addendum: "Some call the tomb of Alyattes a monument of prostitution" (*Geogr.* 13.4.7 [Jones, LCL]).[25]

---

24. In stark contrast to Grotius's seventeenth-century portrayal of Lydia as a "weaving woman," evoking the distaff and spindle, the universal trope of feminine industriousness and propriety, see §1.1.2.

25. In another story of a Lydian monument connected with prostitution, Athenaeus, quoting Clearchus (ca. 450–401 BCE), recounts that the Lydian king Gyges erects a giant monument in memory of his concubine: "Clearchus, in the first book of his *Love Stories* says: 'Gyges, the king of Lydia, became notorious for his devotion to his mistress, not only during her lifetime, giving himself and his empire entirely into her hands; but more than that, when she died he gathered all the Lydians of the country together and reared the monument which is to this day still named after the 'Com-

In Latin literature, the poet Horace wrote four odes to Lydia (*Carm.* 1.8; 1.13; 1.25; 3.9.),[26] where each "Lydia" is primarily characterized as a courtesan.[27] By the next century, Martial wrote a coarse and lewd epigram featuring a sexually promiscuous "Lydia."

> Lydia is as spacious as the arse of a brazen horseman, ... as an old shoe soaked in muddy water, as the wide-meshed nets that wait for stray thrushes, and as the ugly throat of a pelican of Ravenna. I am said to have f____d her in a marine fishpond. I don't know; I think I f____d the fishpond. (Martial, *Epig.* 11.21 [Bailey, LCL])[28]

Athenaeus also wrote of Lydian women in terms of sexual immorality.

> The Lydians went so far in wanton luxury that they were the first to sterilize women.... Xanthus says in the second book of his *Lydian History* that Adramytes, the king of Lydia, was the first to spay women and employ them in the place of male eunuchs. (Athenaeus, *Deipn.* 12.515d [Gulick, LCL])[29]

Athenaeus goes on to describe how Lydian Queen Omphalē (who, in myth, cross-dressed with Hercules)[30] forced the daughters of Lydian freemen to

---

panion' ['Εταίρας], raising it high so that when he made his royal progresses within the region of Mt. Tmolus, wherever he chanced to turn, he could see the monument, and it was visible to all the inhabitants of Lydia" (Athenaeus, *Deipn.* 13.573a–b [Gulick, LCL]).

26. "Lydia: the exotic name suggests luxury and voluptuousness." Robin G. M. Nisbet and Margaret Hubbard, *A Commentary on Horace: Odes, Book 1* (Oxford: Clarendon, 1970), 110.

27. See also Virgil, *Dirae* 12 (Fairclough, LCL); *Lydia*. "Was I the first who dared to sully the chaste purity and assail the hallowed fillet [ribbon] of his love [Lydia]" (*Lydia* 53 [Fairclough, LCL]).

28. Expletive present in the original.

29. Another version from the Suda lexicon (late tenth century CE) implies that the procedure was intended as a youth enhancing measure, "Suidas s. Ξάνθος gives a different account: πρῶτος Γύγης ... γυναῖκας εὐνούχισεν ὅπως αὐταῖς χρῷτο ἀεὶ νεαζούσαις" (Athenaeus, *Deipn.* 319 n. f).

30. "In all the Latin sources he [Hercules] carries out the typical women's work of spinning wool and wears women's clothes; Omphalē on her part appropriates the lion's skin and club (e.g. Ov. Fast. 2,319–326; Ov. Epist. 9,53–128; Prop. 4,9,45 and 3,11,17; Herc. O. 371–377; cf. Lucian. *Dialogi deorum* 15,2)" (Katharina Waldner, "Omphale," BNP).

"lie with their slaves" and ends the account with "But it is not merely the women of Lydia who were allowed free range among all comers, but also those ... tribes in general which dedicated their daughters to prostitution" (*Deipn.* 12.516a–b [Gulick, LCL]). Perhaps the basest allusion to the Lydian woman stereotype in ancient literature is also the earliest, from a text of Hipponax's (mid-sixth century BCE) recounted by Ian Morris: "The dung-covered hero of fr. 92 found himself in a toilet with a woman who performed an obscure act on his anus while beating his genitals with a fig branch. The fragment ends with a cloud of dung beetles whirring out of the filth. The woman was *Ludizousa*, 'speaking in a Lydian fashion' [ηὖδα δὲ λυδίζουσα]."[31] Overall, in a broad spectrum of writings ranging from the classical period to well into antiquity, the ethnography of Lydian woman and "Lydias" features prostitution, sexual licentiousness, and impropriety. Moreover, far from being a localized topos, the degenerate Lydian woman was pervasive and enduring throughout different literary genres and across spans of historical periods.

4.2.3. Topos of "Lydian Disease"

The topos of immoral Lydian women stems from a broader ethnographic stereotype of Lydians as a luxury-loving, degenerate people whose lifestyle led to a demasculinization of their men. Physiognomically, beginning in the earliest classical period, "Lydian" was a byword for a love of luxury and general "softness." The *New Pauly* succinctly describes the enduring ethnographic depiction of Lydians: "The Lydians had a reputation for a hedonistic way of life [τρυφή] ...; Ionians and Athenians, who imitated them, were accused of being soft [ἁβροσύνη] ... or mocked them for suffering from the 'Lydian disease.'"[32]

Athenaeus explains that "the Lydians were notorious for luxurious living; in fact the word 'Lydian-living' in Anacreon is understood to mean the same as 'luxurious living'" (*Deipn.* 15.690b–c [Gulick, LCL]).[33] The

---

31. Ian Morris, "The Strong Principle of Equality and the Archaic Origins of Greek Democracy," in *Dēmokratia: A Conversation on Democracies, Ancient and Modern*, ed. Josiah Ober and Charles W. Hedrick (Princeton: Princeton University Press, 1996), 35; Hipponax, *Fragmenta* 92. See also Kurke, *Coins, Bodies, Games and Gold*, 27.

32. Hans Kaletsch, "Lydia," *BNP*.

33. See Anacreon (*Frag.* 136), also recited in "Scholiast on Aeschylus, *Persae* ('soft-living Lydians'): The Lydians do live softly, whence the expression in Anacreon, people

association between Lydians and decadent *luxuria* was well-established in ancient times and has been attested in both literature and art.³⁴ Men who succumbed to *luxuria* became "soft" and unmanly. As a result, effeminacy was another element that often cojoined with luxury in depicting its degenerative power on masculinity, as is evident in Athenaeus's scathing portrayal of Midas, who "in effeminate luxury lay in his purple robes, or helped the women at their looms to work the wool" (*Deipn.* 12.516b [Gulick, LCL]).³⁵ Clearchus's version of the Lydians' decline into effeminacy through luxury is recounted by Athenaeus.

---

living in Lydian style, i.e. in luxurious style" (Campbell, LCL). Ἀβοδιαίτων ... Λυδῶν ... ἀβροδίαιτοι δὲ οὗτοι, ὅθεν καὶ τὸ παρ᾽ Ἀνακρέοντι λυδοπαθεῖς τινες ἀντὶ τοῦ ἡδυπαθεῖς (Oskar Dähnhardt, *Scholia in Aeschyli Persas* [Lipsia: Teubner, 1894], 22, as quoted in Campbell, LCL); Νῦν δὲ μνηστέον ἱστορίας δηλούσης ὅτι τε ἡδυπάθειαν οἱ Μήονες, ταὐτὸν δ᾽ εἰπεῖν οἱ Λυδοί, ἐφίλουν, ὅθεν, φασί, καὶ Ἀνακρέων τὸν ἡδυπαθῆ <<Λυδοπαθῆ>> ἔφη (Eustathius [fl. 1175]: Eustathius Thessalonicensis, *Commentarii ad Homeri Iliadem*, ed. M. van der Valk [Leiden: Brill, 1987], 4:180, lines 16–18).

34. Keith de Vries, "The Nearly Other: The Attic Vision of Phrygians and Lydians," in *Not the Classical Ideal: Athens and the Construction of the Other in Greek Art*, ed. Beth Cohen (Leiden: Brill, 2000), 338–63; Isaac, *Invention of Racism*, 263 n. 29. "In earlier times again, there were the rulers of Lydia, Media, and still further back, Assyria; not a single variety of pleasure was left untried by them" (Athenaeus, *Deipn.* 12.545d [Gulick, LCL]). Tyrants are depicted as having succumbed to the degenerative effects of Lydian luxury: "I think first of Tiberius and how he turned power into something inhuman and cruel; then of his successor Gaius, and the way he acted like one possessed, wore oriental dress [λυδίζων τὴν στολήν; lit. clothed in Lydian fashion], and won nonexistent wars, making a disgusting revel of the whole government of Rome" (Philostratus, *Vit. Apoll.* 5.32.2 [Jones et al., LCL]). Also, from a physiognomic perspective, the land of Lydia was depicted as being naturally endowed with life's good things. In trying to motivate his troops to take Lydia, the Persian king Cyrus speaks of Lydia's natural bounty: "Seeing that we are to contend not for Syria only, where there is an abundance of grain and flocks and date-palms, but for Lydia as well; for in that land there is an abundance of wine and figs and olive oil, and its shores are washed by the sea; and over its waters more good things are brought than any one has ever seen" (Xenophon, *Cyr.* 6.2.22 [Marchant et al., LCL]). "In the twenty-first book of his *History of Philip* Theopompus says that the Umbrian nation (who live near the Adriatic) are pretty effeminate and live a life comparable to that of the Lydians, possessing good land which caused their advance in prosperity" (Athenaeus, *Deipn.* 12.526f–527a [Gulick, LCL]).

35. A more subtle connection between the unmanning of warriors and contact with Lydian luxury and purple is found in Virgil's *Aeneid*, as its hero, Aeneas, diverts from his mission to found a "new Troy" (Rome) when he falls in love with Queen Dido and remains with her in Tyrian Carthage (Tunis) "in wanton ease ... enthralled by shameless passion," where he, "with his eunuch train, a Maeonian band [i.e., Lydian

The Lydians in their luxury laid out parks, making them like gardens, and so lived in the shade, because they thought it more luxurious not to have the rays of the sun fall upon them at all. And proceeding further in their insolence they would gather the wives and maiden daughters of other men into the place called, because of this action, the Place of Chastity, and there outrage them. And finally, after becoming thoroughly effeminate in their souls, they adopted women's ways of living. (*Deipn.* 12.515e–f [Gulick, LCL])

Lydian men, rhetorically depicted as having succumbed to luxury, not surprisingly were also known for their effeminacy.

A different, earlier etiology of Lydian effeminacy came from Herodotus. In this version, the Lydians had just been defeated by the Persian king Cyrus, who naively had left a just-conquered Lydian in charge of the renowned Lydian treasury in Sardis while Cyrus left for other battles. Upon Cyrus's return and discovery that the Lydian had attempted an uprising by use of some of the treasury funds, the Lydian king Croesus, fearing that Cyrus might sell the Lydians into slavery and pillage the treasury city, offered him an alternate (ultimately acceptable) proposal.

Let the Lydians be pardoned; and lay on them this command, that they may not revolt or be dangerous to you; send, I say, and forbid them to possess weapons of war, and command them to wear tunics [κιθῶνας] under their cloaks and buskins [κοθόρνους] on their feet, and to teach [παιδεύειν] their sons lyre-playing and song and dance and huckstering [καπηλεύειν]. Then, O king, you will soon see them turned to women instead of men; and thus you need not fear lest they revolt. (*Hist.* 1.155 [Godley, LCL])[36]

---

headband] propping his chin and essenced locks, grasps the spoil." When Jupiter finally intervenes to recall Aeneas to his original mission, Aeneas is found wearing a cloak "ablaze with Tyrian purple"—a gift from Dido—and is asked whether he has become "a wife's minion" (Virgil, *Aen.* 4.191–194, 215–217, 262–263, 266–267 [Fairclough, LCL]. For Philo, virtue cannot "take root" in an emasculated soul: "Toil is bitter and stiff and hard, yet from it springs goodness, and therefore there must be no softening. For he who flees from toil flees from the good also, but he who patiently and manfully endures what is hard to bear is pressing on to blessedness. For in the voluptuous livers, whose souls are emasculated and whose bodies run to waste with ceaseless luxury prolonged from day to day, virtue cannot make its lodging" (Philo, *Mos.* 2.183–184 [Colson et al., LCL]).

36. Similar versions of Herodotus's account of the effeminization of Lydian war-

In Herodotus's telling, the Lydian men experienced nothing short of a complete inversion of gender, for prior to Croesus's bargain, Herodotus writes, "there was no nation in Asia more valiant or warlike than the Lydian. It was their custom to fight on horseback, carrying long spears, and they were skilled in the management of horses" (*Hist.* 1.79 [Godley, LCL]).

The process by which warrior Lydians transformed into womanly Lydians became a universalized template for the potential danger of being contaminated by the "Lydian disease."[37] A nation could be undone by its contact with Lydians, as portrayed in Athenaeus's account of the people of Colophon (*Deipn.* 12.526a–d).[38] The theme of Lydian disease emerged in

---

riors also appears in two later historical works (Polyaenus of Macedonia, *Str.* 7.6.4; Justinus, *Ep. hist. Phil.* 1.7.11–13), as well as in a handbook of exercises in rhetorical declamation, where it forms a point of departure for a declamation exercise (Choricius of Gaza, *Decl.*, 3 [14]: The Lydians), pointing to the account's enduring nature. "When the Lydians again revolted after the capture of Sardis, Cyrus on the march to Babylon sent Mazares the Mede with orders to destroy the Lydians' arms and horses when he captured the place, to compel them to wear feminine attire and no longer to learn either archery or riding but to weave and sing. He preferred, as it seems to feminize their souls with these amusements. Of course the Lydians, formerly most bellicose, have become the most unmilitary of barbarians" (Polyaenus, *Str.* 7.6.4 [Krentz and Wheeler]).

37. A warrior's key virtue was his courage, and to be courageous, by definition, meant to be a man. Stephen D. Moore and Janice Capel Anderson explain: "ἀνδρεία derives from ἀνήρ ('man'), so that its root meaning is 'manliness.' Indeed, given that ἀνδρεία and its cognates (ἀνδρεῖος, ἀυρείως, ἀνδρίζομαι, etc.) frequently mean just that—'manliness' and its cognates ('manly,' 'manfully,' 'To play the man,' etc.)—in both classical and *koine* Greek, it is not too much to suggest that built into the language itself was the notion that to act courageously was to act as befits a man. Thus, courage was conceived of as essentially a masculine virtue" (Stephen D. Moore and Janice Capel Anderson, "Taking It Like a Man: Masculinity in 4 Maccabees," *JBL* 117 [1998]: 253). "Ancient texts often regard a man or group of men as effeminate by definition, when they are reputedly cowardly. Courage is regarded as one of the essential ingredients of masculinity, while cowardice is by definition part of the female nature" (Isaac, *Invention of Racism*, 154).

38. "The people of Colophon, according to Phylarchus, were in the beginning rigid in their discipline, but after they had drifted into luxury they contracted friendship and alliance with the Lydians.... They used to walk to the place of assembly clad in robes all of purple.... Consequently, by reason of this kind of regimen they became involved in tyranny and party quarrels, and were destroyed, fatherland and all" (Gulick, LCL).

poetic form in one of Horace's "Lydia" odes, which laments the unmanning of a warrior after he had isolated himself with Lydia at her home.

> In the name of all the gods, tell me, Lydia, why thou art bent on ruining Sybaris ... why he rides no more among his soldier mates.... Why does he shun the wrestling-oil more warily than viper's blood, nor longer show his arms bruised with weapon practice, he who once was famed for hurling, oft the discus, oft the javelin, beyond the farthest mark?" (Horace, *Carm.* 1.8 [Bennett, LCL])

Feminine Lydian men, together with sexually immoral Lydian women (who, by their "shamelessness," degraded the honor of their husbands and fathers),[39] produced an overall ethnographic image of the decadent, immoral, pleasure-seeking Lydian. The stereotype of soft, luxury-seeking Lydians was one of the most prevalent and entrenched in antiquity. In a survey of Hellenistic proverbs, Antony Spawforth lists the following:

> "A Lydian is keeping shop," evoking the attempt by Cyrus to feminize Lydian men by forcing them to dress in womanly garb and be shopkeepers; "A Lydian closed the door," proverbial for stupid thieves (*mōrokleptai*); the popular proverb (listed in no fewer than four collections) "A Lydian (plays) at noon," for sexual license, since (according to the paroemiographer's gloss) "the Lydians are represented in comedy as gorging on sexual pleasures with their own hands."[40]

---

39. "A man's honor is involved in the sexual purity of his mother (although his father has the main obligation in this regard), wife, daughters, and sisters—but not in his own sexual purity. According to this pattern, then, *the sexual purity or exclusiveness of the female is embedded within the honor of some male*. The man is responsible for the maintenance of this sexual exclusiveness; it is delegated to the man" (Malina, *New Testament World*, 48, emphasis original).

40. Antony Spawforth, "Shades of Greekness: A Lydian Case Study," in *Ancient Perceptions of Greek Ethnicity*, ed. Irad Malkin, Center for Hellenic Studies Colloquia 5 (Cambridge: Harvard University Press, 2001), 383. In his physiognomic handbook, Polemo, when relating character to a person's eyes, describes two Lydian men, the first displaying the ethnographic stereotype of effeminacy and sexual degeneracy, and the second of avarice: "If, then, that red is strong and you see in the eye the like of red dots or yellow or green ... [detailed description continues] if, then, you see this eye know that you will not find another eye which is more perfectly evil than that.... The owner of this eye takes no rest from interest in evil and from those things which are great sins and the crudities of nature. I have not seen the like of this type, though I did see one man, and he was from Lydia.... He had eyes like those I have described to

Critical elements found in Lydia the purple seller's Lydian ethnography have lain dormant, unseen by modern interpretive eyes, as the history of interpretation has remained blinkered by questions of social status. In antiquity, however, the Lydian elements of sexual immorality, decadence, luxury, and effeminacy would have seized an audience's attention and raised very pertinent questions as to what connection this type of woman might have with a "place of prayer."

4.2.4. Topos of Purple: Deepening the Topos of Luxuria

The preoccupation in commentaries with Lydia's status has often drawn on connotations of wealth and royalty symbolized by the color purple. It is true that the use of purple could symbolize elite status, but also by early antiquity the elite status symbolically encoded in purple was often rhetorically inverted into a code for "degenerate living" resulting from luxurious extravagance.[41] A Lydian female evoking culturally ascribed degenerate immorality would naturally connect with this underbelly of purple's symbolism.

Rhetorical discourse with luxury as its concern often deployed the element of "purple" in developing its argument. For example, in his invective against Verres's corruption, Cicero joins the topos of luxury together with purple in order to display the depths of Verres's degeneracy.

> There is another thing for which he [Verres] had an incredible passion.... There was not one wealthy house in Sicily where he did not set up a weaving establishment. At Segesta there is a lady of wealth and rank

---

you.... He had an effeminate mouth, was boastful in his speech ... his stomach was large, protruding, even, and fleshy.... He laughed in a high voice, and his spirit seemed ablaze. So I knew that this individual was full of evil, and he was always interested and thinking about plotting and learning vile deeds.... He would often speak of fornication, of young men and women, and that he desired no trappings but bastard children" (Polemo, *Physiogn.* A11 [Hoyland]). "I once saw a man who had eyes that were small, red, and goggling like the eyes of a crab. He was from the land called Lydia.... So I saw him at his house, and I found that he had neither understanding nor intellect, but was a man of a most cutting tongue, and he was covetous of evil, hardly able to see anything without desiring it for himself. He had eyes that quivered a lot and they were small, and in their redness they did not look like other people's eyes" (Polemo, *Physiogn.* A13 [Hoyland]).

41. Reinhold, *History of Purple*, 56.

named Lamia, who for three years had her house full of looms making woven fabrics for him, and the whole of them dyed with purple. There was the wealthy Attalus at Netum, Lyso at Lilybaeum, … time is too short to give you all their names. "He provided the purple himself; his friends supplied the labour only." Well, possibly; parts of his misconduct I am willing for the present to pass over; and one would think it enough for me to accuse him of being able to provide all that purple, of planning to take so much out of the country, and finally of doing what he admits he did—making use of his friends' work—people for such purposes as this. (Cicero, *Verr.* 2.4.26.58–59 [Greenwood, LCL])

In another situation, Diodorus of Sicily recounts how a lawmaker strategically deployed purple as a foil against immoral living.

Whereas everywhere else wayward wives were required to pay fines, Zaleucus stopped their licentious behaviour by a cunningly devised punishment. That is, he made the following laws: a free-born woman may not be accompanied by more than one female slave, unless she is drunk; … she may not wear gold jewellery or a garment with a purple border, unless she is a courtesan; and a husband may not wear a gold-studded ring or a cloak of Milesian fashion unless he is bent upon prostitution or adultery. Consequently, by the elimination, with its shameful implications, of the penalties he easily turned men aside from harmful luxury and wanton living; for no man wished to incur the sneers of his fellow citizens by acknowledging the disgraceful licentiousness. (*The Library of History* 12.21 [Oldfather et al., LCL])

In Juvenal, fathers of old passed on traditional maxims to their sons to help ward off the "fierce craving for unbounded wealth" that could lead to corruption, including a maxim that equated purple with this poisonous passion: "The man who is not ashamed to wear high boots in time of frost, and who keeps off the East wind with skins turned inwards, will never wish to do a forbidden thing; it is purple raiment, whatever it be, foreign and unknown to us, that leads to crime and wickedness" (*Sat.* 14.173–189 [Ramsay, LCL]). Like the effects of "Lydian disease," a desire for purple could also contaminate a heart with a passion for luxurious living and thereby lead to degenerate, unmanly, and corrupt living.

The dichotomy between the "royal" status of purple and its rhetorical use as sign of immorality is also found in biblical narratives. The high status of purple is particularly recurrent in descriptions of the making of curtains for the tabernacle, for example: "You shall make the tabernacle with ten curtains of fine twisted linen, and blue, purple, and crimson yarns" (Exod 26:1). This context of weaving for the tabernacle is incorporated into an account of the annunciation of Mary in the apocryphal Protevangelium of James, where "she took the purple and sat down on her seat and drew out [the thread]" (11.1). Neyrey points out that Mary's working with "purple" elaborates on an earlier portion of the narrative in which Mary had been "selected to spin and weave a cloth for the Temple to cover the Holy of Holies."[42] In this configuration of the deployment of the purple element, Mary is depicted "in appropriate female space (house) and proper female labor (cloth production)."[43] Pieter A. van Stempvoort suggests that the emphasis on Mary's propriety as she spins purple responds to Celsus's claim that not only was Jesus not born of a virgin but also his mother was "a woman that spins for daily hire." The Protevangelium therefore stresses that Mary "was of royal descent; she spun but only for making the temple-veil."[44]

As with other elements and topoi, the salient rhetorical features of "purple" are activated by their connection to elements contained within its shared network. When temple purple cojoins with proper feminine activity—weaving—conducted in appropriate space—household—it evokes royal, refined status. So, too, the industrious wife of Prov 31:10–31, working day and night for the well-being of her household, dresses her family in scarlet and herself in purple fine linen that she has produced as she "seeks wool and flax, and works with willing hands" (Prov 31:13), and "puts her hands to the distaff, and her hands hold the spindle" (Prov 31:19). She sells off the abundance of her household production to merchants, as would be appropriate in an agrarian economy (Prov 31:24). Notably, although she sells her excess production to merchants, she herself is not one of the merchants, who in this passage, similarly to Zech 14:21, are metaphorically called "Canaanites" because of their reputation as being the world's first (purple) traders (σινδόνας ἐποίησεν καὶ ἀπέδοτο περιζώματα δὲ τοῖς

---

42. Referring to Prot. Jas. 10.2; Jerome H. Neyrey, "Maid and Mother in Art and Literature," *BTB* 20.2 (1990): 66–67.

43. Ibid., 66.

44. Pieter A. Van Stempvoort, "The *Protevangelium Jacobi*, the Sources of Its Theme and Style and Their Bearing on Its Date," in *Papers Presented to the Second International Congress on New Testament Studies Held at Christ Church, Oxford, 1961*, ed. F. L. Cross, SE 3 (Berlin: Akademie, 1964), 414.

Χαναναίοις: Prov 31:24 LXX).⁴⁵ In contrast with its use with the "good wife" in Proverbs and with Mary in the Protevangelium, when purple appears in the story of the rich man and Lazarus (Luke 16:19), it does so with the familiar first-century evocation of sumptuousness; and when it clothes the harlot Babylon (Rev 17:4), it unquestionably exploits the fullness of an immorality topos.

Purple not only frequently evoked elements of immorality and *luxuria*, but also by the first century was influenced by the sham purple industry. James Arieti explains: "So great was the demand that imitation of the Tyrian dye appeared, notably the *fucus* of Tarentum. The word *fucus* comes to be synonymous with deceit and simulation (e.g., *Sat.* 1.2.83) because it is an imitation or faking of the true *purpura*."⁴⁶ Dyeing as a sign of deception was a common topic in ancient discourse. Moreover, with purple being the prototypical color of dyes, purple especially featured prominently as a deceptive element. For example, in Plutarch's attack against Herodotus, he alleges that the purple-dyed clothing of the deceptive Persian spies in one of the *Histories*' episodes was analogous to Herodotus's deceptive version of history.⁴⁷ Purple dye, fakery, and deception commonly clustered together in rhetorical discourse.⁴⁸ A Lydian

---

45. In the first century, the "ethnicon 'Canaanite' [had] acquired the connotation 'merchant' in Biblical Hebrew because of the renowned commercial activities of the Phoenicians" (Michael C. Astour, "The Origin of the Terms 'Canaan,' 'Phoenician,' and 'Purple,'" *JNES* 24 [1965]: 347).

46. James Arieti, "Horatian Philosophy and the Regulus Ode (*Odes* 3.5)," *TAPA* 120 (1990): 214.

47. "Might one not suitably apply to Herodotus himself the remark that he puts in the mouth of the Ethiopian? In reply to the offerings of perfume and purple clothing Herodotus makes him say: 'Full of guile are the unguents and full of guile are the Persian garments.' So one might say of him: 'Full of guile are the statements and full of guile the whole treatment of history in Herodotus'" (Plutarch, *Her. mal.* 863D–D [Perrin et al., LCL]).

48. Other examples where dyed clothing is considered an analogue to deception include Herodotus, *Hist.* 3.22; Plutarch, *Table Talk* 646B; *Quaest. rom.* 270F; Clement of Alexandria, *Strom.* 10.48.5; Athenaeus, *Deipn.* 15.686e–687a; Philostratus, *Vit. Apoll.* 1.32. Mark Bradley describes Pliny's consternation over Tyrian purple's being used to obfuscate an object's true identity. Bradley writes: "Pliny proceeds more generally to attack Rome's habit of 'readulterating nature's adulterations' (*ipsa adulterare adulteria naturae*) and berate the artificial character of dyes ([9.65]139). On the dye '*amethystinus*' he comments that it is not enough simply to have stolen the name of a gem (*non est satis abstulisse gemmae nomen amethystum*): *amethystinus*—'soberstone'

woman's purple not only suggested decadent luxury, but also elements of deception and false appearances, elements that become foregrounded by joining with the rhetorical profiling of merchants.

4.2.5. Topos of Seller: "Hucksterism"

To date, inscriptions have yielded only one instance of πορφυρόπωλις, in this instance from "what is apparently a husband/wife team" from the island of Cos.[49] More common was the Latin *purpuraria*, "which could mean 'purple-dyer' as well as 'purple-seller'; but there seems to have been no single Latin word as specific as πορφυρόπωλις."[50] Since πορφυρόπωλις is all but absent from material and literary artifacts outside of the Cos inscription and Acts 16-related writings,[51] and while references to purple dyers can be found in inscriptional evidence, historical-critical discussions of Lydia's occupation have typically moved into the arena of purple dyeing and purple dyers.[52] In addition to "dyer," Lydia's occupation has been variously portrayed, including weaver, merchant trader, or "something of a

---

in Greek—can be 'made drunk' (*inebriatur*) with Tyrian purple to produce a twofold luxury (*duplex luxuria*) and the shameless category (*improbum nomen*) '*Tyriamethystinus*'. The contrived nomenclature, alongside the intellectual difficulties posed to perception and understanding by such blends, echoes the parodies on categories (*nomina*) in discussions of cloth-dyes in Plautus' *Epidicus* and Ovid's *Ars Amatoria*. The point, though, was a serious one for Pliny: categories (*nomina*) represent our understanding of what we perceive, and all these dye names were contrived and synthetic. He does not let the point drop: the derivation '*Tyriamethystinus*' was accidental, the result of dissatisfaction (*paenitentia*) with an unsatisfying *color* (i.e. *amethystinus*) which the dyer fixed with a further layer of Tyrian purple, so that one colour might be concealed by another (*ut color alius operiretur alio*). With this artificial synthesis, how can one tell what one is seeing?" (Mark Bradley, *Colour and Meaning in Ancient Rome*, CCS [Cambridge: Cambridge University Press, 2009], 196). For a general discussion of Roman attitudes toward dyeing and cosmetics, see 161–88.

49. Horsley, "Purple Trade," 27.
50. Ibid.
51. The term πορφυρόπωλις is only used of Lydia in Acts 16. Later commentaries or homilies on Acts will use the term in reference to Lydia, and it will appear in later lexicons. The masculine πορφυροπώλης is also not found in early extant texts. The synonym ἁλουργοπώλης is used by Aristotle (see note 70) and also appears in later lexicons. Neither term enjoyed common currency.
52. For example, Ernst Haenchen, *Acts of the Apostles*, 494 n. 9; Jean-Pierre Sterck-Degueldre, *Frau namens Lydia*, 213–30.

first-century Avon lady or Mary Kay representative."[53] Yet the compound term πορφυρόπωλις specifically means purple-selling woman, clearly understood as such in the tenth-century lexicon *Suda*: πορφυρόπωλις: ἡ τὰ πορφυρᾶ πωλοῦσα (*Suidae Lexicon* 2101).

Strong cultural stereotypes found in πώλης, "seller," were consistently operative in antiquity, regardless of gender. The appropriate salient features of the "seller" component of "purple seller" can be better isolated by first culling other occupational descriptors that commentators have attached to Lydia in the past. Beginning with one of the most common, Lydia is not called a πορφυροβάφισα, purple dyer, a weaver, or indeed any form of cloth worker or artisan. However, since Lydia has so frequently been associated with cloth production in commentary, it is important to first distinguish between the social and cultural understanding of some of these occupational descriptors and that of a πορφυρόπωλις.

From a social-status perspective, dyers and others who were required to practice a τέχνη, a handicraft or trade, were on the low end of the social scale, mainly because they needed to work for their subsistence and were therefore not "free."[54] In addition to not being of the leisure class, tradespeople such as purple dyers often worked in ungenteel environments.[55] While the social status of a trade worker was low, the rhetorical characterization of tradespeople was limited to this low status. That is, while tradespeople could be markers of low social status, as in Celsus's portrayal of Mary, their rhetorical profile centered on vulgarity, coarseness, and uncouthness associated with this low status, rather than moral character per se.[56]

---

53. The quote comes from F. Scott Spencer's portrayal of Lilian Portefaix's characterization of Lydia: F. Scott Spencer, "Women of 'the Cloth' in Acts: Sewing the Word," in *A Feminist Companion to the Acts of the Apostles*, ed. Amy-Jill Levine and Marianne Blickenstaff, FCNTECW 9 (Cleveland: Pilgrim, 2004), 148; Lilian Portefaix, *Sisters Rejoice: Paul's Letter to the Philippians and Luke-Acts as Seen by First-Century Philippian Women*, ConBNT 20 (Stockholm: Almqvist & Wiksell, 1988).

54. "Not to work at a vulgar trade [βάναυσον τέχνην] [is honourable]; for it is characteristic of a free man not to live in dependence on another" (Aristotle, *Rhet.* 1367a27 [Kennedy] [first bracket mine, second in translation]).

55. Born, "Purple in Classical Antiquity," 114. Pliny gives a recipe for purple dye that involves mixing the juices with equal quantities of "human urine" (Pliny the Elder, *Nat.* 9.64 [Rackham, Jones, and Eichholz, LCL]).

56. E.g., "Vulgar are the means of livelihood of all hired workmen whom we

Where past interpretations have cast Lydia as a textile worker, this low-status marker has been used to either support a liberationist reading or has been "overridden" by the presumed high economic status of the purple she was selling. Whichever the direction of these interpretations, the pivotal element has been social status. As I have argued, economically derived social status in the case of Lydia is indeterminate and was not a feature of her rhetorical profile. By reconfiguring Lydia into a textile worker, interpretations have destroyed the rhetorical fabric of the text by removing another of her fundamental descriptors: that of "seller."

Formal physiognomic handbooks were primarily occupied with external bodily signs that indicated a person's inner character since their genesis came from a scientific/medical orientation. In rhetoric, any conventional stereotypes, be they ethnically, bodily (gender included), or occupationally based, were regular features of rhetorical compositions.[57] When a person's occupation played a rhetorical role in an ancient work, her or his occupational category was typically as laden with conventional assumptions and stereotypes as were physical appearance or ethnicity.

In rhetorical depictions, merchants were susceptible to the corrupting influence of money and were particularly prone to deception in its quest. Only in certain isolated cases—those normally dealing with an ἔμπορος, or large-scale merchant—might a rhetorical portrayal be somewhat more nuanced. The ἔμπορος was "a merchant, wholesaler, dealer ... distinguished from the retail trader (κάπηλος) by his making voyages and importing goods himself."[58] This type of mercantile trader was a socially ambivalent figure, in great part due to the financial and social, mutually beneficial reciprocal relationships that could exist between wealthy merchants and elites.[59] Lydia's occupation, described by the compound term πορφυρόπωλις, belongs in the category of "local retail trader" rather than an ἔμπορος, merchant trader. However, even merchant traders, if portrayed

---

pay for mere manual labour, not for artistic skill; for in their case the very wage they receive is a pledge of their slavery" (Cicero, *Off.* 1.42.150 [Miller et al., LCL]).

57. A good example of a nonscientific handbook of stereotypes is Theophrastus, *Characteres*.

58. LSJ, s.v. ἔμπορος; also see Winfried Schmitz, "Kapelos," *BNP*.

59. Jerome H. Neyrey, "The Social Location of Paul: Education as the Key," in *Fabrics of Discourse: Essays in Honor of Vernon K. Robbins*, ed. David B. Gowler, L. Gregory Bloomquist, and Duane F. Watson (Harrisburg, PA: Trinity Press International, 2003), 127–30.

positively, still needed the benefit of apologetic rhetoric to help neutralize the universal stereotypes associated with merchants of any category.

Cicero, for example, claims that large-scale trade potentially could be respectable as long as it is conducted without "misrepresentation" and ideally is merely a temporary means to achieving the truly honorable lifestyle of a retired country-estate holder (*Off.* 1.42.151).[60] Whether apologetic or not, rhetorical portrayals of merchants consistently contained elements of guile.

Merchants, whether wealthy import-export traders, vendors at fairs, shopkeepers, or itinerant travelers, all shared in common various degrees of a rhetorical stereotype that centered on greed and deceptiveness. In Theophrastus's catalog of various negative character types, the market vendor is located in a profile of "shamelessness":

> The shameless man is the sort who ... ruins his reputation, vilifies the powerful, in his character is like a market-vendor, coarse and ready for anything.... He is apt to keep an inn or run a brothel or be a tax collector, and he rejects no disgraceful occupation.... He lets his mother starve, is arrested for theft, and spends more time in jail than at home. (*Char.* 6.1–6 [Rusten, Cunningham, and Knox, LCL])

When Plato debates the pros and cons of either inland or maritime locations for the ideal model city, he cautions about the maritime's vulnerability to moral contamination from the inevitable concentration of merchants that would be attracted by its ports.

> For if the State was to be on the sea-coast ... it would need a mighty saviour and divine lawgivers, if, with such a character, it was to avoid having a variety of luxurious and depraved habits.... For the sea is, in very truth, "a right briny and bitter neighbour," although there is sweetness in its proximity for the uses of daily life; for by filling the markets of the city with foreign merchandise and retail trading, and breeding in

---

60. "Trade, if it is on a small scale, is to be considered vulgar [*sordida*]; but if wholesale and on a large scale, importing large quantities from all parts of the world and distributing to many without misrepresentation, it is not to be greatly disparaged. Nay, it even seems to deserve the highest respect, if those who are engaged in it, satiated, or rather, I should say, satisfied with the fortunes they have made, make their way from the port to a country estate, as they have often made it from sea into port" (Miller et al., LCL).

men's souls knavish and tricky ways, it renders the city faithless and loveless, not itself only, but to the rest of the world as well. (*Leg.* 4.704d–705a [Lamb et al., LCL])

Wealthy merchants, together with all other types of merchants, were profiled as deceptive and immoral due to their desire for profit.[61]

Deception was a particular characteristic of merchants, in great part because of the knowledge imbalance between a buyer and seller that characterizes what cultural anthropologist Clifford Geertz has called a "bazaar economy." Geertz stressed that while "under whatever skies, men prefer to buy cheap and sell dear," a bazaar economy operates primarily through knowledge imbalance rather than comparative pricing.[62] The disparity between a seller's and a buyer's knowledge about the quality of, and appropriate pricing for, a product, be it wool or a slave, provided sellers with the potential to exploit their "insider information" at the expense of the buyer. The underlying social relations that govern a bazaar economy are an appropriate analogue for the first-century Greco-Roman economy.[63]

---

61. "Vulgar we must consider those also who buy from wholesale merchants to retail immediately; for they would get no profits without a great deal of downright lying" (Cicero, *Off.* 1.42.150 [Miller et al., LCL]). Profit is equated with sin in Sirach because of its corrupting influence: "A merchant [ἔμπορος] can hardly keep from wrongdoing, nor is a tradesman (κάπηλος) innocent of sin. Many have committed sin for gain, and those who seek to get rich will avert their eyes. As a stake is driven firmly into a fissure between stones, so sin is wedged in between selling and buying" (Sir 26:29–27:2). See also Ben-Zion Rosenfeld and Joseph Menirav, "Commerce and Marketers, as Viewed by the Sages," in *Markets and Marketing in Roman Palestine*, trans. Chava Chassel, JSJSup 99 (Leiden: Brill, 2005), 180–81.

62. "To start with a dictum: in the bazaar information is poor, scarce, maldistributed, inefficiently communicated, and intensely valued.… The level of ignorance about everything from product quality and going prices to market possibilities and production costs is very high, and much of the way in which the bazaar functions can be interpreted as an attempt to reduce such ignorance for someone, increase it for someone, or defend someone against it" (Clifford Geertz, "The Bazaar Economy: Information and Search in Peasant Marketing," *AmER* 68.2 [1978]: 29).

63. The analogue between the bazaar economy and the Roman economy has also been developed in the work of Peter F. Bang, "Imperial Bazaar: Towards a Comparative Understanding of Markets in the Roman Empire," in *Ancient Economies, Modern Methodologies: Archaeology, Comparative History, Models and Institutions*, ed. Peter F Bang, Mamoru Ikeguchi, and Harmut G. Ziche, Pragmateiai 12 (Bari, Italy: Edipuglia, 2006), 51–88. Also supported by the following: "One of the 'accusations' leveled by the Romans against market vendors was that the vendors' knowledge was greater

Moreover, bazaar economy imbalances are exacerbated in a limited-goods environment, such as in Mediterranean antiquity, where, either in reality or perceptually, "all goods in life exist in finite, limited quantity and are always in short supply," and therefore one person's gain is perceived to be another's loss.[64] From the perspective of a limited-goods society, it is always a sellers' market at the buyer's expense.[65]

In an economy with limited and uneven access to market information, the potential for dishonestly misrepresenting product quality, and exploitative pricing, resulted in a stereotype of merchants "associated with conniving, cheating, and greed" where the topos of "merchant" evoked "thief, swindler and liar."[66] The element of deception evoked by merchants applied to all categories of merchants, whether a slave dealer[67] or a sausage

---

than that of their customers and they could use this knowledge to deceive them. Even Diocletian's Edict branded merchants as scoundrels who were involved in business, who could read the future in the stars (and hence were aware of future price developments)" (187).

64. Malina, *New Testament World*, 89.

65. Ibid., 95.

66. Rosenfeld and Menirav, "Commerce and Marketers," 180. Leslie Kurke offers textual support for "the enduring power of the equation of trade with deceit" from the classical period to antiquity in Kurke, "ΚΑΠΗΛΕΙΑ and Deceit: Theognis 59–60," *AJP* 110 (1989): 537. It is important to note that such stereotypes do not infer that historically this is how all merchants actually behaved, for trust was a key component of sustaining longer-term relationships between buyers and sellers. For example, the general cultural perception was that "to deceive with oaths ... is general practice in the market place," although in reality "the proper use of oaths must have outweighed the misuse; otherwise no contract of sale, no alliance ... could ever have had any force." The difference lies between "cultural wisdom" found in rhetorical portrayals and sociohistorical practice. On oaths in the marketplace, see Walter Burkert, "Polis and Polytheism," in *Greek Religion*, trans. John Raffan (Cambridge: Harvard University Press, 1977), 253–54; see also Nicholas Rauh, *The Sacred Bonds of Commerce: Religion, Economy, and Trade Society at Hellenistic Roman Delos, 166–87 BC* (Amsterdam: Gieben, 1993).

67. "The art of a slave-dealer is a flattery of gymnastic, for they produce a false complexion by the use of paint [*qui colorem fuco*] and a false robustness by puffing them out with fat" (Quintilian, *Inst.* 2.15.25 [Butler, LCL]). "Slave-dealers hide under some sort of finery any defect [of the slave] which may give offence, and for that reason the very trappings arouse the suspicion of the buyer. If you catch sight of a leg or an arm that is bound up in cloths, you demand that it be stripped and that the body itself be revealed to you" (Seneca, *Ep.* 80.9 [Gummere et al., LCL]). See also Albert J. Harrill,

seller (ἀλλαντοπώλης), whom Aristophanes sardonically depicts as the new choice for state leader:

> How can I, a sausage-selling chap, become a Man [ἀνήρ]?
> Why, that's the very thing will make you great, your roguery [πονηρός], impudence [θρασύς], and agora-training.... To be a Demus-leader is not now for lettered men, nor yet for honest men, but for the base and ignorant. (*Eq.* 177–181 [Rogers, LCL])[68]

Trickery was ascribed to wool sellers, who were accused of wetting their wool in order to increase its weight (Aristophanes, *Ran.* 1385–1388),[69] as well as to purple sellers, who were known to doctor their scales (Aristotle, *Mech.* 849b85).[70]

The rhetorical profile of a Greco-Roman female seller conscripted all of the deceptive hucksterism of the male, augmented by the perceived shamelessness of a female engaged in speech and purposeful action in public space.[71] This rhetorical perception of female vendors is succinctly put in Eve D'Ambra's interpretation of a relief of a female seller excavated from a Roman marketplace: "What we see is the most public and characteristic activity of the women in their stalls appealing to passersby. This is also the

---

"The Vice of Slave Dealers in Greco-Roman Society: The Use of a Topos in 1 Timothy 1:10," *JBL* 118 (1999): 106.

68. The sausage seller's name, Agoracritus (Αγοράκριτος), is an example of *antonomasia*. Although it literally translates to "agora judge" it refers to the type of "market smarts" needed to distinguish what price one could optimally buy or sell goods for. Agoracritus explains his name by "an agora-life I lived, and thrived by wrangling" (Aristophanes, *Eq.* 1258 [Rogers, LCL]), where "wrangling" is actually κρινόμενος. The need for "market smarts" is particularly acute in a Greco-Roman "bazaar economy."

69. "His scale sinks down. Why, how came that about? He threw a river in, like some wool-seller [ἐπιοπωλικῶς] wetting his wool, to make it weigh the more" (Rogers, LCL).

70. "This is how sellers of purple [ἀλουργοπῶλαι] arrange their weighing machines to deceive, by putting the cord out of the true centre, and pouring lead into one arm of the balance, or by employing wood for the side to which they want it to incline taken from the root or from where there is a knot" (Rackham et al., LCL). The lexical entry for ἀλουργοπωλική: "considered the same as πορφυροπωλική" is found in five archaic lexicons: Harpocration (second century CE), Pseudo-Zonaras (thirteenth century CE), Photius (ninth century CE), *Suda* (tenth century CE), and *Lexica Segueriana*.

71. One of the Greek words for "prostitute" was "πόρνη, from πέρνημι, to sell." See Elke Hartmann, "Prostitution, Classical Antiquity, " *BNP*.

part of the job that made the women appear disreputable and degraded to elite men, who saw them as aggressive, shameless, and surely willing to sell their bodies as easily as they would hand over a head of garlic."[72]

The Hellenistic proverb referring to a Lydian "keeping shop" pointed to the degree to which Lydia's ethnographic profile was further amplified by the rhetorical profile of her occupation, for it touches on another Lydian stereotype: selling. In Herodotus's account of the demilitarization of Lydian men, Croesus also proposed that, along with other effeminizing measures, Lydian men should learn retail trade, καπηλεύω (Herodotus, *Hist.* 1.155). In fact, as we discussed earlier, Herodotus ascribed the invention of both coin minting and retailing to Lydians (*Hist.* 1.94).

The term κάπηλος, along with its synonyms, was most closely connected with petty trades and regularly evoked hucksterism, "petty roguery," trickery, and cheating.[73] As a result, the element of "seller" contained in Lydia's profile as a πορφυρόπωλις cojoins with general Lydian ethnography. A blend of a huckster topos with that of sexual immorality appears in the work of Josephus, who augmented a list from Lev 21:7 of the types of "impure" women that priests would be forbidden to marry, namely, prostituted and profaned women and divorcées, with those who "gain their livelihood by hawking [καπηλείας] or innkeeping [πανδοκεύειν]" (Josephus, *Ant.* 3.276 [Thackeray et al., LCL]).[74]

Even without her Lydian ethnic profile, Lydia as a seller would have readily shared in the negative cultural stereotype. While general decep-

---

72. Eve D'Ambra, *Roman Women*, Cambridge Introduction to Roman Civilization (Cambridge: Cambridge University Press, 2007), 140.

73. Leslie Kurke has astutely pointed out that Herodotus contrasts the components of Persian education with those proposed by Croesus for Lydian boys where Persian "truth-telling" corresponds and contrasts with Lydian "retail trading." Persian *paideia* is described as follows: παιδεύουσι δὲ τοὺς παῖδας ἀπὸ πενταέτεος ἀρξάμενοι μέχρι εἰκοσαέτεος τρία μοῦνα, ἱππεύειν καὶ τοξεύειν καὶ ἀληθίζεσθαι. "They educate their boys from five to twenty years old, and teach them three things only, riding and archery, and truth-telling" (Herodotus, *Hist.* 1.136 [Godley, LCL]). As Kurke observes, "Croesus' advice is clearly intended to stand in contrast to the program of Persian education: each passage uses the phrase *paideuein (-ousi) tous paidas* with three bare infinitives. *Kitharizein* contrasts with *hippeuein*, *psallein* 'to pluck' replaces *tokseuein*, and *kapêleuein* [huckstering] provides the climactic contrast to *alêthizesthai* [truth-telling]" (Kurke, "ΚΑΠΗΛΕΙΑ and Deceit," 539).

74. Ben-Zion Rosenfeld, "Innkeeping in Jewish Society in Roman Palestine," *JESHO* 41 (1998): 142.

tiveness was a rhetorical attribute of any kind of merchant, ethnographically the Lydians as originators of καπηλεία were standard-bearers for this stereotype. When we add Lydia's Lydian ethnographic profile to the topoi of "purple" and seller, it erupts into a full-blown rhetorical profile that embodies hucksterism and deception.

4.2.6. Lydia's "Reverence": Topoi of Προσευχή and Σεβομένη τὸν θεόν

Lydia is encountered in the spatial context of the Pauline group's looking for a "place of prayer" (προσευχή) and temporally within a frame of "Sabbath" (Acts 16:13). When the disciples sit down with the women, their purposeful action of sitting with an assembled group on the Sabbath evokes a "temple-dialogue" literary motif[75] and echoes two similar Sabbath-day settings: Jesus's preaching in the synagogue in Nazareth (Luke 4:16–28) and Paul's preaching in the synagogue in Antioch (Acts 13:14–42). In both of these two preceding synagogue scenes, the term εὐαγγελίζομαι is featured (Luke 4:18; Acts 13:32), helping to support the portrayal of the assembly on the outskirts of Philippi as a reenactment of prior synagogue assemblies.[76] Contributing to the synagogue-esque sense of the assembly by the river is the epithet σεβομένη τὸν θεόν (Acts 16:14) as the final of Lydia's descriptive attributes.

Almost universally, it has been assumed that "worshiper of God" in this passage designates Lydia as a "Godfearer," that is, a proselyte to Judaism. Representative of most commentaries is the suggestion that "the phrase 'worshiper of God' is equivalent to the technical term 'fearer of God' which the Septuagint routinely uses to describe the house of Israel."[77] From this understanding, Lydia is de facto Jewish, and, like Cornelius in Acts 10 (a φοβούμενος τὸν θεόν 10:2, 22), "converts" to Christianity from Judaism. Implicitly, a religious social identity of "Jewish woman" infers

---

75. On the temple dialogue as a literary form, see Vernon K. Robbins, *Jesus the Teacher: A Socio-rhetorical Interpretation of Mark, with a New Introduction*, 2nd ed. (Minneapolis: Fortress, 1992), 104–5, 178–79; David E. Aune, *Prophecy in Early Christianity and the Ancient Mediterranean World* (Grand Rapids: Eerdmans, 1983), 399–400 n. 93.

76. A common inference found in scholarship is as follows: "According to Ac. 16:13 ff. there was a synagogue at Philippi which Paul visited with his companions to preach the Gospel there to the Jews" (Heinrich Greeven, "Εὔχομαι," *TDNT* 2:808).

77. Malina and Pilch, *Social-Science Commentary*, 117.

that Lydia's piety is located within a normative framework of Jewish customs and values.⁷⁸ Framed by the Sabbath, it is easy to see how the gathering of women might be understood as fitting an established pattern of synagogue visits and preaching. However, the pattern shatters with the substitution of the uncommon term προσευχή for synagogue, the socially inappropriate, purposeful action of first-century Mediterranean men sitting down to talk with women, and most particularly with a women-only gathering represented by Lydia.

From a historical perspective, in addition to there being no firm evidence to date for the existence of a Jewish community in Philippi in the first century, the category of "Godfearers" or "God-worshipers" as a definable class of proselytes remains a matter of debate.⁷⁹ In addition, while some commentators understand the use of θεός in the singular in Lydia's epithet as necessarily pointing to the monotheistic God of Israel, the singular θεός is used quite regularly in Greco-Roman literature, where the god's identity is determined by how it is contextualized. When Herodotus recounts how an Egyptian Pharaoh was delivered by his god, the use of θεός would naturally infer the Egyptian divinity for an Egyptian reader (*Hist.* 2.141). However, when Herodotus—a Greek—names the god in question, he uses the Greek name Hephaestus rather than the Egyptian Ptah. When Josephus recounts the same story, his use of θεός intends the

---

78. There has been some conjecture that the riverside locale implies a Jewish gathering since "women ... had to do ritual ablutions after their monthly period in order to be considered clean and able to attend Jewish worship" (Witherington, *Acts of the Apostles*, 490; see also Malina and Pilch, *Social-Science Commentary*, 116), but these readings ignore the association between water and other cults, such as that of the healing god Asclepius, as well as the somewhat unlikely scenario that the disciples, looking for a place of prayer, sat themselves down among a group of women washing their genitalia. "*Asclepieia* are usually located outside settlements, occasionally on river banks or on the sea shore; statements from antiquity justify this by means of practical and religious considerations. Water installations and the incubation room (*enkoimtērion*) are specifically associated with healing. Water plays a major role in this healing cult, all *Asclepieia* have ready access to a source of fresh water, including those located at the sea" (Fritz Graf, "Asclepius," *BNP*). Apollonius of Tyana claims that like the poet Sappho, another poet, Damophyle, would gather women together in order to compose poems and hymns (Philostratus, *Vit. Apoll.* 30). The constitution of the gathering of women in Acts 16 remains ambiguous.

79. This descriptor is only found in Acts in the New Testament ("Godfearer[s]": 10:2, 22; 13:16, 26; "worshiper of God": 16:14; 18:7).

God of Israel (*Ant.* 10.5–17).[80] In both Herodotus and Josephus, the god in question is simply referred to as a singular θεός since the audience would have automatically filled in the god's identity. When Plutarch wrote of the oracles at Delphi, θεός in the singular is normative throughout the work, since Apollo is self-evidently the god in sight.[81] The use of θεός in the singular does not automatically suggest a monotheistic belief but rather that it is clear what god is in view.

Rhetorical factors also prevent a facile substitution of "Jewish-gentile" for σεβομένη τὸν θεόν. The only place that προσευχή, "prayer," is used as a spatial reference to suggest prayer house in the Bible is in this rhetorical unit (Acts 16:13, 16). Yet this rare use of προσευχή has drawn only passing remarks from commentators, where the gathered women have been regarded as some type of oddity falling outside of the strict bounds of synagogue but constituting normative Jewish religio-social space nonetheless.

While προσευχή is used on its own only in Acts 16:13, 16, to designate a place, it is used with a spatial qualifier in the Old Testament in 1 Macc 3:46; 7:37; 3 Macc 7:20; and Isa 56:7 (x2); 60:7, and in the New Testament in Luke 19:46 (synoptic parallels Matt 21:13 and Mark 11:17). In 1 Macc 3:46, the designation "place of prayer" (τόπος προσευχῆς) is found in a situation of conflict within military discourse describing the battles between the Maccabees and the forces of Antiochus Epiphanes (1 Macc 3:43–46),[82] and so too in 1 Macc 7:37 the reference to the temple as a "house of prayer and supplication" occurs within Jewish-gentile conflict. In 3 Macc 7:20, the Jews dedicate a "place of prayer" (τόπον προσευχῆς) as a thanks offering for a triumphant rescue from an enemy as their former Egyptian persecutor radically transforms into their benefactor after God's salvific intervention.

In Isa 56:7, the "house of prayer" marks the apocalyptic enjoining of all who live in accordance with God's precepts, including the eunuch and

---

80. See pp. 171–72.

81. Among other numerous examples of references to θεός in the singular, see Diodorus of Sicily, *The Library of History* 32.10.2; Xenophon, *Oec.* 7.22.

82. "But they said to one another, 'Let us repair the destruction of our people, and fight for our people and the sanctuary.' And the congregation assembled to be ready for battle, and to pray and ask for mercy and compassion. Jerusalem was uninhabited like a wilderness; not one of her children went in or out. The sanctuary was trampled down, and the sons of aliens held the citadel; it was a lodging place for the Gentiles. Joy was taken from Jacob; the flute and the harp ceased to play. So they assembled and went to Mizpah, opposite Jerusalem, because Israel formerly had a place of prayer in Mizpah."

the foreigner, into God's temple and this apocalyptic theme continues in Isa 60:7, when, at Israel's promised redemption, God's "house of prayer" shall be glorified. In Luke 19:46 and parallels, προσευχή is used spatially to designate the temple and is situated within a context of intense conflict. Jesus, while driving out the temple sellers (τοὺς πωλοῦντας), condemns the temple leadership by contrasting what the temple ought to be—a "house of prayer" (οἶκος προσευχῆς)—with what it has become: "a den of robbers" (σπήλαιον λῃστῶν).[83]

The term is not found in non-Jewish Greek literature, but it is used with this meaning by Jewish-Hellenistic writers Philo and Josephus.[84]

---

83. Military imagery is not that far removed here either: "λῃστής, originally 'the one who takes booty'" (Karl Heinrich Rengstorf, "λῃστής," *TDNT* 4:257).

84. Philo, *Flaccus* 41; 45; 47, 48; 49; 53; 122; *Embassy* 132; 134; 137; 138; 148; 152; 156; 157; 165; 191; 346; 371. Josephus, *Life* 277; 280; 293; *Ant.* 14.258; *Ag. Ap.* 2.10. The Roman author Juvenal's use of the Latin transliteration *proseucha* (*Sat.* 3.295) is regularly cited as evidence that a gentile author uses the term for a Jewish prayer house; however, the term is used in the questioning of a gentile Roman without any explicit presumption of Jewishness attached to it. Juvenal's third *Satire* is concerned with the demise of the "honorable Roman of old" who has been replaced by self-serving, political "flatterers" who, through their corrupt behavior, have become powerful and wealthy at the expense of long-established "true" Romans. Most of this *Satire* contrasts the values and lifestyle of this "new Roman rich" with the now poor, authentic Roman. The Roman of old, due to his poverty, has become vulnerable to life's various indignities from which the rich are insulated. As one example, Juvenal describes how this Roman, out at night, is an easy target for a roving bully: "'Where are you from?' shouts he [the thug]; 'whose vinegar, whose beans have blown you out? With what cobbler have you been munching cut leeks and boiled wether's chaps?—What, sirrah, no answer? Speak out, or take that upon your shins! Say, where is your stand? In what prayer-shop [*proseucha*] shall I find you?' Whether you venture to say anything, or make off silently ... he will thrash you just the same.... Such is the liberty of the poor man: having been pounded and cuffed into a jelly, he begs and prays to be allowed to return home with a few teeth in his head!" (*Sat.* 3.290–300 [Ramsay, LCL]). The entire passage deals with age-old baiting tactics used by bullies that begin with demands for the victim to identify his or her affiliations. The first question, "Where are you from?" is the key one. Since the first-century personality was defined by one's social group, the bully's interrogation is aimed at answering the question, "Who are you?" determined by whom the victim associates with. It is possible that, implicitly, Juvenal's thug is wondering whether the poor Roman is a Jew. When Juvenal does refer to Jews, he portrays them as poor (*Sat.* 3.13–14; 6.542–547), so it is within the realm of possibility that Juvenal is suggesting that the poor Roman may be mistaken for a Jew by the fact of his poverty, but such an interpretation is inferential at best and not the main point of the passage.

Conflicted control over, and classification of, the προσευχή marks Josephus's depiction of the προσευχή. He calls Apion "a liar" for claiming in his *History of Egypt* that Moses erected "prayer-houses [προσευχάς] ... in the various precincts of the city, all facing eastwards, such being the orientation also of Heliopolis" and had them outfitted according to Egyptian customs of piety (Josephus, *Ag. Ap.* 2.10-11 [Thackeray et al., LCL]). Moreover, an underlying theme of conflict is also present in three of Josephus's four other references to προσευχή that deal with a struggle for political power between his adversaries and himself (i.e., *Life* 277, 280, 293). In one of these passages, Josephus, writing autobiographically in the first person, describes how he entered a prayer house armed as if for battle.

> For my part, on the following day I ordered two of my bodyguard, of the most approved valour and staunch loyalty, to accompany me, with daggers concealed under their dress, for self-defence in the event of an assault on the part of our foes. I wore a breastplate myself and, with a sword so girt on as to be as little conspicuous as possible, entered the Prayer-house [προσευχήν]. (*Life* 293 [Thackeray et al., LCL])[85]

Although both Josephus and Philo designate a prayer house with προσευχή, it is by far Philo who makes most frequent use of the term. Yet even Philo uses προσευχή in only two of his thirty-eight extant works (*The Life*; *On the Embassy to Gaius*), where, in both, the same issue is profiled—growing conflict over whether Gaius's image and other trappings of the imperial cult would be allowed in Jewish prayer houses. The προσευχή in Philo is contested space over how it will be classified, through the God of Israel or Gaius, and over who will have control of the space: the Jews or their opponents like Flaccus (who was trying to garner Gaius's favor by persecuting the Jews).

A term rarely used to designate space in Greek literature—προσευχή—is used as such on its own only by two Jewish-Hellenistic authors, and in nearly all cases it is used within situations of violence and/or intense conflict. When it appears in the Bible with spatial qualifiers, it never does so within a context of peaceful community worship. Rather, in 1 Maccabees it

---

85. Heather A. McKay notes: "This account of exciting and violent events in a προσευχή in Tiberias belies any image we may have of a quiet and orderly 'house of prayer'" (Heather A. McKay, *Sabbath and Synagogue: The Question of Sabbath Worship in Ancient Judaism*, RGRW 122 [Leiden: Brill, 1994], 81).

is found in the course of battle sequences and ongoing conflict; in 3 Maccabees it is a dedication of victory; in Isaiah it is an apocalyptic image found within a promise of salvation; and in Luke it is the scene of Jesus's most violent purposeful action. The term προσευχή, therefore, echoes Jewish community scenes of military and political conflict. Rhetographically, the term προσευχή would evoke Jewish community space, while at the same time this space would be marked by an element of intense conflict.

Socio-scientific modeling suggests that territoriality is concerned with "classification of place, communication of this classification, [and] control of the place so classified."[86] Sellers as an occupational category feature once in Luke and once in Acts. In Luke, their presence has contaminated the "house of prayer" and transformed it into a den of robbers (Luke 19:46).[87] The sole, explicitly designated seller of Acts, Lydia, is closely associated with the space from within which she is encountered. In an implied sacred temporal setting of Sabbath, it is easy to see how an extreme issue of classification would permeate any "place of prayer" that might accommodate Lydia the seller.

Finally, the basic meaning of σεβομένη τὸν θεόν is someone who reveres or worships divinity and can be intended as such in the most general sense.[88] There has been a propensity in Judeo-Christian scholarship to ascribe specific Judeo-Christian meaning to terms that might, but do not necessarily, carry these meanings. Abundant Greco-Roman references to reverence for, or worship of, a god or gods using the verb σέβω with θεός as its object (or the adjective θεσεβής, or noun εὐσέβεια) clearly show that

---

86. Jerome H. Neyrey, "'Teaching You in Public and from House to House' (Acts 20:20): Unpacking a Cultural Stereotype," in *The Social World of the New Testament: Insights and Models*, ed. Jerome H. Neyrey and Eric C. Stewart (Peabody, MA: Hendrickson, 2008), 184.

87. Jesus's charge of "den of robbers" evokes one of the most common character slurs in antiquity: "temple robber." "The emotional charge attaching to the offence was sufficient to make 'temple-robber' a term of everyday abuse; orators exercised ingenuity in devising ways in which their opponents had deprived the gods of their due and so fell into the abominated category. Disrespect for sacred money was a mark of extreme social decay, the behavior of a tyrant or barbarian" (Robert Parker, *Miasma: Pollution and Purification in Early Greek Religion* [Oxford: Clarendon, 1983], 170–71).

88. Even Cornelius, who is often identified as a "Godfearer," is first described in the general language of piety, "a devout man who feared God [εὐσεβὴς καὶ φοβούμενος τὸν θεόν] with all his household, gave alms liberally to the people, and prayed constantly to God" (Acts 10:2).

reverence for divinity and piety was a preoccupation of the wider first-century world and that the god in view was determined by the context of the text. Piety could range from conventional displays of culturally appropriate worship to deeply held reverence for divinity. Conventional displays of piety were shown by Alexander, who having decided independently to invade Asia, enacted customary reverential protocols that effectively served to launch his military campaign, making "lavish sacrifices to the gods at Dium in Macedonia and held the dramatic contests in honor of Zeus and the Muses … and put his army in a fine humour" (Diodorus of Sicily, *Library of History* 17.16.3–4 [Oldfather et al., LCL]).[89] At the other end of the piety spectrum, lawmaker Zaleucus[90] proposed that faith in the divine should be the first legislative principle: "That the inhabitants of the city should first of all assume as an article of their creed that gods exist … that they should revere the gods [σέβεσθαί τε τοὺς θεούς] as the cause of all that is noble and good in the life of mankind" (Diodorus of Sicily, *The Library of History* 12.20.2 [Oldfather et al., LCL]).[91]

---

89. A display of piety was a preliminary requisite to any military campaign: "The first duty is to sacrifice to the gods and pray them to grant you the thoughts, words and deeds likely to render your command most pleasing to the gods and to bring yourself, your friends and your city the fullest measure of affection and glory and advantage. Having gained the goodwill of the gods, you have then to recruit a sufficient number of mounted men that you may bring the number up to the total required by law" (Xenophon, *Eq. mag.* 1.1–2 [Marchant et al., LCL]). See also *Anab.* 1.11.1–8. Josephus describes how an adversary attempted to use a show of piety as a ruse to disarm him: "Now a certain one of them by the name of Ananias, a vile and wretched man, proposed publicly to the masses that a fast before God be appointed for the following day. He directed that, having disarmed themselves, at about the same time and in the same place they should appear openly before God; for they understood that if they should not receive assistance from him, all weaponry would be useless. Yet he was saying these things not out of piety, but for the purpose of taking me and my [people] unarmed. And indeed I complied out of necessity, so that I should not appear to disdain this admonition concerning piety" (Josephus, *Life* 290–291 (Barclay; translator's brackets).

90. "Legendary 7th/6th cent. BC legislator from Locri in Lower Italy," R. WO., "Zaleucus," *BNP*.

91. That Zaleucus intended authentic rather than superficial piety (at least in Diodorus's telling) is underscored by the following: "They [the citizens of Locri] should keep the soul pure from every kind of evil, in the belief that the gods take no pleasure in either the sacrifices or costly gifts of the wicked but in the just and honourable practices of good men" (Diodorus of Sicily, *The Library of History* 12.20.2 [Oldfather et al., LCL]).

In the New Testament, Lydia is the first to be described by the epithet σεβομένη τὸν θεόν, and there are no immediate indicators as to where along the piety spectrum Lydia might be located. Rather than affirming the assembly by the river as a Jewish synagogue by placing a pious Jewish woman into it, the descriptor "worshiper of God" clashes with Lydia's earlier descriptors and calls into question how the element of piety fits with Lydia's profile.

While there are no descriptions of women-only gatherings constituting a Jewish synagogue, Philo does describe an idealized ascetic community—the Therapeutae—where women regularly joined the men in a "common sanctuary" (κοινὸν σεμνεῖον) meeting every seven days and listening to an elder expound on doctrine (*Contemp. Life* 30–32).[92] Although they joined the men, the women were separated from them in their own

---

92. On the basis of inscriptional evidence where women bear titles such as "head of synagogue," "leader," "elder," "mother of the synagogue," and "priestess," Bernadette Brooten has argued that women performed leadership roles in synagogue services. Brooten's argument looks for evidence of the presence of women in *male* synagogue services. At issue is the degree to which women participated in the synagogue. So, for example, Brooten searched for evidence in support of intermingled, rather than segregated, seating. The underlying normative model is a male-constituted synagogue and arguments are sought to establish that women both attended synagogue services and fully participated. For Brooten, the issue is over the degree of women's participation in synagogue services, but nowhere does Brooten argue for a women-only synagogue assembly. In the case of Acts 16, Brooten simply refutes the suggestions of others that the gathering of women could not have constituted a Jewish synagogue. She writes: "I believe that the real reason for the hesitancy is that the only congregants mentioned are women. One can see that this is a circular argument: on the assumption that women did not attend or only rarely attended synagogue services, a text which speaks of women attending services is taken as not referring to genuine synagogue worship. None of the three reasons is convincing, and this text is therefore a further attestation of women's presence at Jewish worship services." Bernadette J. Brooten, *Women Leaders in the Ancient Synagogue: Inscriptional Evidence and Background Issues*, BJS 36 (Chico, CA: Scholars Press, 1982), 140. A similar case in found in Lee Levine's comments regarding the role of women in the synagogue. Levine writes: "A number of sources from the first to the seventh centuries C.E. and from Palestine as well as the Diaspora indicate that women were regularly present in the synagogue during worship. Paul traveled throughout much of the Diaspora, and he invariably went to local synagogues, where he often spoke to women.... The fact that pagan women in Damascus were especially attracted to Judaism seems to be an almost certain indication that they attended the synagogue regularly; otherwise, it would be hard to imagine how this attraction would have been effected, expressed, and maintained" (Lee I. Levine,

chamber by a partitioning wall. This wall had a gap at the ceiling ensuring that "the modesty becoming the female sex is preserved while the women sitting within ear-shot can easily follow what is said since there is nothing to obstruct the voice of the speaker" (Philo, *Contempl. Life* 33 [Colson et al., LCL]). By the river outside of Philippi, contravening any normative Sabbath synagogue practices, the we-group sits down with an assembly of women.

In fact, not only is the tone of propriety marking the Sabbath setting of the Therapeutae fundamentally different from the one where Lydia is encountered, but also the rhetorical profile of the female members of the Therapeutae forms a stark contrast to that of Lydia. Avowed lifelong virgins,[93] the Therapeutae gather with men on holy feast days, dressed in undyed simple garments, singing hymns with uplifted hands, signaling that their hands were "clean from gain-taking and not defiled through any cause of profit-making of any kind" (*Contempl. Life* 66 [Colson et al., LCL]). In contrast to the sumptuous "purple-covered couches" found at Greek banquets, the Therapeutae recline on "plank beds of the common kinds of wood, covered with quite cheap strewings of native papyrus" sitting "by themselves on the left" while the men sit on the right (*Contempl. Life* 69 [Colson et al., LCL]). A female Therapeutae's rhetorical profile formed the stark opposite to Lydia's. Rather than supporting a view of the women by the river in Acts 16 as a pious Jewish Sabbath gathering, the only narrated example of a group of Jewish women gathered in a synagogue setting (although not without men), by nature of its contrast, emphasizes the social and cultural inappropriateness of the we-group's joining with the women.

Interpretations have generally assimilated προσευχή with synagogue and harmonized the events by the river with established narrative patterns. The disciples enter a town; on the Sabbath they find a synagogue

---

The Ancient Synagogue the First Thousand Years [New Haven: Yale University Press, 2000], 472–73).

93. "The feast is shared by women also most of them aged virgins, who have kept their chastity not under compulsion, like some of the Greek priestesses, but of their own free will in their ardent yearning for wisdom. Eager to have her for their life mate they have spurned the pleasures of the body and desire no mortal offspring but those immortal children which only the soul that is dear to God can bring to the birth unaided because the Father has sown in her spiritual rays enabling her to behold the verities of wisdom" (Philo, *Contempl. Life* 8.68 [Colson et al., LCL]).

gathering; and they preach to a Jewish assembly, gaining new adherents as a consequence. Such a pattern will explicitly resume in Thessalonica (Acts 17:1-4); Philippi, however, retains expected familiar elements while concurrently altering them. For a gathering of women outside of the city of Philippi, together with the we-group's uncertainty over where a place of prayer might be found, the use of the uncommon term προσευχή, as well as this first use of σεβομένη τὸν θεόν, and most especially Lydia's "huckster" profile, provide a less-than-firm foundation for asserting that Lydia is encountered in pious Jewish space and is its appropriate representative member.

4.2.7. Lydia and the Topos of Hospitality

Lydia's offer to the disciples (Acts 16:15) invokes the social model of hospitality. Typically commentators have inferred that this social model affirms Lydia's role of "hostess." However, by this point in our intertextual analysis, the problems with inferring a hostess image will have become abundantly clear. Nonetheless, the social model of hospitality *does* play an important role within the rhetorical development of the text, albeit through alternate elements. Rather than introducing an element of hostessing, the emotion-fused actions of character evaluation and recognition are the salient elements of hospitality that connect with the topoi associated with Lydia.

As heralds of a divine salvific message, the Pauline group settles into Philippi woefully bereft of any evident stamp of divine sanction. No dazzling clothes, miraculous deeds, shows of physical or rhetorical prowess, or any other conventional clues help to spotlight their connection to the divine. As they make their way to the river, they remain strangers, unknown and unrecognized, uncertain over the location of the place of prayer, and clearly without the benefit of a personal escort. Such cases of strangers visiting new territory, either divinities or agents of a divinity, were regularly depicted in ancient narratives. In these stories, offers of hospitality often functioned as a litmus test by which either the recognition, or rejection, of the divine visitor was displayed.

Narratologists have called such familiar narrative episodes "type scenes,"[94] but from a rhetorical perspective these could be understood

---

94. Expanding on the work of Robert Alter, O. Wesley Allen has suggested the following definition: "Type-scenes are stereotyped scenes which recur within a cultural-literary milieu. The presentations consist of conventional details used to describe a

as distinguishable clusters of conventional elements found in a culture's recurring stories. Rhetorical type scenes were essentially a network of topoi that could be employed within a variety of rhetorical contexts. Rhetorical type scenes encompass multiple elements, which can help frame events or settings within conventional expectations.

A key point of tension in these divine-human encounters was the question of whether the human would recognize the divine identity of the stranger. Ann Pippin Burnett notes that "gods often wandered on earth incognito,"[95] and a host's ability to perceive the presence of a divine visitor constituted a mark of "innate piety," since anyone "who has a true sense of the divine will presumably feel, if only dimly, the physical presence of a god."[96] An offer of hospitality signaled "right-sightedness," while rejection signaled impious blindness.

From the perspective of stranger-god rhetorical type scenes, Lydia's offer to the disciples suggests that she fits within a pattern of those who recognize divine visitors through hospitality. However, when Lydia calls for an evaluation of her fidelity to God within the form of her offer of hospitality, she introduces an element of reciprocity. For not only does Lydia's offer of hospitality suggest that she perceives the presence of a divinity (through God's agents), but also, in return, God's agents are asked to assess whether Lydia authentically reveres God.

Oral-scribally, the Lydia passages resonate most closely with Luke 24:13–32, sharing the highest concentration of lexical and contextual similarities. Where in the case of Acts 16 Lydia's heart (καρδία) is opened (διανοίγω) by the Lord to Paul's preaching (Acts 16:14), in Luke 24 Jesus "opens" (διερμηνεύω: Luke 24:27) the Scriptures to the disciples on the road to Emmaus after first accusing them of being "slow of heart to believe" (βραδεῖς τῇ καρδίᾳ τοῦ πιστεύειν: Luke 24:25); later they will recall that

---

certain narrative event requiring neither verbatim repetition nor a specific formula content" (O. Wesley Allen, *The Death of Herod: The Narrative and Theological Function of Retribution in Luke-Acts*, SBLDS 158 [Atlanta: Scholars Press, 1997], 34–35).

95. Anne Pippin Burnett, "Pentheus and Dionysus: Host and Guest," *CP* 65 (1970): 24.

96. Ibid., 25. See also Weaver, *Plots of Epiphany*, 32–44. Much as Zeus and Hermes stressed that there was no need for Philemon and his wife Baucis to kill a goose for their supper (Ovid, *Met.* 8.684–690); the angel in Judges refuses Manoah's offer of food (Judg 13:15–16); and in Luke, the risen Jesus vanishes before any bread has been eaten in Emmaus (Luke 24:30–31); offers of hospitality to divine guests showcase the otherworldly nature of the guest.

their "hearts burned (or were "kindled") inside them" (Οὐχὶ ἡ καρδία ἡμῶν καιομένη: Luke 24:32). The parallels between the disciples' request to Jesus to come and stay at their home and Lydia's to the we-group are so strong that Acts 16:15 could almost be considered a recitation of Luke 24:29. When the two offers are compared, they both seem to make the same request using very similar language.

Παρεβιάσαντο αὐτὸν λέγοντες, Μεῖνον μεθ' ἡμῶν, ὅτι πρὸς ἑσπέραν ἐστὶν καὶ κέκλικεν ἤδη ἡ ἡμέρα. καὶ εἰσῆλθεν τοῦ μεῖναι σὺν αὐτοῖς. (Luke 24:29)

Παρεκάλεσεν λέγουσα· εἰ κεκρίκατέ με πιστὴν τῷ κυρίῳ εἶναι, εἰσελθόντες εἰς τὸν οἶκόν μου μένετε· καὶ παρεβιάσατο ἡμᾶς. (Acts 16:15)

Both offers are introduced as a strong request (παραβιάζομαι/παρακαλέω) and open their direct discourse with the present active nominative participle of λέγω, and both ask that the "guest(s)" come to their homes and stay (μένω).[97] Making the connection especially compelling is the use of παραβιάζομαι in both Luke 24:29 and Acts 16:15, the only two occurrences in the New Testament.

One clear difference, however, marks the two offers of "hospitality." The offer in Luke conforms to other biblical accounts where travelers enter a new town and upon their arrival are provided with hospitality (e.g., Gen 18:1–8; 19:1–3; Josh 2:1; Judg 19:3–4, 20–21; Acts 10:23). The situation in Luke 24 is clearly one of travel, where having reached town the resident disciples worry that their fellow traveler might continue on into the night's dangers. "Stay with us, because it is almost evening and the day is now nearly over" (Luke 24:29) is the clearly expressed rationale for the offer. A "traveler" element explicitly underlies the premise of their offer, since the offer is made once they have reached town after journeying there together and results from the disciples' concern over Jesus's intentions to travel on ("he appeared to be going further": Luke 24:28).

In contrast, when Lydia's offer is made, the traveler element is all but absent since the group has previously arrived in Philippi and has been

---

97. Andrew Arterbury notes that "the phrase εἰς τὸν οἶκον, often in conjunction with the verbs ἄγω or ἔρχομαι, commonly marks the ratification of the hospitality relationship ... μένω and its cognates describe the guest's decision to stay or remain in a hospitable home" (Andrew E. Arterbury, *Entertaining Angels: Early Christian Hospitality in Its Mediterranean Setting*, NTMo 8 [Sheffield: Sheffield Phoenix, 2005], 188).

staying there for "some days," a situation that is underscored by the we-group's going outside of, instead of entering, Philippi. There is no rationale provided for why Lydia makes her offer; no day is drawing to its end; no traveler has journeyed to town without a place to spend the night.[98] Instead, the salient component of Lydia's offer becomes her request to have her fidelity to the Lord acclaimed.

The verb παρεβιάσατο (παραβιάζομαι) has been translated as "prevailed," and thus these translations suggest that παραβιάζομαι means something akin to "invite persistently until the guest capitulates." Some translations even more explicitly suggest the successful ratification of Lydia's offer by ending the passage with "and she persuaded us" (CEB, NET, NIV) or "and she would take no refusal" (NJB).[99] However, παραβιάζομαι was, first and foremost, a term associated with violent forcing or constraining, usually appearing in a military context.[100] When παραβιάζομαι was found in cases dealing with the zone of emotion-fused thought, it normally implied a forceful attempt to turn or break someone's decision, will, or values.[101]

---

98. Compare Acts 16 with Paul's being received by Onesiphorus when he and his traveling companions go to Iconium in The Acts of Paul and Thecla (second century CE). Onesiphorus (along with his wife and children) stations himself along the road to Lystra and scans the travelers looking for the Pauline group, going only by a description of Paul given to him by Titus, so that "he might receive him to his house" (Acts Paul 1–4, in Wilhelm Schneemelcher, ed., *New Testament Apocrypha*, trans. R. McL. Wilson, 2 vols. [Cambridge: Clarke, 1991], 2:353).

99. Some (e.g., Sterck-Degueldre, *Frau namens Lydia*, 172) argue that the aorist of παρακαλέω in Acts 16:15 infers success and confuse the call with the ratification of the call. The implicit notion of "would take no refusal" contained within a translation of "prevailed" leads to the following type of comments: "Paul had been very particular not to be a charge to the believers in cities where he went. He was perhaps unreasonably touchy on this point, but here he could not refuse. The stronger will of the well-to-do, peremptory, and hospitable woman [Lydia] prevailed" (Sabine Baring-Gould, *A Study of St. Paul: His Character and Opinions* [London: Ibister, 1897], 213, brackets added).

100. "Do a thing by force against nature or law; use violence" (LSJ, s.v. παραβιάζομαι).

101. "Like βία and its Sanskrit cognates, βιάζομαι always denotes a forced as distinct from a voluntary act. πείθειν is expressly contrasted with it.... Whether the reference is to compulsion by higher powers (nature or fate), or whether man compels himself or natural forces, there is always the effective achievement of an act of force or an attempt at such. In the rich use in relation to military action, maltreatment, compulsion of various kinds and even religious constraint, we can see clearly this basic sense of the exercise of hostile force" (Gottlob Schrenk, "βιάζομαι," *TDNT* 1:609).

The New Testament (Matt 11:12, Luke 16:16) employs the uncompounded βιάζομαι in two Q-derived theological passages dealing with taking or entering the kingdom of heaven by force.[102]

In a use not known to Greco-Roman literature, a social type of forcing was found in a few biblical cases where παραβιάζομαι, or its uncompounded form βιάζομαι/βιάζω, concerned the urging of a host upon a guest. A hospitality context for παραβιάζομαι is found in the Septuagint when Manoah urges the angel of the Lord to stay and have a meal in his home (Judg 13:15, 16 LXX). In the New Testament, παραβιάζομαι occurs only one time other than in Acts 16:15—in Luke 24:29. When the disciples from Emmaus invite Jesus in for the night, "they constrained [παρεβιάσαντο] him, saying, 'Stay with us'" (Luke 24:29).

Three other Old Testament cases find βιάζομαι or its cognates used by hosts: the doomed and terrified Saul is urged to eat by the witch of Endor and his servants (1 Sam 28:23 LXX), and the Levite in Judges is urged by his concubine's father to delay his departure and continue enjoying his father-in-law's hospitality (Judg 19:7 LXX). Notably, in both of these cases hospitality is a precursor to violence and death. Finally, a stranger-god type scene blends with the violent flavor of βιάζομαι when in Sodom Lot "urges" (κατεβιάζετο) the angels of the Lord to come and stay the night and the town's men "press hard against" (παρεβιάζοντο) the host, Lot, as they try to force their way into his home and attack his guests (Gen 19:3, 9 LXX).

Lydia's παραβιάζομαι links to the question of whether she will be assessed as being "faithful to the Lord." The form of Lydia's offer is essentially a call for judgment of Lydia's inner character. It is here that the use of παραβιάζομαι amplifies the relevant element from the social model of hospitality: hospitality implied a mutual evaluation between host and guest.

---

102. Matthew also has the noun βιαστής ("the violator, the man of force who achieves his desires by theft," Schrenk, *TDNT* 1:614). Some understand βιάζομαι as a "forceful invitation" into the kingdom of heaven rather than violence against the kingdom; for a summary of views, see Joseph A. Fitzmyer, *The Gospel according to Luke (X–XXIV): Introduction, Translation, and Notes*, AB 28A (Garden City, NY: Doubleday, 1985), 1117–18. Given the basic sense of violence contained by βιάζομαι, far likelier is Schrenk's interpretations that "refers the βιάζεσθαι to the enemies of the divine rule.... The meaning indicated by the βία is 'violently to assault the divine rule, and to rob those who come to it of its blessing'" (Schrenk, *TDNT* 1:613–14).

Andrew Arterbury's comprehensive study of the convention of hospitality depicted in Greco-Roman, Jewish, and early Christian literature finds that "the Greek stem of ξεν-, due to its association with the stranger, is the most common Greek semantic marker for Mediterranean hospitality."[103] An important social intertextural element of the stranger-host hospitality relationship is that "bystanders repeatedly judged the moral character of the host and the guest to be roughly equivalent,"[104] and therefore hospitality involved a mutual positive evaluation. As a result, any offer of hospitality required a mutual assessment of ethos between potential host and guest. As Malina and Pilch point out, once a stranger becomes the guest of a host, the honor of the stranger becomes "embedded in the honor of the host."[105]

One important clarification needs to be raised regarding the social model of hospitality—it assumes that both host and guest are men since hospitality as a social norm functioned between men. If a woman was present, she was not the host proper, but rather a wife or housekeeper who would tend to the men's meals and comforts in a gender-appropriate domestic fashion. A male stranger could not have his honor embedded in the honor of a female host since a woman, by definition, was not vested with her own honor; she could maintain the honor of her household's patriarch in which she herself was embedded only by protecting his honor from any potential shame.[106] Within the social model of hospitality, any male, by becoming a guest, "places himself in a non-male (actually quasi-female) situation in the household of the host."[107] If, on the other hand, a male were to become the guest of a female, the model suggests that his own honor would be assessed culturally as one level beyond female, perhaps to that of a slave.

If a high-status woman was a widow, or her husband was away at war, then it might be possible that she could respectfully act as host. But if so, then she implicitly would bear her family's honor, honor that would

---

103. Arterbury, *Entertaining Angels*, 187. I am also indebted to Arterbury for sharing with me his paper "The Case for the Custom of Hospitality in Ancient Narratives" (paper presented at the Annual Meeting of the Society of Biblical Literature, Washington, DC, 20 November 2006).
104. Arterbury, *Entertaining Angels*, 148.
105. Malina and Pilch, *Social-Science Commentary*, 215.
106. Malina, *New Testament World*, 48–51.
107. Malina and Pilch, *Social-Science Commentary*, 215.

remain defined through its lineage of men, where the stranger would still be considered a guest of the, albeit absent, male. For this reason, women who did not appear to be embedded in any man's honor, if they hosted a male guest, were presented as already transgressing social norms, and their "hosting" arrangements were marked not by social but rather alternate systems of exchange.

One example is the medium of Endor who hosts Saul before he goes off to his death. Like Lydia she too "urges" hospitality on her "guest" denoted by the verb παραβιάζομαι (1 Sam 28:23 LXX). The medium of Endor illustrates how the social model of hospitality cannot simply be invoked each time a guest or guests enter the house of another. Seeking out the medium, Saul is not a traveler looking for lodging; he is a desperate king looking to procure alternate forms of divine communication to help assuage his anxiety over the prospects of facing an attacking army. Saul is hosted by a woman who is "beyond the pale," because, at that point, he too has been ejected from his community and has accordingly had every vestige of honor stripped from him, as soon, too, will be his life. The underlying system of exchange between Saul and the medium is not the social model of hospitality, but rather a form of economic exchange whereby Saul puts the medium back in business by his visit (he had previously expelled all mediums), and she cements her future credentials by foretelling the death of a king. Both "host" and "guest" are devoid of honor from the perspective of prevailing social norms.

Another "hostess" is the prostitute Rahab, who lodges Joshua's spies in Jericho (Josh 2:1–21). Although she does have a father and brothers, from the perspective of the honor/shame model of social status, Rahab is "shameless" and devoid of honor through her role of prostitute, as is her entire family.[108] Once again, when men enter the home of a woman unsupported by a man's honor, it is not the social model of hospitality that governs the "hosting" arrangement, but rather economic and utilitarian exchange. Men visiting prostitutes are not "guests"; they are customers.

The spies, as outsiders, enter the one house that any man can enter freely. Notwithstanding New Testament portrayals of Rahab as one who has been "justified by works" (Jas 2:25) or as an exemplar of faith (Heb 11:31), she is depicted in Joshua primarily as someone who perceives that

---

108. "Certain families and institutions (e.g., husbands serving as pimps, first-century tavern and inn owners, actors, prostitutes as a group) are considered irretrievably shameless" (Malina, *New Testament World*, 51).

her city's rout is imminent (Josh 2:9) and accordingly strikes a bargain to ensure her family's security. Each side keeps its oath, and she and her family are relocated to the appropriate space for army prostitutes, on the outskirts of the army's camp (Josh 6:23). Despite the markers of hospitality—an overnight stay, a hostess protecting the security of her guests—the prevailing system of exchange is based on economic/military rather than social norms. Accordingly, a mutual assessment of social honor between host and guest does not apply to such a model. In its stead, a different form of mutual evaluation governs these exchanges; rather than gauging each other's honor, "host" and "guest" discern each other's capacity to fulfill their sides of the economic bargain.

Lydia, a potential "hostess" devoid of any man's honor, would present a significant challenge to the social honor of any male guest, even without the other elements of her rhetorical profile. Once again, Lydian ethnography helps to illuminate the depth of the chasm between a man's honor and a "hostess" like Lydia. Innkeeping too was closely connected with the Lydians,[109] and the term κάπηλος could, along with retailer, also mean tavern keeper or innkeeper. As Theophrastus emphasized in his character profiles, innkeepers were located squarely within the "shameless" category,[110] since inns typically lodged those who could not be hosted through either kinship or hospitality social relations and were renowned as places of drinking, prostitution, and general debauchery.

When Josephus recites the categories of "impure women" prohibited from marrying priests (Lev 21:7), he adds women who "gain their livelihood by hawking [καπηλείας] or innkeeping [πανδοκεύειν]" (*Ant.* 3.276 [Thackeray et al., LCL]).[111] In Josephus's list of profaned women, "hawking or innkeeping" represent two dimensions of a single category, apparently reflecting an understanding similar to the targum's, which "commonly translates the Hebrew *zonah* 'harlot' by the word *pundokita* (derived from the verb πανδοκεύειν)."[112] When Josephus retells the story of the prostitute Rahab (*Ant.* 5.7–15), he characterizes her home, which houses her whole household, as an inn (καταγώγιον), making Rahab an innkeeper.[113]

---

109. Kaletsch, "Lydia."
110. Recall that "shameless" means the incapacity to have concern for reputation.
111. See p. 143.
112. Josephus, *Jewish Antiquities, Books 1–4*, trans. Henry St. J. Thackeray, LCL (Cambridge: Harvard University Press, 1930), 450 n. b.
113. Rosenfeld, "Innkeeping in Jewish Society," 141–42.

This term for inn (καταγώγιον) is synonymous with πανδοκεῖον, and the πανδοκεύς, or at other times "host," was literally one who would take "all" into his or her home.[114] As a "hawker," Lydia's forceful, and seemingly persistent, offer to the Pauline group of men would have echoed with the type of aggressive behavior expected from the kind of woman who would take "all" into her house. Indeed, if the curious phrase εἰσῆλθον πρὸς τὴν Λυδίαν (Acts 16:40)—literally, "they went into the Lydian"—might seem to carry an ironic note of sexual innuendo, it likely does, for in the Septuagint such phrases do refer to sexual penetration.[115] Rather than "hostessing," Lydia's invitation to the we-group would far more evoke a frame of sexual "hucksterism."

4.2.8. Conclusion: Intertextural Analysis of Lydia

The intertextural analysis of Lydia's narrative attributes has uncovered that first-century readers would have seen Lydia through an interplay of elements found in Lydian ethnography, stereotypes of sellers, and purple's "degenerate" symbolism. Lydians were rhetorically depicted as carriers of the "Lydian disease" that led to a desire for sumptuous, immoral living. The profiling of Lydian women carried this stereotype into the sphere of sexual degeneracy and prostitution. Linked to the Lydian topos, Lydia's occupation of seller inferred deceptive moral character. Completing this network of elements was purple's symbolic association with corrupting luxury. From this blend, we can see that Lydia's cultural profile would have shaped her image into an immoral, huckstering, "harlot-type" figure.

Once the culturally contextualized image of Lydia comes into view, it becomes possible to appreciate just how highly incongruous her final descriptive attribute "worshiper of God" is with her Lydian purple-selling profile. The reader is left to wonder how to make sense of these two clashing yet juxtaposed images. Moreover, already a puzzling setting, the gathering of women by the river only grows in ambiguity when Lydia becomes its featured member. The literary echo of προσευχή as agonistic space becomes even more pronounced as a result.

---

114. Πανδοκεύτρια, the term for "hostess," was used metaphorically with φάλαινα for "sea-monster, ready to take all in" (LSJ, s.v. πανδοκεύτρια).

115. "In the Septuagint it [εἰσέρχομαι] is used for 19 Heb words. The sexual use is common as well as the local: εἰσέρχεσθαι πρὸς γυναῖκα, πρὸς ἄνδρα (Heb. בוא)" (Johannes Schneider, "Εἰσέρχομαι," TDNT 2:676).

When Lydia forcefully urges the Pauline group to come to her home, she only adds to her profile of impropriety. Hospitality was a social model between men and involved a mutual assessment of character and honor between host and guest. Here, instead, the audience would see a "shameless" woman pressing a group of men to come into her home. When Lydia asks the Pauline group to judge her fidelity to God within the form of her offer of hospitality, the reader would immediately appreciate the difficulty such a request would pose. Establishing criteria for assessing fidelity to God becomes the focal point of the ensuing episodes.

Fulfilling Lydia's request for evaluation in Acts 16:15, the Pauline group "stays" at Lydia's and encourages those assembled there to stay in faith (16:40). I will show in the next section that the call of the Macedonian man would have been understood from within the language of military aid and alliances. Strikingly, no reader could have possibly guessed that the type of military alliance that the Macedonian's call for aid would have produced would have been an alliance with a Lydian woman. Yet once we become aware of Lydia's physiognomic profile, then we can begin to negotiate the rhetorical progressive texture of this passage by examining how other key topoi interact with those of Lydia the Lydian purple seller.

4.3. Paul's Vision of the Macedonian Man: Military Topoi

In the upcoming sections, I will show that, first and foremost, Paul's vision would have been located by early audiences within a military-discourse frame.[116] By military discourse, I mean a rhetorical mode of discourse that concerns the motives, strategies, and responses of leaders, their advisors, and their fighting units to an expectation of violent confrontation between groups of people, as well as the events of these confrontations, for example, battles, sieges, and their outcomes. We can identify the presence of military discourse when we see a conglomeration of some of the following types of topoi: warriors, arms, armies/navies, military campaigns, battles/warfare, military supplies, victory/defeat, and allies/enemies.

Much as Lydia's profile is shaped by a conglomeration of elements that work together to form rhetographically powerful topoi, so too the military backdrop to Paul's vision comes into view only through the interplay of

---

116. The term "frame" is understood as an organizing structure for the elements found within it; see p. 61.

the elements associated with the vision and the we-group's response to it. Only by way of standing together do the elements evoked by Paul's vision group into a military-discourse frame. I will visit each of these operative elements in turn in the following sections.

The presence of military discourse would not be unexpected; in fact its absence would be suspect in ancient historiography. As J. E. Lendon put it so accurately: "War eclipses all other subjects in the classical historians."[117] Moreover, war had its own mode of discourse, and as Lendon astutely points out, it was a rhetorical mode that reflected culture as much as, or perhaps more than, it reflected the actual events of the battlefield.[118] In fact, as Lendon explains, "The way ancient authors describe the details of battle can tell us about the mental rigging of the societies in which they lived."[119]

A subset of military discourse might be considered to be "holy war" discourse. Holy war discourse concerns violent confrontation on a cosmic scale that is expected to lead to eschatological victory between those who are characterized as divinely sanctioned "righteous" and the forces of evil. In addition to those topoi that might be found in military discourse generally, holy war discourse is evidenced by the following kinds of topoi: warrior god (directly and/or through agency), holiness/righteousness, judgment/punishment, evil/corruption, and eschatological end times. By evoking a military-discourse frame through the network of elements associated with Paul's vision, Luke draws on messianic "holy war" expectations that, evidenced by the disciples' hopeful question "Lord, will you at this time restore the kingdom to Israel?" (Acts 1:6), have permeated Acts from its opening chapter.[120]

As I will discuss further in chapter 5, "Ideological Texture," it is especially such topoi of "expectations" inherently found in holy war discourse that are used rhetorically in Luke-Acts. Luke's concern for the means of

---

117. J. E. Lendon, "The Rhetoric of Combat: Greek Military Theory and Roman Culture in Julius Caesar's Battle Descriptions," *ClAnt* 18 (1999): 273.
118. Ibid., 275.
119. Ibid.
120. For an investigation of the "holy war" topos in Luke-Acts, see L. Gregory Bloomquist and Priscilla Geisterfer Nyvlt, "Rhetorical Strategies for 'Holy War' in Some Second Temple Texts: Overview, Analysis, and Implications" (paper presented at Rhetorics, Violence, and Evil conference, University of Redlands, Redlands, CA, 23–24 January 2004).

salvific victory is at the heart of the discourse inaugurated by Paul's vision. It provides the rhetorical force that generates a dialectical tension between victory achieved and victory yet to be realized.[121] We have seen the author develop this dialectical tension throughout Luke-Acts. In the Gospel of Luke, for example, Jesus frames the decision-making process as to whether to commit to discipleship in terms of a king taking stock of his military strength and gauging the chances of his army's success in battle (Luke 14:31–33). Yet as Jesus argues, strength in discipleship will come from "renouncing all," and "success" will involve a willingness to follow Jesus to the cross. We will see that the episode in Philippi elaborates this contrast between conventionally expected means of battle and benefits of military victory and the means and outcome of God's salvific victory.

From within this trajectory of anticipated salvific victory, we shall see how Luke continues to draw on a gentile topos in the rhetorical unit, a topos that evidences apocalyptic discourse and that has been recurrent throughout Luke-Acts.[122] Although the episode with Cornelius explicitly engages with the role of the gentile topos, Luke 7:1–10 foreshadows the breakthrough with Cornelius and forms part of the trajectory of argu-

---

121. Some commentators have missed the dialectical argumentation that the blend of frames evoked by Paul's vision puts into motion. John Miller points to the work of Alfred Wikenhauser as representative of interpretations that see Paul's vision as a call to Alexander-style conquest: "Wikenhauser compares Luke's description of Paul's vision to those attributed to a number of key historical figures. He discusses the visionary impetus of Alexander described by Josephus (*Ant.* 11.322–339), and also the apparition that compelled Julius Caesar to cross the Rubicon (Suetonius, *Jul.* 32).... He likens Paul to Alexander and Caesar, and Paul's vision and its result to those of Alexander and Caesar. In this analysis, Paul's crossing into Macedonia takes on the monumental importance of Alexander's conquest of the East and Caesar's decision to claim power in Rome" (John B. Faulkenberry Miller, *Convinced That God Had Called Us*, 68–69; see Alfred Wikenhauser, "Religionsgeschichtliche Parallelen zu Apg 16, 9," *BZ* 23 [1935–1936]: 180–86). The rhetorical effect of the blended military frames will be discussed in chapter 5, "Ideological Texture."

122. For Luke's rhetorical use of gentile topoi in apocalyptic discourse found in Luke-Acts, see L. Gregory Bloomquist, "Rhetorical Argumentation and the Culture of Apocalyptic: A Socio-rhetorical Analysis of Luke 21," in *The Rhetorical Interpretation of Scripture: Essays from the 1996 Malibu Conference*, ed. Stanley E. Porter and Dennis L. Stamps (Sheffield: Sheffield Academic, 1999), 173–209; Bloomquist, "The Intertexture of Lukan Apocalyptic Discourse," in *The Intertexture of Apocalyptic Discourse in the New Testament*, ed. Duane F. Watson, SymS 14 (Atlanta: Society of Biblical Literature, 2002), 45–68; Bloomquist, "Role of the Audience," 157–73.

mentation involving universal access to salvation that employs gentile and military topoi in Luke-Acts. The centurion, introduced in the narrative through his relationship to the Jewish community, humbles himself and calls Jesus by the honorific "lord." In response, Jesus asserts that he has never found such faith "even in Israel." In this manner, Luke inductively frames the Roman military leader as a "faithful Israelite" and hints at what will become explicit in Acts. In Acts 10:1–48, Peter's encounter with Cornelius punctuates the narrative's development of the topos of universal access to salvation and provides a jarring, visual image of the topos. It is in the subsequent chapters, however, including those that take place in Macedonia, that we begin to see evidence of the fuller implications of this universal access. Gentiles will be seen to be not merely recipients of salvation but also increasingly to be members of the salvific community that *mediates* that very salvation. With the we-group's entry into Philippi, Luke will emphasize this growing shift to gentile territory through his use of particularly Hellenistic, Greek, and Roman elements in the rhetorical unit.

4.3.1. Topos of Troas: Military Launching Point

The Pauline group's sweep through a large swath of geographic territory on its approach to Troas followed by a Hellespont sea crossing resonates with historiographic descriptions of the movement of armies. Troas, the location for Paul's vision, evoked other legendary Hellespont crossings between East and West within military campaigns. Not only was Troas legendary from Homer's account of the Trojan War, but also significantly it was located at a natural crossing point bridging East and West, where such crossings featured regularly in expansionary military campaigns.[123] For example, Alexander the Great enjoyed his first military success in a battle at Troas after crossing over from Macedonia, gaining his foothold in Asia.[124] As a result of its prominence in Homer's epics and its historic, strategic, geographic location, Troas developed a conventional association with military campaigns and was also known as a site of "numerous tombs of heroes."[125]

---

123. Herodotus lists the Phrygians, Macedonians, Lydians, Mysians, and Bithynians in his catalog of armies and navies mobilized by Persian king Xerxes in his crossing of the Hellespont (*Hist.* 7.73–75).

124. "Troas," *ODCW*.

125. Jennifer K. Berenson, "The Allusive Man of Macedonia" (paper presented at the Annual Meeting of the Society of Biblical Literature, Boston, 24 November 2008).

4.3.2. The Macedonian Topos

The Macedonian identity of Paul's visionary visitor is highly significant. Discussions about Macedonia in ancient writing most commonly featured "kings and conquests," where two of the most famous Macedonians were Philip II and his son, Alexander the Great.[126] Moreover, Alexander continued to loom large in writers' imaginations in early antiquity, and audiences would have naturally associated a militarily configured Macedonian male, if not with Alexander specifically, then at least with that of an Alexander-type warrior (see Plutarch, *De Alexandri magni fortuna aut virtute*; Arrian, *Anabasis*; Josephus, *Ant.* 11.304–347).[127] The close link between Macedonians and warriors is well illustrated in Josephus's description of a fighting unit that was self-named "the Macedonians" not due to their ethnicity but rather to how they were "armed and trained in the Macedonian fashion." When this unit was unsuccessful in its affront on Jerusalem, Josephus sardonically concluded that "even genuine Macedonians, if they are to conquer, must have Alexander's fortune [τύχης]" (Josephus, *J.W.* 5.465 [Thackeray et al., LCL]).

The appearance of a Macedonian man, when framed within military discourse, distinctly evoked powerful warriors. Moreover, the conquering warrior image evoked by the Macedonian further develops through Philippi's name. The city's moniker came from Philip II, father of Alexander the Great, after he subsumed the former Crenides under his growing dominion.[128] It was the site of two battles in 42 BCE when Octavian and Mark Antony defeated Cassius and Brutus, subsequent to which it was made a Roman colony, and following Octavian's defeat of Antony in 31

---

126. Robert Malcolm Errington, "Macedonia, Macedones," *BNP*.

127. While several commentators have mentioned a possible link between Paul's vision in Acts 16 and Josephus's account of Alexander the Great's at Dium, Bloomquist has more closely focused on the possibility of a correspondence in a work dedicated to the issue. Points of resonance between Alexander's vision and Paul's include Alexander's Macedonian identity, each seeing a man, each vision needing interpretation, and each vision being interpreted as a divine commission requiring a sea crossing between Asia and Macedonia. See L. Gregory Bloomquist, "A Parallel to Paul's Vision in Acts 16:9?" (unpublished paper, 2008). I am indebted to Bloomquist for sharing his insights regarding Paul's vision and Alexander's.

128. "This seems to be the first instance of the practice, later so common, of naming cities for a king" (Diodorus of Sicily, *Library of History*, trans. C. H. Oldfather et al., 12 vols., LCL [Cambridge: Harvard University Press, 1933–1967], 7:243 n. 5).

BCE (battle of Actium), renamed Colonia Julia Augusta Philippensis after Augustus's daughter.[129]

4.3.3. Topos of Sanctioning Dream-Visions

Paul's dream-vision might fall into one of two common dream-vision categories: salvific and political/military. Salvific dream-visions concerned the rescue of an individual or a people from imminent or potential harm. Such salvific dream-visions, notes Bloomquist, "dramatically narrate divine interventions to save or safeguard holy places."[130] More generally, salvific dream-visions concerned the rescue of an individual or a people under divine favor from imminent or potential harm. An example of individual rescue includes a dream-vision warning issued to Themistocles from "the Mother of the Gods," which thwarts a plot against his life (Plutarch, *Them.* 30).[131] In the normal course of events, it was the dreamer who either individually, or along with his or her community, benefited from rescue from danger. In Paul's case, however, not only will Paul the dreamer be physically harmed in Philippi, but also, as I will discuss in ideological texture, his prison experience will be marked by "stay" rather than rescue. Salvation will feature in Paul's dream-vision, but it will do so by blending with other elements, most notably with the element of εὐαγγέλιον. The element of salvation *will* be introduced through the we-group's interpretation of Paul's dream-vision but not by the dream-vision itself.

Prior to its interpretation, Paul's dream-vision most closely resembled other similar messenger dream-visions involving a man or woman who stood over a general or political leader and encouraged the dreamer's next decisive steps. Authors such as Herodotus commonly recounted how a general or a statesman was moved to take military action, often constituting the next step in a campaign, on the basis of information conveyed through a dream-vision. For example, the Persian king Xerxes is visited by a vision of "a tall and goodly [εὐειδής] man" who urges an attack on the

---

129. Joseph H. Hellerman, *Reconstructing Honor in Roman Philippi: Carmen Christi as Cursus Pudorum*, SNTSMS 132 (Cambridge: Cambridge University Press, 2005), 65.
130. Bloomquist, "Parallel to Paul's Vision," 13.
131. "The Mother of the Gods" refers to "Rhea, Cybele, Magna Mater, called also Dindymené from Mount Dindymon, Phrygia" (*Plutarch*, trans. Bernadotte Perrin et al., 28 vols. LCL [Cambridge: Harvard University Press, 1914–2004], 2:83 n. 1).

Greeks (Herodotus, *Hist.* 7.12). Suetonius describes how a vision assuaged Caesar's doubt before he decided to take action against Pompey.

> On a sudden there appeared hard by a being of wondrous stature and beauty, who sat and played upon a reed; and when not only the shepherds flocked to hear him, but many of the soldiers left their posts, and among them some of the trumpeters, the apparition snatched a trumpet from one of them, rushed to the river, and sounding the war-note with mighty blast, strode to the opposite bank. Then Caesar cried: "Take we the course which the signs of the gods and the false dealing of our foes point out. The die is cast," said he. Accordingly, crossing with his army.... (Suetonius, *Jul.* 32–33 [Rolfe, LCL])

Such dream-visions moved a leader to action expressly because the dreamer anticipated divine support.[132]

Visions communicated divine sanction and, as a result of this perceived divine support, strengthened the courage of leaders and/or troops. Alexander, who is usually depicted as receiving visions and/or oracles that simply affirm his own prior decisions, nonetheless is "further persuaded" in his plan to attack Tyre by a dream-vision of Hercules stretching out his right hand and "conducting him into the city" (Arrian, *Anab.* 2.18.1 [Brunt, LCL]). Even authors who did not give credence to dream-visions nonetheless related them as a conventional element used by leaders to strengthen the courage and resolve of their warriors. Polybius (who personally scoffed at the credibility of dream-visions; *Frag.* 21) relates that when the Roman general Scipio wished to rally his troops, he first outlined the benefits of success and then promised rewards to those who displayed acts of courage, ending with the assurance "that it was Neptune [Poseidon] who had first suggested this plan to him, appearing to him in his sleep,

---

132. Dream-visions are covered by Cicero in a list of topoi dealing with divine testimony: "The testimony of the gods is covered thoroughly enough by the following: first, utterances, for oracles get their name from the fact that they contain an utterance [*oratio*] of the gods; secondly, things in which are embodied certain works of the gods. First, the heavens themselves and all their order and beauty; secondly, the flight of birds through the air and their songs; thirdly, sounds and flashes of fire from the heavens, and portents given by many objects on earth, as well as the foreshadowing of events which is revealed by the entrails (of sacrificial animals). Many things also are revealed by visions seen in sleep. The testimony of the gods is at times adduced from these topics *in order to win conviction*" (Cicero, *Top.* 20.77 [Miller et al., LCL], emphasis original).

and promising that when the time for the action came he would render such conspicuous aid that his intervention would be manifest to the whole army" (*Hist.* 10.11.7–8 [Paton, LCL]). Scipio's persuasive speech generated the intended effect: "great enthusiasm and ardour" in the troops (*Hist.* 10.11.7). Biblically, we have the example of Judas Maccabeus, who encouraged his troops by recounting a vision.

> Onias, who had been high priest … was praying with outstretched hands for the whole body of the Jews. Then likewise a man appeared, distinguished by his gray hair and dignity, and of marvelous majesty and authority. And Onias spoke, saying, "This is a man who loves the brethren and prays much for the people and the holy city, Jeremiah, the prophet of God." Jeremiah stretched out his right hand and gave to Judas a golden sword, and as he gave it he addressed him thus: "Take this holy sword, a gift from God, with which you will strike down your adversaries." (2 Macc 15:12–16)

As a final example, Plutarch describes a dream-vision that the Roman general Lucullus experienced at Troas that immediately prompted his setting out to sea for battle.

> Lucullus, in the first place, entered Cyzicus in triumph, and enjoyed the pleasant welcome which was his due; then he proceeded to the Hellespont, and began to equip a fleet. On visiting the Troad, he pitched his tent in the sacred precinct of Aphrodite, and in the night, after he had fallen asleep, he thought he saw the goddess standing over him and saying: "Why dost thou sleep, great lion? The fawns are near for the taking." Rising up from sleep and calling his friends, he narrated to them his vision, while it was yet night. And lo, there came certain men from Ilium, with tidings that thirteen of the king's galleys had been seen off the harbour of the Achaeans, making for Lemnos. Accordingly, Lucullus put to sea at once. (Plutarch, *Luc.* 12.1–3 [Perrin et al., LCL])

As these examples illustrate, dream-visions in a political/military context all functioned in a similar manner: they inferred divine sanction for the vision, and as a result they helped to fortify the courage of a leader and/or troops and thus moved a leader to take immediate military action.

Judas Maccabeus's address to his troops in 2 Macc 15 provides an excellent biblical illustration of how a military leader could blend good news of past victories with an expectation of divine help, supported by a divine vision, in order to ready his troops for battle. Judas, confident "that he would get help from the Lord," "exhorted [παρεκάλει] his men not to fear the attack of the Gentiles, but to keep in mind the former times when help [βοηθήματα] had come to them from heaven, and now to look for the victory which the Almighty would give them" (2 Macc 15:7–8). Buoyed by the promise of divine help, the courage of the troops was aroused (2 Macc 15:9). Building on this, Maccabeus moved on to the standard warrant of divine favor accorded to military leaders—the divinely sent dream-vision (2 Macc 15:12–16). Judas's address to his men garners the expected response: "Encouraged by the words of Judas, so noble and effective in arousing valor and awaking manliness [i.e., courage] in the souls of the young, they determined not to carry on a campaign but to attack bravely, and to decide the matter, by fighting hand to hand with all courage" (2 Macc 15:17). The result of the battle is victory for Judas's army.

Accounts of divine salvation were as common in Greek and Roman culture, and elements of divine favor and promises of victory worked in similar manner transculturally. Josephus offers an illustrative and fascinating example of how the framework of divine salvation from military conflict functioned panculturally as he interweaves his own version of the account of Jerusalem's rescue from the Assyrians together with Old Testament accounts, a story from Herodotus, and an account from Berosus.[133] Three accounts in the Old Testament (2 Kgs 18–19; 2 Chr 32:1–23; Isa 36–37) tell of the threat of a looming attack from Assyrian king Sennacherib facing Judah's king Hezekiah. Hezekiah relies on the courage-inducing anticipation of God's salvific intervention.

> He set combat commanders over the people, and gathered them together to him in the square at the gate of the city and spoke encouragingly to them,[134] saying, "Be strong and of good courage. Do not be afraid or dismayed before the king of Assyria and all the horde that is with him; for there is one greater with us than with him. With him is an arm of flesh; but with us is the Lord our God, to help us and to fight our battles." And the people took confidence from the words of Hezekiah king of Judah. (2 Chr 32:6–8)

---

133. "Priest of Bēl/Marduk, contemporary of Alexander the Great's, author of Chaldean history in three volumes for Antiochus 1" (Beate Pongratz-Leisten, "Berosus," *BNP*).

134. The idiom used in the LXX is literally "spoke into their hearts" (ἐλάλησεν ἐπὶ καρδίαν) and functions as a synonym of παρακαλέω.

In each version, Sennacherib mocks the ability of God to rescue his people and points out that no one else's gods have managed to stave off the Assyrian advance. Hezekiah prays to God for help (2 Kgs 19:14–19; 2 Chr 32:20; Isa 37:14–20), and in response God sends "an angel of the Lord" to rout the Assyrian army, leaving Sennacherib to withdraw in defeat.[135]

Josephus refers to Hezekiah's deliverance in *Jewish Antiquities* but varies the Old Testament accounts. In Josephus, Sennacherib retreats upon hearing that "Tharsikēs, the king of Ethiopia, was coming to the aid of the Egyptians with a large force and had decided to make the journey through the desert and fall upon the Assyrians suddenly" (*Ant.* 10.17 [Thackeray, LCL]). According to Josephus, it is the news of auxiliary military aid that delivers the people. However, careful not to supplant the divine element entirely, Josephus blends the Old Testament account with a story told by Herodotus of the deliverance of the Egyptian pharaoh from Assyrian attack and then follows this with an account from Berosus.

In Herodotus's version, the Egyptian pharaoh Sethos had earlier alienated the Egyptian warriors. When Sennacherib marches his army against the Egyptians, the Egyptian warriors refuse to form an army (expressed though language of βοηθέω: οὔκων δὴ ἐθέλειν τοὺς μαχίμους τῶν Αἰγυπτίων Βοηθέειν). Sethos goes into his temple, cries to the god (Ptah/Hephaestus),[136] where, falling asleep, in a vision he sees

> the god standing over him and bidding him take courage [θαρσύνειν], for he should suffer no ill by encountering the host of Arabia: "Myself,"

---

135. "That very night the angel of the Lord set out and struck down one hundred eighty-five thousand in the camp of the Assyrians; when morning dawned, they were all dead bodies" (2 Kgs 19:35); "And the Lord sent an angel who cut off all the mighty warriors and commanders and officers in the camp of the king of Assyria" (2 Chr 32:21); "Then the angel of the Lord set out and struck down one hundred eighty-five thousand in the camp of the Assyrians; when morning dawned, they were all dead bodies" (Isa 37:36).

136. The god in question is the Egyptian god Ptah, "an ancient deity of Memphis, creator of the universe, god of artisans, and husband of Sekhmet" ("Ptah," in *The Oxford Dictionary of English*, ed. Catherine Soanes and Angus Stevenson, rev. ed. [Oxford: Oxford University Press, 2005]), who was known by the Greeks as Hephaestus (the name used in Herodotus's account), the Greek god of fire, artisans, and blacksmiths (Fritz Graf, "Hephaestus," in *The Oxford Companion to Classical Civilization*, ed. Simon Hornblower and Antony Spawforth [Oxford: Oxford University Press, 1998]).

said the god, "will send you champions [τιμωρούς]."¹³⁷ So he trusted the vision, and encamped at Pelusium with such Egyptians as would follow him, for here is the road into Egypt; and none of the warriors would go with him, but only hucksters [καπήλους] and artificers [χειρώνακτας] and traders [ἀγοραίους]. Their enemies too came thither, and one night a multitude of fieldmice swarmed over the Assyrian camp and devoured their quivers and their bows and the handles of their shields likewise, insomuch that they fled the next day unarmed and many fell. And at this day a stone statue of the Egyptian king stands in Hephaestus' temple, with a mouse in his hand, and an inscription to this effect: "Look on me, and fear the gods [εὐσεβὴς ἔστω]." (*Hist.* 2.141 [Godley, LCL])

Josephus situates Herodotus's story within the Assyrian advance on Judah and reconfigures Herodotus's version, which speaks of the Egyptian ruler crying out to Hephaestus/Ptah, and instead has the pharaoh cry out to God, who then harkens to his prayer by sending the mice (*Ant.* 10.18–19). Herodotus's account is then followed by Berosus's (no extant version remains), which claimed that the 180,000 Assyrians fell due to a "pestilential sickness" that had been visited on them by God (*Ant.* 10.21). Josephus finishes off by noting the requisite thanksgiving for salvation and referring to God as a military ally: "Having been thus wonderfully delivered from the fate which he feared, King Hezekiah together with all the people offered sacrifices of thanksgiving to God, for the destruction of some of the enemy and the removal of the rest from Jerusalem had no other cause than the aid given by their ally God" (*Ant.* 10.24–25 [Thackeray et al., LCL]). By telling his own version of the Old Testament accounts along with Herodotus's Sethos story and Berosus's version, Josephus manages to distance the cause of the salvation from a purely miraculous supernatural intervention without removing the divine salvific element entirely.

Paul's dream-vision begins as a military/political dream-vision, and once the we-group characterizes it as a call from God to convey "good news," the element of anticipated divine support becomes more pronounced.¹³⁸ Without the we-group's interpretation of Paul's dream-vision

---

137. More accurately, "defenders" or "avengers."

138. Shaye Cohen proposes three means of soteriological divine military intervention: "The gods could personally participate in the battle (e.g., the Dioscuri might temporarily assume human form and join the ranks of the victorious army); natural and supernatural phenomena could be turned against the enemy (e.g., lightening, thunder, rainstorm, boulders from heaven and so forth); or less commonly, the god

as a call from God to announce "good news," the visionary experience of a Macedonian man's call lacked the requisite divine element. When the call of the Macedonian is coupled with a perceived call from God through the element of εὐαγγελίζομαι, however, the sense of divine involvement expands from a dream-vision's sanctioning agent to a participating warrior-God who intervenes directly. When the Pauline group sets off to Philippi, they do so not only with the expectation of divine favor but also, through the military frame contextualizing εὐαγγελίζομαι, of a manifestation of divine victory. When instead Paul and Silas will find themselves beaten and publicly dishonored, the rather delicate issue of how it is they can claim divine salvation without clear signs of victory, an issue that confronted Christianity from its earliest inception, will become a pressing concern.

4.3.4. Topos of Military Call for Aid

The Macedonian man's plea for "help," βοηθέω, which "starts from the military sense, so common in Greek historians,"[139] triggers a swift sea crossing and emphasizes its etymological origin—"to run on a call to help."[140] In fact, in the narrative of the Macedonian's request to Paul two terms are used, παρακαλέω, "to call to one's side," and βοηθέω, which were exceedingly common to the point of being formulaic, either together or separately, in requests for support of military campaigns. Polybius's account of a number of peoples calling for Philip V of Macedon's military help during the First Macedonian War is representative of many such accounts using these terms.

> The Aetolians ... were terrorizing and threatening everyone by land while the Romans and Attalus were doing the same by sea. The Achae-

---

might appear in a dream either to the pious defenders (with a message of encouragement or advice) or to the insolent aggressors (with a message of warning)" (Shaye J. D. Cohen, "Alexander the Great and Jaddus the High Priest according to Josephus," *AJSR* 7.8 [1982–1983]: 49). The first two of Cohen's categories can be accepted as proposed, but the third unwittingly slips away from the means through which divine salvation is effected to forms of divine encouragement. Direct salvific divine intervention that was salvific in and of itself needs to be distinguished from divine intervention that acted upon human participants as a motivating force. I am indebted to Bloomquist's "Parallel to Paul's Vision" for directing me to Cohen's work.

139. "βοηθέω," MM, s.v.
140. Friedrich Büchsel, "βοηθέω," *TDNT* 1:628.

ans therefore came to Philip to beg [παρακαλοῦντες] for his help [βοηθεῖν], for they were not only in dread of the Aetolians but of Machanidas, as he was hovering with his army on the Argive frontier. The Boeotians, who were afraid of the enemy's fleet, begged [ᾔτουν] for a commander and for succour [βοήθειαν], but the inhabitants of Euboea were the most energetic of all in their instances to Philip to take precautions against the enemy. The Acarnanians made the same request.... The Aetolians also had occupied the pass of Thermopylae ... feeling sure that they thus shut out Philip and prevented him from coming to help [παραβοηθεῖν] his allies beyond the pass. (*Hist.* 10.41.1–6 [Paton, LCL])[141]

From this perspective of divinely assisted military victory, we see Josephus recount 2 Sam 18:19, 28.

Then Achimas, the son of the high priest Sadok, went to Joab and asked him for permission to go and announce the victory to David and bring him the good news [εὐαγγελίσασθαι] that he had obtained help [τοῦ θεοῦ βοηθείας] and guidance from God.... Achimas appeared and did obeisance to the king, and, in answer to his inquiry about the battle, announced the welcome news of a decisive victory [νίκην εὐαγγελίζεται καὶ κράτος]. (*Ant.* 7.245, 250 [Thackeray et al., LCL])

The Septuagint also includes examples of βοηθέω in requests for military aid.

So King Adoni-bezec king of Jerusalem sent to Elam king of Hebron, and to Phidon king of Jerimuth, and to Jeptha king of Lachis, and to Dabin king of Odollam, saying, "Come up and help me [δεῦτε ἀνάβητε πρός με καὶ βοηθήσατέ μοι], and let us take Gabaon; for the Gabaonites have gone over to Joshua and to the children of Israel." (Josh 10:3–4 LXX)

Due to its military frame, the Macedonian's call evoked a specific type of request: "send fortifying support for a military campaign." It was not a

---

141. A sample of cases where βοηθέω refers to military aid and support includes Thucydides (ca. 455–400 BCE), *P.W.* 5.67.3, 4, 6; 68.2; Plutarch, *Per.* 29.1, 2, 3; *Arat.* 49.2; Polybius, *Hist.* 2.51.1; Herodotus, *Hist.* 5.89 (now at the Thebans' call [ἐπικαλεομένων] the Aeginetans came readily to the aid [ἐβοήθεον] of the Boeotians); Herodotus, *Hist.* 7.145 ("praying aid for Hellas," κελεύσοντας βοηθέειν τῇ Ἑλλάδι); Josephus, *J.W.* 4.229; *Life* 287–288.

general call for "help" or rescue as might come from a drowning person or from a city that has been struck by a natural disaster.

Typically, the requisitioned lack involved material or human resources, such as food, troops, arms, ships, or any other goods, or fighting men that the party involved in the conflict was deficient in.[142] By responding positively to a call, the respondent concurrently entered into alliance with the party calling, so that in most cases a call for aid was also a de facto call for alliance. To render "joint aid," συμβοηθέω, meant to ally in combat, making military "help" synonymous with "alliance." One such example is found in 1 Kgs 21:16 LXX, where English translations (1 Kgs 20:16) alternately refer to the collective of thirty-two kings who, together with "their horses and chariots," fought alongside King Ben-hadad of Aram as "those who helped [συμβοηθοί] him" (RSV) or "those who allied with him" (NRSV). Responding in "help" drew the respondent together with the caller into a military alliance.[143]

Military alliances, even in times of peace, were highly focused on delineating between friend and enemy. Most especially, military calls for aid, being in their essence calls for resources, were acutely concerned with dedicating the sought-after resources to friends and withholding them from common enemies. For example, according to Josephus, when Alexander calls to the Jewish high priest for fortifying aid in support of his siege of Tyre, his call explicitly also demands a shift of alliance.

> And Alexander, coming to Syria, took Damascus, became master of Sidon and besieged Tyre; from there he dispatched a letter to the high priest of the Jews, requesting him to send him assistance [συμμαχίαν] and supply his army with provisions and give him the gifts which they had formerly sent as tribute to Darius, thus choosing the friendship of the Macedonians, for, he said, they would not regret this course. But the high priest replied to the bearers of the letter that he had given his oath to Darius not to take up arms against him and said that he would never

---

142. One example is found in the Sicilian Gelon's response to a Greek call for help: "I am ready to send to your aid [βοηθέειν] two hundred triremes [war ships], twenty thousand men-at-arms, two thousand horse, two thousand archers, two thousand slingers, and two thousand light-armed men to run with horsemen; and I undertake that I will furnish provision for the whole Greek army till we have made an end of the war" (Herodotus, *Hist.* 7.158 [Godley, LCL]).

143. For συμβοηθός; συμβοηθέω; συμβοήθεια, see also Thucydides, *P.W.* 2.82.1; 3.105.2; Xenophon, *Ages.* 1.38.

violate this oath so long as Darius remained alive. (*Ant.* 11.317-318 [Thackeray et al., LCL])

In another example, Croesus, in his war with Cyrus, intends to "invite help from the Egyptians [παρακαλέσας μὲν Αἰγυπτίους] in fulfillment of their pledge (for before making an alliance [συμμαχίη] with the Lacedaemonians he had made one also with Amasis king of Egypt)" (Herodotus, *Hist.* 1.77 [Godley, LCL]). So tightly clustered were elements of military aid and alliance that the term for alliance—συμμαχέω—could also mean military aid or help, as it does in Alexander's call above, whereas the noun συμμαχία could even more directly mean "allied or auxiliary force."[144] Military help and military alliance were simply two sides of the same coin.[145] Responses to calls for military aid defined who was friend and who was enemy in a conflict, since in delivering aid a party also allied itself with the petitioner. The Macedonian man calls for aid in language reminiscent of numerous calls for help in military and political initiatives.[146]

---

144. LSJ, s.v. συμμαχέω, συμμαχία. Two examples from Josephus: "When Jerusalem, our capital, was besieged, and the Temple, which was common to us all, was in danger of falling into the enemy's hands, they sent no assistance [συμμαχίαν οὐκ ἔπεμψαν], wishing to avoid all suspicion of having borne arms against the Romans" (*Life* 348 [Thackeray et al., LCL]); "After he [Senacheirimos] had spent a great deal of time on the siege of Pelusium, and the earthworks which he was raising against the walls had already reached a great height, and he was on the point of attacking, he heard that Tharsikēs, the king of Ethiopia, was coming to the aid of the Egyptians with a large force [πολλὴν ἄγοντα δύναμιν ἐπὶ συμμαχίᾳ τοῖς Αἰγυπτίοις] and had decided to make the journey through the desert and fall upon the Assyrians suddenly" (*Ant.* 10.17 [Thackeray et al., LCL]).

145. Examples of alliance interwoven with military aid can also be found in the Old Testament and LXX: "Your wives, your little ones, and your livestock shall remain in the land that Moses gave you beyond the Jordan. But all the warriors among you shall cross over armed before your kindred and shall help them [συμμαχήσετε αὐτοῖς]" (Josh 1:14). "They helped [συνεμάχησαν] David against the band of raiders for they were all warriors and commanders in the army" (1 Chr 12:21; 12:22 LXX). "Now then you will do well to send me men who will help me [συμμαχήσουσίν μοι], for all my troops have revolted" (1 Macc 11:43). "And Simon sent to Antiochus two thousand picked men, to fight for him [συμμαχῆσαι], and silver and gold and much military equipment" (1 Macc 15:26).

146. Discovering intertexturally that fortification and alliance constitute the two key elements of the Macedonian's call complements the findings of innertextural analysis that the παρακαλέω progressive sequence, which begins with the call in Acts 16:9, is the unit's foundational progression as well as its unusually high concentration of

4.3.5. Topos of Strengthening Courage by Expectation of Victory (Εὐαγγέλιον)

Calls for military aid were interested in the physical material stuff of war, and yet, most unconventionally, the we-group makes ready to respond to such a call by supplying self-expressive speech ("proclaim the good news to them": Acts 16:10). This unusual response of a nonmaterial resource will be the subject of ideological texture, but for the purposes of intertexture, it is important to recognize that one form of self-expressive speech, εὐαγγελίζομαι, not only appeared regularly in military discourse but also performed a military function. Its most common usage in Hebrew, Greek, and Hellenistic-Jewish texts related to "'bringing news of victory' or 'declaring a victory'" of battle, as, for example, "many ... sailed to Cornelia in Lesbos with the glad tidings [εὐαγγελιζόμενοι] that the war was at end" (Plutarch, *Pomp.* 66.3).[147] From a military understanding, εὐαγγελίζομαι was a term first and foremost associated with news of military victory or, at a minimum, of a fortunate turn of affairs in a conflict involving leaders. As well, εὐαγγελίζομαι frequently concerned the news of either the downfall of an enemy or competitor, the victory of a leader, or other news fortunate to a military campaign,[148] and so too did the nouns εὐαγγέλιον/εὐαγγέλια, which could also refer to a thanks offering to a divinity or a reward given to a messenger of the fortunate news.[149]

If the conflict was still ongoing, then the εὐαγγέλιον often helped to fortify the courage of troops, an effect some leaders exploited to the point of fabricating false accounts of "good news" in order to keep their men in fighting spirits.[150] For example, when Agesilaus learned that one of his

---

ἔρχομαι-prefixed verbs. Coming together and separating apart describes the narrative's main movements.

147. Gerhard Friedrich, "Εὐαγγελίζομαι κτλ," *TDNT* 2:707–37. See Josephus, *Ant.* 7.245, 250; Plutarch, *Pomp.* 66.3.

148. See Josephus, *J.W.* 1.607; 3.143, 503; *Ant.* 18.228.

149. See Josephus, *J.W.* 2.420; 4.618, 656; *Ant.* 18.229; Diodorus of Sicily, *The Library of History* 15.74.2; Plutarch, *Sert.* 26.3; *Pomp.* 41.3; *Phoc.* 16.6; 23.4.6, 11; *Cat. Min.* 51.1; *Vit. X. orat.* 846E; *Dem.* 22.2; *Reg. imp. apophth.* 184A; 188D; *Ages.* 33.5; *Demetr.* 17.5; *Glor. Ath.* 347D; *Art.* 14.3, 4; Philostratus, *Vit. Apoll.* 8.27.1.

150. See Xenophon, *Hell.* 4.3.14; Plutarch, *Ages.* 17.3; *Demetr.* 11.3; *Prae. ger. rei publ.* 799F; *Sert.* 11.1. "Often the news does not correspond to the facts. In time of war especially false stories of victory are circulated to boost the morale of tired soldiers. News comes to be treated with suspicion and the term loses its value, so that it can be

naval forces had been defeated at sea and its leader Peisander killed, he changed the report of defeat to one of victory, reporting that although Peisander had died, the navy had been victorious in its battle.[151] As a result of the fabricated good news, Agesilaus's troops remained loyal and courageous, "so that when a skirmish with the enemy took place, the troops of Agesilaus won the day in consequence of the report that the Lacedaemonians [Spartans] were victorious in the naval battle" (Xenophon, *Hell.* 4.3.13–14 [Marchant et al., LCL]. News of victory functioned to strengthen loyalty and courage, two of a warrior's most necessary and valued characteristics.[152]

Ever present was a risk that news accepted as true would later turn out to be false. Rejoicing in the news of the demise of an enemy could lead to a tragic reversal of fate if the good news turned out to be untrue.[153] The authority and credibility of the messenger would be established once the good news was authenticated. Moreover, the credibility of the news account was intimately connected with the credibility of the messenger delivering it.

We can see, then, that there was a particular form of self-expressive speech that, while not typically the object of a military call for aid, was commonly found in military discourse. "Good news" was a specific type of self-expressive speech, and it always carried an element of victory within it. As such, it was a valuable military "resource," as it were, deployed by leaders to strengthen the courage of their troops. Encouragement of morale and strengthening of courage by displaying and emphasizing victory was

---

consciously used in an ironical inversion. Nero wanted his mother killed and she was able to save herself and thus to send him the good news of her deliverance" (Friedrich, "Εὐαγγελίζομαι κτλ," 2:711).

151. King of Sparta from 399 BCE. "Agesilaus," *The Concise Oxford Companion to Classical Literature*, ed. M. C. Howatson and Ian Chilvers (Oxford: Oxford University Press, 1996).

152. "Courage," "enthusiastic zeal," and "tactics" are three critical elements in military discourse; see Lendon, "Rhetoric of Combat."

153. In 4 Maccabees, rejoicing over false "good news" becomes the trigger for Antiochus Epiphanes's persecution of the Jews: "For when he [Antiochus] was warring against Ptolemy in Egypt, he heard that a rumor of his death had spread and that the people of Jerusalem had rejoiced greatly. He speedily marched against them, and after he had plundered them he issued a decree that if any of them should be found observing the ancestral law they should die" (4 Macc 4:22–23).

seen by ancient writers as one of the strategies that generals employed in order to advance their chances of future victory.[154]

4.3.6. Conclusion: Intertextural Analysis of Paul's Vision

As seen in the previous chapter, a call, emphasized by the first παρακαλέω of the unit's foundational progressive sequence (Acts 16:9), triggers the narrative's progression. Intertextural analysis situates this call within the context of similar calls for aid found in historiographies where such calls sought auxiliary resources and alliances. The petitioner is explicitly identified as a Macedonian man, suggesting that it is the Macedonian and his group's initiative that the we-group was being asked to join with. The we-group's intention to deliver εὐαγγέλιον indirectly discloses what the Macedonian group lacks, namely, the "good news" that could play a key role in fortifying the warriors' courage and loyalty. As a result, these two qualities—courage and loyalty—constitute the auxiliary aid requested by the Macedonian man.

But how is what ensues a fulfillment of the call for aid? This is not a surprising question; what *is* surprising is that commentators have not asked this question. Normally, a call for aid would clearly define the resources in question. The Macedonian, in contrast, does not. Instead, as would be expected with dream-visions, which are often paradoxical,[155] the we-group must interpret the message of the vision. The unfolding events, and their interpretation, nuanced the vision to be a call from God to deliver good news of divine victory, but a victory that will be delivered through the channels of auxiliary aid. Ideological texture will take up the richness of the ideological blend found in Paul's vision and the we-group's reaction to it. Moreover, as will be apparent by now, this richness becomes shaded with yet greater complexity following the we-group's encounter with the first recipient of the "good news" proclamation, namely, Lydia.

4.4. Social Power in Roman Philippi

After Paul and the we-group encounter Lydia in the episode, the Python-spirit-woman event shows how social power works in Philippi. Relations

---

154. Lendon, "Rhetoric of Combat," 291–94.
155. See Scott Noegel, *Nocturnal Ciphers: The Allusive Language of Dreams in the Ancient Near East*, AOS 89 (New Haven: American Oriental Society, 2007).

within a polis were structured by social alliances. Notably, when the slave owners level their accusation against Paul and Silas, they make no mention of the harm (loss of profit) that they suffered as a result of Paul's act against their slave. What essentially should be a property-damage case instead is presented as a clash between "us-Romans" and "Jews" (Acts 16: 20–21). The slave owners' unproved, ambiguous charge was sufficient to move the magistrates and crowds to violent action instantly and, as a result, implicitly shows the network of loyalties that undergirded Philippi's structure of social power. Also implicit to the charge is an appeal to Roman honor, for harm to Roman custom would infer harm to Roman social identity. In an honor/shame society, any affront to honor required a commensurate counterresponse. What began as a confrontation between two spiritual beings, the Python spirit and the divine power behind "the name of Jesus Christ" (Acts 16:18), proceeds within the earthly realm of social honor. In Philippi, the instrument best able to restore honor to a dishonored Roman Philippian who also was part of the Philippi's social leadership network was its system of punishment.

4.4.1. Topos of Roman Physiognomy

Despite the fact that the Pauline group was summoned by a Macedonian, it is a Roman and not Macedonian identity that is key to the slave owners' charges against Paul and Silas. They frame their charges in the language of ἔθος, the customs and habits of an ethnic people, and they thereby invoke social and cultural ethnographic codes. In their self-representation, the Roman people were first and foremost a victorious people.[156] Vitruvius claimed that "the divine mind has allotted to the Roman state an excellent and temperate region in order to rule the world" (*Arch.* 6.1.11 [Granger, LCL]).[157] Vitruvius's use of physiognomic warrant supported the prevailing Roman ideology that it had been divinely endowed as "a suitable nucleus for universal rule."[158] This right of hegemonic rule was further supported by an embedded social and cultural ideology that ascribed peace, right order, harmony, and prosperity to its effects. In a survey of literary and

---

156. "The altar of the *Gens Augusta* from Carthage proclaimed Augustus as the one graced by Victory and before whom the world has poured forth her riches" (L. Gregory Bloomquist, "Rhetoric, Culture, and Ideology," 131).
157. See also Evans, "Physiognomics in the Ancient World," 20 n. 19.
158. Isaac, *Invention of Racism*, 85.

material artifacts from the imperial age, Bloomquist cites recurrent rhetorical representations of Augustus as one who was "truly *divi filius* and the great restorer of order."[159] This ideology is clearly illustrated as Plutarch retrojects Augustan thinking into his biography of Alexander, claiming that the truly blessed were the ones fortunate enough to have been conquered by Alexander. Plutarch writes: "Those who were vanquished by Alexander are happier than those who escaped his hand; for these had no one to put an end to the wretchedness of their existence, while the victor compelled those others to lead a happy life" (*Alex. fort.* 328E [Perrin et al., LCL]). An important aspect of an ideology that saw itself not only as the restorer but also as the future source of order relates to the body-zone model where character and identity were somatically encoded.[160]

The Roman sociocultural "body" was morally constituted, and as such, it perceived the contagion of immorality as one of its greatest threats. Thus, while the "essence of Roman identity and the source of its greatest strength was felt to be in the moral contrast between Romans and other peoples,"[161] contact with "other peoples" held the possibility of moral contamination and a consequent degeneration of the Roman body. For this reason, literary examples abound of Romans taking care to ensure that they are not exposed to infectious possibilities.

Many of these threats came from the possibility of contact with *luxuria* or carriers of *luxuria* as demonstrated by the Roman poets' assertions that "the Golden Age did not yet know the wicked art of seafaring" (Lucretius, *Rerum nat.* 5.1004–1006; Ovid, *Met.* 1.94–96).[162] Athenaeus, applauding the expulsion of Epicureans, who were stereotypically carriers of pleasure-seeking degeneracy, writes: "The Romans, therefore, the most virtuous of men in all things, did a good job when they banished the Epicureans Alcaeus and Philiscus from the city … because of the pleasures they introduced (*Deipn.* 12.547a [Gulick, LCL]).[163] It was imperative for Roman men to avoid contact with the "disease of effeminacy" and general

---

159. L. Gregory Bloomquist, "Whose Rhetoric? Whose Empire? The Subversion of Augustan Rhetoric in the Gospel of Luke" (paper presented at the University of Ottawa and Carleton University, 15–16 March 1996), 6–7.

160. For body-zone model, see pp. 44–45.

161. Isaac, *Invention of Racism*, 305.

162. Ibid., 241.

163. For the rhetorical profile of Epicureans, see L. Gregory Bloomquist, "Epicurean Tag in Plutarch."

"softness" that contact with *luxuria* might inculcate. As the discussion of Lydian ethnography highlighted, the "demasculinized" body was no longer the body of a warrior, and therefore it could not, or would not, defend its state. Polybius argues that although the Romans were not as skilled as the (trading) nation of Carthage in naval warfare, they readily overcame this disadvantage through their inherent courage and strength, which thus "turned the scale in favour of [Roman] victory," implicitly attributable to not having been affected by trading-derived luxury's softening influence (*Hist.* 6.52.8–11 [Paton, LCL]). Juvenal critiqued the perceived loss of "true Roman" values and satirically suggested that if a Roman "new-age" son was too "soft" for the life of a warrior, he could be counseled to turn instead to moneymaking: "If you are too lazy to endure the weary labours of the camp, if the sound of horn and trumpet melts your fearful soul within you, buy something that you can sell at half as much again" (*Sat.* 14.198–201 [Ramsay, LCL]). Using the language of ἔθος, the slave owners invoke Roman custom and present themselves as standard-bearers of the Roman ideal. This ideal centered on the courageous, victorious, and morally constituted Roman male.

4.4.2. The Structure of Power in the Polis of Philippi: Topoi of Mantics, Punishment, and Honor

In her investigation into the system of punishment in classical Greece, Danielle Allen underscores that juries were swayed not only by witness reports but even more so by the nature of a litigant's social alliances.[164] No less so, in Roman times crowds, who essentially could replace a jury in determining the outcome of a claim, would assess a litigant's social networks and the degree to which supporting or opposing those networks would be in the crowd's favor.[165] Legal actions displayed not only social alliances but also the very structure of power within a community. Given

---

164. "The jurors assessed a litigant's claims on the basis of the nature of his support group and friendship network and thereby assessed not only the content of social memory but also the structure of social relations in the city" (Danielle S. Allen, *The World of Prometheus: The Politics of Punishing in Democratic Athens* [Princeton: Princeton University Press, 2000], 106).

165. On the power of the crowd in legal actions, see Brian Rapske, *Paul in Roman Custody*, vol. 3 of *The Book of Acts in Its First Century Setting*, ed. Bruce Winter (Grand Rapids: Eerdmans, 1994), 122–23.

the slave owners' immediate, violent response to seeing the effects of Paul's exorcism, we can infer that the profit-generating activities of the slave woman with the Python spirit were shown to be fully integrated within Philippi's structure of power.

The slave woman's mantic spirit is identified as "Python" (πύθων), who in mythology was a dragon killed by the god Apollo and whose consequently rotting body gave Apollo his name of "Pythian," since πύθω means "cause to rot."[166] The most Greek of gods, Apollo was the lord of the oracular temple at Delphi, considered the navel—omphalos—of the Greek-speaking world.[167] In addition to the specific cultural connection between Python and Delphic Apollo, two general attributes of mantics contribute to our appreciation of the role of the mantic slave woman in the narrative: the profitability of oracular activities and the role of mantics as an instrument of political agendas.

In ancient literature, the association between mantics and money is prevalent. Euripides tells another version of the story of Apollo killing Python and then goes on to describe how Earth in revenge sent prophetic dream-visions to humans so that they no longer had need of Apollo's mantic services. When Apollo, who is still a child here, runs off to beg his father Zeus to remove the prophetic visions from humans, Zeus is amused that Apollo had already developed a keen taste for "worship that pays in

---

166. LSJ, s.v. πύθω. Since the slave woman practices divination (μαντεύομαι), her having the spirit of Python would have implied to an audience that her mantic practice was inspired by Apollo. "And the holy strength of Helios made her rot away there; wherefore, the place is now called Pytho, and men call the lord Apollo by another name, Pythian; because on that spot the power of piercing Helios made the monster rot away" (*Homeric Hymns to Pythian Apollo* 370 [Evelyn-White, LCL]). It is also not outside the realm of possibility that the author of Acts intended to pun on πύθω, "rot," when identifying the spirit. Particularly since the message of "salvation" that the slave woman announces the Pauline group to be proclaiming is one of immortality, which contrasts with "corruption" (in Acts 13:34, 35, 36, 37, through the term διαφθορά). Moreover, oral-scribally, the passage with the closest lexical connection to that of the mantic slave woman is the story of the Gerasene demoniac (Luke 8:26–39) who lives in the tombs, a place of decay.

167. "Omphalos," *ODCW*. Connections between Python, Apollo, and Delphi were so strong that Πυθώ could be metonymically substituted for Delphi (LSJ, s.v. Πυθώ). One example of substituting "Pytho" for Delphi comes from Clement of Alexandria, *Exhortation to the Greeks* 1.2P (Butterworth, LCL).

gold" (πολύχρυσα θέλων λατρεύματα σχεῖν: *Iph. taur.* 1275).[168] In Euripides's *Bacchae*, the Theban prince Pentheus accuses the priest Teiresias of acting in self-interest in worshiping the newly arrived Dionysus: "By introducing a new god, you hope to advance your augerer's business, to collect more fees for inspecting sacrifices" (*Bacch.* 257 [Vellacott]).

The symbiotic relationship among gods, mantics, and rulers is well illustrated in Herodotus's description of Lydian king Croesus's exchanges with the Delphic oracle. Before his attack on the Persians, Croesus made extravagant sacrifices and sent lavish treasure to Delphi in order to "win the favour of the Delphian god" (Herodotus, *Hist.* 1.50–52).[169] Later, Croesus sent messengers to the oracles in order to ask whether he should proceed with an attack against the Persians. When the answer came back "that if he should send an army against the Persians he would destroy a great empire," Croesus interpreted it as a signal of his assured success and went ahead with his attack (*Hist.* 1.53–54 [Godley, LCL]). When it turned out that it was his own great Lydian empire that fell to the Persians, Croe-

---

168. A similar version of this story is also attributed to Aesop. See B. E. Perry, "Demetrius of Phalerum and the Aesopic Fables," *TPAPA* 93 (1962): 299–300.

169. "He offered up three thousand beasts from each kind fit for sacrifice, and he burnt on a great pyre couches covered with gold and silver, golden goblets, and purple cloaks and tunics; by these means he hoped the better to win the aid of the god, to whom he also commanded that every Lydian should sacrifice what he could. When the sacrifice was over, he melted down a vast store of gold and made of it ingots of which the longer sides were of six and the shorter of three palms' length, and the height was one palm. These were an hundred and seventeen in number. Four of them were of refined gold, each weighing two talents and a half; the rest were of gold with silver alloy, each of two talents' weight. He bade also to be made a figure of a lion of refined gold, weighing ten talents…. When these offering were made, Croesus sent them to Delphi, with other gifts besides, namely, two very great bowls, one of gold and one of silver. The golden bowl stood to the right, the silvern to the left, of the temple entrance…. Moreover, Croesus sent four silver casks, which stand in the treasury of the Corinthians, and dedicated two sprinkling-vessels, one of gold, one of silver. The golden vessel bears the inscription 'Given by the Lacedaemonians,' who claim it as their offering. But they are wrong, for this, too, is Croesus' gift. The inscription was made by a certain Delphian, whose name I know but will not reveal, out of his desire to please the Lacedaemonians…. Along with these Croesus sent, besides many other offerings of no great mark, certain round basins of silver, and a golden female figure three cubits high, which the Delphians assert to be the statue of the woman who was Croesus' baker. Moreover he dedicated his own wife's necklaces and girdles" (Godley, LCL).

sus sent envoys reproaching the god for his "thanklessness." The priestess emphasized that Apollo had done what he could; although he could not alter destiny, he had apparently forestalled the fall of Sardis (i.e., Lydia) for three years. Whether acting in self-interest or being themselves coerced, mantics were frequently portrayed as intimately integrated with the economic, social, and political agendas of human figures of power. In taking action against the Python spirit, Paul pressed on the nerve center of Philippi's structure of power and in so doing activated one of the principal instruments of power: the penal system.

Following Paul's exorcism, when the slave owners purposefully dragged the (now publicly reputed) representatives of the "Most High God" through the streets of Philippi, they themselves suffered no repercussion for what in other circumstances would have been perceived as a case of bald hubris. Instead, they were rewarded by the ready acquiescence of the crowd in the agora and most especially by Philippi's leaders.[170] Having the ability to punish was a crucial marker of power in any Greco-Roman city, one that Aristophanes satirically depicts when his "sausage-seller" in *Equites* is promised all the trappings of power including the ability to imprison at will.

> You shall be over-lord of all those people,
> The Agora, and the Harbours, and the Pnyx.
> You'll trim the Generals, trample down the Council,
> Fetter, imprison, make the Hall your brothel. (*Eq.* 165 [Rogers, LCL])

---

170. "There was however a specific offence called 'hubris' in Attic law. Anyone who stuck, pushed or restrained another person might put himself in danger of a prosecution for hubris. This prosecution was not a private lawsuit for damages, but an indictment for an offence against the community as a whole, and it was open to a jury to concur in a prosecutor's demand for the infliction of the death penalty. Indictments for hubris coexisted with private claims for damages arising out of simple assault, but to establish that an act of violence was hubris rather than assault it was necessary to persuade the jury that it proceeded from a certain attitude and disposition on the part of the accused: that is to say, from a wish on his part to establish a dominant position over his victim in the eyes of the community, or from a confidence that by reason of wealth, strength or influence he could afford to laugh at equality of rights under the law and treat other people as if they were chattels at his disposal" (Kenneth J. Dover, *Greek Homosexuality* [Cambridge: Harvard University Press, 1978], 35).

Punishment was the handmaiden of power in a city, and the slave owners clearly had this instrument at their disposal.[171] Not only were the slave owners instantly able to mobilize the leaders and people of Philippi, but also they managed to do so, not by proving that they had sustained an unjust injury from Paul's actions but instead through issuing an enigmatic charge against the accused of promulgating undefined "un-Roman" customs. The very arbitrariness of the slave owners' charges against Paul and Silas displays their unquestioned access to Philippi's system of punishment and testifies to the power vested in them.[172]

In the first-century Mediterranean world, any relations transacted within a framework of power by definition also implicated issues of honor. Punitive competitions, that by their very nature functioned through established power structures, formed a particular type of struggle for honor.[173] Indeed, the etymological connections between punishment and honor further emphasize the intimate relationship between the two, as Allen remarks.

> Greek words for punishment reveal the centrality of honor to the process of punishing. The most common word for "punishment" was *timoria* and for "to punish," *timoreisthai*, which we might translate as "to assess and to distribute honor." The words *atimia* and *atimos* ("dishonor" and "dishonored") referred to the specific penalty of political disfranchisement and were originally used to describe the exile who had been cast entirely outside the community.[174]

---

171. Equally valid in the first century are Allen's remarks on classical Athens: "Punishment established structure of power. In addition, those people who claimed to hold power could only prove that they did by punishing and by forcing their world views on someone who had rejected them" (Allen, *World of Prometheus*, 87). "Public violence on selected bodies becomes an instrument of social coercion. More than a deterrent, it effects a *forcible realignment of subjectivity* to identify with the enforcing power" (Maud W. Gleason, "Truth Contests and Talking Corpses," in *Constructions of the Classical Body*, ed. James I. Porter, The Body, in Theory: Histories of Cultural Materialism [Ann Arbor: University of Michigan Press, 1999], 300).

172. "The Roman criminal justice system may have presented to its subjects a face as arbitrary, as inexplicable, even as malign—as Fortuna herself. But its very incomprehensibility comprehended a message. Arbitrariness is an effective way to dramatize power" (Gleason, "Truth Contests and Talking Corpses," 299).

173. Allen, *World of Prometheus*, 61.

174. Ibid.

Through a reciprocal act of "casting out," the slave owners sought to remove Paul and Silas's previous publicly proclaimed status as agents of the "Most High God." If we consider that "honor expresses one's public standing," then we can see that the honor of the Pauline group suffered a precipitous drop following the Python spirit's exorcism.[175] This loss of honor, however, was not limited to the men involved but also implicated the God they were proclaiming. By identifying Paul and Silas as "Jews" (Acts 16:20), the slave owners also gave identity to the "Most High God" as the God of Israel. The exorcism, rather than functioning as a healing miracle in the context of this unit, functioned as a challenge and triggered a competition for public honor. The challenge was met, in true first-century fashion, by a commensurate response.[176] Where Paul's exorcism attacked a sensitive element of the slave owners' source of honor—mantic activities that had generated significant profit—the slave owners in turn attacked the honor of Paul and Silas's God by bodily attacking his agents.

4.4.3. Conclusion: Intertextual Analysis of Social Power in Roman Philippi

If indeed the Pauline group had expectations that it would evangelize "important cities in the contemporary Roman empire" beginning with Philippi,[177] then by all appearances their merger with the slave woman would have testified to the fulfillment of their mission. Mediating a divinity associated with the preeminent Greek god Apollo, the slave woman belonged to some of Philippi's most powerful men. Her public proclamations that the disciples were agents of the Most High God and were empowered to deliver salvation situated the disciples and their God in a position of honor within the city of Philippi.

Yet, instead of presenting a successful ongoing alliance with powerful Philippians, Luke portrays break and rupture, as Paul first expels the slave owners' source of profit and is then himself expelled from Philippian society. The cause of this rupture—profit— comes to the fore. Ethnography too is featured once again. Where previously the threat of Lydian contamina-

---

175. Neyrey, "Loss of Wealth," 88. A predominantly male value, honor "is a claim to worth *and* the social acknowledgement of that worth" (Malina, *New Testament World*, 30).

176. For the role of challenge-response in contests of honor in the first-century agonistic culture, see Malina, *New Testament World*, 33–36.

177. Fitzmyer, *Acts of the Apostles*, 583.

tion was introduced with Lydia, now the question of the Roman physiognomic standard surfaces in the charges against Paul and Silas.

Topoi of power and honor, and their physical manifestations through a key tool of a city's power structure and its penal system, figure prominently. Punishment served to dishonor the accused and expelled him from society. The emotion-fused element of anger, an element rarely recognized in discussions of this unit, plays a catalytic role as the anger of the slave owners shows itself sufficient for activating the people, magistrates, and lictors against Paul and Silas.[178] Whereas many have approached the exorcism of the Python spirit as a sign of "the triumph of Christianity over pagan Greco-Roman practices,"[179] ignoring the resultant humiliation and dishonoring of the we-group and their God, the exorcism instead plays a crucial role in unveiling the interconnected links of Philippi's social structure of power, ranging from a spiritual divinity (by implication Apollo) to Philippi's earthly chief leaders.

4.5. Topoi of Prison

Terms associated with prison form one of the densest conglomerations of repetitive *lexica* in this passage. Inner textural analysis has also shown that Lydia and the jailer are connected progressively, particularly through the repetitive term οἶκος, although it is not immediately clear how. In analyzing the relationship between suffering and joy developed by Paul in his Letter to the Philippians, Bloomquist has emphasized the radical differences between an experience of prison in antiquity and that of a modern North American one. Pointing to the need for an intertextural understanding of this difference, Bloomquist writes:

> Most of us have no experience of prison. But, even if we did, imprisonment would have been profoundly different from almost any North American experience of prison today. Prison in antiquity was not a "holding cell," but a place to impose greater suffering on the wrongdoer

---

178. Allen's analysis of the role of anger in classical Greece carries into Greco-Roman cities: "We will discover first of all that in Athens anger and personal interest provided the only truly legitimate basis for an attempt to punish someone. Punishments inspired by anger provided a means of recalibrating status and honor in the city after a wrongdoing. This recalibration especially benefited the punisher" (*World of Prometheus*, 35).

179. Fitzmyer, *Acts of the Apostles*, 583.

than the wrongdoing had caused.... Moreover, we would be shocked that torture was common ... and prison was an opportunity to enable torturers to hurt those accused of hurting others and to do so with increasing savagery and ferocity.[180]

Paul's exorcism precipitated his and Silas's incarceration.

4.5.1. Physiognomy of Jailers: Brutalization and Torture

The occupational physiognomy of jailers evoked savagery as much as other instruments of the Roman penal system, such as the fasces, did.[181] Philo writes that jailers, endowed with "an uncivilized and unsoftened nature," become hardened through their daily contact with "thieves, burglars, men of violence and outrage, who commit rape, murder, adultery and sacrilege," thereby forming "a single body of evil, a fusion of every sort of pollution" (*Joseph* 84 [Colson et al., LCL]). The end result is the brutalizing jailer: "Everyone knows how full of inhumanity and cruelty gaolers are; pitiless by nature and case-hardened by practice, they are brutalized day by day towards savagery, because they never even by chance see or say or do any kindness, but only the extremes of violence and cruelty" (*Joseph* 81 [Colson et al., LCL]). Philo's description of a jailer is a case study of physiognomical thinking. It begins with an innate predisposition[182] and

---

180. L. Gregory Bloomquist, "Subverted by Joy: Suffering and Joy in Paul's Letter to the Philippians," *Int* 61 (2007): 274–75.

181. The Roman lictors, the ῥαβδοῦχοι (Acts 16:35, 38), technically the fasces bearers (where the fasces were the ancient equivalent to modern batons used by riot police), are found only in Acts 16 in the Bible. The element of the fasces is emphasized by the verb ῥαβδίζω, which describes Paul and Silas's beating by rods in Acts 16:22. "The *fasces* were not merely decorative or symbolic devices carried before magistrates in a parade of idle formalism. Rather, they constituted a portable kit for flogging and decapitation. Since they were so brutally functional, they not only served as ceremonial symbols of office but also carried the potential of violent repression and execution" (Anthony J. Marshall, "Symbols and Showmanship in Roman Public Life: The Fasces," *Phoenix* 38 [1984]: 129–30; see Loretana de Libero, "Fasces," *BNP*).

182. This natural predisposition, in physiognomical terms, is best understood as "barbarianism": "There are occasional suggestions that 'Scythian' public slaves were charged with policing and guarding the *polis* in Greco-Roman antiquity. This premise is sourced in the historic use of 'Scythian archers' in the late fourth–early fifth century BCE to keep order in Athens and sometimes referred to as a police force. This group was disbanded in the fourth century BCE and there is nothing to suggest a connec-

augments it with the effects of further contaminating contact "with every sort of pollution," thereby forming the end product of a stereotypical hardened jailer.

True to type, the Philippian jailer goes above and beyond his orders to secure Paul and Silas by fastening them "in wood."[183] Brian Rapske notes that although fastening prisoners in stocks may have formed part of an evening "lockdown" routine in prison, the jailer's placing Paul and Silas in stocks immediately upon their incarceration suggests that "more than security may have been in mind," as the use of stocks "could also be a form of torture."[184] Evidence that torture rather than security provided the jailer's most probable motive is further emphasized by the text's specifying that Paul and Silas were incarcerated in the innermost cell, where the possibility of escape would have been highly unlikely.

Through bribery, it was possible to motivate jailers toward greater or lesser degrees of humane treatment. For example, Antiphilus's friend Demetrius gives a portion of his daily wages to Antiphilus's jailer, "thus rendering him tractable and peaceful," whereas previously the jailer had exercised "his authority over Antiphilus with a heavy hand" (Lucian, *Tox.* 31 [Harmon, Kilburn, and MacLeod, LCL]). In the Acts of Paul and Thecla, Thecla gives her bracelets to the prison's doorkeeper and a silver mirror to the jailer in order to gain access to the imprisoned Paul (Acts Paul 18).[185] Prisoners were dependent on relatives or friends to bring them

---

tion between Scythian ethnicity and policing in subsequent years. Nonetheless by the Byzantine period, the term *Skythai* was used indiscriminately to describe barbarian peoples from the north and east" (Peter J. Rhodes, "Scythians," *BNP*). It is this element of "barbarianism" that forms the stereotype of prison guards. "The B[arbarian] image is encapsulated in the terms *feritas, immanitas, inhumanitas, impietas, ferocia, superbia, impotentia, furor, discordia, vanitas, perfidia* and *imprudentia*" (Volker Losemann, "Barbarians," *BNP*). Third and Fourth Maccabees characterize Scythians as cruel torturers: "They also led them out with harsh treatment as slaves, or rather as traitors, and, girding themselves with a cruelty more savage than that of Scythian custom, they tried without any inquiry or examination to put them to death" (3 Macc 7:5); "Since they were not able in any way to break his spirit, they abandoned the instruments and scalped him with their fingernails in a Scythian fashion" (4 Macc 10:7).

183. Stocks "often consisted of a long piece of wood pierced at regular intervals with notches or holes and split along the length so that the feet of the prisoner could be set it and secured" (Rapske, *Paul in Roman Custody*, 126–27).

184. Ibid., 127. See Allen, *World of Prometheus*, 200–201.

185. In Acts 24:26, the hope of receiving a bribe sustains Felix's continued discussion with the imprisoned Paul.

food, and bribes were often the avenue by which access to prisoners could be gained.[186]

Although literature portrays jailers as innately brutish, their hardness was all but ensured by a brutal system that showed no leniency to jailers who may have been remiss in their duties. The Philippian jailer did not hesitate in moving toward his own death when he had supposed that the postearthquake open doors implied that the prisoners had escaped (Acts 16:27), for he understood that to have allowed an escape would likely have brought about his own torture and death as it had done for Peter's jailers (Acts 12:19). Not only were jailers to ensure that prisoners did not escape, but they also were expected to see to the ongoing suffering of their charges. The very thought of friendship between prisoners and jailers would have been ludicrous.

4.5.2. Space of Prison: Suffering and Death

The space of a first-century prison evoked suffering, filth, disease, and death. Suffering that resulted from the threat or realization of physical maltreatment at the hands of one's jailer was aggravated by prison's inhumane living conditions.[187] Diodorus of Sicily writes of the dire conditions of a prison at Alba Fucens.

> This prison is a deep underground dungeon, no larger than a nine-coach room, dark, noisome from the large numbers committed to the place, who were men under condemnation on capital charges, for most of this category were incarcerated there at that period. With so many shut up in such close quarters, the poor wretches were reduced to the physical appearance of brutes, and since their food and everything pertaining to their other needs was all foully commingled, a stench so terrible assailed anyone who drew near that it could scarcely be endured. (*The Library of History* 31.9.2)[188]

Lucian portrays similar conditions in his story of Antiphilus's imprisonment.

---

186. Rapske, *Paul in Roman Custody*, 209–13. Cf. Matt 25:36, 39, 43, 44.
187. See Matthew L. Skinner, *Locating Paul: Places of Custody as Narrative Settings in Acts 21–28*, AcBib 13 (Atlanta: Society of Biblical Literature, 2003), 81–84.
188. Quoted in Rapske, *Paul in Roman Custody*, 197–98.

> He [Antiphilus] slept on the ground and at night could not even stretch out his legs, which were confined in the stocks. By day, to be sure, the collar was sufficient, together with the manacles upon one hand; but for the night he had to be fully secured by his bonds. Moreover, the stench of the room and its stifling air (since many were confined in the same place, cramped for room, and scarcely able to draw breath), the clash of iron, the scanty sleep—all these conditions were difficult and intolerable for such a man. (*Tox*. 30 [Harmon, Kilburn, and MacLeod, LCL])

Wretched suffering to the point of death was a prominent element of the first-century prison, and the conditions of Philippi's prison would not have been any less so.

Since prisons were spaces of suffering, disease, and death, there was a form of rhetorical type scene—prison escape—that showcased a divinity's superior power through the miraculous escape of prisoners under divine favor. Earthquakes, along with other violent natural phenomena such as thunder and lightning, were closely associated with manifestations of divine power in the ancient world.[189] When serving to "open doors," earthquakes were subsumed under a broader topos of "door miracles," which involved cases of closed doors opening miraculously.[190] Prison-escape rhetorical type scenes blended door miracles with the topos of imprisonment. They functioned to exhibit the release of divinely sanctioned prisoners. An illustrative example comes from Artapanus's account of Moses's imprisonment by the Pharaoh.

> The king of the Egyptians learned of Moses' presence, summoned him and asked for what purpose he had come. He responded that the master of the universe had ordered him *to release the Jews*. When the king learned this, he confined him in prison. But when night came, all the doors of the prison opened of themselves, and some of the guards died, while others were relaxed by sleep and their weapons were broken. Moses came out and went to the royal chambers. (*Mos*. 23–24 [Collins, *OTP*], emphasis original)[191]

---

189. Stefan Maul and Fritz Krafft, "Earthquake," *BNP*; Richard Seaford, "Thunder, Lightning and Earthquake in the *Bacchae* and the Acts of the Apostles," in *What Is a God? Studies in the Nature of Greek Divinity*, ed. Alan B. Lloyd (London: Duckworth, 1997), 139–51.

190. Joachim Jeremias, "θύρα," *TDNT* 3:175–76.

191. As preserved in Eusebius, *Praep. ev*. 9.27.1–37.

4. INTERTEXTUAL ANALYSIS 193

Numerous scholars have remarked on the similarities between the prison scenes in Acts (5:17–42; 12:1–19; 16:19–40) and those found in Euripides's *Bacchae*.[192] Elements of the imprisonment in Philippi, in particular, resonate uncannily with the *Bacchae*, and many of these commonalities have been long recognized despite a lack of awareness of further support provided by Lydian ethnography.[193]

When the Thebian prince Pentheus is told that a new god has arrived, he dismisses him as "a juggling sorcerer from Lydia-land" (*Bacch.* 234 [Vellacott]). Although Pentheus attempts to imprison Dionysus's Maenads, they become "loosed from bonds ... the fetters from their feet self-sundered fell ... doors, without mortal hand, unbarred themselves" (*Bacch.* 440–449 [Vellacott]). Pentheus captures Dionysus by commanding: "track down that effeminate [θηλύμορφον] foreigner" (*Bacch.* 353–354 [Vellacott]).[194] Dionysus, offering no resistance, is easily captured and brought to Pentheus, who orders Dionysus's hands to be untied since he poses no physical threat: "You are no wrestler, I can tell from these long curls cascading most seductively over your cheek" (*Bacch.* 455–458 [Vellacott]).[195] Subsequently, Pentheus does have Dionysus bound and

---

192. A list compiled by John Weaver includes Otto Weinreich, "Gebet und Wunder," in *Genethliakon Wilhelm Schmid*, TBAW 5 (Stuttgart: Kohlhammer, 1929), 169–464; Richard I. Pervo, "The Literary Genre of Acts of the Apostles" (ThD diss., Harvard University, 1979), 54–90; Pervo, *Profit with Delight: The Literary Genre of the Acts of the Apostles* (Philadelphia: Fortress, 1987), 18–24; Reinhard Kratz, *Rettungswunder: Motiv-, traditions- und formkritische Aufarbeitung einer biblischen Gattung*, EHST 123 (Frankfurt am Main: Lang, 1979), 446–99; Wilhelm Nestle, "Anklänge an Euripides in der Apostelgeschichte," *Phil.* 59 (1900):46–57. Weaver, *Plots of Epiphany*, 12–21, 133.

193. For a table of common narrative elements between Acts 16 and the *Bacchae*, see Weaver, *Plots of Epiphany*, 270.

194. "Just as the *Iliad* calls Paris γυναιμανής [mad for women], so a Homeric hymn uses the same term for Dionysus. In Aeschylus he is called contemptuously 'the womanly one' (ὁ γύννις); in Euripides, 'the womanly stranger' (θηλύμορφος). At times he is also called 'man-womanish' (ἀρσενόθηλυς). The Christians sneer at his effeminacy to which the strange story of his encounter with Prosymnus can also bear witness [Clement of Alexandria, *Exhortation to the Greeks* 2.30P]. Indeed, there is a tale that Hermes gave the infant Dionysus to Ino with the stipulation that she rear him as a girl" (Walter F. Otto, *Dionysus: Myth and Cult*, trans. Robert B. Palmer [Bloomington: Indiana University Press, 1965], 176, square brackets my own).

195. Similarly, Edonian king Lycurgus asks about the newly arrived Dionysus,

imprisoned in his palace dungeon. In the darkness, displaying his divine power, Dionysus frees himself by an earthquake and fire (*Bacch.* 616–640).

Although most commentators have pointed to the similarities between Paul and Silas's imprisonment and Dionysus's, Philippi skips out of the groove in a number of key areas. It is precisely these differences that point to areas of intense rhetorical interest. Luke's reconfiguration of the prison-escape rhetorical type scene and its rhetorical impact will be discussed in ideological texture.

Whereas miraculous prison escapes functioned to display divine power, another series of stories associated with the topos of prison shifted focus to the prisoner. In these texts, the topos of prison functioned as a locus of testing.[196] Two examples from ancient literature illustrate how imprisonment could test, and consequently display, a person's character. In *Toxaris*, Lucian's anthology of stories of loyal friendship, one story is told of how imprisonment demonstrated exemplary loyalty between friends Antiphilus and Demetrius. When Antiphilus is unjustly incarcerated, he finds himself abandoned by all except for his loyal friend Demetrius. Demetrius searches out the languishing Antiphilus[197] and begins to tend to his care.

> He bade him have no fear, and tearing his short cloak in two, put on one of the halves and gave the remainder to Antiphilus, after stripping from him the filthy worn-out rags he was wearing. From that time forth, too, he shared his life in every way, attending and cherishing him; for by hiring himself out to the shipmen in the harbour from early morning to noon, he earned a good deal of money as a stevedore. Then, on returning from his work, he would give part of his pay to the keeper, thus rendering him tractable and peaceful, and the rest sufficed well enough for the maintenance of his friend. Each afternoon he remained with Antiphilus, keeping him in heart; and when night overtook him, he slept just in front of the prison door where he had made a place to lie and

---

Ποδαπὸς ὁ γύννις, "Where does this effeminate fellow come from?" (Aeschylus, *Frag.* 31; ca. 525–ca. 456 BCE), quoted in Weaver, *Plots of Epiphany*, 38.

196. For example, in Revelation the Ephesians are encouraged: "Do not fear what you are about to suffer. Behold, the devil is about to throw some of you into prison, that you may be tested, and for ten days you will have tribulation. Be faithful unto death, and I will give you the crown of life" (Rev 2:10).

197. The wretchedness of Antiphilus's conditions was narrated on p. 192 above.

had put down some leaves. (Lucian, *Tox.* 30–31 [Harmon, Kilburn, and MacLeod, LCL])

When he can no longer bribe his way into prison, Demetrius claims to have been an accomplice to the crime of which Antiphilus had been wrongfully accused and thus joins Antiphilus, managing to get himself secured in the same set of irons. Despite now falling ill himself, Demetrius continues to try to ease Antiphilus's discomfort: "So they bore their discomforts more easily by sharing them with each other" (*Tox.* 32 [Harmon, Kilburn, and MacLeod, LCL]). Eventually, several prisoners manage to file through their chains, and all but Demetrius and Antiphilus escape, killing the guards in the process. Demetrius and Antiphilus choose to remain in prison since they are innocent.[198] When, at daybreak, they are discovered as the only remaining prisoners, they are praised for staying and set free. However, "they were not the men … to be content with being released in that way," since the public perception of their guilt would have remained. To clear their names, Demetrius insists on an inquiry. When the investigation affirms their innocence, the magistrate

> commended them, expressing very great admiration for Demetrius, and in dismissing them [ἀφίησι] condoled [παραμυνθησάμενος] with them over the punishment which they had undergone through their unjust imprisonment and presented each of them with a gift out of his own pocket, Antiphilus with ten thousand drachmas and Demetrius with twice as much. (*Tox.* 33 [Harmon, Kilburn, and MacLeod, LCL])

Demetrius shows himself to be a paragon of loyalty through a prison trial.[199]

---

198. They also seize the actual perpetrator and keep him from escaping.

199. Both Cicero and Diodorus of Sicily retell a different story of laudable loyalty between friends that is demonstrated through the prison topos. Cicero writes: "They say that Damon and Phintias, of the Pythagorean school, enjoyed such ideally perfect friendship, that when the tyrant Dionysius had appointed a day for the execution of one of them, and the one who had been condemned to death requested a few days' respite for the purpose of putting his loved ones in the care of friends, the other became surety for his appearance, with the understanding that if his friend did not return, he himself should be put to death. And when the friend returned on the day appointed, the tyrant in admiration for their faithfulness begged that they would enrol him as a third partner in their friendship" (Cicero, *Off.* 3.10.45 [Miller et al., LCL]). Relating a similar version, Diodorus writes: "While Dionysius was tyrant, and a certain Phintias, a Pythagorean, who had formed a plot against the tyrant, was

Philo too uses prison to highlight exemplary character in his story of Joseph's imprisonment (Gen 39:20–23). In Genesis, the more succinct version of the account has the Lord coming to the unjustly imprisoned Joseph's aid, resulting in the jailer's turning over the management of the prison to Joseph. In Philo's expanded and modified version, due to Joseph's abundance of virtue, both the prisoners and the jailer have their natures converted, and through the example of Joseph's character the very space of prison is converted as well. After describing the brutish nature of jailers,[200] Philo writes:

> Nevertheless one of this kind, tamed by the nobility of the youth [Joseph], not only allowed him some security from violence and hardship, but gave him the command of all the prisoners; and thus while he remained nominally and for the sake of appearance the keeper of the gaol, he resigned to Joseph the actual office, which thus became the source of no small benefit to those who were in confinement. Thus even the place, as they felt could not rightly be called a prison, but a house of correction [σωφρονιστήριον]. For instead of the tortures [βασάνων] and punishments which they used to endure night and day under the lash or in manacles or in every possible affliction, they were rebuked by his wise words and doctrines of philosophy, while the conduct of their teacher effected more than any words. For by setting before them his life of temperance and every virtue, like an original picture of skilled workmanship, he converted even those who seemed to be quite incurable. (Philo, *Joseph* 85–87 [Colson et al., LCL])

Through the shining example of his virtuous nature, Joseph converts both the jailer and the prisoners, and transmutes the space of prison into a space of wisdom.

---

about to suffer the penalty for it, he asked Dionysius for time in which to make such disposition as he wished of his private affairs; and he said that he would give one of his friends as surety for his death. And when the ruler expressed his wonder whether such a friend was to be found as would take his place in prison, Phintias called upon one of his acquaintances, a Pythagorean philosopher named Damon, who without hesitation came forward at once as surety for his death" (Diodorus of Sicily, *The Library of History* 10.4.3–4 [Oldfather et al., LCL]).

200. See §4.5.1.

4.5.3. Conclusion: Intertextural Analysis of the Topos of Prison

The penal system, instrumental to the enforcement of the power structure of a polis, functioned by exerting physical violence and extreme hardship. Within this system, the inhumane conditions of prison, enforced by their equally inhumane keepers, made a stay in prison a form of torture even in instances where torture was not formally applied. Prison and jailers evoked elements of torture, suffering, and filth.

Forming an ultimate tool of dominance, prisons could appear as a testing ground for differentiating between divine and opposing power in literature. Miracles of independent door-openings enabled the triumphant release of their divinely sanctioned prisoners, and when they occurred they heralded the imminent demise or loss of power of impious leaders. In Philippi, however, an earthquake does not facilitate a prison escape; instead all prisoners stay. Ideological texture will investigate how Paul and Silas's prison stay is used rhetorically in the passage.

4.6. Conclusion: Intertextural Analysis

Our investigation of intertextural analysis first discovered that Lydia's descriptive attributes take on their meaning through the connectivity between elements of Lydia's Lydian ethnography, her purple; and her occupation as a seller brings forth topoi of sexual immorality, degenerative luxury, profit-seeking, and hucksterism. This is in stark contrast to the narratively framed expectations of a setting of Jewish piety. The rhetorical force of the analysis suggests that Lydia risks contaminating the Pauline group and "effeminizing" them. If indeed she represents the group of women that gather with her on the outskirts of Philippi, then the rhetorical nature of the assembly by the river would be far closer to a "den of robbers" than to a "house of prayer" (Luke 19:46).[201]

Second, the social topic of hospitality, long used by commentators to classify Lydia as a "hostess," instead operates rhetorically to profile the need for mutual evaluation between host and guest. Importantly, hospitality functioned through male social codes, for the honor of the guest would

---

201. "If an individual who is a member of a group has become a symbol of this group his behavior will be regarded as more important, because it is more representative, than that of other members of the same group" (Perelman and Olbrechts-Tyteca, *New Rhetoric*, 333).

be embedded in the honor of the host for the duration of the stay. Far from suggesting hostessing, "shameless" Lydia's offer presents a severe challenge to the ethos of the Pauline group and thereby to their message of good news. Dissonant with her Lydian purple-selling profile, Lydia speaks in the language of fidelity; yet the possibility of discovering fidelity in a Lydian woman remains a question throughout and is in fact left unanswered until the unit's final verse.

Third, we found that the rhetorical unit opens with topoi common to military discourse, including the sweep of territory preceding the vision; the legendary site of Troas that featured in other military Hellespont crossings; the Macedonian identity of the man that suggested conquering heroes; Paul's vision that evoked the dream-visions of military leaders; and the form of the Macedonian's words as a military call to aid. The call of the Macedonian man resonates with other dream-visions found in military discourse that motivate a leader or general to action. Unlike other calls for auxiliary military aid, however, the Macedonian petitioner does not disclose the nature of his want. It is left to the we-group to perceive that self-expressive speech delivering fortunate news of victory will supply the requisitioned aid. In situations of conflict, this type of "good news" regularly served to fortify the courage of troops. Moreover, as with other such calls, the request assumes that some type of alliance will be formed between the petitioner, who is human rather than divine, and the respondent. This analysis of intertexture provides grounds for suggesting that "fortifying courage" and alliance arise as two key objectives of Paul's vision.

Fourth, although the exorcism of the Python spirit from the rhetorical unit's second featured woman, the mantic slave woman, might be interpreted as another show of the superior power of Paul's God over a "pagan" god, the consequent punishment and dishonoring of Paul and Silas argue against such a reading. Instead, the exorcism unveils Philippi's power structure as the slave owners handily mobilize Philippi's penal system through their anger. This power structure and penal system are both clearly Roman. Roman ethnography becomes operative through the charges of the slave owners who present themselves as Roman men, with Paul and Silas as potential contaminants to Roman values.

Fifth, the physiognomic profile of the moral, powerful, and victorious Roman male contrasts with the dishonored, beaten, and incarcerated Paul and Silas, who, though finding themselves in prison—a place of filth, torture, and suffering—are given the means of escape, but instead remain along with the other prisoners. This is in contrast to other stories of prison escapes, particularly those involving Dionysus; the Philippi imprisonment does not follow expected events. Downplaying any explicit reference to divine intervention, the element of "stay" rather than escape evidences steadfast stability through courage, resolve, and solidarity.

Sixth, the physiognomic profiling of jailers suggests that the jailer makes for no more of a welcome, or potentially wholesome, convert and host than did Lydia. Brutishness, savagery, and a nature that understands only the language of bribes form the elements of the rhetorical profile of jailers. Combined with Lydia, the jailer's conversion suggests that the "growth of the Christian church" resembles more the growth of decays and molds rather than the frequently occurring images of pious house churches.

Throughout history up until the mid-twentieth century, most commentators have signaled a keen awareness of the ethnographic implications of Lydia's Lydian background.[202] In the process, dissonant elements such as Lydia's ethnographic profile have been smoothed out and blended with ideologically generated conventions, essentially disappearing from view.[203] However, to a first-century audience these and other seemingly inconspicuous elements would have jumped out and demanded attention.

As is becoming increasingly clear, there is no place here for a triumphalist reading of Acts 16. Through intertextural analysis, I have investigated the background of the "networks of meaning" found in the unit's elements. My analysis of ideological texture will now suggest how the author has structured these rhetorically in order to develop the unit's rhetorical impact.

---

202. This can be seen by revisiting chapter 1.
203. Such interpretations are evidence of what Perelman and Olbrechts-Tyteca call "psychical and social inertia," the "equivalents in consciousness and society of the inertia of physics"; inertia harmonizes incongruous elements with the normal and habitual (*New Rhetoric*, 105).

5
Ideological Texture

5.1. Introduction to Ideological Texture

The earlier investigation of inner texture provided a blueprint of the rhetorical unit's topographical profile through examining key repetitions, progressions, narrational/sensory-aesthetic, and argumentative textures. Through intertexture, I fleshed out rhetorically significant elements by situating these in their appropriate literary, social, cultural, and historical backgrounds; by observing which elements connected with each other and formed into topoi; and by noting certain forms of discourse that employed these topoi. Identifying the rhetorical landscape, while procedurally a critical feature of SRI, was but a means for reaching the main goal of this analysis, namely, determining how the topoi function argumentatively and for what purpose. Function, rather than form, and specifically rhetorical function, is the main concern of SRI. Using the inventory of topoi, elements, and argumentative threads gathered through the first two phases of analysis, I will explore how the author of Acts has deployed these rhetorically in developing the ideological texture of the text.

Earlier discussion in argumentative texture pointed out that since argumentation so frequently relies on intertextural elements, a full-bodied representation of a text's argumentative flow depends on the audience having access to "off the page" topoi from either its shared knowledge and/or the benefit of intertextural analysis. The analysis of ideological texture can reengage argumentative texture in order to determine how seemingly disparate topoi such as Lydian woman, purple seller, hospitality, military call for aid, dream-visions, place of prayer, mantics, and prison are joined rhetorically.

Once intertextural topoi are linked to the argumentative texture of the text, I will affirm that much of the rhetorical unit's ideological texture is developed through the synkratic use of rhetography.[1] Rhetography conscripts mental images for rhetorical purpose, but the argumentation does not unfold as a pastiche of discrete images; rather, rhetography works dynamically, linking, blending, and transforming into new possibilities. Cognitive science's approach to conceptual blending offers a helpful model for investigating how rhetographically sourced argumentation operates, since its focus is on how humans make meaning through cognitive mental images. Especially beneficial for examining ideological texture is the concept of "framing."

When a frame functions as an organizing structure, it specifies "the nature of the relevant activity, events, and participants."[2] The perspective of frames allows us to look at discourse and its topoi from within these three categories—activity, events, and participants—in order to bring the particular nature of each rhetorical frame into relief.

New understanding emerges from blends of frames, which often produce "emergent structure." Emergent structure, the result of certain blends, develops when audiences mentally fuse elements of frames together, "fill in" background information evoked by the blends, and elaborate further possibilities that arise from the blend. Fauconnier and Turner point out that "emergent structure arises in the blend that is not copied directly from any input," and therefore it opens a new horizon of possibilities for the audience.[3]

The task of charting ideological texture will be accomplished in part by looking for relevant conceptual blends that are evoked by the text and that are guided by *synkrisis*. More specifically, I will refer to the notion of what I term "Lydian touchstone *synkrisis*," a form of comparison through testing that will be discussed in greater detail below. As this discussion of ideological texture will maintain, the author formed an argumentative path by the παρακαλέω progression and thereby has structured a series of synkratic events that present the critical criteria for judging the basis for the coming together and separating apart (underscored by the unit's abundant recurrences of ἔρχομαι, "come, go" prefixed terms) of those who might mediate or obstruct the delivery of salvific "good news." Along this path, the author will rhetographically argue that the aid requested by the

---

1. For rhetography, see §2.1.3.1.3.
2. Fauconnier and Turner, *Way We Think*, 123.
3. Ibid, 48.

Macedonian man—fortifying loyalty and courage—can be delivered only by the mutual joining together of those who are "authentically" faithful.

An equally important, and parallel, task is protecting the news of salvation from contamination. Lydia's physiognomic profile suggests that Lydia would present an obstacle to the successful transmission of that which the Macedonian calls for. However, given that appearances can often be deceptive, Luke presents a number of illustrative cases that can help the reader discern the difference between genuine and "counterfeit" faith. Each of these explicit and implicit points of *synkrisis* are triggered through a progression of "παρακαλέω events" that will constitute the structural framework for the investigation of this rhetorical unit's ideological texture. I will turn to each of these sequentially, but first I will explain how a particular form of *synkrisis* emerged from another uniquely Lydian phenomenon: the Lydian touchstone.

5.1.1. Lydian Touchstone *Synkrisis*

Lydia's offer to the we-group presented a dilemma common to Greco-Roman discourse concerned with distinguishing between what potentially could be deceptive external appearances and a human's true inner essence. Such challenges were often expressed in literature through the metaphor of the Lydian touchstone, or testing stone. The material touchstone, reputed to come from the Lydian river Tmolus, separated false gold from pure and led to metaphorical "touchstone" comparisons that distinguished the true from the false, particularly between sincere moral character and its hypocritical manifestation. Touchstone comparisons were not invoked for general forms of character assessments, such as displaying who might have a more generous character compared to one more miserly, but specifically for distinguishing between corrupt, deceptive, counterfeit character and that of genuine, true, and pure. Touchstone comparisons sought to uncover who or what was trustworthy.

Touchstone rhetoric operated through *synkrisis*, what Fauconnier and Turner term "disanalogy," that is, the comparison of differences through similarity.[4] Fauconnier and Turner explain:

---

4. For *synkrisis*, see pp. 102–3.

We are not disposed to think of a brick and the Atlantic Ocean as disanalogous, but we are disposed to think of the Atlantic Ocean and the Pacific Ocean as disanalogous. Disanalogy is coupled to Analogy. Psychological experiments show that people are stymied when asked to say what is different between two things that are extremely different, but answer immediately when the two things are already tightly analogous.[5]

Touchstone *synkrisis* distinguished between what looked the same on the surface but was fundamentally different at its heart.[6] While normally touchstone *synkrisis* concerned cases where a corrupt inner core was masked by deceptive external appearance, Lydia's physiognomic profile presented an opposite, but equally challenging, difficulty. Luke directs the rhetorical force of Lydia's profile at distinguishing between an external corrupt physiognomic profile and the heart of a "worshiper of God." Lydia's offer to the we-group rhetographically asks that the quality of her loyalty to the Lord be put to the Lydian touchstone.

Greco-Roman social environments that were preoccupied with the dangers of hypocrisy, false friends, and deceptive appearances often produced literature that expressed a desire for the ability to see inside a human heart in order to verify external markers of character by comparing them to an internal essence.[7] For example, Athenaeus yearns for the

---

5. Ibid., 99.

6. As Leslie Kurke points out, the issue with counterfeit coins was not that they were a mixture of good and bad but rather that they appeared as pure but were to their core base. As an example, Theognis complains: "Nothing is harder to know than a man who is counterfeit, Kyrnos, nor does anything require more caution [than this]. The delusion of counterfeit gold and silver is endurable, Kyrnos, and easier for a wise man to discover. But if the mind of a man who is a friend, in his breast escapes [your] notice being false, and he has a tricky heart in his breast, this is the most counterfeit thing the god has made for mortals and this is the most grievous of all things to find out" (Theognis 117–124, quoted in Kurke, *Coins, Bodies, Games and Gold*, 54, brackets in translation). Referring to Theognis's observation, Kurke writes: "For Theognis is not concerned with the indistinguishable mixing of good and bad qualities in the *kakos anēr*, but with a thoroughly base interior (heart or soul) concealed beneath an apparently noble surface" (ibid.).

7. Referring to the first-century Mediterranean social environment, John Pilch writes: "This is a world where 'hypocrisy' is a constant plague, with the consequence that people are actually deceiving others by hiding their inner, evil thoughts behind a facade of orthopraxis (Luke 6:42; 12:1, 56; 13:15). They are like actors (the literal

faculty of vision that would permit a person to see into another's heart: "Would that, to see what sort of man each is, we could open his breast and look at his mind, then locking it up once more, regard him surely as our friend" (*Deipn.* 15.694e [Gulick, LCL]). This interest in finding a means of separating appearance from reality regularly found its metaphorical expression in the topos of the Lydian touchstone, another Lydian topos related to Lydian gold, which can trace long and deep roots beginning in the preclassical period and continuing through antiquity.

Theophrastus, the author of *Characteres*, also wrote *De Lapidibus*, a treatise on rocks and minerals. In it he tells of a stone, found only in the Lydian river Tmolus, that was used to test the quality of gold: "It is said that a stone has now been discovered which is far superior to the kind previously known, and detects the quality not only of refined gold, but also of copper alloyed with gold or with silver.... All stones of this kind are found in the river Tmolus" (*Lap.* 7.46–47 [Eichholz]). Pliny repeated Theophrastus's description and also explained that this stone, known as a "touchstone," was called by some a "Heraclian stone and others Lydian" (Pliny the Elder, *Nat.* 33.43 [Rackham, Jones, and Eichholz, LCL]). Despite Pliny's mention of a "Heraclian" name, the touchstone was most commonly known as a "Lydian touchstone" because of its reputedly being sourced from the gold-carrying Lydian river.[8] Gold's quality was tested by rubbing the object in question on the touchstone and then comparing the color of the streak deposited by it to another left behind by pure gold.

In ancient poetry and literature, metaphorical references to the Lydian touchstone featured regularly in discourse concerned with the display of truth. As early as the sixth century BCE, Theognis wrote: "If you would wash me, the water will flow unsullied from my head; you will find me in all matters as it were refined gold, red to the view when I be rubbed with the touchstone; the surface of me is untainted of black mould or rust, its

---

meaning of the Greek word *hypokritēs*) who refuse to be their authentic selves and instead play another role" (John J. Pilch, "Healing in Luke-Acts," in *The Social World of the New Testament: Insights and Models*, ed. Jerome H. Neyrey and Eric C. Stewart [Peabody, MA: Hendrickson, 2008], 213).

8. "*Pierre Lydienne* ce que nous nommons *Pierre-de-touche*, parce que les premières de cettes espèce avoient été tirées du fleuve *Tmolus* en Lydie" (Anne Claude Philippe Caylus, *Recueil d'Antiquités Égyptiennes, Étrusques, Grecques, Romaines et Gauloises* [Paris: Chez Desaint & Saillant, 1752], 5:135, emphasis original).

bloom ever pure and clean" (Theognis 447–452).⁹ In similar manner, Plato has Socrates ask:

> If my soul had happened to be made of gold, Callicles, do you think I should have been delighted to find one of those stones with which they test gold, and the best one; which, if I applied it, and it confirmed to me that my soul had been properly tended, would give me full assurance that I am in a satisfactory state and have no need of other testing? (*Gorg.* 486d–e [Lamb et al., LCL])

The poet Bacchylides wrote: "For the Lydian stone [Λυδία λίθος] reveals gold, but all-powerful wisdom and truth cross-examine the excellence of men" (*Frag.* 10).¹⁰ His contemporary Pindar wrote, "But, even as gold showeth its nature when tried by the touchstone [βασάνῳ], so it is with an upright mind [νόος ὀρθός]" (Pindar, *Pyth.* 10.68 [Sandys, LCL]).

A test of purity, the Lydian touchstone would display the true quality of goodness of a human's inner heart. In these cases, the result of the touchstone test would function as warrant of true character, a seal of excellence. The touchstone topos came from the language of economic exchange, the language of moneychangers and merchants from within which flowed an undercurrent of possible deception and where discerning true value was an ongoing concern.

While display of purity was one function of the touchstone topos, the metaphorical analogy to its metallurgical purpose further extended the touchstone topos beyond simply identifying a degree of purity, for touchstones regularly operated as "judgment stones" that were used to distinguish between counterfeit and real. Euripides has Medea implore: "O Zeus, why when you gave to men sure signs of gold that is counterfeit, is there no mark on the human body by which one could identify base men?" (*Med.* 516–519 [Kovacs, LCL]).¹¹ The touchstone, or testing stone, thus separated counterfeit from genuine, authentic from artifice. Cicero, for example, assumes his audience's familiarity with the touchstone topos when he writes: "By the exercise of care a fawning friend may be separated and distinguished from a true friend, just as everything pretended and false

---

9. Quoted in Page duBois, *Torture and Truth* (New York: Routledge, 1991), 12.
10. Preserved in Stobaeus, *Anthology* (on truth) and quoted in duBois, *Torture and Truth*, 14 n. 11.
11. Διειδέναι οὐδεὶς χαρακτὴρ ἐμπέφυκε σώματι.

may be distinguished from what is genuine and true" (*Amic.* 25.95 [Miller et al., LCL]). Separating false from true by way of the Lydian touchstone topos also found its way into Christian literature as Clement of Alexandria contrasted the discernment capabilities of a Christian "expert" with that of one sourced in faith alone, through the Lydian touchstone analogy.

> We approve of the sea-captain who has had plenty of experience and has visited "the cities of many peoples," and the doctor who has treated many patients. This is how some people form the idea of "the empirical doctor." Anyone who brings every experience to bear on right action, taking models from Greeks and non-Greeks alike, is a highly skilled hunter of truth. He really is "many-wiled." Like the testing stone (a stone from Lydia that was believed to distinguish genuine from false gold), our "man of many skills," our Christian Gnostic, is also competent to distinguish sophistry from philosophy, superficial adornment from athletics, cookery from pharmacy, rhetoric from dialectic, and then in Christian thought, heresies from actual truth. (*Strom.* 1.9.44.1–4 [Ferguson])

The touchstone topos functioned in two interrelated ways: it displayed purity of character, and it functioned as an instrument of separation that distinguished artificial from genuine, corrupt from pure. Touchstone tests unveiled those who had attempted to disguise their true natures by taking on the appearance of "the real thing." Like Lydian physiognomy, Lydian touchstone rhetoric was also associated with Lydian legend; but rather than invoking vitriolic characterizations of Lydian degeneracy, it instead was concerned with the other side of the coin, as it were, distinguishing corrupt from genuine.

Metaphorical use of the Lydian touchstone bridged biblical and Greco-Roman discourse through the common element of testing of character framed within a language of metallurgy. In comparing the biblical book of Proverbs with the collection of gnomic sayings ascribed to Theognis, John Pairman Brown observes that the two books share "their most common imagery" in "the *testing of gold* as a symbol of men's character, with actual common vocabulary."[12] The refining fire and test by touchstone led to the same end: distinguishing the genuine and pure from the corrupted and false. Theophrastus writes:

---

12. John Pairman Brown, "Proverb-Book, Gold-Economy, Alphabet," *JBL* 100 (1981): 169, emphasis original.

> The nature of the stone that tests gold is remarkable [θαυμαστή], for it seems to have the same power as fire, for that also tests gold. On that account some people are puzzled by this, but not too aptly, for the stone does not test in the same way. But fire [works] by changing and altering the colors, while the stone [works] by friction. For it appears to have the power to bring out the essential nature of each [metal].... And all such stones are found in the River Tmolus. (*Lap.* 45, 47)[13]

The touchstone element continued to circulate through antiquity, common to rhetoric concerned with separating the hypocrite from the true friend. Theognis writes: "Seek as I will, I can find no man like myself that is a true comrade[14] free of guile; and when I am put to the test and tried even as gold is tried beside lead, the mark of pre-eminence is upon me" (Theognis 415–418 [Edmonds, LCL]). Plutarch, again employing a rhetoric of economic exchange, evokes the touchstone by comparing a false friend to a counterfeit coin.

> For it is cruel to discover friends that are no friends at a crucial time which calls for friends, since there is then no exchanging one that is untrustworthy and spurious for the true and trustworthy. But one's friend, like a coin, should have been examined and approved before the time of need, not proved by the need. (Plutarch, *How to Tell a Flatterer from a Friend* 49C–E [Perrin et al., LCL])

With the threat of deceptive appearances presented by hypocrisy or flattery, the touchstone was an instrument that could enable right-sightedness.[15]

---

13. Quoted in Kurke, *Coins, Bodies, Games and Gold*, 57–58, brackets in translation.
14. Πιστὸν ἑταῖρον.
15. Herodotus tells of how after the Persian ruler Xerxes had decided to invade Athens, he gathered "the noblest among the Persians," ostensibly to consider their various opinions on his purposed attack on Greece, and yet, having made clear that attack was his favored course of action and one that was also "the will of heaven," he, like other similar rulers, implicitly expected to hear his plan affirmed rather than challenged. As expected, most of his advisors simply flattered his opinion. One, however, Artabanus, decided to speak an opposing opinion and in so doing presented it within the touchstone analogy: "If opinions opposite the one to the other be not uttered, it is not possible that choice should find the better, but that one which has been spoken must be followed; but even if they be spoken, the better can be found; even as the purity of gold cannot of itself be discerned, but when gold by rubbing is compared with gold, we then discern the better" (Herodotus, *Hist.* 7.10 [Godley, LCL]).

This claim that a Lydian touchstone topos is deployed in structuring the argumentation of the unit has support not only through common elements suggested by Lydia's physiognomic profile and the pervasive question of her loyalty but also by lexical clues suggested by Lukan oral-scribal intertexture, through the term βάσανος, "test, trial or torture." Page duBois has analyzed the etymological move from Lydian touchstone to that of truth-seeking through torture and begins by pointing out that βάσανος, originally referring to testing by touchstone, later developed the meaning of testing by torture: "The ancient Greek word for torture is *basanos*. It means first of all the touchstone used to test gold for purity; the Greeks extended its meaning to denote a test or trial to determine whether something or someone is real or genuine. It then comes to mean also inquiry by torture."[16] Test by physical torture or suffering within the language of metals became a way for early Christians to express the manifestations of steadfast faith. For example, 1 Peter encourages the audience through the hope of salvation to endure nearer-term suffering in order to display the

---

16. DuBois, *Torture and Truth*, 7. "βάσανος: *the touch-stone*, Lat. lapis Lydius, a dark-coloured stone on which pure gold, when rubbed, leaves a peculiar mark, hence 2. generally, *a test, trial whether a thing be genuine or real*, 3. *inquiry by torture, the 'question,' torture*, used to extort evidence from slaves. 2. *torture of disease*, N.T. (Deriv. uncertain)" (LSJ, s.v. βάσανος). The term, βάσανος (verbal βασανίζω), occurs in Luke-Acts in two places, in the stories of the rich man and Lazarus and of the Gerasene demoniac (Luke 8:28; 16:23, 28). The rich man not only shares with Lydia a rhetorical profile evoking degenerate luxury but also the only occurrences in Luke-Acts of the term "purple" (Luke 16:19; Acts 16:14) as well as the term διαβαίνω. He also shares with the rhetorical unit infrequently occurring terms such as κακός (Luke 16:25; Acts 16:28) and τράπεζα (Luke 16:21; Acts 16:34). In the story, the rich man, of course, fails the test and is relegated to the "excluded from salvation" frame.

The story of the Gerasene demoniac shares lexical connectivity with the repetitive texture of the rhetorical unit, including an abundance of ἔρχομαι prefixed terms, prison-related terms, and common points such as "calling out in a loud voice" (Luke 8:28; Acts 16:28), as well as the only two times in Luke-Acts that someone calls out the epithet τοῦ θεοῦ τοῦ ὑψίστου (Luke 8:28; Acts 16:17). Like Philippi, Gerasa is framed as gentile territory, it evokes Roman space through Latin loanwords (λεγιών: Luke 8:30; κολωνία: Acts 16:12), where spirits as well as instruments of profit are driven out (python spirit, pigs), leading the inhabitants of each city to "fear" and ask the exorcist in question—Jesus in Gerasa, Paul in Philippi—to leave (Luke 8:37; Acts 16:38–39). The analysis of oral-scribal intertexture suggests that elements evoking the Lydian touchstone not only are found through Lydia, but also lexically with two units in Luke that have a high degree of correlation with the rhetorical unit.

purity of their faith: "In this you rejoice, though now for a little while you may have to suffer various trials, so that the genuineness of your faith, more precious than gold which though perishable is tested by fire, may redound to praise and glory and honor at the revelation of Jesus Christ" (1 Pet 1:6–7). Whether by fire or by touchstone, the end result was the same: separation of the corrupt from the uncorrupted. The contrary states did not simply appear, however, as if in contact with a magic potion. They could distinguish themselves only through testing, through either melting or rubbing. As a result of this crucial element of testing, the element of the assayer's refining fire commonly described God's judgment.[17] While testing by refining fire was often a topos in apocalyptic discourse,[18] the notion of testing was used more broadly in various forms of discourse to convey the process by which God discerned a person or people's true nature. The inner person became unveiled in God's sight when tested by fire.[19] In Greco-Roman literature, the Lydian touchstone test revealed the inner person.

It is within a touchstone-*synkrisis* argumentative framework that the author of Luke-Acts has positioned Lydia and her request for the assessment of her loyalty to the Lord. We can imagine this *synkratic* movement of "rubbing away" false exteriors, or affirming essential interiors, as a horizontal back-and-forth, as two characters rub against each other in the narrative for comparative effect. Each synkratic event of inner character unveiling charts a course through the narrative by way of the rhetorical unit's principal progressive sequences: the παρακαλέω progression.[20] Each of the cases of the rhetorical unit's παρακαλέω "events" involve alliance or rupture with the Pauline group. The basis for one or the other is revealed through the comparative process of *synkrisis*.

---

17. E.g., Ps 66:10; Prov 17:3; Jer 6:27; 9:7; Zech 13:9; Jas 5:3; 1 Pet 1:7; Rev 3:18.
18. Robbins, *Invention of Christian Discourse*, 203.
19. The Epistle of James condemns "the rich" for having failed the test and encourages the others to hold firm in faith despite their sufferings: "Your gold and silver have rusted, and their rust will be evidence against you and will eat your flesh like fire" (Jas 5:3).
20. For the παρακαλέω progression, see §3.2 above.

5.2. The Παρακαλεω of the Macedonian Man: Blending Military Frames

The "military" category situates the rhetorical unit's discourse generally, but when we examine the particular topoi that intertextual analysis discovered in Paul's vision, and the we-group's response to it, it is possible to suggest that within a general category of military discourse there are three distinct organizing frames introduced by Paul's vision: military call for aid; sanctioning divine dream-vision; and delivery of "good news" (εὐαγγελίζομαι). Also, a fourth frame of a warrior-God emerges from the we-group's interpretation of the vision as a call from God.

The four frames, while equally at home in military discourse, concern distinct events, activities, and participants. These distinctions not only differentiate the organizing principle of the frames but also in some cases are incompatible with elements found in other frames. The frames are not easily blended: for example, how does self-expressive speech—the activity of "announcing good news"—fit together with the expectation of material, auxiliary help evoked within a military call-for-aid frame? Yet the author of Acts does blend the four and by so doing develops a reconfigured frame that forms the rhetorical backdrop to the unit's ensuing occasions of παρακαλέω.

Although four military-discourse frames can be identified in the opening of the rhetorical unit, they are not presented independently but rather through a blend that privileges certain elements, diminishes or removes others, and ultimately forms a reconfigured frame that draws on its source conventions, all the while moving beyond these into a new framing structure. The blend occurs by bringing together some of the key topoi of the frames, like military aid, victory, and divinely sanctioned initiative, and also by incorporating absent or incongruous elements like the nonspecific nature of the call, the absence of divine elements in the vision itself, and conceptually resolving clashing elements like the incompatible roles of the main participants of each frame. In examining how the frames are blended, I will highlight incongruities and clashes in order to see how they also influence the formation of a new framing structure. This emergent frame privileges the call-for-aid frame, from within which successful discernment of the divinely sanctioned good news of victory will provide the sought-after resource of steadfast courage and faith.

5.2.1. Blending for Rhetorical Effect: A Call from God to Announce "Good News" Comes as a Call for Military Aid from a Macedonian

If indeed the Macedonian man would evoke great conquering heroes—and given the audience's historical context, he likely would—then the we-group's rush to assist would have created an image of auxiliary aid to a Macedonian campaign destined for massive conquest. Conquest, that is, Alexander-style. As Bloomquist has pointed out, the rhetorical impact of Paul's vision would have suggested to an audience that the disciples were involved in "a new war, with new battles and a new people to bring into subjection."[21] As the we-group runs to help the Macedonian, the audience might almost taste the victory at hand. However, from the beginning, the author undermines a facile reading of the vision's implications by incorporating incompatible elements and omitting anticipated ones.

The Macedonian man is apprehended within the locus of Paul's emotion-fused thought—emphasized by elements of vision and sight (ὅραμα, ὁράω: Acts 16:9, 10)—and not, as would be expected, in the external audible world (nor by its material proxy: a letter). In fact, if the man's request were to be situated outside of a dream-vision context, it would fit with regular interhuman communication; a person speaks and the receiver of the speech deduces the speaker's intended meaning. This seeming clash between two communicative channels is resolved by the way that divine dream-visions were understood to operate in the ancient world. Divinely sent messengers regularly communicated in human self-expressive fashion within the dreamer's zone of emotion-fused thought. For, as Peter Struck observes, "dreams are perhaps the ancient world's most-traveled bridge between the heavens and the individual."[22] The divine dream-vision normalizes what otherwise would be an abnormal communicative encounter.

Yet the divine dream-vision frame, while normalizing the communication process between the Macedonian man and Paul as a form of divine communication, at the same time finds itself clashing with the profile of the Macedonian man due to his geo/ethnographic human, rather than other-

---

21. Bloomquist, "Parallel to Paul's Vision in Acts 16:9," 17.
22. Peter Struck, "Viscera and the Divine: Dreams as the Divinatory Bridge between the Corporeal and the Incorporeal," in *Prayer, Magic, and the Stars in the Ancient and Late Antique World*, ed. Scott Noegel, Joel Walker, and Brannon Wheeler, Magic in History (University Park: Pennsylvania State University Press, 2003), 125.

worldly, portrayal. Strikingly absent in Paul's dream-vision is any appearance of a spiritual-being character. Divine visions catalyzed action precisely because the leaders receiving them understood that a contemplated, or suggested, plan had divine warrant; in this the divine element was crucial. The Macedonian man grounds the divine-vision frame, as it were, and in so doing removes the critical element of assured divine support.

The first effect of dream-visions was not purposeful action; rather, prior to purposeful action, the basic effect of such visions was to encourage and motivate the emotion-fused heart of a leader. In its unhesitating immediacy, the response of the Pauline group remains fully consistent with other responses to divine dream visions: an enthusiastic emotion-fused decision to act. The setting and event—a vision experienced during the night in Troas—is consistent with the activities triggered by divinely sent dream-visions decisively seeking to move into new geographic territory. However, the content of the vision, a Macedonian man rather than divine being, is out of place with the divine dream-vision frame. Clashes of elements between frames such as those introduced by the Macedonian's human emphasis in a call-for-aid frame with the expected, yet absent, requisite divine element in the dream-vision frame blend together in a way that synthesizes, and innovatively reconfigures, the clash into a new blend. In their blend, the frames of military call for aid and divine dream-vision bring a geo/ethnically defined human element to prominence while evoking a spiritual-world communicative medium.

The typical roles of participants in divinely sent dream-visions and military calls for aid also introduce incompatibilities with Paul's vision, for the role of a person who received a divinely sent dream-vision differed from the role of a person receiving a call for aid. In divinely sent dream-visions, the receiver of the dream was a leader who initiated military action, whereas in calls for aid it was the caller. In the case of Paul's vision, however, the Macedonian man is the initiator, while Paul, who as dreamer would typically be the leader, here instead is the respondent to the Macedonian's initiative. Moreover, when the author introduces the "we-group" narrational character, another normative shift is introduced. Ordinarily, a leader would experience a vision, and either he or a dream interpreter would infer the meaning of the vision and then relay the meaning—typically direction to action—to his troops. Once again, in Paul's vision roles are blended: one leader becomes many.

The first action of the we-group is one of interpretation: "concluding [συμβιβάζοντες] that God had called us to proclaim the good news to them" (Acts 16:10); and it is through this act that the we-group first comes into existence as a narrative character in Acts. The term συμβιβάζω, which "means strictly 'to cause to stride together,'"[23] is used to describe the first formative act of the we-group—deducting and inferring the meaning of the vision. This first instance of "knitting together"[24] as a narrational voice comes from the we-group's hearing (stressed by καλέω in the compound) God's narratively absent voice as a response to a human's call for aid emitted from within one person's dream-vision. The emotion-fused act of hearing within the collective's emotion-fused heart forms the lever for enabling the delivery of the Macedonian's sought-after aid. This complex shift from one to several takes place not through working together in purposeful action, nor by self-expressive speech, but rather through the zone of emotion-fused thought. Within a dream-vision frame, the we-group's emotion-fused response subsumes the role regularly reserved for a military leader.

Each of the four military frames introduced by Luke lacks normative elements: the dream-vision is absent any explicit divine elements; the call of the Macedonian does not specify the resource requested, nor does it name an enemy, and further, it is conveyed through an emotion-fused dream; the respondents conclude that a nonmaterial resource, εὐαγγέλιον, will supply the auxiliary aid; a group, rather than a single leader interprets the dream; and a salvific warrior-God is "heard" through the Macedonian's request. Through these incongruities, Luke develops a rich cognitive blend by structuring an emergent frame for the means of salvation. The participants are Macedonian warriors, the we-group, and God; the event is an earthly/spiritual victory blend; and the activity is delivering auxiliary military aid through preaching.

A closer look at the function of the resource to be delivered, εὐαγγέλιον, is an early indicator that, from the beginning, the author intends to suggest that this victory will take an unanticipated path toward an unconventional outcome. In essence, the Macedonian man requisitions a resource that is expected to bring victory to the Macedonians. Through this element of victory, εὐαγγέλιον, the call from the Macedonian man fuses with the perceived call from God. In this unusual fusion of a παρακαλέω from a militarily imaged man with the προσκαλέω from God, the element of εὐαγγέλιον as

---

23. Gerhard Delling, "Συμβιβάζω," *TDNT* 7:763.
24. LSJ, s.v. συμβιβάζω.

a fortifying resource in military conflict will be used by Luke to present his ideological understanding of the nature of εὐαγγέλιον as divine salvation.

Good news was a form of nourishment of the heart, strengthening inner resolve and eagerness of spirit to take on the enemy. At the same time, within a gospel framework, good news was the news of God's salvation through Jesus. By blending a military call for aid with a response of good news, Luke signals his major ideological claim: faithful courage is the salient fortifying resource that is required for salvation. The author employs a response to a military call for aid to illustrate how the bestowal of divine salvation was to be delivered. Moreover, by requiring the we-group to interpret the meaning of Paul's vision, Luke positions the emotion-fused act of discernment as a critical mode of delivery of salvation. Finally, in their role of responders, the we-group is positioned to assist others, namely, the "Macedonians," to develop this crucial faculty of discernment that would lead to faithful courage.

5.2.2. Conclusion: Ideological Texture of the Παρακαλέω of the Macedonian Man

A call from a Macedonian man catalyzes a renewed sense of direction in the Pauline group and motivates their crossing into new geographic territory. Almost immediately, the man's call is fused with a perceived call from God, creating an analogous relationship: a call for military aid is as a summons from God to bring "good news." By bringing together four military-discourse frames—call for aid, divinely sent dream-vision, announcement of victorious good-news, and warrior-God—Luke both introduces salvific expectations while concurrently plants seeds of incompatibility that will grow in prominence, destabilize cultural presumptions, and reconfigure and create a new image of salvation.

Incompatible elements begin to unsettle an otherwise standard account of divinely directed campaigns. Most importantly, Paul's vision does not contain any elements that might suggest a message from a spiritual being. Instead, the narrative's emphasis on the Macedonian's earthbound origin removes the crucial element of implied divine sanction for a leader's future actions. The we-group responds, however, as if it had heard the voice of God, despite having heard only the voice of the Macedonian. Moreover, instead of compelling a leader's initiative, the vision compels a response to the initiative of another. The we-group is called to join forces, and from the outset Luke brings the notion of alliance into prominence.

Not only does Paul's vision shift his role from the convention of leader to responder, but also the vision's interpretation and response further shifts leadership from a single person to a group, a group that "hears" the voice of their ultimate leader—God—in the zone of their emotion-fused thought. These subtle shifts from normative accounts of dream-visions and calls for aid could be easily overlooked by an audience ready to hear of grand victorious sweeps. Soon, however, mounting incompatibilities will become too jarring and incongruous to ignore. The Macedonian man is a figure of irony that will begin to unravel with the introduction of the women by the river.

5.3. The Παρακαλεω of Lydia: Discerning a "Worshiper of God"

The Macedonian man calls the Pauline group to himself and his fellow Macedonians, and then, progressively, Lydia calls the we-group to her home. The Macedonian's call is framed within a military call for aid, whereas Lydia's is framed within the social model of hospitality (Acts 16:9, 15). Although the two frames do not appear to share any common elements beyond the lexical, Luke blends the frames by fusing elements of the Macedonian's call with Lydia's. Through the blend, elements that are found in the emergent military frame blend, such as alliance, fortifying resource of faithful courage, victory, and salvation, emerge in new form as the author develops the notion of who can rightfully be called a "worshiper of God," and, in the collective sense, form a "house of prayer."

Framed by military discourse, the we-group's first move in Philippi invokes a new frame when, instead of heading toward a battlefield or army camp, it goes out in search of a προσευχή, "place of prayer," in Acts 16:13. Once the place-of-prayer frame is introduced and begins to take on prominence in the narrative, it does not simply erase the military opening, but rather the frame blends with the military opening to evoke other cases where military discourse blended with "place of prayer." Jewish religio-political issues concerned with territoriality are at the heart of these military/house of prayer blends.[25] The frame of military aid, when blended with προσευχή, would raise expectations that the we-group would find either a Jewish or, perhaps due to the Macedonian element, a Jewish/gentile community engaged in some form of territorial political/military con-

---

25. For discussion of προσευχή and territorial conflict, see §4.2.6 above.

flict. The audience would expect that, called by God, the we-group would embolden a socioreligious community in its struggle against a common enemy. Within these expectations raised by the blend between the call-for-aid frame and place of prayer, Lydia's profile will introduce further incompatible elements, and consequently will again destabilize the blend.

5.3.1. Clash of Frames: Προσευχή, Lydia, and Fortifying Resource of Εὐαγγέλιον

Given that the space of "synagogue" was a normative Jewish posttemple Sabbath setting, it is not surprising that the elements of Sabbath and place of prayer have often attached themselves to Lydia's descriptor as a "worshiper of God." When the phrase "worshiper of God" (σεβομένη τὸν θεόν) has been linked to conventional Sabbath activity, it has imaginatively transformed the setting by the river into a Jewish synagogue assembly made up of pious Jewish women. The entrenched nature of this type of characterization shows through the NRSV's having shifted "worshiper of God" to first place in Lydia's list of descriptors following her name, despite the fact that it is found last in the Greek text.[26] The move belies a premise that "worshiper of God" functions as an inaugural framing element in Lydia's profile rather than the incompatible clash that it actually is.

For although at first glance it may seem that the gathering in Philippi implies "business as usual," for the we-group, there exist problems with presuming a Jewish pious identity for the group gathered by the river and for Lydia. The difficulty with facile portraits of Lydia as a pious gentile who worships the God of Israel is that the assembled women, through their representative member Lydia, are not cast as pious Jewish women resembling Philo's *Therapeutae*, or as the pious disciple Tabitha (Acts 9:36), whose purposeful action is devoted to works of charity toward widows, or as a Jewish mother of a disciple (16:1), or as a Jewish wife and loyal teacher of the Way such as Priscilla (18:26). If indeed a representative member of a group can illuminate a group's character, and from a first-century collective understanding of personality it would, then Lydia's rhetorical profile (as a huckstering, Lydian, profit-seeking woman) would frame the assembly as corrupt space rather than a synagogue. Since interpretations

---

26. "A certain woman named Lydia, a worshiper of God, was listening to us; she was from the city of Thyatira and a dealer in purple cloth" (Acts 16:14 NRSV).

have not taken into account the physiognomic profile activated by Lydia's preceding descriptors—Lydian purple seller—the jarringly incongruent ending of "worshiper of God" is lost.

A frame of Jewish prayer-house assembly can contain elements such as prayer, Jewish people, pious gentiles, Scripture, community leaders, and God of Israel and can even quite readily blend in military elements such as Josephus's breastplate and sword, or Philo's account of increasing hostilities with Gaius, but it cannot retain its integrity as an organizing structure by incorporating an element such as Lydia. The spatial frame of Prayer house and character frame of Lydian purple-selling female, using the language of cognitive science, clash as frames—they cannot readily blend together because they contain too many incompatible elements. Especially when character and frame are inextricably linked through a physiognomic profiling such as Lydia's, the prayer-house frame clashes profoundly with Lydia's.

Ambiguous and multivalent meanings of typically unvarying sacred terms have been discovered as one of the repetitive features of the rhetorical unit, and the river gathering becomes the omphalos of this ambiguity. On an earlier Sabbath in Antioch, in stark contrast with the incongruous setting outside of Philippi, the Pauline group had entered a clearly designated synagogue,[27] sat down, and, after the reading of Scripture, delivered their message (to either all men or a group containing some men)[28] a message that was framed within the history of Israel. Within this unequivocally conventional Jewish space, Paul spoke to Jews and to proselytes who were explicitly identified as such, that is, "pious proselytes."[29] When σέβω was used again in Antioch, the spatial reference point shifted from the synagogue to the city, where its prominent men[30] and leading (presumably gentile) women of propriety[31] (Acts 13:50) were roused by "the Jews" to expel Paul and Barnabas.[32] The next time σέβω is used, it refers to Lydia. The space in which she is encountered is defined by a gathering of women by the river, which may or may not be the (uncommonly named) place of

---

27. τὴν συναγωγήν (Acts 13:14).
28. Ἰσραηλῖται καὶ οἱ φοβούμενοι.
29. τῶν σεβομένων προσηλύτων.
30. τοὺς πρώτους τῆς πόλεως.
31. τὰς σεβομένας γυναῖκας τὰς εὐσχήμονας (13:16).
32. In each of the Antioch cases, σέβω is attributive.

prayer. Within this ambiguous space, rather than designating women of propriety, σέβω designates a Lydian purple seller (Acts 16:14).

While the history of interpretation has generally sanitized Lydia's image, an alternate reaction is found in the works of Ephrem and Ishoʻdad of Merv, who excised any mention of Lydia from their commentaries. Most especially, the comments of Arator and the Venerable Bede display the intense clash with normative piety that is presented by Lydia.[33] Arator skips from his explicit commentary on the Macedonian man to the slave woman, but between each of these, in the space where comments about Lydia should be located, he indirectly tackles the very issue Lydia's profile raises.

In suggesting why the disciples were precluded from preaching in Asia, Arator first raises a question regarding the universality of salvation and asks, "If the Almighty filled with bountiful generosity, proclaims, 'I have not come to destroy mankind but rather to save it,' what occasion brings it about that this is denied to some and given to others, though the rich mercy of Jesus wills that it come to the aid of everyone jointly?"[34] Arator's answer seems to be that while some are ready to hear the words of salvation, others, because of their taint, will need to wait until they are more suitably endowed. Singling out the suitability of potential hearers of the salvific word, Arator writes: "The Master who cleanses deep within knows which hearts now bear the word [and] whom evil error is still blocking up inwardly, so that teaching may then serve its function when it comes safely, which He says [thus], 'Let dogs not undertake to do violence to holy things, and let pigs laden down with mire not turn their contagion against pearls.'" Without explicitly naming Lydia as the potential contaminant, Arator refers obliquely to another remaining "difficult matter" and continues to develop his argument that the word of salvation should be protected from the "contagion" of "pigs" mired in filth.

Connecting purple with sexuality, Arator begins to expound on how the "holy Chief Priest" dressed in clothing "ornamented with purple and gold borders" also wears "a similar garment on the thigh, by which he may put a covering upon his private parts when going forth to the temple, and as a priest may strive to approach the mysteries chastely with bound loins." Lest there be any doubt about which "private parts" are in question,

---

33. For dates and references, see pp. 12–13.
34. All quotes from Arator, *Arator's On the Acts of the Apostles*, 69–70, translators' brackets.

Arator elaborates that these are "those bound members which dark lust possesses," that should only be "freed for marriage." The text then moves to develop an analogous relationship between conjugal creativity to sharing the effects of the word: "For Paul also rather often said that offspring can be given the seed of the word, by his mentioning 'my little children.'" Moving to his conclusion, Arator makes his point clear: just as semen must be reserved for its appropriate role (procreation) with an appropriate woman (a wife), so too the words of a (sexually chaste) priest should be reserved for cleansed hearts: "It is pleasing then for procreative eloquence to be subdued for a little while and for the teacher to control his eagerness, moderating the forces of his talent for a time and carrying them bound up, keeping holy things for the cleansed lest the profane wear them away underfoot as they are poured out." Having developed and concluded his argument that in essence claims that "pigs" will need to wait to hear the good news, Arator then carries on to the Python-spirit episode. Lydia is never named, and no mention is made of the we-group sitting down with women and sharing their self-expressive speech. But the invective found in the space between comments on the call of the Macedonian man and the ensuing Python-spirit episode is likely the truest representation of how Luke would have imagined the rhetorical impact of Lydia on his audience.[35]

The Venerable Bede, who "used Arator frequently,"[36] also excises any mention of Lydia but, like Arator, brings in an allusion to dogs in reference to the people of Asia (Lydia's place of origin) as well as to the Syrophoenician woman's crumbs. Bede writes:

---

35. It is not surprising to learn that Arator's interests were directed toward supporting apostolic succession (motivated by his patron) over the universalization of the gospel. François Bovon writes: "A l'encontre de l'auteur des Acts, sa préférence va à Pierre plutôt qu'à Paul. Cet intérêt porté aux apôtres n'est du reste pas historique, mais il reflète son affection pour celui qu'il considère comme le sucesseur de Pierre, Le pape Vigile, auquel il dédie son ouvrage.... Toute l'histoire de Corneille démontre, selon lui, l'autorité et le prestige de Pierre: les derniers vers consacrés à notre péricope ne sont pas une louagne à Dieu pour avoir appelé les Gentils à l'Évangile, mais un éloge de Pierre, qui, le premier, out conscience de leur élection et, tel un chasseur, partit à leur recherche. Certes, le thème de l'élection des nations n'est pas oublié mail il est subordonné à la personne de Pierre" (François Bovon, *De Vocatione Gentium: Histoire de l'Interprétation d'Act. 10, 1–11, 18 dans les Six Premiers Siècles*, BGBE 8 [Tübingen: Mohr Siebeck, 1967], 14–15).

36. Arator, *Arator's On the Acts of the Apostles*, 3.

Cornelius, who devoted himself to prayers and almsgiving, was shown the way of salvation as his reward. And God, who knows hearts, on account of his kindness, withdrew [his] teacher from Asia lest, if what is holy were given to dogs, the error of their wicked heart might be judged more reprehensible on account of their disregard of his preaching. On the other hand the Macedonian legate, whom we believe to have been the angel of that people, asked the apostles, who were concerned with other matters, that crumbs of the Lord's bread might be offered to them.[37]

The pious Cornelius was worthy to receive the aid of salvation, but "dogs" with wicked hearts were not. Faced with Lydia's ineligibility to receive the message of salvation, excising and indirectly condemning was one response to the conundrum presented by Luke's account. The alternate response that turned Lydia into a modest hostess was much less vitriolic, but in a way even more distorting of Lydia's rhetorical impact.

Arator's comments hit the rhetorical target of Lydia: a contagion will befoul the words of salvation. In doing so, the contagion becomes an enemy in the battle for salvation. Luke's concern over the ethos of the good news and accordingly its messengers does indeed become a major point of focus for the unit. Yet, quick to spot the enemy as a result of their own ideological agendas, commentators such as Arator discounted the Lord's sanction of Lydia as a chosen recipient of the Macedonian's call.

5.3.2. Divine Sanction of Lydia's Heart

By having her emotion-fused heart opened by the Lord in order to grasp the meaning of the good news, Lydia becomes the first narrated recipient of the Macedonian's requisitioned aid. As a recipient of military aid, she would have received the lacking fortifying resource and would consider herself allied with the providers of the resource: the we-group. As much as these are the frames, topoi, and elements that are argumentatively blended into the narrative, there are a number of sociocultural difficulties with bringing Lydia into this framework. Not only did her physiognomic profile deem her unsuitable for house-of-prayer membership, but also, from the perspective of a military call for aid, Lydia would have been equally out of place with the profile of a Macedonian warrior, yet she is progressively

---

37. Bede, *The Venerable Bede: Commentary on the Acts of the Apostles*, trans. and ed. Lawrence T. Martin, Cistercian Studies (Kalamazoo, MI: Cistercian, 1989), 135–36.

linked with such a figure. In fact, by all accounts Lydia would doubly be excluded from any consideration of warrior status on account of both her female gender as well as her retail-trading occupation.

In a military call-for-aid frame, not only were women out of place, but their presence was also antithetical to the very notion of any military configuration. A similarly incongruent element is situated in Lydia's retail-trading occupation. Herodotus's story of how the Egyptian pharaoh had been abandoned by his warriors, and in desperation could march out to meet the Assyrians only with the market people including the retailing hucksters, spotlights the stark contrast between warriors and retail traders. Without the nocturnal appearance of the salvific mice, Sethos would surely have been doomed.[38] A legendary warrior such as the image formed by the Macedonian man would not only be incompatible with the image of a woman or retail-trader but also in the cultural blends of these topoi would form their antithesis.

Yet Luke consummates the response to the Macedonian's call by the good news being announced to Lydia. It is not any easy blend. In fact, it is one that many would have considered as humorous a concept as the Egyptian Sethos's army of market people, and therefore it might function as a form of satire (Herodotus, *Hist*.2.141). Satire, as Olbrechts-Tyteca points out in *Le Comique du Discours*, is a form of indirect argumentation that works through inductive rather than deductive argumentation. Satire introduces incompatibilities with norms and conventions and is a form of the "ridiculous." Olbrechts-Tyteca distinguishes the inductive incompatibilities found in the "ridiculous" from contradictions within

---

38. See pp. 171–72. Separately, Herodotus emphasized the distinction between warriors and retail traders when he cataloged Egyptian social classes on the basis of occupation, and included "hucksters" (οἱ κάπηλοι) and warriors. He then elaborates: "Those who learn trades and their descendents are held in less esteem than the rest of the people, and those who have nothing to do with artisans' work, especially men who are free to practice the art of war, are highly honoured." This dichotomy between market people and warriors is, according to Herodotus, an opinion "held by all the Greeks" (Herodotus, *Hist*. 2.164–167 [Godley, LCL]). This culturally understood clash between warriors and sellers is also found in playwright Aeschylus's description of a fearsome warrior who has not come "to do any petty trading in the battle [οὐ καπηλεύσειν μάχην]" (Aeschylus, *Sept*. 545 [Smyth]) that, as LSJ informs, idiomatically means will not "fight half-heartedly" (s.v. καπηλεία).

formal logic that she calls the "absurd."[39] From this perspective, Lydia is a ridiculous figure, wholly incompatible with the Macedonian man due to sociocultural conventions governing the profiles of warriors and Lydian retailers and yet whose call is tied, by its progressive characteristics, with the Macedonian's.[40]

In the stark opposition between a Macedonian warrior and Lydia, Luke begins to turn audience expectations on their head by linking what should be two antithetical figures through a progressive inductive relationship. For although a military call-for-aid frame would have raised expectations in the audience that the we-group would deliver its fortifying resource and form an alliance with Alexander-type warriors, their encounter with Lydia displays a rather different understanding. Argumentative textural analysis had noted that the we-group does not pause, even for a moment, when they discover the women by the river. Instead, in a breach with cultural gender protocols, they unhesitatingly perform a socially unnatural act—they sit with the women and begin a Sabbath-day discourse with them. In the purposeful act of sitting down with the women and offering them their self-expressive speech, the we-group fulfills their response of delivering the "good news" to the "Macedonians," yet not even remotely in a manner that would meet audience expectations.

Significantly, it is this particular act of the we-group that receives divine sanction when the Lord opens Lydia's heart. While an expected element of divine sanction was notably absent from Paul's vision, sanction instead appears through the Lord's taking action within Lydia's heart, validating, but not inciting, the group's interpretation of the vision. Paul's vision does evoke divine communication; however, it does not supply the foolproof seal of divine sanction. Instead, the group hears a Macedonian's call for aid as if it were a summons from God to deliver good news. The Lord, by joining in with the Pauline group's initiative with the women by the river through opening Lydia's heart, affirms that the we-group got it right.

The nature of a Lydian purple seller's heart would be viewed through the lens of Greco-Roman physiognomy as a center of deceptive, luxury-loving guile. The physiognomic profiling of Lydians invoked a topos that

---

39. Lucie Olbrechts-Tyteca, *Le Comique du Discours*, Sociologie Générale et Philosophie Sociale (Brussels: Éditions de l'Université de Bruxelles, 1974), 159–61, 185.

40. "A statement is ridiculous as soon as it conflicts, without justification, with an accepted opinion" (Perelman and Olbrechts-Tyteca, *New Rhetoric*, 206).

perpetuated one of the most durable transcultural century-spanning ethnographic stereotypes. In Greco-Roman thinking, a Lydian purple seller was a contaminating threat, a degenerative influence on civic society. However, in the case of Lydia of Thyatira, Luke does not direct the threat of contamination at the polis of Philippi (which later argumentation will demonstrate had already degenerated), but rather at the community group rhetorically contextualized as a "prayer house." Yet Lydia's heart, instead of being purified, is opened by the Lord much as the disciples' hearts were also opened on the way to Emmaus.[41] The Lord's purposeful action mirrors Jesus's, except that whereas Jesus both opened the disciples' eyes and filled their hearts with his self-expressive speech (Luke 24:31–32), in the case of Lydia, while the Lord opens (διήνοιξεν) her heart, it is Paul who fills it with his self-expressive speech (Acts 16:14).

Pauline baptism inferred that the baptized would have heard the Christ content of the "good news." Baptism ensured that, at a minimum, the newly baptized would have heard through their ears the self-expressive speech of salvation. What was less certain was whether the words delivered by self-expressive speech simply remained superficially heard words or whether the speech was ultimately processed within the zone of emotion-fused thought and thereby allowed to transform the listener's heart. With examples such as Simon the Magician and Ananias and Sapphira, it would seem that many, to paraphrase Philo, kept the good news lodged "just outside the ears" and did not allow it to pass through to their hearts.[42] When the Pauline group begins speaking to the women by the river, the text remains silent on the content of the speech; however, Lydia's baptism signals that the group would have been preaching about "Jesus and the resurrection" (Acts 17:17), that is, the "good news."

By opening Lydia's heart, the Lord enables the words that she hears to pass through to her zone of emotion-fused thought so that not only are

---

41. The intertextural parallels between Lydia and the disciples from Emmaus in Luke 24 are discussed on pp. 154–56.

42. Philo describes how the *Therapeutae* engaged with the teachings of Scripture: "But every seventh day they meet together as for a general assembly and sit in order according to their age in the proper attitude.... Then the senior among them who also has the fullest knowledge of the doctrines which they profess comes forward and with visage and voice alike quiet and composed gives a well-reasoned and wise discourse..., and this does not lodge just outside the ears of the audience but passes through the hearing into the soul and there stays securely" (*Contempl. Life* 31 [Colson et al., LCL]).

the "strange things" (Acts 17:20) heard, but also their meaning can come to light. In this way, Lydia is treated by God in precisely the same way that Jesus treats the disciples on the road to Emmaus, and this, of course, would be an affront to any traditional standard of piety. For, while the Lord treats Lydia as if she were an authentic disciple of Jesus, she is culturally profiled as a contaminant in need of expulsion or purification. Yet, instead of being expelled, Lydia is drawn into the innermost proximity with the Lord through the gold standard of discipleship—a heart equipped to integrate fully the content of Paul's self-expressive speech.[43]

The unit's sequence begins with the we-group coming together by hearing the voice of God in the Macedonian's call. The emotion-fused process of apprehending God's voice is common to the we-group and Lydia. By having her heart opened by the Lord, Lydia becomes an exemplary community member, but this move, while readily accomplished at the narrative level, socioculturally remains an unfathomable blend. The cognitive-rhetorical conundrum remains: how can an unpurified woman with Lydia's profile fit within a community frame of place of prayer? Moreover, while Lydia's profile clashes with that of the place of prayer, the problem presented by her profile goes well beyond issues of purity.

Although it might be tempting to suggest that a Lydian woman infers a concern for Jewish purity issues drawn from general categories of "clean" and "unclean" and points to a discourse of sexual immorality, Greco-Roman physiognomy helps to refine such an understanding. Lydian disease was spread by person-to-person contact, either by trade or by ingratiating friendship within social networks. Interpersonal relationship was the means through which Lydian disease could take hold, and it is this very risk that Lydia's offer presents when she presents her invitation to the we-group—"come to my house and stay" (Acts 16:15). If seen as infected, the we-group, as representatives of the Christ movement, would become suspect of mediating a false divinity. As with any good news of

---

43. The biblical heart metaphorically referred to the seat of the innermost part of the human being and was the location of thinking, understanding, feeling, and volition, encompassing a human's character and intellect. Since the biblical heart included faculties of reasoning, emotion, and will, in some cases biblical versions translate καρδία as "mind" instead of "heart." As is the case in Acts 16:14, a person "hears" the words spoken by another with her or his heart, thinks (Luke 2:19) and also understands (Deut 29:4 [29:3 LXX]) with the heart. The heart was a major "organ" in the zone of emotion-fused thought; it housed the essence of a person's true character.

victory brought by messengers, the news was only as credible as its messenger, for the veracity of the news could never be assumed.

Good news, beyond the subject of the news itself, tended to feature an underlying concern with the credibility of its messenger and accordingly of the message. Good news could indeed fortify; in fact, more than that, good news could save; but in order for the news to be efficacious it had to be accepted as true.[44] Although the we-group clearly understood itself to have divine sanction in its mission to Philippi, thereby rendering its "good news" authentically salvific, Luke will seemingly remove all conventional markers that would typically authenticate the veracity of good news: recognition, reward, and honoring of the messenger; victory and celebration; and, most importantly, evidence of a defeated enemy.[45] In upsetting expected elements normally found in discourse dealing with announcements of "good news," the "good news" itself becomes suspect.

Into this conundrum Luke delivers Lydia—a full-bodied threat to the integrity of the good news—and yet positions her as an emblematic first recipient of the type of aid that the audience might have expected a Macedonian warrior to receive. It was not possible to have a call for aid without a concurrent understanding of who constituted the foe, yet in the Macedonian's call no enemy is specified. Within Greco-Roman concerns over *luxuria* and hypocrisy as well as Judeo-Christian concerns over πορνεία, a character such a Lydia would make for a natural enemy, yet she is instead set squarely within the we-group's army camp. As further discussion will show, the question over who constitutes enemy does not simply disappear, but its definition, along with who constitutes "friend," will increasingly be displayed by Luke according to a new set of criteria.[46]

---

44. "We often find σωτηρία and εὐτύχημα, εὐτυχία combined with εὐαγγελίζομαι. Victory over enemies is the salvation of the city" (Gerhard Friedrich, "Εὐαγγελίζομαι," *TDNT* 2:711).

45. These elements are present in ancient discourse (sometimes in their negation) even when the news turns out to be fabricated or the messenger is punished rather than rewarded.

46. Sensitivity to dividing lines between those who could and could not receive salvific good news is acutely expressed in Mark's Gospel account of Jesus's initial reaction to the Syrophoenician woman's request for the healing of her daughter (Mark 7:24–30; Matt 15:21–28). Divinely wrought salvation, constituting the ultimate military resource leading to the ultimate victory, clearly was not intended for the ethnically delineated "dogs." The story is not found in Luke's Gospel (it is designated as part of the "great omission" in Luke), but Acts does contain an equally ethnically des-

Given past New Testament patterns, two solutions would normally present themselves in situations analogous with bringing Lydia into a προσευχή frame: expulsion or purification. In stark contrast to established patterns, Lydia is neither expelled nor purified; instead the Lord "opens" her heart so that she can fully engage herself with Paul's words. At this point, what may have begun as a humorous blend, a Macedonian warrior's request fulfilled in a Lydian purple seller, once blended with the prayer house and delivery of salvation, quickly moves outside of the comedic and into the scandalous.

5.3.3. The Rhetographical Argumentative Structure of Lydia's Offer: Worshiper of God Is as Loyalty to the Lord

As discussed in argumentative texture, the argumentation of Lydia's conditional offer ("If you have judged me to be faithful to the Lord, come to my house and stay": Acts 16:15) is not structured by cause and effect. That is, Lydia's being assessed as faithful does not cause the disciples to come to her home, but rather the condition is one of evidence-inference. If the disciples do go to Lydia's, the audience can infer that Lydia has been judged as faithful to the Lord. The evidence-inference structure helps to stress the difference between the context of Lydia's offer and the semantically similar one put to Jesus by the disciples returning to Emmaus (Luke 24:29). Lydia's offer frames the remainder of the rhetorical unit since the condition's affirmation in Acts 16:40 closes the unit. In this manner, a complete argument is presented: if the we-group goes into Lydia's home and stays, then she will have been judged as being faithful to the Lord (Acts 16:15); the we-group, despite being asked to leave Philippi by its leaders, goes into Lydia's house; therefore, Lydia is judged as being faithful to the Lord (Acts 16:40).

Although the argumentative structure of Lydia's offer could be formulated by an enthymeme, its rhetorical impact comes from rhetography rather than rhetology.[47] The verbal argumentative structure forms a logos-grounded platform from which the rhetographical argument supplying the energy for the passage's rhetorical force is launched. The challenge

---

ignated "shameless" woman, sharing a common link through the element of purple trading, who also self-expressively tries to force her will on an agent of God. This woman, however, unlike Mark's Syrophoenician, automatically receives the means of divine salvation.

47. For rhetography and rhetology, see §2.1.3.1.3.

presented by Lydia's offer resides primarily in the rhetographical realm: a Lydian woman who is a purple seller evokes elements that clash with the conclusion to the verbal argumentative conditional enthymeme.

Physiognomically, a female Lydian purple seller is an unfaithful woman, and this physiognomical characterization is located in the zone of emotion-fused thought. Lydia, the unfaithful "huckster" (stereotypically speaking), self-expressively speaks the language of faith ("If you have found me to be faithful to the Lord": Acts 16:15) after divine intervention in the nucleus of emotion-fused thought—her heart. Lydia's request to the Pauline group, hinging on a positive evaluation of her faithfulness, remains unanswered until the very end of the Philippi visit when the we-group "stays" after being expelled from Philippi and instead of leaving goes to Lydia's (Acts 16:40). In between Lydia's request and the final visit to her house, the question of the relationship between Lydia's Lydian purple selling profile and her "fidelity to the Lord" remains in motion.

The element of fidelity, central to Lydia's offer, is not the only element that is dissonant with Lydia's profile. As argued above, the designation "worshiper of God" (Acts 16:14), rather than establishing Lydia's character, raises the question as to how a woman such as Lydia can be authentically reverent. The two points of incongruity with Lydia's ethnographic profile, found in two adjacent verses—"worshiper of God" and "faithful to the Lord"—fuse with each other through their divine sacred elements, θεός in the case of verse 14 and κύριος in verse 15, forming the object of Lydia's reverence and faith respectively. Through an analogous relationship, the process of evaluating Lydia's loyalty also informs the process of determining what constitutes a "worshiper of God."

Luke suggests that if Lydia is judged to be faithful to the Lord, then so too would the quality of her reverence be authenticated, for if genuinely faithful, then she would also be an authentic worshiper of God. Moreover, there would be no question as to the God in view, for if Lydia's faithfulness is to be judged by the Pauline group, the Lord of Lydia categorically would need to be the same as the God of Paul. However, there is an argumentative clash presented within the enthymeme, for according to physiognomic logic, Lydia must be assessed as not faithful to God. Yet God's divine initiative in this unit is solely focused on enabling Lydia's heart to understand the message of salvation. By presenting a cultural clash within the argumentative framework of Lydia's offer, Luke throws the reader into confusion: on what basis can Lydia be considered to have embodied the good news. In order to help the audience work their way through a seemingly intractable evaluative challenge, Luke develops the ideological texture of the text within the framework of an inductive analogy that precedes, and is necessary for, the completion of the syllogism invoked by Lydia's offer. The author provides the audience with an argumentative aid in the form of an inductive analogy: a person is a worshiper of God as a person is faithful to the Lord.

Perelman and Olbrechts-Tyteca divide the structure of analogies into two relations, one being the *phoros* that bears the weight of the analogy, here "faithful to the Lord," and the theme clarified by the *phoros*, "worshiper of God."[48] Connecting fidelity with reverence to a divinity was a standard religious principle in Old Testament, New Testament, and Greco-Roman understanding, indeed one of the preeminent religious principles.[49] So foundational was this connection between faith and reverence that it would be possible to argue that the relationship "worshiper of God is as faithful to the Lord" functions as an illustrative example since in a proper analogy "it is necessary that the theme and the *phoros* belong to different spheres."[50] In the language of cognitive science, the *phoros* and theme would need to belong to different frames, but, certainly from an ancient understanding, both faith in the Lord as well as reverence to God would both be framed by a singular notion of piety.[51] Examples of faith and reverence in these cases would "represent two particular cases of a single rule" and would illustrate or clarify an established preexisting understanding.[52] Analogies, in contrast to illustrative examples, "facilitate the development and extension of thought";[53] they establish new rules, new emergent blends. Luke does indeed seek to establish new rules by calling Lydia a worshiper of God. For a worshiper of God, as the history of interpretation of Lydia has affirmed, would imply to the audience a fit

---

48. Perelman and Olbrechts-Tyteca, *New Rhetoric*, 373.

49. Zeba A. Crook, "BTB Readers Guide: Loyalty," *BTB* 34.4 (2004): 167–77; Bruce J. Malina and Jerome H. Neyrey, "Ancient Mediterranean Persons in Cultural Perspective: Portrait of Paul," in Neyrey and Stewart, *Social World of the New Testament*, 257–75.

50. Perelman and Olbrechts-Tyteca, *New Rhetoric*, 373.

51. "Where Latin has the single term to refer to loyalty, Greek has a range of words. One of these is *eusebeia*. That *eusebeia* is typically translated as 'piety' tells us a great deal about the relationship between loyalty and piety, and it reveals in addition that like loyalty, piety too was an action in essence" (Crook, "Loyalty," 168).

52. Perelman and Olbrechts-Tyteca, *New Rhetoric*, 373.

53. Ibid., 385.

with sociocultural standards of Jewish piety. By suggesting that an "unpurified" Lydian can fit within a worshiper-of-God frame, Luke destabilizes the constitutive elements of the frame. As the rhetorical unit progresses, the author will provide a number of illustrative test cases for what elements can form a reconstituted worshiper-of-God frame. Of these, Luke will offer "steadfast loyalty" as the preeminent criterion.

Not only in divine/human relations but also in both military alliances and social alliances, like those formed through the social model of hospitality, loyalty was a central value. In fact, discourse dealing with calls for aid and military alliances was preoccupied with the question of fidelity and whether the parties involved would remain loyal to agreed friend-enemy divisions. Lexically, the terms πιστός and πίστις often occurred in military discourse concerned with questions of loyalty in alliances.[54]

Fidelity, in contrast to "abstract values, such as justice or truth," is a "concrete value ... attaching to a living being, a specific group, or a particular object, considered as a unique entity."[55] In military calls for aid, fidelity was an exceptionally concrete value, for staying within the lines of common friends and common enemies was a paramount criterion for military loyalty. As did the Jewish high priest with Alexander, leaders regularly rebuked calls for aid on the grounds that a favorable response would result in disloyalty to a prior ally.[56]

As the rift between Paul and Barnabas over John Mark illustrates, loyalty continued to be a pressing concern for the author of Acts, and an assessment of loyalty forms the cornerstone of Lydia's offer of hospitality to the Pauline group. In Acts, the frame of fidelity to God increasingly destabilizes from traditional biblical understanding. Shortly before the events at Philippi, Paul separates from John Mark and Barnabas over the issue of fidelity raised by John Mark's perceived defection that, from Paul's perspective, disqualified him from discipleship and yet from Barnabas's did not. Circumcision, the landmark material sign of Jewish fidelity, becomes a topic of intense debate as it relates to gentiles (Acts 15:1–29) and yet remains a critical material marker of Timothy's discipleship in the transitional unit preceding Philippi (Acts 16:3). As fidelity to certain customs and protocols becomes less of a sure marker of reverence, the need for establishing essential markers of fidelity increases. Within this context of

---

54. J. H. Quincey, "Orestes and the Argive Alliance," *ClQ* 14.2 (1964): 191.
55. Perelman and Olbrechts-Tyteca, *New Rhetoric*, 77.
56. See §4.3.4.

growing volatility regarding who qualifies and who does not, as a Christian "believer," Lydia is encountered by the we-group. When the Pauline group meets Lydia, they are presented with a new challenge: how to assess the authenticity of her loyalty, for only upon such an assessment could she be evaluated a worshiper of God and therefore a rightful member of the house of prayer.

5.3.4. Lydia's Παραβιάζομαι: Urging Judgment

When Lydia makes her overture to the Pauline group in Acts 16:15, she does so in the classical language of social alliance.[57] While Lydia asks to have her claim of loyalty ratified, the narrative offers no immediate signals as to whether the we-group moves to further its alliance with her and instead closes the unit with Lydia's urging.[58] As we know from intertextural discussion of divine-stranger rhetorical type scenes, divine recognition was typically a one-way action in which the host was to recognize the guest. By adding a reverse call for recognition, Luke develops an inferential argument that a genuine worshiper of God will recognize not only divine presence but also, most importantly, the nature of the divinity. Implicitly, if Lydia is found to be faithful to Paul's God, then a process of mutual recognition would have been successfully concluded. For if Lydia is found to be faithful to Paul's God, then by inference she must genuinely "see" the true nature of Paul's God, since it is only with this "right-sightedness" that genuine faith can be manifested. Reverence takes on its own particular form in the rhetorical unit, as it increasingly features the ability to recognize not simply the presence but also the nature of a divinity.

---

57. "We are so accustomed to translating the word πίστις as 'faith' in terms of religious creed that we tend to miss its basic meaning as 'faithfulness' or 'loyalty'" (Malina and Neyrey, "Ancient Mediterranean Persons," 265). "Ancient Mediterranean people identified and defined themselves as situated in and embedded in various others persons or unities. Such unities were groups held together by the social glue of loyalty or solidarity and were symbolized by blood, birth, or fictive birth. Ancient Mediterraneans considered themselves embedded in a range of in-groups with varying degrees of loyalty: family, fictive family (school, faction, guild, clientele), *polis*, and the like" (260). See also Zeba A. Crook, *Reconceptualising Conversion: Patronage, Loyalty and Conversion in the Religions of the Ancient Mediterranean*, BZNW 130 (Berlin: de Gruyter, 2004), esp. 199–250.

58. Καὶ παρεβιάσατο ἡμᾶς (Act 16:15).

5.3.5. Delineation between Friend and Enemy: Physiognomy and Character Assessment

In essence, Lydia's offer calls the we-group to read her emotion-fused heart, while at the same time the author calls on the audience to resolve the clash of frames introduced by attempts to harmonize Lydia's physiognomic profile with "worshiper of God." The challenge of appraising "human surfaces to human depths"[59] is precisely the challenge presented by Lydia, for her profile places her in an "enemy" camp. While Lydia and her household were baptized and were therefore included into the community of the baptized, baptism did not inoculate against unfaithfulness, nor did it prevent newly baptized members from becoming unsuitable for long-term church membership. For Judas, Ananias and Sapphira, Simon, and John Mark, death or separation became the only options for preserving the integrity of the Christ movement.[60]

Unlike the centurion's or Jairus's requests to Jesus to come to their homes in order to perform a specific task of healing (Luke 7:2–10; 8:41–42), Lydia's request to the Pauline group to come and stay at her home is weighted toward interpersonal relationship, specifically through the social model of hospitality. Moreover, although Lydia's request to "stay" suggests social alliance, she does not come with publicly recognized credentials, unlike the centurion, whose reputation is vouched for by the Jewish community, or Jairus, who is a synagogue leader. Her lack of credentials is only amplified when we consider the social impropriety of a woman's pressing invitation of "hospitality" to a group of men.

The book of Revelation will argue that anyone who buys or sells has been marked by the beast of the earth (Rev 13:16–17). What mark, then, would a purple seller bear? While Timothy can adopt a material mark of belonging for the benefit of public perception (Acts 16:3), Luke challenges

---

59. Gleason, *Making Men*, 55.

60. Paul's rejection of John Mark for future missionary work in Acts 15:37–39 signals the issue, profiled in the narrative, regarding increasingly blurred criteria for assessing who can be considered a loyal believer and on what basis someone is to be assessed as falling outside of the limits of acceptability for discipleship. Judas's actions clearly would have been seen and understood as an act of betrayal. John Mark, on the other hand, was still accepted as a legitimate disciple by Barnabas, yet not by Paul. Through the difference of opinion between Barnabas and Paul, Luke rhetographically demonstrates the growing upheaval to internal sociocultural logic that marked the transition toward universal access to salvation.

the audience to wrestle with the question of how Lydia, a woman, can demonstrate a heart "circumcised by faith." How to gauge a cleansed heart in a person physiognomically characterized within a πορνεία frame presented a dilemma precisely due to the conventions evoked by this figure.

Stereotypes develop by a process of mental compression where, from a wide field of possible elements, certain elements are condensed into "perceivable units" that allow humans to make sense of their world.[61] Like any other topoi derived from a cluster of elements, stereotypes look for points that are rich in connectivity; they draw together similarities and discard unique features. Malina and Neyrey explain: "Experiencing life in terms of stereotypes means to approach everyday reality with its persons and things by using general conceptions rather than by taking time to construct customized designs.... Stereotypes simplify real-world persons and groups, while allowing us to prescind from the rich reality that persons and groups actually have."[62] In the language of cognitive science, stereotypes are formed by a cognitive blending process that yields a "human-scale" compression.[63] Physiognomy is an exemplar of human-scale compression that takes wide groups of people and condenses their perceived characteristics and behaviors into standard human character types. Typically, deep-rooted social and cultural biases and prejudices supply a substantial portion of those compressed elements that blend into stereotypes. Although physiognomy constructs profiles of human character, the biases contained in these profiles distort "any individual features that [people and groups] may actually have."[64] For example, Paul's need for Timothy to be circumcised was driven by physiognomic logic. Timothy's already solid, public reputation is subsumed by a traditional stereotypical marker of group identity—circumcision—thereby maintaining the generic religio-ethnic standard as the salient feature of Timothy's character. Privileging biased generalizations over actual individual character was exacerbated in social environments characterized by group orientation.

Stereotypical "standard mental pictures" function cognitively; they form "reliable cognitive maps of the world" that allow humans to "assess and evaluate the territories involved." The primary vantage point for

---

61. Malina and Neyrey, *Portraits of Paul*, 169–70. For compression of elements, see Fauconnier and Turner, *Way We Think*, 312–28.
62. Malina and Neyrey, *Portraits of Paul*, 170.
63. Fauconnier and Turner, *Way We Think*, 322–24.
64. Malina and Neyrey, *Portraits of Paul*, 170.

assessing characters and events came from a group's ethnic identity, which itself was sourced from a "geographically oriented label."[65] A group's own ethnic identity stemmed from a form of geocentrism that located one's place of origin as the "center of life for oneself and one's ethnic group."[66] Known as either the "omphalos myth" or the notion of a "mother *polis*," a geocentric sensibility involved the view that one's ethnic group set a standard for human norms and nature. Malina and Neyrey explain: "The view that place is the original center of life for oneself and one's ethnic group was symbolized by the image of the center as the navel of the social body. This is 'geocentrism' replicated in ethnocentrism—the belief that my ethnic group represents normative human nature."[67] Since religion was embedded in all aspects of first-century social life, cognitive maps were also embedded within religious space, for while Delphi was the omphalos of the Greek-speaking world, it was more specifically Apollo/Python's temple that designated its true center. So, too, while Jerusalem was the center of the Jewish world, its nucleus of identity was found in the temple. Timothy's circumcision was therefore a reminder that the navel of the Jewish social and religious body was still firmly centered on the Jerusalem temple, and moreover that at a minimum Paul's own geocentric location in Acts 16:1–5 or at least his perception of the communities' common geocentric location remained rooted there.

The analysis of innertexture noted that the plural form pervades the rhetorical unit, including the only plural occurrences of κύριος in Acts, and the notable first appearance of the "we-group" as a narrative character in its own right. Within groups such as Macedonians, Romans, women, and Jews, only one—the we-group—stands alone as lacking a clear stereotype-derived cognitive identity map. Physiognomy could be relied on as a dependable tool only for as long as a social body's cognitive maps were firmly centered on its geographic origin. Luke's narrative, however, dislocates the center.

From the outset, Luke presents a paradox, one that influences the rhetorical movement of the entire unit. As the Jerusalem-centered cognitive map destabilizes, the we-group is called on to assess a request from an ethnically defined group of strangers: the Macedonians, yet without having

---

65. Malina and Neyrey, "Ancient Mediterranean Persons," 113.
66. Ibid., 121.
67. Ibid.

the security of its own cognitive map.[68] Without these maps, physiognomically derived logic is disabled. At the same time, however, Luke continues to present challenging situations that stress the need for interpretation, perception, and judgment.

In discussing the mutability of notions, where notions arise out of "passage from the word to the idea," Perelman and Olbrechts-Tyteca observe that any notions that apply to future events, even the most ostensibly scientific ones, will always contain a degree of ambiguity. They write: "A perfectly clear notion is one of which all cases of application are known so that it does not admit of a new unforeseen use. Only divine knowledge or knowledge limited by conventions satisfies such a requirement."[69] Acts 16 removes both conditions of certainty. Traditional media for transmission of divine knowledge fall silent in the rhetorical unit. Paul's vision is absent any instruction from God; the prison earthquake is without explicit divine elements; the space for mediation of the divine—the "prayer house"—is obscured. Moreover, conventions of physiognomic reasoning are upended, sending formerly clear notions into liminal territory. By recurrently profiling the emotion-fused faculty of discernment, the author employs ambiguity for rhetorical purpose in this unit.

As a result of Luke's deliberate use of ambiguity, Philippi becomes an earthquake zone in Acts 16, where all standard-bearing cognitive maps destabilize. Although it is a Macedonian man who calls for the Pauline group and Macedonia is emphasized through repetition, no one subsequently is identified as Macedonian in Philippi. Philippi is characterized as a colony and thus suggests Rome as its center, but although the Latinized term for colony is used, the narrative describes the city as a "first" within Macedonia, not Rome.[70] The slave woman with the Python spirit

---

68. "The process of socialization outfits human beings with the cognitive maps shared by their groups in order to make meaningful social, human living possible" (ibid., 170).

69. Perelman and Olbrechts-Tyteca, *New Rhetoric*, 131.

70. Although κολωνία is usually translated as "Roman colony" in Acts 16:12, the qualifier "Roman" is absent from the Greek text. Nonetheless the Latinized term does specifically evoke a Roman colony rather than a colonial settlement generally. Hugh Mason surveyed the use of κολωνία in documents as well as literature and found that the literary use was extremely rare. It was instead more commonly used as a technical term in documents in order to specify the distinctly Roman nature of the colony. While Mason suggests that only Acts uses the term "casually," more correctly the use in Acts is rhetorical: the term deliberately mirrors other examples where it functions

evokes Greek Delphic Apollo, yet she is found on the streets of Roman Philippi, where eventually her spiritual center, the spirit, is cast out. While the slave owners speak on behalf of Roman custom, they, along with the mob in the agora, act from anger and not from legal process as should have been Roman custom. Later Paul, labeled a Jew by the slave owners, presents himself as a Roman citizen and calls into question the lack of customary Roman jurisprudence. Lydia is identified as an Asian foreigner to Philippi, and the space in which she is encountered is outside rather than inside the city. From all geocentric and ethnic perspectives, Philippi and its inhabitants suggest outlying, ambiguous, and decentered territory. As the we-group's cognitive map begins to take on its own distinct framing structure, concurrently so too will Luke increasingly expose the "enemy" within this emerging territorial profile, as "ally" also develops its own unique characteristics.

Mikeal Parsons has argued that Luke employed physiognomic conventions, ultimately, in order to subvert common prejudices governing the first-century world. Thus those considered outcasts because of their external appearance and/or physiognomic profiles are welcomed into a "radically inclusive community."[71] Citing the Ethiopian eunuch in Acts 8:27–39 as one example, Parson argues that Luke draws on ethnographic, anatomical, and zoological physiognomy to characterize the eunuch as ethnographically inferior, sexually effeminate, and ambiguous, and as somebody who yet nonetheless is brought into the fold of a salvific community. Parsons writes:

> Luke's own moral vision was formed, not by the dominant cultural values espoused by his teachers of rhetoric, but rather by the teaching of Israel's scriptures—"The LORD does not see as mortals see; they look on the outward appearance, but the LORD looks on the heart" (1 Sam. 16:7)—and the teachings of Jesus himself (e.g., the Good Samaritan in Luke 10).
>
> The Ethiopian eunuch would have been viewed by Luke's auditors as sexually ambiguous, socially ostracized, and morally evil (greedy and cowardly). Yet when the eunuch asks, "What is to prevent me from being

---

as a proper name, metonymically evoking Philippi's full Roman name of Colonia Julia Augusta Philippensis. It situates Philippi within Rome, where "Roman" is a recurring term. See Hugh J. Mason, *Greek Terms for Roman Institutions: A Lexicon and Analysis*, ASP 13 (Toronto: Hakkert, 1974), 108–9.

71. Mikeal C. Parsons, *Body and Character in Luke and Acts: The Subversion of Physiognomy in Early Christianity* (Grand Rapids: Baker Academic, 2006), 14–15.

baptized?" Luke's response is surely that neither the eunuch's physical condition, nor his place of origin, nor his likeness to a sheared sheep prevents his entrance into the eschatological community in fulfillment of the Abrahamic promise of a blessing to "all the families of the earth" (Acts 3:25; cf. Gen. 22:18). In that community "God shows no partiality." (Acts 10:34)[72]

Parsons's work in demonstrating how a physiognomic understanding shapes characterization in Luke and Acts has contributed significantly to raising awareness to its prevalent use in these texts. Moreover, Parsons quite rightly makes 1 Sam 16:7 the salient lens for interpreting why an author such as Luke invoked physiognomic profiling. Not only does Luke-Acts emphasize that the Lord looks on the heart rather than outward appearance; increasingly at issue in Acts is a growing tension between what were thought to be reliable external markers of the inner heart and a person's true inner essence. While God may show no partiality in cases of pious, righteous, upstanding members of the community such as Cornelius or in the case of extortionists who are willing to repent such as Zacchaeus, there are nonetheless examples of other cases that are not nearly as welcome into the community. By looking from the Lukan perspective at what turns people into outcasts, it is possible to further refine Parsons's thesis that, from its liberationist perspective, tends to overlook those who are cursed or ultimately barred from the new community, and who thereby form the de facto enemy.

5.3.6. Conclusion: Ideological Texture of the Παρακαλέω of Lydia

One woman, Lydia, fully receives what the Macedonian man implicitly requested: the "good news." Most significantly, Lydia had not only heard Paul's self-expressive message through her ears but also was endowed, through divine intervention, with the capacity to apprehend it fully within her emotion-fused heart. The good news could point the way to its salvific source only if it were genuinely appropriated within a listener's heart. By this defining characteristic, the ability to perceive Paul's God, Luke positions Lydia as an ideal core member of the newly forming church.

---

72. Ibid., 141. For the eunuch as a symbol of sexual transgression, see also J. David Hester, "Eunuchs and the Postgender Jesus: Matthew 19.12 and Transgressive Sexualities," *JSNT* 28 (2005): 13–40.

A "worshiper of God," however, would necessarily be loyal to the Lord, for this was a constitutive religious principle. Yet culturally Lydia was not only "not warrior" and "not appropriate gender to constitute synagogue," but also, her physiognomic profile would render her "immoral, unfaithful, and deceptive" and therefore "not faithful." Physiognomic logic would suggest that Lydia ought to be either expelled or purified in order to protect the integrity and therefore the salvific efficacy of the good news, yet neither action is taken in Lydia's case. Instead, the Lord opens Lydia's heart, much as Jesus helps to open the hearts of the first disciples on the road to Emmaus. Luke portrays Philippi as liminal territory that challenges the audience to restructure the internal logic that guides its discernment of who qualifies for membership in the forming "right-sighted" community of God.

Consistent with Parson's thesis, Luke disassembles physiognomic logic as a governing criterion for determining who qualifies as an in-group member. Indeed Lydia, despite her rhetorical profile, is assessed as faithful by the end of the Philippian episode. The case of Lydia, however, is not nearly as simple as a final warrant of her fidelity might suggest. For she raises the question, if physiognomic logic can no longer function as a trusted indicator of who is a suitable member of Paul's community and who is not, for not all are, then what, in its stead, is to become the new criterion of inclusion or exclusion? To this question, Lydia's other descriptor, "worshiper of God," holds a partial answer. Luke fuses the two phrases "worshiper of God" and "loyal to the Lord" together in order to form the unit's main analogous structure: "One is a worshiper of God as one is loyal to the Lord."[73]

A worshiper of God would necessarily be situated within a community of those who share the same perception of divinity, most especially in the first century, when group alliances constituted a person's identity.

---

73. While "loyal" is essentially synonymous with "faithful," the quality of steadfast allegiance to God is emphasized more strongly by the choice of "loyal" in the inductive analogy that governs how Lydia's status as a believer will be judged. As I will argue, Paul and Silas demonstrate how "staying in faith" illustrates the quality of steadfast loyalty to Paul's God, even if this loyalty will result in physical suffering, or public humiliation and dishonor. It is the quality of unwavering allegiance that would be found in an ideal warrior. This form of loyalty connects with the "resource" of steadfast courage that the we-group understands itself called to deliver to the Macedonians and also connects with Paul's final act of encouragement at Lydia's home.

5. IDEOLOGICAL TEXTURE

Describing a human as a worshiper of God immediately brought forth two elements, the God in view, and the socioreligious body formed through this God. This integral aspect of interrelationship holds the key to the challenge presented by Lydia's offer, for other discourse, whether biblical or Greco-Roman, that clustered elements of Lydians, prostitution, sexual immorality, purple, and trade—the constellation of elements that would have been evoked by Lydia's profile—was concerned with a corrupt social body that had formed through mercantile rather than sacred or honorable exchange systems.[74] Moreover, corrupt bodies often masqueraded as pure, honest, or divinely constituted bodies. Separating the diseased body from the wholesome one was not a simple task. Lydia's physiognomic profile makes her a natural enemy of a synagogue or temple; she presents the danger of a contaminating influence that can corrupt the good news and render it an ensnaring trap for "mammon" rather than a path to God. God, however, sanctions Lydia by opening her heart.

At stake for the we-group was the very essence of their salvific message. For like any announcement of military "good news," the news first would need to be authenticated, and here the ethos of the messenger was key. If the self-expressive speech of the we-group was to retain its power to save, then the socioreligious body through which it would by necessity be mediated needed to be devoid of corruption.

The analysis of the ideological texture of the text suggests that by bringing Lydia into a setting that should be constituted as a Jewish synagogue but is instead ambiguous, Luke develops the rhetoric of Acts 16 to radically reconfigure the criteria for evaluating who can claim rightful membership to the "right-sighted" community of God. This reconfiguration will be accomplished by a series of test cases that illustrate the nature of "true" and, contrasting, "counterfeit" faith. The criteria for "right-sightedness" are displayed by Lydian touchstone *synkrisis*.

5.4. The Implicit Παρακαλεω of the Slave Woman

When the slave woman connects sequentially with Lydia, her encounter with the Pauline group will set off a chain of illustrative comparisons that will serve to examine what loyalty to the Lord looks like and

---

74. Elements of purple, mercantilism, and harlotry are found in a wide range of prophetic/apocalyptic biblical and apocryphal texts: Ezekiel, Isaiah, Jeremiah, Hosea, Zechariah, the Epistle of Jeremiah, and Revelation in particular employ these elements.

who embodies it. It is precisely the challenge of perceiving the seemingly imperceptible differences that holds Luke's rhetorical interest in this unit. For only by its transmission through uncorrupted channels would the "good news" retain its salvific capacity.

As soon as the narrative leaves Lydia behind, the slave woman with the Python spirit encounters the disciples, mirroring Lydia by speaking directly, and lexically by the participle λέγουσα (Acts 16:16–17), and spatially by the context of the we-group going to a place of prayer. Each woman is acted on internally by a divinity—in Lydia's case through the Lord's opening of her heart and in the slave woman's by the Python spirit's work within her. These similarities have prompted scholars to contrast Lydia with the slave woman on the basis of the god that each ostensibly reveres. Lydia the "good woman" converts to Christianity and contrasts with the "bad" slave woman who proclaims a "pagan" god.[75] Accordingly, Paul's casting out of the Python spirit is displayed as a triumph of his Christian God.

If this passage were to be viewed from a history of interpretation, then such a reading would be entirely consistent with claims of triumphant evangelization; however, when viewed from the perspective displayed by the text itself, three incompatible factors leave open the question of the basis for the slave woman's sequential connection to Lydia. The first is that Lydia's physiognomic profile does not comfortably fit with the image of a "good" woman, and the question regarding the quality of her "conversion" frames the entire episode. Second, far from displaying the superior power of their God, Paul and Silas are publicly humiliated, violated, incarcerated, and driven out of town as a consequence of Paul's having cast out the Python spirit. Third, Paul had tolerated the spirit's proclamation for "many days" (Acts 16:18). In other words, there had not seemed to be any immediate need on Paul's part to purge Philippi of a spiritual adversary.

As might be expected with rhetoric structured by touchstone *synkrisis*, Lydia and the slave woman do appear to be deliberately juxtaposed. The slave woman speaks—as did Lydia—and the content of her proclamation

---

75. One example, drawn from traditional scholarship, comes from Joseph A. Fitzmyer: "The exorcism of the possessed slave girl is used by Luke to depict the triumph of Christianity over pagan Greco-Roman practices" (Fitzmyer, *Acts of the Apostles*, 583). Another example comes from postmodern scholarship: Staley sees the text as juxtaposing "Lydia the 'good' woman with the pythonic 'bad' girl" ("Changing Woman," 186).

suggests that she too has heard the "good news." As Lydia drops out of the narrative and the slave woman takes center stage, the audience might begin to wonder if now the we-group had finally found an authentic "worshiper of God" whose own divine spirit had recognized, and in a sense had willingly become, "subject to" the deity of Paul. Perhaps Lydia, true to type, will be exposed as the profit-seeking huckster that stereotype would expect, but the slave woman, so consistently and publicly supporting the disciples' mission, will turn out to be "the real thing."

The slave woman speaks words of truth: "These men are servants of the Most High God, who proclaim to you a way of salvation" (Acts 16:17). In this manner, the slave woman herself fulfills the type of role ascribed to messengers of good news; moreover, she seems to continue with the παρακαλέω trend as she vociferously calls the people of Philippi to the disciples.[76] The disciples, understanding themselves to be called by God to supply military fortification through allied efforts by way of announcing the news of salvation, seemingly find their ideal ally.

From a first-century perspective that viewed others according to the groups they appeared to be embedded in, the slave woman would appear to be fully embedded within the Pauline group. Moreover, group-centered eyes would have extended the perceived Pauline–slave woman alliance to the source of the slave woman's proclamations—the Python spirit—as well as the slave woman's owners—her "lords" (κύριοι). This presumed alliance, however, comes to an unexpected end when the slave woman's Python spirit is abruptly cast out.

When Paul casts out the Python spirit, the effect of the exorcism bears none of the hallmarks of other healings through exorcism in Luke-Acts: exhibiting a postexorcism healed body and the awed reaction of a witnessing crowd.[77] The slave woman simply disappears from the narrative; moreover, in the near future she is likely destined to suffer significant bodily hardships, now having become a profit-draining, rather than a profit-

---

76. The term σωτηρία was often combined with εὐαγγελίζομαι in announcements to a city of its salvation through victory. See note 44.

77. Other exorcisms are clearly presented within a healing context, and their effect usually results in an awed reaction from the crowd, thereby increasing the authority and honor of the worker of the exorcism: Luke 4:33–36, 40–41; 6:18; 7:21; 8:2, 35; 9:42; 11:14; 13:11–12; Acts 5:16; 8:6–8; 19:12.

generating, slave.[78] In contrast with other exorcisms, there is no sense of bodily healing conveyed by the casting out of the Python spirit.

Also, crowds are not awed, or at least put into a state of reverential fear, by the exorcism. Instead, as a consequence of the exorcism, the crowds will turn on Paul and Silas, publicly beating, humiliating, and thereby "effeminizing" them. Rather than functioning to demonstrate the supernatural healing capacity of the Pauline disciples in order to increase their public authority and honor, the exorcism is used by Luke to inaugurate a process of separation. Through this separation will begin the unveiling of "authentic," in contrast to counterfeit, allies of God.

5.4.1. The Slave Woman's Owners: Unveiling an Enemy

The exorcism fundamentally changes the apparent configuration of the we-group; it visibly breaks any perceived alliance with the Python spirit/slave woman and with the slave owners.[79] While loyalty was the bonding agent that held together social alliances, this bond regularly became "unglued" if more favorable circumstances could be found elsewhere. It is from within this notion of loyalty as an integral feature of social alliances that Luke presents a major twist. For it is Paul who precipitates the rupture by casting out the Python spirit—this despite many days of publicly witnessed cooperation with the slave woman. Paul betrays the bonds of loyalty first and thereby creates an enemy.

In creating an enemy, however, Paul displays the enemy's inner emotion-fused heart. As had been the case from the inception of the rhetorical

---

78. The probable unfortunate fate of the slave woman has vexed commentators in the past, and as a result the woman is either "healed" from her possession and/or some have suggested that Paul effects her manumission. The tougher reality is that while she is free from the influence of the Python spirit, the prognosis for her bodily well-being does not seem favorable. In addition, while many who have received the message of the kingdom of God will suffer bodily harm as a result of this message, Jesus, Stephen, James, and Paul included, their suffering comes as a result of their having "accepted the cross" as it were. The slave woman, because of her utter passivity in this regard, does not fit with the profile of others who take on the consequences of the message of salvation. While difficult to reconcile with liberationist theology, the slave woman seems to be presented more as an instrument, in this case a medium of profit, than as a human being.

79. It may therefore rhetorically not be a coincidence that the we-group ceases to be a we-group after Acts 16:17 until it reappears in 20:5.

unit, Luke continues to target the zone of emotion-fused thought as the slave owners "see," ἰδόντες, rather than hear, that their hope of profit had departed and then respond with purposeful action. In this manner, two hopes are brought side by side, a hope of salvation and a hope of profit, each residing within the emotion-fused heart. By a disloyal act to the κύριοι (lords) through the name of his Lord (Acts 16:18, 31), Paul unveils the bonds of loyalty that had motivated the slave owners—profit—and thereby shows that these lords are in fact "lovers of mammon."

While both Matthew and Luke use the maxim "You cannot serve God and mammon" to contrast an orientation toward material wealth with spiritual, Luke subtly shifts the frame into one more sharply targeted at competing loyalties as a corrupting force on a religious group that is responsible for mediating God's word to the people.[80] More specifically, in the Gospel, Luke's use of the *gnōmē* moves in on his target—the Pharisees—who are "lovers of money," φιλάργυροι (Luke 16:14).[81] But the audience, of

---

80. Mammon here is used with the first-century understanding as explained by Kenneth Hanson and Douglas Oakman: "Gold and silver were employed regularly as media for storing 'value' by those who had precious metals to hoard. The Mediterranean peoples of the eastern Roman Empire would tend to consider money value in light of the core cultural values of Mediterranean societies: honor and shame. Wealth, the Aramaic term for which is *mamona*, would be the storage of resource values for creating, preserving, displaying, or recovering public reputation ('honor'), and for protecting the economic integrity of family and household" (Kenneth C. Hanson and Douglas E. Oakman, *Palestine in the Time of Jesus: Social Structures and Social Conflicts* [Minneapolis: Fortress, 1998], 122). From this definition, the term "mammon" is used here to denote all material goods and social activities that are deployed for "creating, preserving, displaying, or recovering public reputation ('honor'), and for protecting the economic integrity of family and household" (ibid).

81. "The play on words in Luke 16:11 (faithless with unrighteous mammon, entrusted with righteous mammon) gives a very powerful indication that Jesus' intention and meaning was closest to root 4—'MN, to trust. From 'MN, we get the familiar English transliteration Amen, truly. What is trustworthy is true; what is untrustworthy is false. This attitude comes from an ancient culture where epistemology is rooted in social relations and strong group perceptions. The meaning of Mammon is bound up with trust and true and false social perceptions of reality" (Douglas E. Oakman, "The Radical Jesus: You Cannot Serve God and Mammon," *BTB* 34.3 [2004]: 123–24). Keeping within the notion of competing loyalties, the Gospel of Thomas expresses a similar sentiment, but now framed by military rather than economic discourse: "Jesus said, 'It is impossible for a person to mount two horses and to bend two bows. Also it is impossible for a servant to serve two masters, or he will honour the one and insult the other" (Gos. Thom. 47.1–2 [DeConick]).

course, would know that it is God whom the Pharisees are to love with all their hearts and souls and strength (Deut 6:5; Luke 10:27). If indeed the target of the Pharisees' love is found within the realm of whatever means might advance their own worldly status (i.e., mammon), then the audience could infer inductively that Luke charges the Pharisees with loving mammon with their hearts, souls, and strength. As a result, by way of their allegiance with the means of increasing mammon, they are in effect "faithful" to mammon and unfaithful to God.

Luke uses Paul's exorcism to illustrate how a maxim such as "You cannot serve God and mammon" plays itself out in the human earthbound world. The exorcism is a signal that slaves of the Most High God cannot coexist in alliances such as that with the Python-slave-woman-lords enterprise. Loyalty to one calls forth the imperative of disloyalty to the other. However, and herein lies Paul's conundrum, those who are enslaved to mammon may well look like servants of God.[82]

It is highly significant that the slave woman's words fully supported the we-group's perceived call from God and that she continued to accompany the disciples, calling the words out for many days. For by having Paul silence the slave woman after a lengthy span of time, Luke establishes that the good news is not simply a matter of proclaiming correct self-expressive words. On the surface, the words of salvation may be quite true. However, the proclaiming "self" that is revealed is the far more important element. In this case the revealed "inner self" of the slave owners turned out to be one driven by profit-seeking rather than service to God.[83] An alliance with an enterprise enslaved by mammon presented an insurmountable obstacle to the Pauline mission, because it would irredeemably taint the good news and thereby render the we-group "hucksters of God's words," those who therefore can longer be expected to speak sincerely "in Christ."[84]

---

82. A similar misrepresentation is voiced in Ezek 33:31: "They come to you as people come, and they sit before you as my people, and they hear your words, but they will not obey them. For flattery is on their lips, but their heart is set on their gain."

83. Repetitive textural analysis already signaled the importance of profit to the unit by noting that ἐργασία repeats (Acts 16:16, 19) and connects with ἀγορά (16:19), both of which occur for the first time in Acts in this unit.

84. In 2 Corinthians, Paul asserts: "For we are not, like so many, hucksters [καπηλεύοντες] of God's word; but as men of sincerity, as commissioned by God, in the sight of God we speak in Christ" (2 Cor 2:17). Speech through Christ is sincere, speech through profit-seeking is false. Apollonius of Tyana explains a similar predicament

The danger of such a taint produced by association with perceived "money-loving prophets" is that the salvific nature of the good news was inextricably bound together with the ethos of the ones proclaiming it. Should it be perceived as tainted, there would be no way to recover "the good news." Each of the we-group and slave-owners-Python group mediated divine communication, and for a time it appeared that both were self-expressively communicating the same divinity. Yet again, distinguishing between them called on Paul's emotion-fused effort of discernment. From the length of time it took for Paul to make his decisive move, the author of Acts leads the audience to infer that the markers distinguishing the two forms of divine communication were far from self-evident.

Paul's action against the Python spirit forms an act of judgment. The spirit is exposed as *not* being "faithful to the Lord" since the "event" underlying the activity of mantic proclamation was profit-making, not salvation. The slave-owners group is not faithful to the Lord, and therefore its members are not worshipers of God. They, then, have rejected the good news and therefore remain outside of the salvific possibilities of the good news. True to the Python's name—rot—the group of profit-induced "corruption" is destined for the opposite of immortality, ultimate rot. Although at this point judgment about another profit seeker, the purple-selling Lydia, remains unanswered, when the slave owners are "rubbed side by side" with Lydia, one form of counterfeit loyalty is exposed. In this manner, following Lydia's offer, Luke presents the first illustrative case of what would be judged as *not* faithful to God: fidelity to mammon.

---

to his audience; Philostratus writes: "But there is also, Majesty, a kind of sham learning and hucksterism that you should not equate with prophecy [μαντικήν], because prophecy is very valuable it tells the truth, though I am not sure it is an art. By 'sham learning' I refer to sorcerers, because to make the nonexistent exist, and the existent to be doubted, all this I ascribe to the beliefs of those they dupe. Whatever learning there is in magic lies in the antiquity of those that are tricked as spectators. The trade consists entirely of money-grubbers [φιλοχρήματοι]. All their boasted devices they have invented for the sake of gain, and they hunt piles of money by inducing others, whatever they desire, to think them omnipotent" (Philostratus, *Vit. Apoll.* 8.7.10 [Jones et al., LCL]).

5.4.2. Conclusion: Ideological Texture of the Implicit Παρακαλέω of the Slave Woman

Although Lydia and the slave woman are linked by their gender, speech, and the context of meeting the we-group on its way to a place of prayer, their linkage is sequential and not progressive. The slave woman does speak, but unlike Lydia, she does not speak her own self-expressive speech. When Paul turns to shut down the mantic operation, he does not speak to the woman; instead, he speaks directly to the Python spirit (Acts 16:18). The slave woman is therefore a vocalization medium, a sound, but not a self-expressive voice. Instead, she gives voice to the self-expressive speech of the Python spirit. For, the Python spirit working through the slave woman generates profit for the gain of the profit-seeking slave owners just as purple generates profit for the profit-seeking purple seller Lydia. The slave woman attaches to Lydia semantically but then sequentially moves the point of comparison to Lydia away from herself and to her profit-seeking owners. At the same time the Python spirit forms an analogous relationship with Lydia's purple. The voice of profit, when sourced in monetized divine communication, expresses itself as if it were degenerate purple, and it is Paul's exorcism that exposes it as such.

Where initially the παρακαλέω of the Macedonian man fused with a perceived προσκαλέω from God, in Philippi the Python spirit, as the self-expressive agent of the slave woman, calls the Philippians to the disciples. However, as an instrument of profit, the Python spirit cannot draw hearers to a source of salvation because salvation, from a Lukan perspective, cannot be found through profit-centered divine mediation. The Python spirit, ultimately, can draw hearers only to death.

The incident with the slave owners suggests that Luke begins to present a "human-scale" apocalypse. Although brought into Philippi on a call for military aid, the Pauline group does not ride in with a warrior God, destroying the enemy and victoriously exhibiting its divinely supported invincibility. But through the judgment stone, the Lydian touchstone, the corrupted hearts, and therefore the doomed nature of the slave owners are exposed. Through their unveiling, the slave owners' hearts are exposed as the enemy, an enemy that, although offered the means of salvation, has rejected it.

5. IDEOLOGICAL TEXTURE

5.5. Paul's Implicit Παρακαλεω in Prison: Bringing to Right-Sightedness by Staying in Faith

As was described in the intertextural analysis, most scholarly attention to the Philippian imprisonment has centered on the notion of divinely assisted prison escape. Yet, while evoking the divinely assisted prison-escape topos, Luke concurrently removes expected elements and introduces others, in a manner similar to the author's prior reconfiguration of the divine dream-vision topos. The Philippian earthquake contains no explicit displays of divine presence and in fact plays with this absence by assigning the frequently theophonic "great voice" to Paul (Acts 16:28) and having the jailer source the lights (Acts 16:29).[85]

Perhaps most significantly, the earthquake does not serve to facilitate Paul and Silas's escape from prison; they are instead released in the morning by the magistrates who seem unaware of the event of the earthquake. In contrast with this and other prison-escape stories, including those of Acts 5:19 and 12:17, manifestations of divine salvific power as the means of escape are absent from the Philippian episode. True, an earthquake occurs that miraculously opens doors and releases bonds without destroying the structure, which would undoubtedly have evoked signs of a divine hand in the audience. But as was the case with the absence of an explicit divine element in Paul's dream-vision, so too the culturally

---

85. The text expresses Paul calling out by the phrase ἐφώνησεν δὲ μεγάλῃ φωνῇ, "he sounded a loud cry," which simply describes him as shouting loudly. Yet at the same time, the phrase ἐν φωνῇ μεγάλῃ commonly appears in divine epiphanies; see Marianne Palmer Bonz, *The Past as Legacy: Luke-Acts and Ancient Epic* (Minneapolis: Fortress, 2000), 97 n. 38; where ἐν φωνῇ μεγάλῃ occurs twenty times in Revelation, describing the calls of heavenly voices (see David E. Aune, *Revelation 1–5*, WBC 52A [Dallas: Word, 1997], 347). Mikeal Parsons notes that one of the reasons that the Lycaonians may have taken Paul and Barnabas for gods is Paul's speaking in a "loud voice," "echoing the view in antiquity that gods spoke with frightfully loud voices" (Parsons, *Acts*, 199). The specific combination the verb φωνέω together with the adjective μέγας and noun φωνή only occurs three other times in the New Testament: the call of the unclean spirit in Mark 1:26, the call of an angel of judgment in Rev 14:18, and Jesus's last words in Luke 23:46. In Philippi, the phrase comes out of a male human's (Paul's) mouth, yet within the context of a seemingly "miraculous" earthquake event. Having the jailer call for lights also contrasts with other cases where the element of light is closely associated with divinity. In the *Bacchae*, Dionysus brings on lightning and fire and makes clear that they have been divinely sent; in Acts 12:7, the appearance of light in Peter's prison cell is clearly a by-product of the arrival of the angel of the Lord.

anticipated explicit manifestation of divinity is absent from the prison scene. Prison escapes involved releases from prison as a direct result of divine rescue, yet Paul's imprisonment is notably absent the element of providential rescue and, beyond the earthquake itself, any other elements associated with spiritual beings. Philippi is a story of prison stay rather than prison escape.

5.5.1. Prison as Touchstone

The space of prison, so prevalent in the rhetorical unit, is used by Luke to present a highly charged topos evoking death and misery. Fauconnier and Turner contend that "physical spaces are already attached by memory to sensations and events in our past."[86] As was highlighted in the intertextural analysis, the space of ancient prison evoked visceral physical sensations of physical pain, hunger, sickness, and suffering as well as emotion-fused sensations of humiliation, sadness, and loss. Prison was a place of darkness, in imagination akin to the ultimate form of corruption—death. In a powerful ideological twist on an age-old type scene, Luke does not employ the prison topos to demonstrate how God's power can rescue a pious believer from the darkness of prison but rather uses the topos as a torturous testing stone.[87]

Prison, so closely associated with torture, featured in accounts such as Lucian's and Philo's as a testing ground, a place where the pure, uncorrupted nature of one unjustly punished would come to light. In these cases, prison formed its own refining fire, or touchstone, where the sterling character of a prisoner would shine forth from the dark pits of torture and death. Much like Lucian and Philo did with Demetrius's and Joseph's prison tests, Luke will also showcase Paul and Silas's exemplary characters by the trials of prison.

Having unveiled the hearts of the slave owners, Paul and Silas are themselves put to the test, not metaphorically, but through the material, physical test of torture. Thematic repetitive elements such as "beating," "blows," and "stocks," further stressed by the *hapax* of ῥαβδοῦχος, "lictors" (Acts 16:35, 38), bring the topos of physical torture to the fore. The narrative suddenly switches from its emphasis on the zones of self-expressive

---

86. Fauconnier and Turner, *Way We Think*, 316.
87. On the relationship between Lydian touchstone and truth-finding through torture, see §5.1.2 above.

speech and emotion-fused thought to that of purposeful action—action that is focused on the objects of its force, Paul and Silas's bodies.

The guard awakens from sleep and yet remains in a dreamlike state by falsely "seeing" in the open door the certainty of escaped prisoners.[88] Once again, Luke uses emotion-fused thought to advance his ideological goals. In supposing the prisoners escaped, the guard makes ready to die. Divinely enabled prison escape would have meant death to the jailer, as underscored by his immediate move to attempt suicide.[89] In fact, the death of guards could complement the divinely assisted escape topos. The death of a guard would surely benefit the successful escape of the prisoners, yet by staying, the prisoners in Philippi secure the life of the guard.

In watching the Pauline group respond to the call of the Macedonian man, the audience readied for clear evidence of a divinely enabled approaching victory. First confounded by the women and Lydia and now by Paul and Silas's imprisonment, the audience cannot help but begin to wonder when Paul's God will make a salvific appearance, for indeed a warrior God rightfully should have crushed an antagonist like the prison guard. The guard had taken the bloodied Paul and Silas and had inflicted even greater suffering on them by fastening their feet in stocks. Yet instead of being killed for harming divinely chosen disciples, the guard is saved. Moreover, Luke will stress that the guard is not saved by a conventional show of divine rescue but rather, quite unconventionally, by the effects of Paul and Silas's steadfast loyalty to their God.

Paul's loud human voice, theophonically framed, "awakens" the jailer a second time, this time from his mortal presumption. Paul's call to the jailer functions as an implicit παρακαλέω: Paul calls the jailer to himself, and consequently to the source of divine salvation. A place of darkness and death transforms to a place of light. By their purposeful act of staying in prison, Paul and Silas bring good news of salvation to the jailer that they had understood themselves called on to deliver.[90]

---

88. The jailer literally "comes out of sleep [ἔξυπνος]," where sleep (ὕπνος) was "the brother of death" in myth (e.g., Homer, *Il.* 14.231).

89. "When the jailer woke and saw that the prison doors were open, he drew his sword and was about to kill himself, supposing that the prisoners had escaped" (Acts 16:27). Torture then death of Peter's guards was in fact one outcome of Peter's divinely enabled escape (Acts 12:19).

90. "'Believe in the Lord Jesus, and you will be saved, you and your household.'

Contra cultural expectations, Luke presents the purposeful act of staying—staying in faith—as the means for bringing the jailer out of his hypnotic dream state to the "right-sightedness" of God. Paul and Silas transform the jailer's sight and "convert" his loyalties by the "nonact" of faithfully remaining in prison. Having been explicitly charged by the magistrates to keep Paul and Silas secure, the faithful jailer dutifully fastens his charges in stocks in the innermost cell but, following the prisoners' purposeful act of staying, transforms into an unfaithful jailer and in an act of pure insubordination leads Paul and Silas out of prison.

It is a pivotal moment in the rhetorical unit. Previously a "slave" of the magistrates (who had shown themselves beholden to the slave owners), the jailer prostrates himself in front of Paul and Silas and addresses them as "lords." Like Lydia, the jailer's heart becomes fully open to receiving Paul and Silas's self-expressive speech, and indeed he does receive it. Moving sequentially from the jailer's previous "lords" to Paul and Silas, now transformed from shamed prisoners into honored "lords," the jailer is led to the one he ultimately should be faithful to, the "Lord Jesus" (Acts 16:31). By way of this progression, the jailer and his household are "saved" since they have received the good news.

Not only is the gold standard of life—immortality—discovered where death should hold sway, but the overall space of the prison compound, including the jailer's house, is replete with elements that could rightfully be found in a place of prayer. On their way to a place of prayer, a second time, Paul and Silas are physically dragged and thrust into one. The term προσευχή, used in an uncommon fashion to denote space in the rhetorical unit, occurs for the final time in Acts 16:16. However, once in prison, Paul and Silas partake in the self-expressive acts of praying and singing hymns (Acts 16:25) while an assembly—the prisoners—listen. The jailer prostrates himself in front of men he calls "lords," evoking a reaction appropriate to an encounter with the holy, much as did Peter, the Gerasene demoniac, and the woman with the hemorrhage in front of Jesus in the Gospel (Luke 5:8; 8:28, 47).[91] Paul and Silas "speak the word of

---

And they spoke the word of the Lord to him and to all that were in his house" (Acts 16:31–32).

91. "The Greek προσκυνεῖν corresponds to the Heb. הׁשתחנה. One bows down before God especially when approaching Him in the sanctuary, so that הׁשתחנה comes to denote the performance of cultic actions at a holy place" (Heinrich Greeven, "Εὔχομαι," TDNT 2:789).

the Lord" to the assembly much as they did to the synagogue in Antioch (Acts 13:14–42; 16:32). Washing and a baptism ensues, and a "table" is set followed by the group's rejoicing that one has come to believe in God.[92] Elements associated with priestly discourse, evoking synagogue or temple space, permeate the prison compound. Space associated with the deepest form of corruption becomes space associated with the holy, and within this space the source of eternal life is mediated.

5.5.2. Conclusion: Ideological Texture of Paul's Implicit Παρακαλέω in Prison

Put to the touchstone of prison torture, Paul and Silas display the nature of authentic faith. The jailer shifts from brutalizer to healer and in so doing undermines Philippi's mechanism of power. The purposeful act of staying melds with the emotion-fused acts of faith and fidelity and produces the means of salvation. The result of the touchstone test unveils the pure gold standard of "faith in the Lord" through Paul and Silas's staying in faith.

When experienced by the jailer, the gold standard of faith performs a transformative function. Prison is not fled; instead, it transmutes from space of death into space of eternal life. Not only do Paul and Silas stay in their cell following the earthquake, but they also insist on staying in the prison compound after they receive word of their release from the magistrates (Acts 16:26–28, 36–37). These two stay events join a thematic progression of "stays" throughout the unit. However, the concept of divinely enabled release remains operative in the text. Just as Luke does not erase the divine dream-vision frame with a Macedonian's call for aid but uses it to create a new blend of frames, the prison-escape frame remains operative as it transforms expectations of divine rescue. A show of divine power does not enable a prison escape here; rather, the prison-escape frame, in evoking the expectation of release, highlights the prisoners' contrasting action of staying. In this manner, "staying" becomes a rhetorically powerful, purposeful action.

In the space of Philippi, the prisoners and the jailer are not only "tamed," as in Philo's account of Joseph, but also given sight of God leading to the source of their immortality. Luke's human-scale apocalypse con-

---

92. Ἀναγαγών τε αὐτοὺς εἰς τὸν οἶκον παρέθηκεν τράπεζαν καὶ ἠγαλλιάσατο πανοικεὶ πεπιστευκὼς τῷ θεῷ (Acts 16:34).

tinues. The pit of death, prison, is transformed into a holy space mediating salvation. However, instead of the usual elements associated with an apocalyptic destruction of evil forces together with divine restoration of goodness and right order, namely, a wrathful, avenging warrior God, the steadfast faith of two men shines forth as if it were refined gold and serves to reorder the forces of evil and life. Just as the Macedonian's ethnic identity grounded Paul's dream-vision, so too does Paul's great voice, the jailer's call for lights, and the purposeful act of staying ground the means of salvation in prison.

This, then, becomes the battle scene. By turning an enemy into an ally by demonstrating the essential trait of a warrior, faithful courage, Paul and Silas *do* bring in the auxiliary aid that leads to victory. True, this is a human-scale victory; no dragon falls from the heavens, no fire consumes the earth. Rather, an enemy is led to shift allegiances but in so doing undermines the very structure of coercive force that had been employed in the attempt to silence the disciples. The space used in service of this victory is not the pure, clean, uncorrupted space typically required for appropriate mediation of the holy, but instead filthy, diseased, corrupted space. For in Luke's ideological shift, the criterion for divine mediation shifts dramatically from conventionally appointed holy space to any space that enables the right sight of God. Authentic worship of God takes places in any space that leads, through the genuine faith of its members, to the right sight of God.

5.6. The Inverted ΠΑΡΑΚΑΛΕΩ of the Magistrates: Separating Apart

Once day dawns, the magistrates now effect Paul and Silas's release following the same channel of communication that led to their incarceration. Earlier, the magistrates had themselves ripped Paul and Silas's clothing and had ordered them flogged, presumably by the lictors.[93] Once beaten by the lictors, the disciples were handed over to the jailer, who secured them in the innermost cell (Acts 16:24). Now a discharge is effected in reverse order. The magistrates send the lictors with word of release, who deliver this word to the jailer, who in turn conveys it to Paul and Silas. In mirroring the incarceration, Luke signals that both the incarceration and the

---

93. Ῥαβδίζω, ῥαβδοῦχος (Acts 16:22).

release form part of a seamless system of punishment. The goal is expulsion, and the message from the magistrates is intended as the final step in ridding Philippi of its presumably now appropriately cowed menace.

Paul and Silas, however, do not respond as prisoners beaten into submission would be expected to, swiftly departing the prison and Philippi, thankful to have escaped further torture. The tables turn, and Paul accuses the magistrates of the very offense that had led to his incarceration—acting against Roman custom and encouraging other Philippians to do so as well. Through Paul's counteraccusation, the magistrates exhibit the fundamental un-Roman emotion, fear, and in so doing Luke casts them within the framework of defeated enemies.

5.6.1. Fear: An Enemy's Self-Defeat

While Paul and Silas's first act of staying in prison served to open the jailer's heart to their words of salvation, their second act of staying serves as a show of judgment against the magistrates. Romans, self-perceived as models of virtue and justice, physiognomically presented themselves as holding to the highest standards of integrity. Contrary to Roman ideals, the magistrates are exposed as having behaved in "un-Roman" fashion by having resorted to mob justice without due legal process.[94]

The magistrates, as Philippi's leaders, function as the polis's representative members. Incited to action through the anger of the slave owners, the magistrates immediately show themselves under the influence of the vengeful slave owners and mob. They conform to the convention of leaders being "enslaved," notionally to the people, but ultimately to passion. Between the slave owners and the magistrates, custom and law are joined together and the customary "law" of Philippi is exposed as being derived from enslavement to vengeful passion.

Moreover, once receiving word of Paul's own claim to "Romanness," the magistrates are afraid. Fear, the most unmanly, and un-Roman, of emo-

---

94. In contrast to the Philippian experience, note how Festus portrays Roman custom: "When I was in Jerusalem, the chief priests and the elders of the Jews informed me about him and asked for a sentence against him. I told them that it was not the custom of the Romans to hand over anyone before the accused had met the accusers face to face and had been given an opportunity to make a defense against the charge" (Acts 25:15–16).

tions, is used only of the magistrates in the rhetorical unit.⁹⁵ Fear becomes the operative emotion-fused motive of the magistrates and, in stark contrast with the outcome of Paul and Silas's test of prison, further condemns them. In military discourse, "fear" was the emotion of an enemy defeated; it most certainly was not the emotion of warriors whose hearts had been strengthened with fortifying aid. In military discourse, fear and confusion in an enemy were the prime markers of defeat.⁹⁶ As J. E. Lendon points out, "Warfare is a contest of masculinity."⁹⁷ Through their cowardly fear, the magistrates clearly display themselves as not having received the fortifying news that could lead to salvation.

Quite deliberately, Luke makes rhetological speech the medium of communication between the magistrates and Paul during the final separation scene. It was the form of legal language that the magistrates could understand, and not surprisingly it evoked weak-kneed fear in them. In place of the reverential fear that emotion-fused perceptive communication might have yielded, had their hearts opened themselves to it, the magistrates instead experience cowardly fear.

The magistrates' final scene with Paul and Silas forms the reverse analogue of the call of the Macedonian man. They reject "military aid" and therefore do not ally themselves with the we-group. As a result, they do not receive the good news of salvation within their hearts; they are outside of those who rightfully could be called "worshipers of God." Most notably, in Acts the term "fear" never appears as a descriptor of reverence in the rhetorical unit (i.e., there are no "Godfearers" here); it is used only of the self-interested fear of the magistrates. Their defeat could not be more complete, and at the same time their defeat could not be more understated. No shows of vengeful divine justice are displayed against Philippi's magistrates. Instead, a city's leadership that had been given every opportunity to see remains unsighted.

In this way, Luke uses the fearful man, the antithesis of masculinity and of the Roman masculine ideal, to define Philippi's leading men. The term παρακαλέω, explicitly occurring here for the third time in the rhetorical unit (Acts 16:39), functions contrary to its essential meaning when it is invoked within the context of the magistrates' fear. Instead of suggesting

---

95. Ἐφοβήθησαν δὲ ἀκούσαντες ὅτι Ῥωμαῖοί εἰσιν (Acts 16:38).
96. Orderly tactics and courage led to victory; see Lendon, "Rhetoric of Combat," 273–329.
97. Ibid., 310.

an act of joining by calling to oneself, παρακαλέω instead becomes a form of cowardly pandering, as the magistrates attempt to drive Paul and Silas out as expeditiously as possible.[98] Ultimately the very men who earlier laid claim to guarding Roman custom are displayed as violating it, with the message being delivered, in true Lukan irony, through the symbolically laden Roman lictors.

Paul's self-expressive speech functions with the magistrates much as it did with the exorcism of the Python spirit: it exposes. Whereas the basis for the slave owners' alliance with the disciples—hope of profit—was unveiled by the departure of the Python spirit, thereby rendering the slave woman's true-sounding words spurious, now Paul's condemnation of the magistrates exposes them as counterfeit Romans. As false Romans, the magistrates' external self-representation does not reflect their inner hearts; their roles as Romans are incompatible with the actions that display their character.

Through Paul's charging the magistrates with having acted against Roman custom, Luke leads the audience to infer inductively that the magistrates are fragmented, or disordered, beings who are no longer "in sympathy" with their own reason.[99] A person "not in sympathy" with her or his reason is a fragmented person, suggesting a state of confusion.[100] Such confusion was a sign of irrationality and therefore of a "false man"—a man in appearance but not in practice. The cause of this confusion was often ascribed to having succumbed to the sorts of disorganizing passions typically associated with the "Lydian disease."[101] In Ephesus a similar scenario will play itself out. Driven by a desire for profit, the Ephesian silversmiths will incite a riotous attack on the disciples. As a result, an impassioned mob forms into an assembly brought together by confusion rather than

---

98. Notice the difference in how the unjustly imprisoned Antiphilus and Demetrius are treated and Paul and Silas. Antiphilus and Demetrius have their innocence affirmed by an investigation and in recognition of the injustice suffered are financially compensated. Paul and Silas's innocence is never acknowledged by Philippi's magistrates, and their παρακαλέω is not one of condolence, but rather an attempt to appease in order to get them out of Philippi as expeditiously as possible. See p. 195 above.

99. For example, see Arrian, *Epict. diss.* 2.9.19–21.

100. Luke presents this as an inaugural sign of the arrival of the kingdom of God: "He has shown strength with his arm; he has scattered the proud in the thoughts of their hearts" (διεσκόρπισεν ὑπερηφάνους διανοίᾳ καρδίας αὐτῶν) (Luke 1:51).

101. For "Lydian disease" see §4.2.3. As examples of discourse that targets passion and *luxuria* as influences that disorder reason, see Arrian, *Epict. diss.* 2.9.2–5; Philostratus, *Vit. Apoll.* 8.7.23.

ordered reason.[102] So too in Philippi, a mob along with the city's leaders joined together in attack in response to enigmatic and unsubstantiated charges against Paul and Silas, incited by the emotion-fused anger of the slave owners and without any process of judgment or discernment.

In military discourse, as in narratives of justice being meted out, the enemy was expected to receive its punitive deserts. So, for example, Origen is challenged by Celsus to explain how it is that the God of Jesus would have allowed the perpetrators of Jesus's death to suffer no ill consequence for their act. In response, Origen (unwittingly displaying the severity of the schism that had by that point developed between Christians and Jews) falls back on a traditional logic of victory and defeat.

> But the one who condemned him did not even suffer any such fate as that of Pentheus by going mad or being torn in pieces, he [Celsus] says. He did not see that it was not so much Pilate who condemned him ... as the Jewish people. This nation has been condemned by God and *torn in pieces*, and scattered over all the earth, a fate more terrible than the rending suffered by Pentheus. (*Cels.* 2.34 [Chadwick], emphasis original; brackets added)

Luke, however, advances a far different ideological message. A people become "like Pentheus" when they choose a system of divine mediation that obscures the right sight of God.[103] This can be any people—Macedonians, Jews, Greeks, Romans, or self-regarded Christians.

Philippi, it must be remembered, became a Roman colony as a result of Antony's and Augustus's win against fellow Romans Cassius and Brutus; the battle of Philippi was fought in the course of a civil war where Roman fought against Roman and, moreover, received its name—Colonia Julia Augusta

---

102. "Now some cried one thing, some another; for the assembly was in confusion, and most of them did not know why they had come together" (Acts 19:32). The term used to describe this ἐκκλησία is συγχύννω, "confused," the same term that the LXX uses in its noun form to denote the place name of "Babel" as a qualifier of the confused state of a pre-Pentecost world: Διὰ τοῦτο ἐκλήθη τὸ ὄνομα αὐτῆς Σύγχυσις ὅτι ἐκεῖ συνέχεεν κύριος τὰ χείλη πάσης τῆς γῆς (Gen 11:9 LXX).

103. The hapless Pentheus, effeminized and dismembered by the end of his battle with Dionysus, was regularly invoked in discourse concerned with the effects of a social body that was fragmented from within. See Clement of Alexandria, *Strom.* 13.57.1–3 (Ferguson); P. Aelius Aristides, *To the Rhodians: Concerning Concord* 37–39 (Behr).

Philippensis—after former allies Augustus and Antony fought each other.[104] The very ground of Philippi remained in social memory spatially associated with Rome's conflicts where like fought with like. Within this spatial background of civil war, Luke presents the Romans Paul and Silas in conflict with self-purported Romans who represent Philippi's social structure of power.

Although Philippi is presented as Roman territory, an image supported by Latinized terms, as well as the charges against Paul and Silas of advocating "un-Roman" customs to "us Romans," Paul's countercharges against the magistrates accuse the city of having unmoored itself from its geocentric social logic, and of devolving into a fragmented, irrational rabble. Within a dyadic society when representatives of a group displayed corrupted or disordered inner hearts, they concurrently pointed to the general corruption of the social body in which they were embedded.[105] Philippi's leaders, no longer in sympathy with their reason as rightful true Roman males, are symptomatic of the diseased social body of the polis of Philippi. Disconnected from its ethnographic source—Rome—the polis of Philippi had disoriented its ground of social logic.[106]

Moreover, unlike the growing movement of Christianity, the Philippians' disconnect with their ethnographic source was not leading to the development of a new logic of discernment but rather to the "blindness" of irrationality. Paul's accusation highlights the irony of the magistrates having succumbed to un-Roman behavior: the judicial process, an osten-

---

104. Appian describes how fellow soldier fought against fellow soldier: "Thus did Octavian and Antony by perilous daring and by two infantry engagements achieve a success, the like of which was never before known; for never before had such numerous and powerful Roman armies come in conflict with each other. These soldiers were not enlisted from the ordinary conscription, but were picked men. They were not new levies, but under long drill and arrayed against each other, not against foreign or barbarous races. Speaking the same language and using the same tactics, being of like discipline and power of endurance, they were for these reasons what we may call mutually invincible. Nor was there ever such fury and daring in war as here, when citizens contended against citizens, families against families, and fellow-soldiers against each other" (*Bell. civ.* 4.137 [White, LCL]). Virgil writes: "Therefore once more Philippi saw Roman armies clash in the shock of brother weapons" (*Georg.* 1.489–490 [Fairclough, LCL]).

105. Bruce J. Malina and Jerome H. Neyrey, "First-Century Personality: Dyadic, Not Individual," in *The Social World of Luke-Acts: Models for Interpretation*, ed. Jerome H. Neyrey (Peabody, MA: Hendrickson, 1991), 76.

106. For the social logic of ethnocentrism, see §5.3.5 above.

sible process of truth-finding, had been subverted by irrational animal-like passion fueled by the anger of the slave owners. Touchstone *synkrisis* continues: rubbed side by side with the Romans Paul and Silas, "Roman" Philippi is exposed as a locus of disordered blindness, in stark contrast with the right sight that had brought the jailer to life.

5.6.2. Conclusion: Ideological Texture of the Inverted Παρακαλέω of the Magistrates

Ironically, in the dawning light of day, the blindness of the magistrates leads them to reject the source of salvation in their midst. The inverted context of the magistrates' παρακαλέω, sending away rather than drawing near, underscores the inverted outcome of their encounter with the disciples. Through their loyalty to the slave owners, the magistrates perform the opposite of Lydia's offer: they ask the disciples to leave. Exposed as Rome-fearers rather than reverential Godfearers, the magistrates do not receive the "good news."

Although the early Macedonian frame suggested battling warriors, the defeat of the magistrates is emotion-fused rather than physical. To outside eyes, there would be little to suggest that an enemy had been defeated, but the analysis of the ideological force of the passage gives us grounds to suggest that, in terms of access to immortal life, it has. The final scene with the magistrates underscores that the good news can fortify the hearts only of those who can perceive its source. In a passage marked by surface-level rhetological argumentation, the impact of Paul's counteraccusation functions rhetographically. From the perspective of military discourse—the unit's inaugural frame—defeat of one party meant the victory of another. The notion of win-win had not yet entered the social psyche of a limited-goods environment. The Macedonian's call for aid left the enemy lines undefined, and now the "defeat" of the magistrates completes their configuration within an "enemy" role. The magistrates are not a physiognomically based enemy, however, and Paul and Silas's earlier ongoing tolerance of the slave woman underscored that point. The magistrates turn themselves into an enemy, and self-inflict their defeat by allying themselves with the slave owners' act of vengeance. Face-to-face with a source of salvation, the magistrates remain blind to its presence and, in that manner, are ultimately undone.

5.7. Paul's Παρακαλεω to the Assembly at Lydia's: Mutual Recognition

When, contra the magistrate's request to leave, Paul and Silas instead "stay" at Lydia's (Acts 16:39–40), they culminate the rupture between themselves and the leading social network of the polis. But Paul and Silas's defiant stay also performs a concurrent and inverse function. When Paul and Silas join with those gathered at Lydia's, their stay performs a cohesive function. Their "stay" argumentatively affirms Lydia's loyalty to the Lord and suggests that she is indeed a worshiper of God. As a worshiper of God, she has received the good news of salvation. Both friend and foe come to light through the final act of staying. Moreover, those gathered at Lydia's are called ἀδελφοί, a term that in the Gospel of Luke can mean kinship relationships but in Acts refers only to religious communities of believers. An alliance has therefore been established, carrying military elements, yet within the context of a group of worshipers of God in a newly developing house of prayer.

5.7.1. Culmination of the Παρακαλέω Progression: "Seeing" and "Encouraging" the Assembly at Lydia's

Paul and Silas's "stay" at Lydia's completes Luke's illustrative test cases that portray various dimensions of authentic and inauthentic faith within the rhetorical unit. Through the disciples' "stay" at her house, Lydia's loyalty is affirmed as being genuine in comparison with Python-sourced corruption. Progressively compared with the slave-owner merchants, touchstone *synkrisis* suggests that a Lydian purple-selling woman, the most likely candidate for exposure as counterfeit, should be considered as an exemplar of authentic discipleship.

If Lydia's loyalty is genuine, then as its representative her house assembly cannot be considered a "den of robbers," but rather as a gathering of worshipers of God—a house of prayer. The house-of-prayer element leads to Luke's rhetorical goal in presenting Lydia as a test case for judgment. For the Christian house of prayer was under increasing pressure from within to rechart its cognitive maps for defining "true" believers. Not unexpectedly, given the primacy of discernment, Paul and Silas's sole actions at Lydia's—"seeing" and "encouraging"—revert the body-zone focus back to emotion-fused thought ("when they had seen [ἰδόντες] and encouraged [παρεκάλεσαν] the believers [ἀδελφοί])": Acts 16:40). It completes the unit's παρακαλέω progression.

Paradoxically, in view of the history of interpretation's insistence on Lydia's role as a material-resource provider, materiality is completely absent in Lydia's case, which instead operates within the zones of self-expressive speech and emotion-fused thought. Lydia does not post bail for Paul as does his host Jason in Thessalonica (Acts 17:9); nor does she bribe her way into prison with her jewelry and silver in order to gain access to Paul as does Thecla (Acts Paul 18); nor, like Antiphilus's friend Demetrius, does she give a portion of her daily wages to the jailer in order to protect the prisoner from the jailer's brutality (Lucian, *Tox.* 31); nor does she bring any form of food or nourishment to Paul and Silas. In contrast, the jailer will bring Paul and Silas into his house, bathe them, and set a meal before them in his role as host (Acts 16:33–34). Lydia's presentation, on the other hand, is devoid of any contribution of material resources. Even the "visit" to Lydia's avoids the material spatial indicator of "house"—Paul and Silas do not go to Lydia's house, οἶκος, in Acts 16:40; rather, they "go to the Lydian"[107] despite οἶκος being a repetitive term in this passage. By the river in Acts 16:14–15, the relationship between Lydia, the Lord, and Paul falls primarily within the framework of emotion-fused thought and self-expressive speech, as does Paul's "stay" at Lydia's (16:40).

The emotion-fused act of sight formed a critical sensory role in ancient thinking that went far beyond visual perception. To really see meant to perceive deeply. "True" sight, that is, sight that can perceive divinity, is ordered sight that leads to genuine clarity. As such, it forms the opposite of false sight and confusion. If a blind, disordered enemy is a defeated enemy, then ordered sight and clarity signal victory for the allies.[108]

Paul and Silas's first act upon entering Lydia's is "seeing," and this act forms an *inclusio* to Paul's first act of "seeing" the vision of the Macedonian in Troas.[109] In each case, Paul's act of seeing infers cognitive perception

---

107. Εἰσῆλθον πρὸς τὴν Λυδίαν.

108. The argument that the rhetorical unit's principal focus is on discerning the difference between counterfeit and genuine and thereby restoring "right sight" supports Bloomquist's suggestion that the unveiling of truth could be considered as one of the characterizing elements of apocalyptic discourse. See L. Gregory Bloomquist, "Methodological Criteria for Apocalyptic Rhetoric: A Suggestion for the Expanded Use of Sociorhetorical Analysis," in *Vision and Persuasion: Rhetorical Dimensions of Apocalyptic Discourse*, ed. Greg Carey and L. Gregory Bloomquist (St. Louis: Chalice, 1999), 199–201.

109. Καὶ ὅραμα διὰ [τῆς] νυκτὸς τῷ Παύλῳ ὤφθη (Acts 16:9); καὶ ἰδόντες παρεκάλεσαν τοὺς ἀδελφούς (Acts 16:40).

and evaluation, and indeed "seeing" the assembly at Lydia's affirms Lydia's claim to faithfulness. In addition to functioning as a faculty of perceptiveness, sight in ancient understanding involved interpenetration; it was not a one-directional faculty. As Danielle Allen explains: "To see was to be seen and to be seen was to see. The processes of vision entailed a two-way physical exchange of what was inside, or in the innards of, both seer and seen."[110] Given the two-way exchange between seer and seen, it is possible to suggest that Paul's "sight" of the assembly at Lydia's removes the taint of Lydia's physiognomic profile, much as the healing exchange between Jesus and the woman with the hemorrhage resulted in the woman being restored to wholeness and health and Jesus's commensurate loss of power (Luke 8:43–48). However, Lydia's physiognomic profile is the key element within such a logic of cleansing, for it is not Lydia the human who is cleansed or purified, but rather the audience's sight of Lydia. As contended, Lydia is treated much as were the disciples on the road to Emmaus—she is accorded the faculty of clear sight within her heart since her heart had been evaluated by God as suitably endowed for perceptive insight. Lydia is not cleansed or purified, but her physiognomic profile of immoral huckstering suggests that she ought to be. By presenting Lydia within a "polluted" cultural profile, yet elevating her rhetorical presentation to one who meets the standards of truest discipleship, the rhetoric of the unit dramatically subverts physiognomic logic as it raises a gold standard—steadfast faith—to prominence.[111]

Through touchstone *synkrisis*, Lydia's claim to faithfulness had been "rubbed" alongside the dross faith of a Python-sourced mediation system. Furthermore, the very notion of "faithfulness" or "fidelity to the Lord" had been illustrated, just like the life-size "painting" of Joseph in prison,[112] by Paul's prison stay. Paul's prison stay defines faith to the Lord. Assessing Lydia's faith meant that this faith, and this faith alone, determined the criterion for inclusion into prayer-house space and not, as might have been expected, any form of ethnocentric and/or gender-derived evaluation.[113]

---

110. Allen, *World of Prometheus*, 79.

111. This conclusion supports Parsons's thesis that Luke and Acts subverts physiognomic logic; Parsons, *Body and Character in Luke and Acts*. In Lydian touchstone rhetoric, pure gold represented steadfast faithfulness: "Gold, that material least liable to corruption, is for him [Theognis] an emblem of extraordinary integrity and stability in human character" (DuBois, *Torture and Truth*, 12).

112. See p. 196.

113. Following on the work of Louise Schottroff, Ivoni Richter Reimer's sociohis-

Luke's radical reconfiguration of markers of right-belonging had already been signaled by Paul and Silas's incarceration. While on Luke's ideological level their prison stay displayed their powers of divine mediation, on a sociocultural level and from within the world of the narrative, they remained to outside eyes dishonored men whose bodies had been socially effeminized.[114] As pointed out above, on the surface, life in Philippi continued on much as it had before the incarceration; Paul and Silas were not as much returned to public honor as they were hustled out of prison, and ultimately out of Philippi, with as little attention as possible. As Jennifer Glancy astutely observes, "in the first century ... scar tissue on a breast pierced in battle was readily distinguished from a crosshatching of weals on a back"—battle wounds were not confused with "disciplinary stripes."[115] Stressing that in physiognomic understanding "social status was somatically expressed," Glancy asks the pressing question, "what is it like to follow an eminently beatable leader?"[116]

The answer, at least according to the author of Luke-Acts, is that following such a leader might lead to similar physical suffering and public dishonor, since such is the consequence of steadfast faith. Moreover, such

---

torical liberationist interpretation of Lydia also concluded that Lydia's act of hospitality constitutes an act of courage. The sociohistorical questions asked of the text did not lead to the rhetorical ones of the role of the physical attack on Paul as well as the cultural understanding of a female Lydian "host"; nonetheless the element of courage is an important insight that is further supported by this sociorhetorical investigation. Reimer writes: "In Lydia's case, the pressure she applies is a sign of her solidarity. She certainly knows the conditions in the Roman colony of Philippi, and the attitude of the Roman authorities toward Jews (Acts 16:19-24). In this situation, her pressing invitation is an attempt to aid the missionaries by taking precautions for their protection. At the same time, she has to be ready to answer to the city authorities for giving them her protection. Should a conflict arise between her guests and the Roman authorities her house would be drawn into a dangerous situation. It is possible that in this case Lydia was unable to offer the protection provided by law, inasmuch as Paul ... finds it necessary to appeal to his own rights as a Roman citizen. The action of Lydia and the others is to be understood, against the background here developed, as 'hospitality,' which included the provision of protection for her guests. To put it another way: hospitality is not abrogated when there is danger, but only at that moment proves itself to be genuine hospitality" (Reimer, *Women in the Acts of the Apostles*, 124).

114. "Dishonorable bodies were whippable; honorable bodies were not" (Jennifer A. Glancy, "Boasting of Beatings [2 Corinthians 11:23-25]," *JBL* 123 [2004]: 109).

115. Ibid., 113.

116. Ibid., 129.

suffering might well come about from challenges to a mammon-bound system of divine mediation. Jesus's own death provided ample testimony for that possibility. Seeing the reality, however, brought the need for fortifying encouragement acutely to the fore. A new social logic carried along with it new consequences. One consequence is that losing one's safety net of conventional social alliances raised the need for courage. Courage is precisely the quality that announcements of good news invoked in troops.

The Macedonian man called for fortification and alliance, and indeed at Lydia's these are delivered. Paul's παρακαλέω is perhaps the most intense of those found in the progression, yet paradoxically the content of the παρακαλέω is not narrated. His is the sort of παρακαλέω a leader would deliver to his troops in order to ready them for further battle; and the basis for the encouragement is faith in the good news of salvation.

Not surprisingly, with the critical role played by resources within military calls for aid, military alliances formed through them were acutely concerned with the question of fidelity, for its actual presence was always tenuous. Military alliances were essentially held together by cost-benefit analyses that were constantly being reevaluated. If at any time the cost of an alliance was perceived to exceed expected benefits, then resources and loyalties would readily shift.[117]

Religious loyalties, also, were far from stable, and Luke-Acts is acutely aware of the fragile nature of religious loyalty. Maud Gleason describes the problem: "People's belief systems seem liable to sudden dislocations, like an unstable knee…. As we have seen, the apocryphal *Acts of Peter* portrays a world in which religious loyalty is extremely labile; both Christians and pagans shift allegiance abruptly, repeatedly."[118] Although Gleason's comments are contextualized by the second century, the Gospels and Acts portray exactly these sorts of shifts of allegiance.

In each case in Acts when the disciples were first enthusiastically received by a community and subsequently driven away by members of the same community, the fragility of loyalty continued to be displayed. One culturally conventional way an author like Luke might have attempted to solidify loyalty among believers would have been to show how high-status members of the community turned to the Christian message as a means of providing the emerging church with high-status endorsement. Another

---

117. Luke 14:31–32 uses the norm of a cost-benefit analysis to highlight that military alliance typically arises from this type of calculus.
118. Gleason, "Truth Contests and Talking Corpses," 302.

would have been to suggest that loyalty would have its material rewards, a hope dangled in front of many a potential military ally. Yet instead, Luke illustrates loyalty by the test of prison and by a Lydian purple-selling woman suggesting, at a minimum, a dire need for a new propaganda advisor, or perhaps, far likelier, a deeply countercultural case for loyalty.[119]

The author of Acts presents loyalty to the Lord as being highly incompatible with cost-benefit analyses, since one consequence of such loyalty is that it can lead to torturous incarceration in prison.[120] Another consequence is that mutually beneficial alliances undergirded by hope of material gain, such as that between the we-group and the slave-woman network, undo the salvific element of the good news. What is good for business and worldly honor is generally not good for the gospel.[121]

---

119. As the stories of Joseph and Antiphilus and his friend Demetrius show, demonstrating fidelity through prison stays was quite present in cultural rhetoric. The heroic nature of these accounts suggests that these too were intended to be countercultural.

120. In his published thesis, Bloomquist explored the role of suffering in Paul's Letter to the Philippians. Bloomquist argues that suffering is not presented as an end, but rather as a consequence of faith. If being faithful to the Lord leads to situations of suffering, then faith prevails. Given the crucial role of loyalty in Acts 16, there may be more elements in common between the letter and Acts than has been historically acknowledged. Bloomquist writes: "Obedience to Paul does not imply veneration of a master or participation with the apostle in religious mysticism, but proclamation: 'he invites people to join with him in the journey on the gospel road.' The same necessity that presses him into a situation that is not necessarily of his plan or desire is that which pressed Christ. And though caught by necessity, Paul, like Christ, is confident of God's ability to bring victory out of apparent tragedy. Again like Christ, Paul seeks simply to act honourably to the end (1.18b–26 and 1.27–30). And so like the one described in 2.6–11, though forced by necessity into a situation not of his own choosing and ultimately confident of God's grace, Paul gives of himself freely and willingly" (L. Gregory Bloomquist, *The Function of Suffering in Philippians*, JSNTSup [Sheffield: Sheffield Academic, 1993], 169–70; see Bloomquist, "Rhetoric of Suffering in Paul's Letter to the Philippians," 195–223).

121. Interestingly, the insight that Lydia's purple selling might be incompatible with forming an association with the Pauline group is only voiced in an early twentieth-century catalog of "women of the Bible," outside the academy of biblical scholarship. Margaret Sangster writes: "It took courage to accept the Cross in the day when Lydia reached out her hand and touched it and said that hereafter she would share it with Jesus in the fellowship of His sufferings. She did the next thing when she asked the servants of Christ who preached the Cross to enter her house. Prudent people might have warned her that her business might suffer, that as a seller of purple she would make less money if she were known to belong to an unpopular sect, and that

5.7.2. Conclusion: Ideological Texture of Paul's Παρακαλέω to the Assembly at Lydia's

If, as argued, traditionally derived cognitive maps could no longer be relied on to determine what constituted a genuine house of divine mediation, then Luke also, through those gathered at Lydia's, begins to illustrate the nature of an authentic sacred-social network. Despite Paul and Silas's public beating, the new believers had not scattered like Pentheus's limbs; they had remained gathered at Lydia's. Moreover, the group at Lydia's is clearly designated by Luke as ἀδελφοί and is therefore characterized as a community of believers. Those at Lydia's are framed within a progression of "stays" as a group that stays.

In contrast to a shaken world broken from within like that of Roman Philippi, the house of prayer at Lydia's is firmly secured and anchored. By mutually recognizing each other's faith in the Lord, the Pauline group and Lydia's group are able to strengthen each other's steadfastness. Although ἰδόντες παρεκάλεσαν τοὺς ἀδελφούς (Acts 16:40) might be read as temporal sequence, much as the RSV has it, "and when they had seen the brethren, they exhorted them," it is far likelier, given the role of sight in antiquity and the Macedonian's call for fortification (subtly distinct from exhortation), that the aorist participle ἰδόντες is contemporaneous with the action of the main verb παρεκάλεσαν.[122] The NRSV comes closer to conveying the emotion-fused act of seeing as coparticipating with an ostensibly self-expressive, yet functionally emotion-fused, act of encouraging: "and when they had seen and encouraged." In the two-way exchange of seeing, the sight of Lydia and those gathered with her as truly faithful to the Lord exchanges with the sight of the Pauline group as sincere servants of God who deliver the source of salvation—neither side are κάπηλοι (2 Cor 2:17). Through this two-way exchange, the message of salvation can travel beyond the ears, lodge in the heart, and by strengthening it, take root.

---

she might better worship the Lord in secret. This was not Lydia's way" (Margaret E. Sangster, *The Women of the Bible: A Portrait Gallery* [New York: Christian Herald, 1911], 340–41).

122. See Wallace, *Greek Grammar*, 624.

5.8. Conclusion: Ideological Texture

This analysis of ideological texture shows that Luke used the basic military notion of παρακαλέω—to call an ally to one's side for auxiliary military aid—as a structuring element that frames an illustrative series of explicit and implicit calls between the disciples and potential new believers, as a rhetographical demonstration of emerging criteria for evaluating which alliances would further, or hinder, the gospel's salvific efficaciousness. Most notably, the investigation of ideological texture provides grounds for suggesting that Luke replaced traditional physiognomic markers, such as ethnicity, with the quality of "steadfast faith" as the principal criterion that distinguishes friend from enemy in the "battle" for salvation. Moreover, the author presents the emotion-fused faculty of discernment, "rightsightedness," as an apocalyptic element that functions in the stead of the traditional topos of an apocalyptic divine refining furnace that separates the allies to salvation from the enemies. By blending incompatible and clashing elements together with traditional frames and topoi, Luke develops a new framework for salvation that, strikingly, does not display a powerful, honored, warrior God as a deliverer of salvific victory, but rather culturally dishonored or shameless disciples, who nonetheless do deliver the victory of salvation through their steadfast faith.

The author of Acts presents a human-scale apocalypse that is focused on emotion-fused inner-human faculties. From the beginning, Luke signals that traditional apocalyptic roles have been shifted in his presentation. A divine trumpet blast does not summon a military leader, but instead a group of disciples responds to a call for military aid from a Macedonian leader, yet within that call it hears God's voice. Consequently, the rhetorical development of the text unfolds through the Pauline group's delivery of the needed resource, fortifying faith and courage to others. However, whereas in a military context this faith and courage would be delivered by explicit assurances of the support of power from a divine warrior God, Luke removes the traditional markers of divine support and replaces these with powerful examples of faith in action.

First, we can see from our analysis of ideological texture that Luke deployed the topos of gender in order to begin to destabilize audience expectations after opening the rhetorical unit with a Macedonian warrior/divine victory blend. Instead of first encountering men, the normative gender of Macedonian warriors and members of Jewish synagogues, the Pauline group not only encounters women but also sits with them, and begins preaching without hesitation, as if they had found a synagogue gathering. Yet, despite the fact that in sitting down with the women the Pauline group transgresses sociocultural honor codes, God affirms their actions by opening the understanding of Lydia's heart to Paul's salvific words. Second, an exorcism does not serve to showcase the superior power of God's agents and their God, as amazed crowds witness a healed and restored body. Instead, God's agents are publicly humiliated, beaten, and incarcerated. The publicly dishonored state of the disciples contrasts sharply with the elevated honor of Philippi's social power network. Yet the profit-motivated mantic industry is also exposed as being a contagion to the good news of salvation. Third, an instrument of Philippi's power network, and an enemy to the bringers of salvation—the jailer—is not killed in a show of divine might as God's messengers are miraculously rescued from prison, but instead he is shown the source of immortal life as the messengers "foolishly" stay on. Fourth, as a result of this faithful steadfast stay, the jailer's heart is opened to see God, and as a consequence of his new faculty of right-sightedness, the jailer acts disloyally to his former lords and thereby undermines Philippi's system of coercive violence. A former locus of suffering and disease, prison, is transformed into a place of salvation. Fifth, enemy leaders are not destroyed, nor is their city ravaged by an avenging god's army, but rather they are given the opportunity to see, and when they reject it, they are eschatologically destined for death, while they continue with their worldly privileges of power and honor. Sixth, Paul and Silas's last act of "defiance," defined by going to Lydia's rather than leaving Philippi as requested by the magistrates, does not reestablish their ethos as honorable men representing an honored God, but instead displays the honorless nature of their own social network. The social code of hospitality only served to highlight how utterly socially inappropriate it would be for a group of men to "stay" with a woman who is not embedded in the honor of any male and moreover who is profiled as culturally "shameless."

Finally, through Lydia's profile, Luke layers the topos of female gender with topoi of Lydian ethnographic immorality, the hucksterism of merchants, and symbolism of purple degeneracy. Together, these topoi found in Lydia's profile formed a minute, human-scale compression of archetypical apocalyptic biblical enemies, such as Tyre in Isaiah and Ezekiel or the harlot of Revelation. A traditional apocalyptic solution would see such characters defeated and destroyed by God's mighty arm. Instead, God enables Lydia to perceive fully the meaning of the message of salvation, and the final act of God's agents is to go to Lydia's house and discover there a place of prayer. The "harlot" is not destroyed, nor driven out, but rather the audience's view of a harlot is righted, so that when the Lydian physiognomic profile is driven out, an authentic worshiper of God comes into view. A divine refining furnace did not separate contaminants from the pure, but rather Lydian touchstone *synkrisis* comparatively distinguished the body that constitutes worshipers of God from that which is corrupt to its core. In the end, there are no purple traders in the house of the Lord (Zech 14:21), but rather the house of a Lydian purple seller is affirmed as a genuine place of prayer composed of right-sighted believers who receive fortifying courage in order to strengthen their salvific steadfast faith.

Conclusion

This sociorhetorical interpretation of Acts 16:9–40 provides grounds for suggesting that Lydia, the purple-selling woman, functions as a highly rhetorical figure in the text.[1] Through intertextural analysis, I uncovered elements drawn from Lydia's Lydian ethnicity, her occupation of "seller," and the symbolism of the color purple that cohere into a deeply rooted topos of Lydian physiognomy, rhetorically amplified by Lydia's name. The Lydian topos shades Lydia as an immoral, deceptive, unfaithful "outsider." As a result of this culturally contextualized vantage point, it became possible to appreciate the critical role that Lydia's profile played in advancing the author's ideological goals.

A woman whose physiognomic profile would suggest an unsuitable fit with the community that constitutes a salvific space of a "place of prayer," Lydia nonetheless ultimately is found within the nucleus of such a community as a representative member. Through the analysis of the ideological texture of the text, we saw that the author of Luke-Acts argues that the physiognomic profile of people exemplified by Lydia has become an unreliable indicator for assessing the suitability of such people to assume representative roles in the church. By casting the episode within a blend between a military call for aid and the gospel message, the author argues for newly emerging criteria for assessing who will contribute to the salvific nature of the nascent church, and who risks contaminating it, and thereby rendering such space either salvific or devoid of such efficaciousness. Moreover, and most significantly, Lydia's acceptance signals the author's view that the Christ movement should conceive of a place of prayer as space that is constituted by those whose hearts, or inner beings, are shaped by their "right-sightedness" of God. The ideological texture of the text dismantles the social logic of ethnic, gender, or other physiognomic profiles

---

1. For a definition of rhetorical figure, see p. 36.

as reliable guides to the inner spiritual character of newcomers to the Christ movement. Instead, Luke proposes that a person takes on her or his identity as a worshiper of God through remaining steadfastly and courageously loyal to God.

We have seen that the rhetorical force of the Philippi passage develops by way of three interconnected argumentative structures: a παρακαλέω progression, *inclusio* of Lydia verses, and Lydian touchstone *synkrisis*. The παρακαλέω progression establishes a series of alliances and ruptures, where the allied parties constitute the salvific space of a "place of prayer," while those separated out are revealed as antithetical to such space. The Lydia verses *inclusio* rhetographically display the spatial shift of a place of prayer from a traditional synagogue setting to any space where worshipers of God can be found gathered together. By way of Lydian touchstone *synkrisis*, the author of Luke-Acts argues that people identify themselves as worshipers of God through faithful adherence to the gospel message, despite the bodily, social, and/or economic harmful effects that may ensue from such loyalty.

The Macedonian's request triggered the unit's παρακαλέω progression as well as the narrative's plot development. Our analysis of intertextures and ideological textures revealed that the author of Acts inaugurated the rhetorical unit through blends of military topoi. Specifically, the Pauline group was called as if it were an army in order to supply auxiliary military aid. However, the requisitioned aid was not in the form of the regular material resources, but instead it performed a strengthening of the heart by supplying fortifying faith and courage. At the same time, Luke blends elements of divine victory and salvation with the response to the call for aid and thereby raises audience expectations of divine victory. However, as seen in the analysis of progressive and narrational textures, almost immediately another key frame emerges as Luke develops the sacred-spatial element of the rhetorical unit through the theme of the we-group's journeying to a place of prayer. In this manner, Luke positions the place of prayer as the space where the salvific aid will be delivered. Yet, most curiously, no space in Philippi is explicitly identified as a place of prayer; instead, spaces of prayer emerge from a prison and a Lydian woman's home.

The rhetorical force expands with Lydia's request to the Pauline group to come to her home and stay, the second παρακαλέω of the unit, as it progressively moves the Macedonian's call for military aid and alliance into the sphere of Lydia's home. We can think of the *inclusio* of the Lydia passages and the verses it contains as a complete response to the Macedonian.

CONCLUSION

That is, if the Pauline group understood itself commissioned to deliver the good news of the gospel in order to ally with an army and fortify it with courage and loyalty so that it might succeed in the battle for salvation, then the makeup of this "army," as first represented by Lydia, and the manner by which it forms into an allied body, permits the conceptual clash between the Macedonian and Lydia to resolve into a new understanding of how the battle for salvation will be won. We have seen that Lydia's call for evaluation of her ongoing loyalty to God is the rhetorical goal of the unit.

As pointed out in the analysis of narrational texture, the narrator never expressly tells the audience that the we-group has reached its destination and therein found a place of prayer. Instead, Luke presents the topos of female gender through the gathering of women and rhetographically presents a crucial question: what is the distinguishing feature of a place of prayer? The author answers this question by introducing Lydia and framing the ensuing rhetorical development of the text through an argumentative *inclusio* structured by her offer to the disciples. Supported by the rhetorical unit's progressive texture and the analysis of intertexture, we can see that the author inductively argues that if Lydia, whose cultural profile fits a character frame of immorality and deception, is assessed as being faithful to God, then the social alliance formed between the disciples and Lydia's "household" would be akin to a military alliance that delivers fortifying salvific aid. It is within the space of such an alliance that a place of prayer can be found.

Although social logic would suggest that Lydia's authenticity be rejected, Luke counters this logic by narrating God's opening of Lydia's heart in order to enable her to understand Paul's preaching fully. In the unit's sole case of explicit divine initiative, God warranted Lydia's heart, yet a surface-level cultural assessment would condemn it. In order to resolve the counterfactual clash between viewing Lydia through sociocultural eyes and God's, the author introduced a number of illustrative examples that could supply the criteria for judging whether a person's heart would be assessed as being "right" before God. This appraisal of Lydia's heart, predicated on the quality of her faithfulness to God, is delivered rhetographically through what I have termed Lydian touchstone *synkrisis*.

In general terms, *synkrisis* produces a series of comparative episodes, while the more targeted variant of touchstone *synkrisis* incorporates rhetoric that was concerned with distinguishing between potentially deceptive appearances and displaying the true makeup of a person's inner being. In the Philippi episode, following a structure of touchstone *synkrisis*, the inner makeup of a number of characters is revealed, and these insights provide a rhetographical gallery of criteria for defining the quality of "faithfulness to God."

First, through the episode with the mantic slave woman with the Python spirit and her owners, the author rhetographically maintains that Lydia the purple seller cannot mediate salvation if her relationship with God is motivated by profit. Second, through Paul and Silas's imprisonment and decision to stay in prison following the earthquake, the author shows how Lydia would not authentically revere God if she displayed ritual piety, such as praying and singing hymns, but ultimately would succumb to "Lydian disease" and not faithfully remain in a situation of hardship and suffering in order to save the life of another. Third, by displaying the basis for solidarity between the magistrates, the slave owners, and the mob of Philippi, Luke demonstrates that Lydia would be unfaithful to God if she were to choose to protect her social alliances over her alliance with God.

When the Pauline group does go to Lydia, the argumentative *inclusio* is completed. Lydia is affirmed as faithful to God as defined through the touchstone *synkrisis*, and therefore her loyalty is not to profit, nor to shows of superficial ritual piety, nor to protecting her personal security, nor to beneficial social alliances. Lydia and those assembled with her have remained in faith, and in Paul's final act of encouragement, the Macedonian's call for aid is fulfilled.

Strikingly, not only does Luke rhetographically use Lydia's call for judgment to introduce a series of evaluative standards and thereby emphasize the emotion-fused acts of discernment and judgment in the text, but also, in contrast with the role ascribed to Lydia by the history of interpretation, any mention of sharing material resources is absent, while self-expressive and emotion-fused acts are salient. Moreover, through intertextural analysis, Lydia's socioeconomic status, although a preoccupation of the history of interpretation, was found to be indeterminate, and accordingly it plays no rhetorical role. Instead, her physiognomic status as a corrupting contagion is paramount.

Moreover, the chasm between Lydia the hostess in the history of interpretation and the culturally contextualized huckster Lydia displays the profound degree of ideological influence operative within biblical commentary. In stark contrast with the rhetoric of Acts 16, Lydia's physiognomic profile has been sanitized by the history of interpretation and transformed into a paradigm of feminine propriety. In addition, the history of interpretation has applied this reconfigured image of Lydia to the social model of hospitality within a context of hostessing and thereby has recast her into a provider of material and other resources. This ideologically driven model of femininity has been further blended with a certain strand of Christian triumphalism that had understood the victory promised by Paul's vision to imply conventional spoils of war, including elevated social status, dominance, and material rewards. Thus the divine sweep of Macedonia has been characterized as having yielded a high-status patroness who used her wealth and status in order to support the "victors."

Notably, our analysis of intertexture unfolded a first-century, physiognomically profiled image of Lydia the degenerate huckster, as Lydia the hostess, the creation of the history of interpretation, disappeared. Framed by Lydia's call to the disciples to evaluate her fidelity to God, Luke launched a series of illustrative examples that distinguished between authentic and spurious fidelity in order to subvert the type of physiognomic social logic that traditionally would have been used to assess whether a person such as Lydia could or could not join the emerging Christ movement and thereby help mediate the spread of salvation.

In contrast to historicizing an ideologically formed figure, as has been the case with the history of interpretation's Lydia the hostess, SRI has revealed the historically contextualized rhetorical event of a figure that challenged traditional stereotype-driven criteria for inclusion into a place of prayer. The victory in Philippi, therefore, stemmed from enabling the right-sight of God to potential worshipers of God and thereby transforming them into the "faithful" and not from securing five-star housing. Also, too, victory was derived from transforming spaces where worshipers of God may be found, such as prison and a Lydian's home, into unlikely yet truly reverential places of worship.

Most significantly, God's direct action of opening Lydia's heart enabled her to perceive Paul's God and thereby accorded her access to the highest standard of discipleship: someone who can "hear, see, and understand" the meaning of the Christ event. When this divine opening of Lydia's heart is coupled with the Pauline group's affirmation of Lydia's faith, we can see how Luke portrays Lydia within a core scriptural understanding of discipleship.

As a result, "Lydia the huckster" offers a radical challenge to gender- and ethnic-based criteria for assessing who can or cannot form a salvific assembly of God and connects Lydia to a network of episodes in Luke-Acts. This network involves examples of people who, according to conventional sociocultural codes, should be considered inherently "blind" to the sight of God and who would thereby obscure the sight of God to others or at a minimum limit access to God. From this perspective, such people carried the danger of "contaminating" the sight of God. Also found in this network are cases of those who, according to these same stereotyped conventions, would be expected to enable the sight of God to others and yet who obscure it. Within this network, Luke draws on topoi found in stereotypes in order to invert the implicit suppositions embedded in the stereotypes as he argues for an alternate basis for evaluation. By including Lydia the Lydian purple seller in a place of prayer, salvific space runs the risk of being contaminated not through foreignness but rather through allegiance to other powers, such as mammon.

This network of episodes includes the case of a Samaritan who demonstrates a true love of God by tending to a wounded traveler and yet, according to prejudicial ethnography, was considered one who would not be eligible for "eternal life" (Luke 10:25–37). Similarly, we have the example of the Samaritan who alone recognized that his healing had come through God's grace and therefore responded in thanksgiving and praise (Luke 17:11–19). We also find within Luke's network of physiognomically based topoi an Ethiopian eunuch who has his understanding opened to scriptural messianic expectations and to the good news that these have been fulfilled (Acts 8:27–39).[2]

With the benefit of our sociorhetorical interpretation of Lydia, we can see that Simon the Pharisee and the woman called a "sinner" in Luke 7:36–50 would also be connected to the constellation of episodes that deal with subverting stereotype-driven sociocultural logic. Although Lydia is not called a sinner, both she and the "sinner" of Luke 7:36–50 are rhetorically portrayed as potential contaminants to the ethos of God's agents. By accepting intimate contact with a woman who is socially categorized as a "sinner," Luke shows that Jesus undermines his credibility as a prophet in the eyes of the Pharisee Simon: within Simon's sociocultural logic, Jesus should demonstrate his prophetic authority by rejecting the woman. Yet Luke has Jesus invert the Pharisee's logic by Jesus's argument that someone

---

2. For the earlier discussion of the physiognomic profile of the Ethiopian eunuch, see pp. 236–37. More broadly, we see this network including anyone within the general category of "gentile," as exemplified by the encounter between Peter and Cornelius (Acts 10:1–48). The only other call for "help," βοηθέω, occurs in Acts 21:8, in ironic events that see Paul removed from the temple and arrested, because he is falsely accused of introducing a "contaminant" there: an Ephesian.

who was heavily burdened by sin would feel the impact of God's grace all the more profoundly. Therefore, by perceiving the magnitude of the woman's sinfulness, yet nonetheless accepting the woman and forgiving her sins, Jesus creates within her a steadfast bond with God and thereby fulfills the ultimate mandate of a prophet.

Moreover, Luke invokes the social code of hospitality not only to demonstrate Jesus's true prophetic nature but also to critique the Pharisee's inability to recognize this nature. As discussed in the intertextural analysis, in the case of Lydia the social code of hospitality is evoked by Luke in order to profile the imperative of mutual character assessment between "host" and "guest." So too a Pharisee *should* recognize Jesus's identity, yet Simon does not. It is the woman's intimate actions that are portrayed as the appropriate form of hosting in this situation. As Luke has Jesus challenge the Pharisee's sight, so too Luke has Lydia challenge the sight of those who would see her as a contaminant to the credibility of God's agents.

Yet again, when we read of the women who traveled with Jesus and the other disciples in Luke 8:1–3, we see Luke rhetorically use the social model of hospitality in order to highlight that the good news of the kingdom of God is advanced through unconventional alliances that subvert physiognomically based social codes. As Elaine Wainwright has observed, the women, particularly Mary Magdalene, are described as previously having been "extremely" afflicted and/or demon possessed, yet by the time they are narrated as having formed part of Jesus's circle they are "healed." Noting that labels such as "possessed" or "afflicted" often expressed society's strictures on those whose behavior deviated from social norms, Wainwright points out that the women who travel with the disciples all the way to Jerusalem are portrayed by Luke as having been restored: "They have been constituted as part of the community." Yet paradoxically, the women are found within a type of "travelling hospitality" frame that stresses the highly itinerant character of their mixed-gender circle.[3] As discussed in the intertextural analysis, people evaluated hospitality alliances through male honor codes in which the status of host and guest was publicly judged to be equal. Luke's use of physiognomic stereotypes, honor codes, and the social model of hospitality rhetorically

---

3. Elaine M. Wainwright, *Women Healing/Healing Women: The Genderization of Healing in Early Christianity*, BibleWorld (Sheffield: Equinox, 2006), 164–72. For the category of "sinner" as a form of social deviance labeling, see Greg Carey, *Sinners: Jesus and His Earliest Followers* (Waco, TX: Baylor University Press, 2009).

challenges those who might reapply deviance labeling to women such as Joanna, Mary Magdalene, and Susanna in view of their unconventional roles within Jesus's good-news-based traveling community.

Luke also used hospitality to profile the faculty of "right-sightedness" in the episode with Jesus and the disciples from Emmaus, the unit that lexically resonates closely with Lydia (Luke 24:13–32). Although the women who had visited Jesus's tomb had proclaimed the good news of his resurrection, they had not been believed, and as a result their good news had no effect. As I have emphasized, the efficaciousness of good news was dependent on the credibility of its messengers. The physiognomic bias against authoritative female proclamation constrained the good news of Jesus's resurrection. In accepting the disciples' offer of hospitality and showing himself as risen, Jesus affirmed the women's proclamation of good news as true.

Luke uses sociocultural conventions of evaluation such as physiognomic stereotypes, topoi of honor and shame, and topoi of hospitality in order to innovate a set of evaluative criteria that require active and engaged discernment outside of the bounds of these conventions. When Luke presents criteria for faith, he concurrently presents an image of the God to whom Paul, Silas, Lydia, and the other disciples are faithful. The author of Acts rhetorically argues that Paul's God does not fit within cultural honor codes that normally would display the highest honor of a divinity. For example, God is not honored by showing how God's agents form alliances with prominent, high-status men, nor by spectacular displays of miraculous escapes, nor by demonstrations of divine might by meting out vengeful punishment to enemies. Instead, Luke shows that Paul's God is honored by the way God's followers willingly sacrifice the opportunity to elevate their own public honor or choose not to preserve their own personal security for the sake of enabling access to salvific good news to others.

At this point, I wish to clarify that the argument that Lydia is a rhetorical figure does not infer that a historic figure has been relegated to the level of symbol, as has been the practice of some past commentators. Symbolization can be found in such cases as when the Venerable Bede dematerialized the widows at Tabitha's bedside (Acts 9:39) into a "repentant soul's holy thoughts."[4] In contrast, the most targeted rhetorical profiling is often

---

4. Bede, *Venerable Bede*, 92.

reserved for the most full-bodied historical figures, frequently in situations of social conflict. For example, a contemporary illustration of rhetorical profiling was acutely depicted by the satirically intended *New Yorker* cover that portrayed then presidential-hopeful candidate Barack Obama dressed in traditional Middle Eastern apparel.[5] The controversial cover, titled "The Politics of Fear," intended to satirize rhetographically how Obama's adversaries were attempting to profile him rhetorically as some form of "terrorist" danger to America. The cover is a stark reminder that physiognomic rhetorical profiling is far from being past ancient practice and reveals the vitriolic nature of a historical, truly rhetorical, situation.[6]

In similar manner, "the Lydian" undoubtedly targeted a woman, or, more likely, various women in varied communities, who were involved in a very real, historical, rhetorical situation.[7] At the core of this rhetorical situation is a call for the assessment of someone who, because of her gender, ethnographic, and occupational profile would be considered unsuitable for acceptance into the inner core of church participation. The rhetorical situation, therefore, signals a historically located debate from within.

A future, deeper investigation of the discourse modes operative in the rhetorical unit may help to clarify better the contours of this community debate. The rhetorical unit blends at least three discourse modes: historiography, biblical apocalyptic, and Greco-Roman "Lydian touchstone *synkrisis*." As this analysis has highlighted, ancient historiography was primarily a discourse of war and political conflict that was especially concerned with relating the causes of victories and losses. Despite frequent evidence of divine support, historiographies essentially told of human armies engaged in earthly battles. On the other hand, apocalyptic discourse inferred conflict on a cosmic scale. Ultimately, the Philippi episode displays apocalyptic expectations of the destruction of corrupt powers enacted through human, earthly agents acting through loyal allegiance to God. The Macedonian man's distinctly military profile, heightened through cultural asso-

---

5. Barry Blitt, illustrator, "The Politics of Fear," *NewY*, July 21, 2008, cover.

6. For "rhetorical situation," see Bitzer, "Rhetorical Situation," 1–14; see Alexandra Gruca-Macaulay, "Distinguishing between Form-Derived Rhetorical Purpose and Lloyd Bitzer's Rhetorical Situation" (paper presented at the Annual Meeting of the Society of Biblical Literature, New Orleans, LA, 21 November 2009).

7. For example, "Jezebel" of Thyatira (Rev 2:20) was clearly seen by some in her community as a leader, yet to John's community as a member of the "synagogue of Satan" (Rev 2:9).

ciations with Alexander the Great, activates the rhetorical impact of the Pauline group's encounter with the women by the river and Lydia. As the initial recipients of the good news from the Pauline group, Lydia and the women are the first to represent "us Macedonians" as recipients of a theologized form of military aid that yields to the allied parties the victorious outcome of "salvation." The clash between the Macedonian's military configuration with that of the women's gender, as well as Lydia's ethnicity and occupation, introduces a point of tension for rhetorical effect. In the language of conceptual blending, delivering to Lydia that which was requested by the Macedonian introduces a counterfactual blend, a transformed way of understanding that which previously would have been conceptually incompatible. By blending the earthly historiographic discourse with apocalyptic elements, Luke presents his belief that apocalyptic battles will be enacted by human agents in the earthly realm. The Lydia *inclusio* presents qualitative argumentation for an apocalyptic moment that is not writ large with cosmic imagery, but rather is delivered by human actors whose hearts are directed toward the gospel.

Luke portrays the means to victory to these apocalyptic human-scale battles within a frame of Lydian touchstone synkratic discourse. Normally Lydian touchstone *synkrisis* operated in civic discourse that was concerned with discerning whether a person was a trusted, sincere political ally, personal friend, or friend of the state. The element of judgment or discernment was prominent and common to both biblical apocalyptic and Lydian touchstone synkratic discourse. It is through the Greco-Roman topos of Lydian physiognomy, a topos that calls for judgment in the rhetorical unit, that Luke blends the three discourse modes. Out of this blend Luke presents the emergent discourse of a salvific "place of prayer" that focuses on the challenge of discerning whether a person could be trusted as a sincere worshiper of God and thereby join the religious-social alliance that could mediate salvation.

The exigence for this discourse comes from *within* a community; it does not arise, as would be the case with either a historiography or biblical apocalyptic alone, from a cohesive community in conflict with an external enemy. It also would be easy to see, based on the slave owners' accusation and Paul and Silas's treatment by Philippi's leaders, how it might appear that the text features a dichotomy between "us Jews" and "us Romans." However, Paul's declaration of his Roman citizenship underscores the murkiness of those boundaries that might establish who is "us" and who is "them." The rhetoric of Acts 16 is concerned with who constitutes "us" from within. A more detailed future focus on the emerging discourse of this unit could help develop a better understanding of the profile of these first audiences of Luke-Acts.

Moreover, in further analyzing Luke's emergent blend, we might gain further insight into the basis for claiming theological unity between Luke and Acts. Most particularly, Bloomquist has argued that Luke employs apocalyptic discourse in order to invert cultural codes that originated within the temple hierarchy.[8] Significantly, precisely because Luke's desired impact was to replace cultural codes that served to preserve the worldly honor and status of those at higher levels of the hierarchy at the expense of mediating God to the people, it was those members of the hierarchy, argues Bloomquist, who had the most to lose if Luke's rhetorical goals were realized and therefore formed the indirect, "peripheral," target of Luke's discourse.[9] Future work should revisit Bloomquist's thesis in order to investigate the "apocalyptic path," as it were, that carries the apocalyptic theme from the cultural code of the temple to that of the synagogue. Lydian touchstone *synkrisis* was concerned with distinguishing the pure of heart from within relatively small social groups. For that reason, while still within the apocalyptic mode, we can see how the code center shifts as the concerns of the Gospel of Luke move through the Acts of the Apostles.

In addition to raising questions about the makeup of the early audiences of Acts, the analysis of the rhetorical figure of Lydia also invites future sociorhetorical exploration into other female figures in Luke-Acts and most particularly the one woman whose heart's emotion-fused action is repetitively featured: Mary (Luke 2:19, 51). God opens Mary's womb and Lydia's heart in two cases of divine initiative within a woman's interior that are not a function of cleansing or healing. Mary and Lydia are further linked by both being women who speak direct discourse in the narrative and by being the only two women in Luke-Acts who have the activity of their hearts specifically highlighted. In one case, Mary treasures Jesus's words in her heart within the context of prior temple teaching (Luke 2:51), whereas Lydia's heart is opened within a "place of prayer" frame. These elements in common raise the question of whether there is an intended authorial link between Mary and Lydia and, if so, then for what rhetorical

---

8. See Bloomquist, "Intertexture of Lukan Apocalyptic Discourse," 45–68; Bloomquist, "Role of the Audience," 157–73; Bloomquist, "Rhetorical Argumentation and the Culture of Apocalyptic," 173–209.

9. Bloomquist, "Role of the Audience," 171.

purpose. Answers to such questions might also contribute to the debate over the basis for unity between Luke and Acts.

At the other end of the characterization spectrum, Lydia's physiognomic profile opens the possibility of future investigation into points of resonance between Lydia and the larger-than-life purple-clad ensnaring harlot Babylon of Revelation. In particular, such an investigation might benefit from looking at the differences in rhetorical responses: biblical apocalyptic in the case of Revelation, and in the case of Acts 16, a historiographic/apocalyptic/Lydian-touchstone-*synkrisis* blend, in order to help us better understand the profile and conflicts of the communities from which the discourse arose. From an analytical perspective, we might use the relationship between discourse modes and the ideological presentation of topoi found within these modes in order to examine comparatively the ideological points of difference or similarity between early church communities.

When I began my search for Lydia the businesswoman, I did not anticipate finding Lydia the huckster. Yet, as interesting as the intertextual insights from the Lydian physiognomic topos may have been, it was with some weariness that I seemed to find myself discovering yet another biblical harlot. However, instead of finding a harlot who is judged and condemned as such, rather unexpectedly I proceeded to discover a departure from conventional patterns in which the "harlot" figure tests the sight of those who can discern her true, authentically God-centered nature. An SRI analysis permits the hope that Lydia the hostess in the history of interpretation can be laid to rest, and in her stead the image of Lydia the perceptive disciple can resume its rightful place as the "rhetorical cognitive images" of the first audiences of Acts join with our own.

Bibliography

Aeschylus. Translated by Herbert Weir Smyth. LCL. London Heinemann 1930.
Allen, Danielle S. *The World of Prometheus: The Politics of Punishing in Democratic Athens.* Princeton: Princeton University Press, 2000.
Allen, O. Wesley. *The Death of Herod: The Narrative and Theological Function of Retribution in Luke-Acts.* SBLDS 158. Atlanta: Scholars Press, 1997.
Appian. *Roman History.* Translated by Horace White. 4 vols. LCL. Cambridge: Harvard University Press, 1913.
Arator. *Arator's On the Acts of the Apostles (De Actibus Apostolorum).* Edited by Richard J. Schrader. Translated by Joseph L. Roberts and John F. Makowski. CRS 6. Atlanta: Scholars Press, 1987.
Arieti, James. "Horatian Philosophy and the Regulus Ode (*Odes* 3.5)." *TAPA* 120 (1990): 209–20.
Aristides, P. Aelius. *Orations 17–53.* Vol. 2 of *The Complete Works.* Translated by Charles Allison Behr. Leiden: Brill, 1981.
Aristophanes. Translated by Benjamin Bickley Rogers. 3 vols. LCL. Cambridge: Harvard University Press, 1924.
Aristotle. Translated by H. Rackham et al. 23 vols. LCL. Cambridge: Harvard University Press, 1926–2011.
Aristotle. *On Rhetoric: A Theory of Civic Discourse.* Translated and edited by George A. Kennedy. 2nd ed. New York: Oxford University Press, 2007.
Arrian. *Anabasis of Alexander.* Translated by P. A. Brunt. 2 vols. LCL 236. Cambridge: Harvard University Press, 1976–1983.
"Artapanus." Translated by John J. Collins. *OTP* 2:889–903.
Arterbury, Andrew E. "The Case for the Custom of Hospitality in Ancient Narratives." Paper presented at the Annual Meeting of the Society of Biblical Literature. Washington, DC, 20 November 2006.

———. *Entertaining Angels: Early Christian Hospitality in Its Mediterranean Setting.* NTMo 8. Sheffield: Sheffield Phoenix, 2005.

Ascough, Richard S. *Lydia: Paul's Cosmopolitan Hostess.* Paul's Social Network. Collegeville, MN: Liturgical Press, 2009.

Astour, Michael C. "The Origin of the Terms 'Canaan,' 'Phoenician,' and 'Purple.'" *JNES* 24 (1965): 346–50.

Athenaeus. *The Deipnosophists.* Translated by Charles Burton Gulick. 7 vols. LCL. Cambridge: Harvard University Press, 1927–1941.

Auerbach, Erich. *Mimesis: The Representation of Reality in Western Literature.* Translated by Willard R. Trask. Princeton: Princeton University Press, 1968.

Augustine. *Saint Augustin: Anti-Pelagian Writings.* In vol. 5 of *The Nicene and Post-Nicene Fathers*, Series 1. Edited by Philip Schaff. Translated by Peter Holmes and Robert Ernest Wallis. 1886–1889. Repr., Grand Rapids: Eerdmans, 1956.

Aune, David E. *Prophecy in Early Christianity and the Ancient Mediterranean World.* Grand Rapids: Eerdmans, 1983.

———. *Revelation 1–5.* WBC 52A. Dallas: Word, 1997.

Bal, Mieke. *Narratology: Introduction to the Theory of Narrative.* Translated by Christine van Boheemen. Toronto: University of Toronto Press, 1985.

Bang, Peter F. "Imperial Bazaar: Towards a Comparative Understanding of Markets in the Roman Empire." Pages 51–88 in *Ancient Economies, Modern Methodologies: Archaeology, Comparative History, Models and Institutions.* Edited by Peter F Bang, Mamoru Ikeguchi, and Harmut G. Ziche. Pragmateiai 12. Bari, Italy: Edipuglia, 2006.

Baring-Gould, Sabine. *A Study of St. Paul: His Character and Opinions.* London: Ibister, 1897.

Bauman, Richard A. *Women and Politics in Ancient Rome.* New York: Routledge, 1992.

Bede. *The Venerable Bede: Commentary on the Acts of the Apostles.* Translated and edited by Lawrence T. Martin. Cistercian Studies. Kalamazoo, MI: Cistercian, 1989.

Berenson, Jennifer K. "The Allusive Man of Macedonia." Paper presented at the Annual Meeting of the Society of Biblical Literature. Boston, 24 November 2008.

Bitzer, Lloyd F. "The Rhetorical Situation." *PhRh* 1 (1968): 1–14.

Bizzell, Patricia, and Bruce Herzberg, ed. "Chaïm Perelman." Pages 1372–74 in *The Rhetorical Tradition: Readings from Classical Times to the Present*. 2nd ed. New York: St. Martin's, 2001.

Black, Robert Allen. "The Conversion Stories in the Acts of the Apostles: A Study of Their Forms and Functions." PhD diss., Emory University, Atlanta, 1985.

Bloomquist, L. Gregory. "Rhetorical Profiling." Conversation with the author. Ottawa, 2007.

———. "The Epicurean Tag in Plutarch: Implications for New Testament Study." Paper presented at the Eastern International Region Meeting of the American Academy of Religion, UQAM. Montreal, Quebec, March 1994.

———. "First-Century Models of Bodily Healing and Their Socio-rhetorical Transformation in Some NT Traditions." Paper presented at the Rhetorics of Healing Conference, Claremont Graduate University, Claremont, CA, 24 January 2002.

———. *The Function of Suffering in Philippians*. JSNTSup. Sheffield: Sheffield Academic, 1993.

———. "The Intertexture of Lukan Apocalyptic Discourse." Pages 45–68 in *The Intertexture of Apocalyptic Discourse in the New Testament*. Edited by Duane F. Watson. SymS 14. Atlanta: Society of Biblical Literature, 2002.

———. "Methodological Criteria for Apocalyptic Rhetoric: A Suggestion for the Expanded Use of Sociorhetorical Analysis." Pages 181–203 in *Vision and Persuasion: Rhetorical Dimensions of Apocalyptic Discourse*. Edited by Greg Carey and L. Gregory Bloomquist. St. Louis: Chalice, 1999.

———. "A Parallel to Paul's Vision in Acts 16:9?" Unpublished paper, 2008.

———. "Paul's Inclusive Language: The Ideological Texture of Romans 1." Pages 165–93 in *Fabrics of Discourse: Essays in Honor of Vernon K. Robbins*. Edited by David B. Gowler, L. Gregory Bloomquist, and Duane F. Watson. Harrisburg, PA: Trinity Press International, 2003.

———. "Rhetography and *Topoi*." E-mail correspondence with the Rhetoric of Religious Antiquity Context group, 6 September 2007.

———. "Rhetoric, Culture, and Ideology: Socio-rhetorical Analysis in the Reading of New Testament Texts." Pages 115–46 in *Rhetorics in the New Millennium: Promise and Fulfillment*. Edited by James D. Hester and J. David Hester. SAC. New York: T&T Clark, 2010.

———. "The Rhetoric of Suffering in Paul's Letter to the Philippians: Socio-rhetorical Reflections and Further Thoughts on a Post-colonial Contribution to the Discussion." *Thf* 35 (2004): 195–223.

———. "Rhetorical Argumentation and the Culture of Apocalyptic: A Socio-rhetorical Analysis of Luke 21." Pages 173–209 in *The Rhetorical Interpretation of Scripture: Essays from the 1996 Malibu Conference*. Edited by Stanley E. Porter and Dennis L. Stamps. Sheffield: Sheffield Academic, 1999.

———. "The Role of Argumentation in the Miracle Stories of Luke-Acts: Towards a Fuller Identification of Miracle Discourse for Use in Socio-rhetorical Analysis." Pages 85–124 in *Miracle Discourse in the Argumentation of the New Testament*. Edited by Duane F. Watson. Atlanta: Society of Biblical Literature, 2012.

———. "The Role of the Audience in the Determination of Argumentation: The Gospel of Luke and the Acts of the Apostles." Pages 157–73 in *Rhetorical Argumentation in Biblical Texts: Essays from the Lund 2000 Conference*. Edited by Anders Eriksson, Thomas H. Olbricht, and Walter Übelacker. ESEC 8. Harrisburg, PA: Trinity Press International, 2002.

———. "Subverted by Joy: Suffering and Joy in Paul's Letter to the Philippians." *Int* 61 (2007): 270–82.

———. "Whose Rhetoric? Whose Empire? The Subversion of Augustan Rhetoric in the Gospel of Luke." Paper presented at the University of Ottawa and Carleton University, 15–16 March 1996.

Bloomquist, L. Gregory, and Priscilla Geisterfer Nyvlt. "Rhetorical Strategies for 'Holy War' in Some Second Temple Texts: Overview, Analysis, and Implications." Paper presented at Rhetorics, Violence, and Evil conference, University of Redlands, Redlands, CA, 23–24 January 2004.

Bonz, Marianne Palmer. *The Past as Legacy: Luke-Acts and Ancient Epic*. Minneapolis: Fortress, 2000.

Born, Wolfgang. "Purple in Classical Antiquity." *CibR* 4 (1937): 111–18.

Bovon, François. *De Vocatione Gentium: Histoire de l'Interprétation d'Act. 10, 1–11, 18 dans les Six Premiers Siècles*. BGBE 8. Tübingen: Mohr Siebeck, 1967.

Bradley, Mark. *Colour and Meaning in Ancient Rome*. CCS. Cambridge: Cambridge University Press, 2009.

Brooten, Bernadette J. *Women Leaders in the Ancient Synagogue: Inscrip-*

tional Evidence and Background Issues. BJS 36. Chico, CA: Scholars Press, 1982.

Brown, John Pairman. "Proverb-Book, Gold-Economy, Alphabet." *JBL* 100 (1981): 169–91.

Bruce, F. F. *The Acts of the Apostles: The Greek Text with Introduction and Commentary*. 2nd ed. London: Tyndale, 1951.

Burke, Kenneth. "Lexicon Rhetoricae." Pages 123–83 in *Counter-Statement*. 2nd ed. Berkeley: University of California Press, 1968.

Burkert, Walter. "Polis and Polytheism." Pages 216–75 in *Greek Religion*. Translated by John Raffan. Cambridge: Harvard University Press, 1977.

Burnett, Anne Pippin. "Pentheus and Dionysus: Host and Guest." *CP* 65 (1970): 15–29. http://www.jstor.org/stable/269179.

Calvin, John. *The Acts of the Apostles 14–28*. Edited by David W. Torrance and Thomas F. Torrance. Translated by John W. Fraser. CalC 2. Grand Rapids: Eerdmans, 1966.

Campbell, David A., trans. *Greek Lyric*. 5 vols. LCL. Cambridge: Harvard University Press, 1982–1983.

Campbell, William Sanger. *The "We" Passages in the Acts of the Apostles: The Narrator as Narrative Character*. StBibLit 14. Atlanta: Society of Biblical Literature, 2007.

Cancik, Hubert. *Brill's New Pauly: Encyclopaedia of the Ancient World*. Leiden: Brill, 2002–2011.

Carey, Greg. *Sinners: Jesus and His Earliest Followers*. Waco, TX: Baylor University Press, 2009.

Caylus, Anne Claude Philippe. *Recueil d'Antiquités Égyptiennes, Étrusques, Grecques, Romaines et Gauloises*. Vol. 5. Paris: Chez Desaint & Saillant, 1752.

Charles, Robert Henry, ed. and trans. *The Apocrypha and Pseudepigrapha of the Old Testament in English*. Vol. 2. Oxford: Clarendon, 1913.

Chrysostom, John. "A l'Evéque Cyriaque Exilé." Letter 125. In vol. 6 of *Oeuvres Complètes de Saint Jean Chrysostome*. Translated by J. Bareille. 21 vols. Paris: Vivès, 1865–1878.

———. *Commentariorum in Matthaeum*. Edited by J.-P. Migne. PG 58. Paris, 1862.

———. *Expositiones in Psalmos*. In vol. 9 of *Oeuvres Complètes de Saint Jean Chrysostome*. Translated by J. Bareille. 21 vols. Paris: Vivès, 1865–1878.

———. *Homiliae in Acta apostolorum*. In vol. 15 of *Oeuvres Complètes de Saint Jean Chrysostome*. Translated by J. Bareille. 21 vols. Paris: Vivès, 1865–1878.

———. *Homiliae in epistulam i ad Corinthios*. In vol. 16 of *Oeuvres Complètes de Saint Jean Chrysostome*. Translated by J. Bareille. 21 vols. Paris: Vivès, 1865–1878.

———. *The Homilies of S. John Chrysostom, Archbishop of Constantinople, on the First Epistle of St. Paul the Apostle to the Corinthians, Translated with Notes and Indices, Part 1, Hom. 1–24*. Translated by John Henry Parker. Library of the Fathers. Oxford: Parker, 1839.

———. *Homilies on Galatians, Ephesians, Philippians, Colossians, Thessalonians, Timothy, Titus, and Philemon*. In vol. 13 of *The Nicene and Post-Nicene Fathers*, Series 1. Edited by Philip Schaff. 1886–1889. Repr., Grand Rapids: Eerdmans, 1956.

———. *Homilies on the Acts of the Apostles and the Epistle to the Romans*. Vol. 11 of *The Nicene and Post-Nicene Fathers*, Series 1. Edited by Philip Schaff. 1886–1889. Repr., Grand Rapids: Eerdmans, 1956.

———. *Homilies on the Epistles of Paul to the Corinthians*. In vol. 12 of *The Nicene and Post-Nicene Fathers*, Series 1. Edited by Philip Schaff. 1886–1889. Repr., Grand Rapids: Eerdmans, 1956.

———. *Homilies on the Gospel of Saint Matthew*. In vol. 10 of *The Nicene and Post-Nicene Fathers*, Series 1. Edited by Philip Schaff. 1886–1889. 14 vols. Repr., Grand Rapids: Eerdmans, 1956.

———. *On the Priesthood; Ascetic Treatises; Select Homilies and Letters; Homilies on the Statues*. Vol. 9 of *The Nicene and Post-Nicene Fathers*, Series 1. Edited by Philip Schaff. 1886–1889. Repr., Grand Rapids: Eerdmans, 1956.

Cicero. Translated by Walter Miller et al. 30 vols. LCL. Cambridge: Harvard University Press, 1913–2010.

Clement of Alexandria. *The Exhortation to the Greeks; The Rich Man's Salvation; To the Newly Baptized*. Translated by G. W. Butterworth. LCL. Cambridge: Harvard University Press, 1919.

———. *Stromateis: Books One to Three*. Translated by John Ferguson. FC. Washington, DC: Catholic University of America Press, 1991.

Cohen, Shaye J. D. "Alexander the Great and Jaddus the High Priest According to Josephus." *AJSR* 7.8 (1982–1983): 41–68.

Crook, Zeba A. "BTB Readers Guide: Loyalty." *BTB* 34.4 (2004): 167–77.

———. *Reconceptualising Conversion: Patronage, Loyalty and Conversion in the Religions of the Ancient Mediterranean.* BZNW 130. Berlin: de Gruyter, 2004.

D'Ambra, Eve. *Roman Women.* Cambridge Introduction to Roman Civilization. Cambridge: Cambridge University Press, 2007.

Dähnhardt, Oskar. *Scholia in Aeschyli Persas.* Lipsia: Teubner, 1894.

De Vries, Keith. "The Nearly Other: The Attic Vision of Phrygians and Lydians." Pages 338–63 in *Not the Classical Ideal: Athens and the Construction of the Other in Greek Art.* Edited by Beth Cohen. Leiden: Brill, 2000.

DeConick, April. *The Original Gospel of Thomas in Translation with a Commentary and New English Translation of the Complete Gospel.* LNTS 287. London: T&T Clark, 2006.

Déniz, Alcorac Alonso. Review of *Coastal Asia Minor: Pontos to Ionia.* Vol. 5A of *A Lexicon of Greek Personal Names,* edited by T. Corsten. BMCR. http://bmcr.brynmawr.edu/2011/2011-01-11.html.

Dio Chrysostom. Translated by J. W. Cohoon and H. Lamar Crosby. 5 vols. LCL. Cambridge: Harvard University Press, 1940.

Diodorus of Sicily. *Library of History.* Translated by C. H. Oldfather et al. 12 vols. LCL. Cambridge: Harvard University Press, 1933–1967.

Dover, Kenneth J. *Greek Homosexuality.* Cambridge: Harvard University Press, 1978.

DuBois, Page. *Torture and Truth.* New York: Routledge, 1991.

Edmonds, J. M., trans. *Elegy and Iambus Being the Remains of All the Greek Elegiac and Iambic Poets from Callinus to Crates Excepting the Choliambic Writers with the Anacreontea.* 2 vols. LCL. Cambridge: Harvard University Press, 1931.

Ephrem. "The Commentary of Ephrem on Acts." Translated by Frederick C. Conybeare. Pages 373–453 in *The Text of Acts.* Edited by James Hardy Ropes. Vol. 3 of *The Acts of the Apostles.* Part 1 of *The Beginnings of Christianity.* Edited by F. J. Foakes Jackson and Kirsopp Lake. London: Macmillan, 1926.

Euripides. Translated and edited by David Kovacs. 8 vols. LCL. Cambridge: Harvard University Press, 1994.

———. *Bacchae.* In vol. 1 of *The Tragedies of Euripides.* Translated by Theodore Alois Buckley. London: Bohn, 1850. http://data.perseus.org/texts/urn:cts:greekLit:tlg0006.tlg017.perseus-eng1.

———. *The Bacchae and Other Plays.* Translated by Philip Vellacott. Harmondsworth, UK: Penguin, 1954.

Eustathius Thessalonicensis. *Commentarii ad Homeri Iliadem*. Edited by M. van der Valk. 4 vols. Leiden: Brill, 1987.

Evans, Elizabeth C. "Physiognomics in the Ancient World." *TAPS* 59.5 (1969): 1–101.

———. "Physiognomics in the Roman Empire." *CJ* 45 (1950): 277–82.

Fauconnier, Gilles, and Mark Turner. *The Way We Think: Conceptual Blending and the Mind's Hidden Complexities*. New York: Basic Books, 2002.

Fitzmyer, Joseph A. *The Acts of the Apostles: A New Translation with Introduction and Commentary*. AB 31. New York: Doubleday, 1998.

———. *The Gospel according to Luke (X–XXIV): Introduction, Translation, and Notes*. AB 28A. Garden City, NY: Doubleday, 1985.

Fraser, P. M., E. Matthews, and the British Academy, eds. *A Lexicon of Greek Personal Names*. 5 vols. Oxford: Clarendon, 1987–2013.

Gasque, W. Ward. *A History of the Interpretation of the Acts of the Apostles*. Tübingen: Mohr Siebeck, 1975. Repr., Eugene, OR: Wipf & Stock, 2000.

Gaventa, Beverly Roberts. *The Acts of the Apostles*. ANTC. Nashville: Abingdon, 2003.

Geertz, Clifford. "The Bazaar Economy: Information and Search in Peasant Marketing." *AmER* 68.2 (1978): 28–32.

Géradon, Bernard de. "L'Homme à l'Image de Dieu." *NRTh* 80 (1958): 683–95.

Gibson, Craig A. *Libanius's* Progymnasmata: *Model Exercises in Greek Prose Composition and Rhetoric*. WGRW 27. Atlanta: Society of Biblical Literature, 2008.

Glancy, Jennifer A. "Boasting of Beatings (2 Corinthians 11:23–25)." *JBL* 123 (2004): 99–135.

Gleason, Maud W. *Making Men: Sophists and Self-Presentation in Ancient Rome*. Princeton: Princeton University Press, 1995.

———. "Truth Contests and Talking Corpses." Pages 287–313 in *Constructions of the Classical Body*. Edited by James I. Porter. The Body, in Theory: Histories of Cultural Materialism. Ann Arbor: University of Michigan Press, 1999.

Graf, Fritz. "Hephaestus." In *The Oxford Companion to Classical Civilization*. Edited by Simon Hornblower and Antony Spawforth. Oxford: Oxford University Press, 1998.

Grant, Robert M. "Early Christian Geography." *VC* 46 (1992): 105–11.

Grant-Davie, Keith. "Rhetorical Situations and Their Constituents." *RhetR* 15 (1997): 264–79.
Grotius, Hugo. "*Ad Acta Apostolorum.*" Pages 579–668 in *Hugo Grotius Opera Omnia Theologica: Faksimile-Neudruck der Ausgabe Amsterdam 1679*. 1679. Repr., Stuttgart-Bad Cannstatt: Frommann, 1972.
Gruca-Macaulay, Alexandra. "De Géradon's Body-Zone Model and Greco-Roman Physiognomy: The Role of Socio-culturally Encoded Bodily Actions in Socio-rhetorical Analysis." Paper presented at the Annual Meeting of the Society of Biblical Literature. San Francisco, CA, 21 November 2011.
———. "Disrupting the *Polis*: Greco-Roman Voluntary Associations and the Conversion of Lydia of Thyatira in Acts 16:14–15, 40." Paper presented at Rhetorics of Social Formation conference. University of Redlands, CA, 20 January 2007.
———. "Distinguishing between Form-Derived Rhetorical Purpose and Lloyd Bitzer's Rhetorical Situation." Paper presented at the Annual Meeting of the Society of Biblical Literature. New Orleans, LA, 21 November 2009.
———. "Reading 'Lydia' in Acts 16: A Figure in Rhetoric or a Rhetorical Figure?" Paper presented at the Annual Meeting of the Society of Biblical Literature. San Diego, CA, 17 November 2007.
Haenchen, Ernst. *The Acts of the Apostles: A Commentary*. Translated by Bernard Noble and Gerald Shinn. Revised by Robert McL. Wilson. 14th ed. Göttingen: Vandenhoeck & Ruprecht, 1965. Repr., Oxford: Blackwell, 1971.
Hamlyn, D. W. "Aristotelian *Epagogue*." *Phronesis* 21 (1976): 167–84.
Hanson, Kenneth C., and Douglas E. Oakman. *Palestine in the Time of Jesus: Social Structures and Social Conflicts*. Minneapolis: Fortress, 1998.
Harrill, Albert J. "The Vice of Slave Dealers in Greco-Roman Society: The Use of a Topos in 1 Timothy 1:10." *JBL* 118 (1999): 97–122.
Hellerman, Joseph H. *Reconstructing Honor in Roman Philippi: Carmen Christi as Cursus Pudorum*. SNTSMS 132. Cambridge: Cambridge University Press, 2005.
Hemer, Colin J. "Thyatira." Pages 106–28 in *The Letters to the Seven Churches of Asia in Their Local Setting*. JSNTSup 11. Sheffield: Sheffield Academic, 1986.
Herodotus. *Histories*. Translated by A. D. Godley. 4 vols. LCL. Cambridge: Harvard University Press, 1920–1925.

Hesiod. *The Homeric Hymns and Homerica*. Translated by Hugh G. Evelyn-White. LCL. Cambridge: Harvard University Press, 1914.
Hester, J. David. "Eunuchs and the Postgender Jesus: Matthew 19.12 and Transgressive Sexualities." *JSNT* 28 (2005): 13–40.
Hester, James D. "Rhetorics in and for the New Millennium." Pages 1–20 in *Rhetorics in the New Millennium: Promise and Fulfillment*. Edited by James D. Hester and J. David Hester. SAC. New York: T&T Clark, 2010.
Hippocrates. Translated by W. H. S. Jones et al. 10 vols. LCL. Cambridge: Harvard University Press, 1923–2012.
Hillier, Richard. *Arator on the Acts of the Apostles: A Baptismal Commentary*. OECS. Oxford: Clarendon, 1993.
Horace. *The Odes and Epodes*. Translated by C. E. Bennett. LCL. Cambridge: Harvard University Press, 1914.
Horsley, G. H. R. "Lydia and the Purple Trade." *NewDocs* 3:53–55.
———. "Addenda to *New Docs 1976–1979*." *NewDocs* 5:135–50.
———. "The Purple Trade, and the Status of Lydia of Thyatira." *NewDocs* 2:25–32.
Howatson, M. C., and Ian Chilvers, ed. *The Concise Oxford Companion to Classical Literature*. Oxford: Oxford University Press, 1996.
Hoyland, Robert, trans. "A New Edition and Translation of the Leiden Polemon." Pages 329–464 in *Seeing the Face, Seeing the Soul: Polemon's Physiognomy from Classical Antiquity to Medieval Islam*. Edited by Simon Swain. Oxford: Oxford University Press, 2007.
"I Can't Operate on This Boy; He Is My Son." Everything2.com. http://tinyurl.com/SBL4818a.
Isaac, Benjamin. *The Invention of Racism in Classical Antiquity*. Princeton: Princeton University Press, 2004.
Isho'dad of Merv. *The Commentaries of Isho'dad of Merv, Bishop of Hadatha (c. 850 A.D.) in Syriac and English*. Vol. 4. Translated by Margaret Dunlop Gibson. HSem 10. Cambridge: Cambridge University Press, 1913.
Jacquier, Eugène. *Les Actes Des Apôtres*. Ebib. Paris: Gabalda, 1926.
Johnson, Luke Timothy. *The Acts of the Apostles*. SP 5. Collegeville, MN: Liturgical Press, 1992.
Josephus. Translated by Henry St. J. Thackeray et al. 10 vols. LCL. Cambridge: Harvard University Press, 1926–1965.
———. *Against Apion*. In vol. 10 of *Flavius Josephus: Translation and Commentary*. Edited by Steve Mason. Translated by John M. G. Barclay. Leiden: Brill, 2007.

Juvenal. *Juvenal and Persius*. Translated by G. C. Ramsay. LCL. Cambridge: Harvard University Press, 1918.

Kennedy, George A. *New Testament Interpretation through Rhetorical Criticism*. Chapel Hill: University of North Carolina Press, 1984.

———, trans. *Progymnasmata: Greek Textbooks of Prose Composition and Rhetoric*. WGRW 10. Atlanta: Society of Biblical Literature, 2003.

Kratz, Reinhard. *Rettungswunder: Motiv-, traditions- und formkritische Aufarbeitung einer biblischen Gattung*. EHST 123. Frankfurt am Main: Lang, 1979.

Kurke, Leslie. *Coins, Bodies, Games and Gold: The Politics of Meaning in Archaic Greece*. Princeton: Princeton University Press, 1999.

———. "Pindar and the Prostitutes, or Reading Ancient 'Pornography.'" Pages 101–25 in *Constructions of the Classical Body*. The Body, in Theory: Histories of Cultural Materialism. Ann Arbor: University of Michigan Press, 1999.

———. "ΚΑΠΗΛΕΙΑ and Deceit: Theognis 59–60." *AJP* 110 (1989): 535–44.

Lausberg, Heinrich. *Handbook of Literary Rhetoric: A Foundation for Literary Study*. Edited by R. Dean Anderson. Translated by David E. Orton. Foreword by George A. Kennedy. Leiden: Brill, 1973.

Le Moyne, Pierre. *The Gallery of Heroick Women*. Translated by John Paulet Winchester. London: R. Norton for Henry Seile, 1652.

Lendon, J. E. "The Rhetoric of Combat: Greek Military Theory and Roman Culture in Julius Caesar's Battle Descriptions." *ClAnt* 18 (1999): 273–329.

Levine, Lee I. *The Ancient Synagogue: The First Thousand Years*. New Haven: Yale University Press, 2000.

Longenecker, Bruce W. *Rhetoric at the Boundaries: The Art and Theology of the New Testament Chain-Link Transitions*. Waco, TX: Baylor University Press, 2005.

Lucian. Translated by A. M. Harmon, K. Kilburn, and M. D. MacLeod. LCL. Cambridge: Harvard University Press, 1913–1967.

MacDonald, Dennis R. "Lydia and Her Sisters as Lukan Fictions." Pages 105–10 in *A Feminist Companion to the Acts of the Apostles*. Edited by Amy-Jill Levine and Marianne Blickenstaff. FCNTECW 9. Cleveland: Pilgrim, 2004.

Malina, Bruce J. *The New Testament World: Insights from Cultural Anthropology*. 3rd rev. and expanded ed. Louisville: Westminster John Knox, 2001.

Malina, Bruce J., and Jerome H. Neyrey. "Ancient Mediterranean Persons in Cultural Perspective: Portrait of Paul." Pages 257–75 in *The Social World of the New Testament: Insights and Models*. Edited by Jerome H. Neyrey and Eric C. Stewart. Peabody, MA: Hendrickson, 2008.

———. "First-Century Personality: Dyadic, Not Individual." Pages 67–96 in *The Social World of Luke-Acts: Models for Interpretation*. Edited by Jerome H. Neyrey. Peabody, MA: Hendrickson, 1991.

———. *Portraits of Paul: An Archaeology of Ancient Personality*. Louisville: Westminster John Knox, 1996.

Malina, Bruce J., and John J. Pilch. *Social-Science Commentary on the Book of Acts*. Minneapolis: Fortress, 2008.

Marshall, Anthony J. "Symbols and Showmanship in Roman Public Life: The *Fasces*." *Phoenix* 38 (1984): 120–41.

Martial. *Epigrams*. Translated and edited by D. R. Shackleton Bailey. 3 vols. LCL. Cambridge: Harvard University Press, 1993.

Martin, Clarice J. "The Acts of the Apostles." Pages 763–99 in *Searching the Scriptures*. Edited by Elisabeth Schüssler Fiorenza. New York: Crossroad, 1993.

Mason, Hugh J. *Greek Terms for Roman Institutions: A Lexicon and Analysis*. ASP 13. Toronto: Hakkert, 1974.

Matson, David Lertis. *Household Conversion Narratives in Acts: Pattern and Interpretation*. JSNTSup 123. Sheffield: Sheffield Academic, 1996.

Matthews, Shelly. *First Converts: Rich Pagan Women and the Rhetoric of Mission in Early Judaism and Christianity*. Contraversions: Jews and Other Differences. Stanford, CA: Stanford University Press, 2001.

McKay, Heather A. *Sabbath and Synagogue: The Question of Sabbath Worship in Ancient Judaism*. WGRW 122. Leiden: Brill, 1994.

Meeks, Wayne A. "The Image of the Androgyne: Some Uses of a Symbol in Earliest Christianity." *HR* 13 (1974): 165–208.

Metzger, Bruce M. *A Textual Commentary on the Greek New Testament: A Companion Volume to the United Bible Societies' Greek New Testament (Fourth Revised Edition)*. 2nd ed. Stuttgart: Deutsche Bibelgesellschaft, 1994.

Meyer, Heinrich August Wilhelm. *Critical and Exegetical Handbook to the Acts of the Apostles*. Edited by William P. Dickson. Translated by Paton J. Gloag. 4th ed. Meyer Commentary Series. New York: Funk & Wagnalls, 1883.

Miller, Carolyn R. "The Aristotelian Topos: Hunting for Novelty." Pages 130–46 in *Rereading Aristotle's Rhetoric*. Edited by Alan G. Gross and

Arthur E. Walzer. Carbondale, IL: Southern Illinois University Press, 2000.

Miller, John B. Faulkenberry. *Convinced That God Had Called Us: Dreams, Visions and the Perception of God's Will in Luke-Acts*. BibInt 85. Leiden: Brill, 2007.

Moore, Stephen D., and Janice Capel Anderson. "Taking It Like a Man: Masculinity in 4 Maccabees." *JBL* 117 (1998): 249–73.

Morris, Ian. "The Strong Principle of Equality and the Archaic Origins of Greek Democracy." Pages 19–48 in *Dēmokratia: A Conversation on Democracies, Ancient and Modern*. Edited by Josiah Ober and Charles W. Hedrick. Princeton: Princeton University Press, 1996.

Moxnes, Halvor. "Patron-Client Relations and the New Community in Luke-Acts." Pages 241–68 in *The Social World of Luke-Acts: Models for Interpretation*. Edited by Jerome H. Neyrey. Peabody, MA: Hendrickson, 1991.

Muilenburg, James. "Form Criticism and Beyond." *JBL* 88 (1969): 1–18.

Nestle, Wilhelm. "Anklänge an Euripides in der Apostelgeschichte." *Phil* 59 (1900):46–57.

Neyrey, Jerome H. "Loss of Wealth, Loss of Family, Loss of Honor: The Cultural Context of the Original Makarisms in Q." Pages 87–102 in *The Social World of the New Testament: Insights and Models*. Edited by Jerome H. Neyrey and Eric C. Stewart. Peabody, MA: Hendrickson, 2008.

———. "Maid and Mother in Art and Literature." *BTB* 20.2 (1990): 65–75.

———. "The Social Location of Paul: Education as the Key." Pages 126–64 in *Fabrics of Discourse: Essays in Honor of Vernon K. Robbins*. Edited by David B. Gowler, L. Gregory Bloomquist, and Duane F. Watson. Harrisburg, PA: Trinity Press International, 2003.

———. "'Teaching You in Public and from House to House' (Acts 20:20): Unpacking a Cultural Stereotype." Pages 183–99 in *The Social World of the New Testament: Insights and Models*. Edited by Jerome H. Neyrey and Eric C. Stewart. Peabody, MA: Hendrickson, 2008.

Nisbet, Robin G. M., and Margaret Hubbard. *A Commentary on Horace: Odes, Book 1*. Oxford: Clarendon, 1970.

Noegel, Scott. *Nocturnal Ciphers: The Allusive Language of Dreams in the Ancient Near East*. AOS 89. New Haven: American Oriental Society, 2007.

O'Day, Gail R. "Acts." Pages 394–402 in *Women's Bible Commentary*. Edited by Carol A. Newsom and Sharon H. Ringe. 2nd ed. Louisville: Westminster John Knox, 1998.

Oakman, Douglas E. "The Radical Jesus: You Cannot Serve God and Mammon." *BTB* 34.3 (2004): 122–29.

Olbrechts-Tyteca, Lucie. *Le Comique du Discours. Sociologie Générale et Philosophie Sociale*. Brussels: Éditions de l'Université de Bruxelles, 1974.

Origen. *Contra Celsum*. Translated by Henry Chadwick. Cambridge: Cambridge University Press, 1953.

O'Toole, Robert T. *The Unity of Luke's Theology: An Analysis of Luke-Acts*. Wilmington, DE: Glazier, 1984.

Otto, Walter F. *Dionysus: Myth and Cult*. Translated by Robert B. Palmer. Bloomington: Indiana University Press, 1965.

Ovid. *Metamorphoses*. Translated by Frank Justus Miller. 2 vols. LCL. Cambridge: Harvard University Press, 1916.

Parker, Robert. *Miasma: Pollution and Purification in Early Greek Religion*. Oxford: Clarendon, 1983.

Parsons, Mikeal C. *Acts*. Paideia Commentaries on the New Testament. Grand Rapids: Baker Academic, 2008.

———. *Body and Character in Luke and Acts: The Subversion of Physiognomy in Early Christianity*. Grand Rapids: Baker Academic, 2006.

Parsons, Mikeal C., and Martin M. Culy. *Acts: A Handbook on the Greek Text*. Waco, TX: Baylor University Press, 2003.

Perelman, Chaïm, and Lucie Olbrechts-Tyteca. *The New Rhetoric: A Treatise on Argumentation*. Translated by John Wilkinson and Purcell Weaver. Notre Dame: University of Notre Dame Press, 1969.

———. *Traité de l'Argumentation: La Nouvelle Rhétorique*. 5th ed. Brussels: Éditions de l'Université de Bruxelles, 1958.

Perrin, Bernadotte. Introduction to *Plutarch's Lives: Theseus and Romulus; Lycurgus and Numa; Solon and Publicola*. Translated by Bernadotte Perrin. LCL. Cambridge: Harvard University Press, 1914.

Perry, B. E. "Demetrius of Phalerum and the Aesopic Fables." *TPAPA* 93 (1962): 287–346.

Perry, Peter S. *The Rhetoric of Digressions: Revelation 7:1–17 and 10:1–11:13 and Ancient Communication*. Tübingen: Mohr Siebeck, 2009.

Pervo, Richard I. "The Literary Genre of Acts of the Apostles." ThD diss., Harvard University, 1979.

———. *Profit with Delight: The Literary Genre of the Acts of the Apostles*. Philadelphia: Fortress, 1987.

Philostratus. Translated and edited by Christopher P. Jones et al. 6 vols. LCL. Cambridge: Harvard University Press, 1921–2014.
Philo. Translated by F. H. Colson et al. 12 vols. LCL. Cambridge: Harvard University Press, 1929–1962.
Pilch, John J. "Healing in Luke-Acts." Pages 203–19 in *The Social World of the New Testament: Insights and Models*. Edited by Jerome H. Neyrey and Eric C. Stewart. Peabody, MA: Hendrickson, 2008.
Pindar. *The Odes of Pindar Including the Principal Fragments*. Translated by John Sandys. LCL. Cambridge: Harvard University Press, 1915.
Plato. Translated by W. R. M. Lamb et al. 12 vols. LCL. Cambridge: Harvard University Press, 1914–2013.
Pliny. *Natural History*. Translated by H. Rackham, W. H. S. Jones, and D. E. Eichholz. 10 vols. LCL. Cambridge: Harvard University Press, 1938–1963.
Plutarch. Translated by Bernadotte Perrin et al. 28 vols. LCL. Cambridge: Harvard University Press, 1914–2004.
Polyaenus. *Stratagems of War*. Translated and edited by Peter Krentz and Everett L. Wheeler. Vol. 2. Chicago: Ares, 1994.
Polybius. *The Histories*. Translated by W. R. Paton. 6 vols. LCL. Cambridge: Harvard University Press, 1922–1927.
Popović, Mladen. *Reading the Human Body: Physiognomics and Astrology in the Dead Sea Scrolls and Hellenistic-Early Roman Period Judaism*. STDJ 67. Leiden: Brill, 2007.
Portefaix, Lilian. *Sisters Rejoice: Paul's Letter to the Philippians and Luke-Acts as Seen by First-Century Philippian Women*. ConBNT 20. Stockholm: Almqvist & Wiksell, 1988.
Quincey, J. H. "Orestes and the Argive Alliance." *ClQ* 14.2 (1964): 191.
Quintillian. *The Institutio Oratoria*. Translated by H. E. Butler. 4 vols. LCL. Cambridge: Harvard University Press, 1920–1922.
Rapske, Brian. *Paul in Roman Custody*. Vol. 3 of *The Book of Acts in Its First Century Setting*. Edited by Bruce Winter. Grand Rapids: Eerdmans, 1994.
Rauh, Nicholas. *The Sacred Bonds of Commerce: Religion, Economy, and Trade Society at Hellenistic Roman Delos, 166–87 BC*. Amsterdam: Gieben, 1993.
Reimer, Ivoni Richter. "Lydia and Her House." Pages 71–149 in *Women in the Acts of the Apostles: A Feminist Liberation Perspective*. Translated by Linda M. Maloney. Minneapolis: Fortress, 1992.

———. *Women in the Acts of the Apostles: A Feminist Liberation Perspective*. Translated by Linda M. Maloney. Minneapolis: Fortress, 1992.

Reinhold, Meyer. *History of Purple as a Status Symbol in Antiquity*. Latomus 116. Brussels: Latomus, 1970.

Renan, Ernest. *Saint Paul*. Histoire des Origines du Christianisme 3. Paris: Michel Lévy Frères, 1869.

Reventlow, Henning Graf. "Humanistic Exegesis: The Famous Hugo Grotius." Pages 175–91 in *Creative Biblical Exegesis: Christian and Jewish Hermeneutics through the Centuries*. Edited by Henning Graf Reventlow and Benjamin Uffenheimer. JSOTSup 59. Sheffield: JSOT Press, 1988.

Robbins, Vernon K. "By Land and by Sea: The We-Passages and Ancient Sea Voyages." Pages 215–42 in *Perspectives on Luke-Acts*. Edited by Charles H. Talbert. PRSt. Special Studies Series 5. Edinburgh: T&T Clark, 1978.

———. *Exploring the Texture of Texts: A Guide to Socio-rhetorical Interpretation*. Valley Forge, PA: Trinity Press International, 1996. Repr., New York: Bloomsbury, 2012.

———. *The Invention of Christian Discourse*. RRA 1. Dorset, UK: Deo, 2009.

———. *Jesus the Teacher: A Socio-rhetorical Interpretation of Mark, with a New Introduction*. 2nd ed. Minneapolis: Fortress, 1992.

———. *Sea Voyages and Beyond: Emerging Strategies in Socio-rhetorical Interpretation*. Edited by Vernon K. Robbins, David B. Gowler, and Robert von Thaden Jr. ESEC 14. Dorset, UK: Deo, 2010.

———. *The Tapestry of Early Christian Discourse: Rhetoric, Society and Ideology*. New York: Routledge, 1996.

———. "Writing as a Rhetorical Act in Plutarch and the Gospels." Pages 142–68 in *Persuasive Artistry: Studies in New Testament Rhetoric in Honor of George A. Kennedy*. Edited by Duane F. Watson. Sheffield: JSOT Press, 1991.

Roberts, John, ed. *Oxford Dictionary of the Classical World*. Oxford Reference Online. http://tinyurl.com/j9lalnc.

Rosenfeld, Ben-Zion. "Innkeeping in Jewish Society in Roman Palestine." *JESHO* 41 (1998): 133–58.

Rosenfeld, Ben-Zion, and Joseph Menirav. "Commerce and Marketers, as Viewed by the Sages." Pages 171–209 in *Markets and Marketing in Roman Palestine*. Translated by Chava Chassel. JSJSup 99. Leiden: Brill, 2005.

Rubinelli, Sara. "The Ancient Argumentative Game: Τόποι and *Loci* in Action." *Argu* 20 (2006): 253–72.
Rusten, Jeffrey, I. C. Cunningham, and A. D. Knox, trans. and eds. *Theophrastus: Characters; Herodas: Mimes; Cercidas and the Choliambic Poets*. LCL. Cambridge: Harvard University Press, 1929.
Sangster, Margaret E. *The Women of the Bible: A Portrait Gallery*. New York: Christian Herald, 1911.
Schneemelcher, Wilhelm, ed. *New Testament Apocrypha*. Translated by R. McL. Wilson. 2 vols. Cambridge: Clarke, 1991.
Schurman, Anna Maria van. *Whether a Christian Woman Should Be Educated and Other Writings from Her Intellectual Circle*. Translated and edited by Joyce L. Irwin. The Other Voice in Early Modern Europe. Chicago: University of Chicago Press, 1998.
Seaford, Richard. "Thunder, Lightning and Earthquake in the *Bacchae* and The Acts of the Apostles." Pages 139–51 in *What Is a God? Studies in the Nature of Greek Divinity*. Edited by Alan B. Lloyd. London: Duckworth, 1997.
Seneca. Translated by Richard M. Gummere et al. 11 vols. LCL. Cambridge: Harvard University Press, 1913–2004.
Skinner, Matthew L. *Locating Paul: Places of Custody as Narrative Settings in Acts 21–28*. AcBib 13. Atlanta: Society of Biblical Literature, 2003.
Soanes, Catherine, and Angus Stevenson, ed. *The Oxford Dictionary of English*. Revised edition. Oxford: Oxford University Press, 2005.
Spawforth, Antony. "Shades of Greekness: A Lydian Case Study." Pages 375–400 in *Ancient Perceptions of Greek Ethnicity*. Edited by Irad Malkin. Center for Hellenic Studies Colloquia 5. Cambridge: Harvard University Press, 2001.
Spencer, F. Scott. "Women of 'the Cloth' in Acts: Sewing the Word." Pages 134–54 in *A Feminist Companion to the Acts of the Apostles*. Edited by Amy-Jill Levine and Marianne Blickenstaff. FCNTECW 9. Cleveland: Pilgrim, 2004.
Staley, Jeffrey L. "Changing Woman: Toward a Postcolonial Postfeminist Interpretation of Acts 16:6–40." Pages 177–92 in *A Feminist Companion to the Acts of the Apostles*. Edited by Amy-Jill Levine and Marianne Blickenstaff. FCNTECW 9. Cleveland: Pilgrim, 2004.
Sterck-Degueldre, Jean-Pierre. *Eine Frau namens Lydia: Zu Geschichte und Komposition in Apostelgeschichte 16, 11–15.40*. WUNT 2/176. Tübingen: Mohr Siebeck, 2004.

Strabo. *Geography*. Translated by Horace Leonard Jones. 8 vols. LCL. Cambridge: Harvard University Press, 1917–1932.
Struck, Peter. "Viscera and the Divine: Dreams as the Divinatory Bridge between the Corporeal and the Incorporeal." Pages 125–36 in *Prayer, Magic, and the Stars in the Ancient and Late Antique World*. Edited by Scott Noegel, Joel Walker, and Brannon Wheeler. Magic in History. University Park: Pennsylvania State University Press, 2003.
Suetonius. *Lives of the Caesars*. Translated by J. C. Rolfe. 2 vols. LCL. Cambridge: Harvard University Press, 1914.
Talbert, Charles H. *Reading Acts: A Literary and Theological Commentary on the Acts of the Apostles*. Reading the New Testament. New York: Crossroad, 1997.
Tannehill, Robert C. *The Acts of the Apostles*. Vol. 2 of *The Narrative Unity of Luke-Acts: A Literary Interpretation*. Minneapolis: Fortress, 1990.
Theophrastus. *De Lapidibus*. Edited and translated by D. E. Eichholz. Oxford: Clarendon, 1965.
Van Stempvoort, Pieter A. "The *Protevangelium Jacobi*, the Sources of Its Theme and Style and Their Bearing on Its Date." Pages 410–26 in *Papers Presented to the Second International Congress on New Testament Studies Held at Christ Church, Oxford, 1961*. Edited by F. L. Cross. SE 3. Berlin: Akademie, 1964.
Virgil. Translated by H. Rushton Fairclough. 2 vols. LCL. Cambridge: Harvard University Press, 1918.
Vitruvius. *On Architecture*. Translated by Frank Granger. 2 vols. LCL. Cambridge: Harvard University Press, 1934.
Wainwright, Elaine M. *Women Healing/Healing Women: The Genderization of Healing in Early Christianity*. Bible World. Sheffield: Equinox, 2006.
Wallace, Daniel B. *Greek Grammar: Beyond the Basics; An Exegetical Syntax of the New Testament with Scripture, Subject, and Greek Word Indexes*. Grand Rapids: Zondervan, 1996.
Weaver, John B. *Plots of Epiphany: Prison-Escape in Acts of the Apostles*. BZNW 131. Berlin: de Gruyter, 2004.
Weinreich, Otto. "Gebet und Wunder." Pages 169–464 in *Genethliakon Wilhelm Schmid*. TBAW 5. Stuttgart: Kohlhammer, 1929.
Wikenhauser, Alfred. "Religionsgeschichtliche Parallelen zu Apg 16, 9." *BZ* 23 (1935–1936): 180–86.
Witherington, Ben, III. *The Acts of the Apostles: A Socio-rhetorical Commentary*. Grand Rapids: Eerdmans, 1998.

———. *Women in the Earliest Churches*. SNTSMS 59. Cambridge: Cambridge University Press, 1988.

Xenophon. Translated by E. C. Marchant et al. 7 vols. LCL. Cambridge: Harvard University Press, 1925–2013.

Zerubavel, Eviatar. *Social Mindscapes: An Invitation to Cognitive Sociology*. Cambridge: Harvard University Press, 1997.

Ancient Sources Index

Hebrew Bible/Septuagint		13:16 LXX	157
		19:3–4	155
Genesis		19:7 LXX	157
11:9 LXX	256 n. 102	20–21	155
18:1–8	155		
19:1–3	155	1 Samuel	
19:3 LXX	157	16:7	236, 237
19:9 LXX	157	28:23 LXX	157, 159
22:18	237		
29:8–18	125	2 Samuel	
39:20–23	196	11:2–4	125
		18:19	174
Exodus		18:28	174
26:1	134		
		1 Kings	
Leviticus		20:16	175
21:7	143, 160	21:16 LXX	175
Deuteronomy		2 Kings	
6:5	244	18–19	170
29:3 LXX	225 n. 43	19:14–19	171
29:4	14, 225 n. 43	19:35	171 n. 135
Joshua		1 Chronicles	
1:14	176 n. 145	12:21	176 n. 145
1:14 LXX	176 n. 145	12:22 LXX	176 n. 145
2:1	155		
2:1–21	159	2 Chronicles	
2:9	160	32:1–23	170
6:23	160	32:6–8	170
10:3–4 LXX	174	32:20	171
		32:21	171 n. 135
Judges			
13:15 LXX	157	Psalms	
13:15–16	154 n. 96	66:10	210 n. 17

Proverbs
- 17:3 — 210 n. 17
- 31 — 16
- 31:10–31 — 134
- 31:13 — 134
- 31:19 — 16, 134
- 31:24 — 134
- 31:24 LXX — 134–135

Isaiah
- 36–37 — 170
- 37:14–20 — 171
- 37:36 — 171 n. 135
- 56:7 — 146
- 60:7 — 147

Jeremiah
- 6:27 — 210 n. 17
- 9:7 — 210 n. 17

Ezekiel
- 33:31 — 244 n. 82

Zechariah
- 13:9 — 210 n. 17
- 14:21 — 134, 268

Deuterocanonical Books

1 Maccabees
- 3:43–46 — 146
- 3:46 — 146
- 7:37 — 146
- 11:43 — 176
- 15:26 — 176

2 Maccabees
- 15 — 169
- 15:7–8 — 170
- 15:9 — 170
- 15:12–16 — 169, 170
- 15:17 — 170

3 Maccabees
- 7:5 — 190
- 7:20 — 146

4 Maccabees
- 4:22–23 — 178 n. 153
- 10:7 — 189 n. 182

Pseudepigrapha

Sibylline Oracles
- 3:170 — 122
- 5:287 — 122
- 5:292 — 122

Ancient Jewish Writers

Artapanus, *Moses*
- 23–24 — 192

Josephus, *Against Apion*
- 2.10 — 147 n. 84
- 2.10–11 — 148

Josephus, *Jewish Antiquities*
- 3.2.276 — 143, 160
- 5.8–15 — 160
- 7.245 — 174, 177
- 7.250 — 174, 177
- 10.5–17 — 146
- 10.17 — 171, 176
- 10.18–19 — 172
- 10.21 — 172
- 10.24–25 — 172
- 11.304–347 — 166
- 11.317–318 — 176
- 11.322–339 — 164 n. 121
- 14.258 — 147 n. 148
- 18.228 — 177
- 18.229 — 177 n. 149

Josephus, *Jewish War*
- 1.607 — 177 n. 148
- 2.420 — 177 n. 149
- 3.143 — 177 n. 148
- 3.503 — 177 n. 148
- 4.229 — 174 n. 141

4.618	177 n. 149	165	147 n. 84
4.656	177 n. 149	191	147 n. 84
5.465	166	346	147 n. 84
		371	147 n. 84

Josephus, *The Life*
277	147 n. 84, 148
280	147 n. 84, 148
287–288	174 n. 141
290–291	150 n. 89
293	147 n. 84, 148
348	176 n. 144

Philo, *Against Flaccus*
41	147 n. 84
45	147 n. 84
48	147 n. 84
49	147 n. 84
53	147 n. 84
122	147 n. 84

Philo, *On the Life of Joseph*
81	189
82–84	189
85–87	196

Philo, *On the Contemplative Life*
31	224 n. 42
30–32	151
33	152
66	152
68	152 n. 93
69	152

Philo, *On the Life of Moses*
2.183–184	128 n. 35

Philo, *On the Embassy to Gaius*
132	147 n. 84
134	147 n. 84
137	147 n. 84
138	147 n. 84
148	147 n. 84
152	147 n. 84
156	147 n. 84
157	147 n. 84

New Testament

Matthew
11:12	157
15:21–28	226 n. 46
21:13	146
25:36	191 n. 186
25:39	191 n. 186
25:43	191 n. 186
25:44	191 n. 186

Mark
1:26	247 n. 85
7:24–30	226 n.46
11:17	146
15:33–39	41

Luke
1:42–55	90 n. 70
1:51	255 n. 100
2:19	225 n. 43, 279
2:51	279
4:16	68 n. 9, 75 n. 38, 95 n. 80
4:16–28	144
4:18	144
4:33–36	241 n. 77
4:38–40	118
4:40–41	241 n. 77
5:8	250
6:18	241 n. 77
6:42	204 n. 7
7:1–10	164
7:2–10	232
7:21	241 n. 77
7:36–50	274
8:1–3	275
8:2	241 n. 77
8:26–39	99 n. 90, 183 n. 166
8:28	209 n. 16, 250
8:28–31	86 n. 64

Luke (cont.)		Acts	
8:30	209 n. 16	24:28	155
8:35	241 n. 77	24:29	155, 157, 227
8:37	209 n. 16	24:30–31	154 n. 96
8:41–42	232	24:31–32	224
8:43–48	261	24:32	155
8:47	250	Acts	
9:42	241 n. 77	1:6	163
10	236	2:8	82
10:25–37	274	3:25	236
10:27	244	4:1	85 n. 63
11:14	241 n. 77	4:2	85 n. 63
12:1	204 n. 7	4:20	82
12:56	204 n. 7	4:36	121
13:11–12	241 n. 77	5:8	77, 117
13:14	68 n. 9	5:16	241 n. 77
13:15	204 n. 7	5:17–42	193
13:16	68 n. 9	5:19	247
14:5	68 n. 9	7:2–53	43
14:31–32	263	7:51	43
14:31–33	164	7:57	43
16:1–8a	43	8:6–8	241 n. 77
16:9	21	8:8–24	102 n. 97
16:11	243	8:27–39	236, 274
16:13	43, 46	9:11	122 n. 20
16:14	243	9:11–12	93 n. 74
16:16	157	9:17	93 n. 74
16:19	135, 209 n. 16	9:36	217
16:21	209 n. 16	9:39	276
16:23	209 n. 16	9:43–10:23	94 n. 79
16:25	209 n. 16	10	144
16:28	209 n. 16	10:1–48	165, 274
17:11–19	274	10:2	144, 145 n. 79, 149 n. 88
19:46	146, 147, 149, 197	10:19–20	93 n. 74
21:1–2	51	10:22	144, 145 n. 79
21:1–4	51	10:23	155
21:3	51	10:34	237
22:42	97 n. 85	10:48	49
23:35–39	105	12:1–19	193
23:46	247 n. 85	12:4	78 n. 44
24	154, 155, 224 n. 41	12:7	247 n. 85
24:4	81 n. 50	12:17	78 n. 44, 247
24:13–32	154, 276	12:19	191, 249 n. 89
24:25	154	13:4	83 n. 59
24:27	154	13:14	68 n. 9, 95 n. 80, 218 n. 27

13:14–42	144, 251	16:11–12a	94
13:16	145 n. 79	16:11–40	43, 65 n. 3, 80
13:26	145 n. 79	16:12	70, 83, 83 n. 55, 209 n. 16, 235 n. 70
13:32	144		
13:34	183 n. 166	16:12b	94
13:35	183 n. 166	16:13	45, 53, 68 n. 9, 69, 69 n. 15, 70, 70 n. 20, 74, 75, 75 n. 37, 76, 77, 79 n. 45, 83 n. 55, 84, 85, 87, 94, 95, 95 n. 80, 98, 104, 144, 146, 216
13:36	183 n. 166		
13:37	183 n. 166		
13:50	218		
14:14–15	99 n. 89	16:13–14	84
14:22	79 n. 45	16:13–15	2, 74, 76
15:1–29	230	16:14	14, 15, 29, 68, 68 n. 7, 70, 70 n. 21, 77, 79, 84, 95, 118, 120, 144, 145 n. 79, 154, 209 n. 16, 217 n. 26, 219, 224, 225 n. 43, 228
15:13	69		
15:19	78 n. 44		
15:29	69 n. 12		
15:37–39	232	16:14–15	1, 4, 5, 33, 76, 77, 84, 117, 260
16	2, 5, 7, 9, 17, 24, 30, 33, 52, 59, 64, 78 nn. 42 and 44, 121, 136, 136 n. 51, 145 n. 78, 151 n. 92, 154, 156 n. 98, 166 n.127, 193 n. 193, 199, 235, 239, 264 n. 120, 272, 278, 280		
		16:15	12 n. 7, 17, 68, 68 n. 10, 69, 69 nn. 11 and 14, 70 nn. 18 and 21, 72, 72 n. 26, 73, 73 n. 29, 74, 74 n. 33, 76, 77, 78, 78 n. 43, 79, 83 n. 55, 84 n. 60, 85, 89, 91, 96, 97, 108, 109, 111, 111 n. 114, 117, 153, 155, 156 n. 99, 157, 162, 216, 225, 227, 228, 231
16:1	73, 78, 217		
16:1–5	78, 78 n. 44, 79, 80, 234		
16:3	78, 230, 232		
16:4	78	16:15a	74
16:5	79	16:15b	11
16:6	93	16:16	100 n. 91, 53, 68, 70 nn. 20 and 21, 77, 85, 98, 100, 104, 105, 146, 189 n. 181, 244 n. 83, 250, 250
16:6–7	83 n. 55, 94		
16:6–10	65 n. 3		
16:6–40	65 n. 3	16:16–17	74, 98, 98 n. 86, 240
16:7	93	16:17	68, 68 n. 9 and 10, 69 n. 11, 70 n. 21, 74, 77, 85, 98, 99, 101, 209 n. 16, 241, 242 n. 79
16:9	68, 68 nn. 9 and 10, 69, 69 nn. 11 and 13, 14, 72, 72 n. 26, 75 n. 37, 80, 81, 82, 83 n. 55, 84, 93, 94 n. 76, 95, 176 n. 146, 179, 212, 216, 260 n. 109		
		16:17–18	83 n. 55
		16:18	68, 68 n. 10, 69, 69 n. 11, 70 n. 21, 83 n. 55, 85, 87, 98, 99, 99 n. 88, 180, 240, 243, 246
16:9–10	68, 75, 80, 81, 82		
16:9–40	5, 9 n. 1, 41, 43, 67, 80, 111, 269	16:18–19	101
		16:19	68, 68 nn. 7 and 9, 69, 69 n. 16, 70 nn. 19 and 21, 75, 75 n. 37, 86, 100, 100 nn. 93 and 94, 105, 244 n. 82
16:10	4, 9, 68, 69, 70, 70 n. 21, 71, 75 n. 37, 75 n. 38, 81, 82, 93, 93 n. 72, 94 n.77, 96, 177, 212, 214		
16:10–17	68 n. 8, 81 n. 52, 82	16:19–24	261 n. 113
16:11	69 n. 16, 70	16:19–40	83 n. 55, 86, 193

Acts (cont.)
  16:20   68 n. 9 and 10, 69 n. 16, 70, 70 n. 19, 83 n. 55, 187
  16:20–21   69 n. 11, 80, 86, 101, 101 n. 95, 109 n. 110, 180
  16:21   68, 68 n. 9, 101
  16:22   68 n. 9, 70 n. 19, 79, 83 n. 55, 189 n. 181, 252, 252 n. 93
  16:22–23   87, 103 n. 104
  16:23   68, 69 n. 16, 70, 70 n. 19, 78, 83 n. 55, 104
  16:23–24   105
  16:24   68, 69 n. 16, 70 n. 19, 78, 87, 104, 252
  16:25   68, 68 n. 7 and 9, 70 n. 19 and 21, 74, 87, 104, 250
  16:26   87, 104
  16:26–28   251
  16:27   68 n. 9, 69, 70, 70 n. 19, 75, 75 n. 37, 78, 83 n. 55, 88, 104, 191, 249 n. 89
  16:27–28   87
  16:28   68, 68 n. 10, 69 n. 11, 83 n. 55, 105, 209 n. 16, 247, 248
  16:29   68, 68 n. 7, 88, 247
  16:30   68, 68 n. 10, 69 nn. 11 and 15, 16, 70 n. 21, 73, 105, 106
  16:30–32   88 n. 66
  16:31   68, 68 n. 10, 69, 70 nn. 18 and 21, 73, 74 n. 33, 78, 83 n. 55, 106, 108, 243, 250
  16:31–32   68, 69 n. 11, 249 n. 90
  16:32   70 nn. 18 and 21, 73 n. 32, 74, 74 n. 33, 78, 85, 106, 251
  16:33   69 n. 16, 74, 74 n. 33, 107
  16:33a   74
  16:33b   74
  16:33–34   88, 106, 260
  16:34   69 n. 16, 70 nn. 18 and 21, 73, 73 n. 32, 74 n. 33, 78, 209 n. 16, 251 n. 92
  16:35   68 nn. 9 and 10, 69, 69 n. 11, 70 n. 19, 83 n. 55, 85 n. 63, 89 n. 67, 107, 189 n. 181, 248
  16:36   68, 68 n. 9, 69, 69 n. 11, 70 n. 19, 85 n. 63, 88
  16:36–37   251
  16:37   68, 68 nn. 9 and 10, 69, 69 nn. 11 and 16, 70 n. 19, 78, 88, 107 n. 108, 109
  16:38   68, 68 n. 9, 70 n. 19, 85 n. 63, 189 n.181, 254 n. 95
  16:38–39   89, 209 n. 16
  16:39   69, 69 n. 16, 70, 72, 73 nn. 27 and 28, 83 n. 55, 110, 111, 254
  16:39–40   259
  16:40   4, 5, 33, 68 nn. 7 and 9, 69, 70 n. 19, 72 n. 26, 73, 73 n. 28, 74 n. 33, 75, 75 n. 37, 76, 77, 78, 79, 80, 83 n. 55, 89, 97, 111, 118, 161, 162, 227, 228, 259, 260, 260 n. 109, 265
  17:1–4   79, 153
  17:1–10a   80
  17:2   75 n. 38, 79 n. 47, 101 n. 96
  17:3   79
  17:4   79
  17:5   79, 80
  17:6   80
  17:9   260
  17:10   80
  17:17   224
  17:20   225
  17:31   78 n. 44
  18:7   145 n. 79
  18:9   69
  18:26   217
  19:2–5   48, 50, 50 n. 44
  19:12   241 n. 77
  19:23–40   102 n. 97
  19:32   256 n. 102
  19:35–41   103
  20:5   242 n. 79
  20:5–15   68 n. 8, 81 n. 52
  20:9   121
  20:20   149 n. 86
  21:1–18   68 n. 8, 81 n. 52
  21:8   274
  21:24   78 n. 44
  21:39   122 n. 20

22:3	122 n. 20	Arator, *De Actibus apostolorum*	
22:4	78 n.44	3	220 n. 36
24:26	190 n. 185	69–70	219 n. 34
25:15–16	253 n. 94		
27:1–29	68 n. 8, 81 n. 52	Augustine, *De praedestinatione sanctorum*	
27:42	106 n. 106	41	10 n. 4
28:1–16	68 n. 8, 81 n. 52		
		Clement of Alexandria, *Cohortatio ad Graecos*	
2 Corinthians			
2:17	244, 265	1.2P	183 n. 167
		2.30P	193 n. 194
Philippians			
1:18b–26	264	Clement of Alexandria, *Stromateis*	
1:27–30	264	1.9.44.1–4	207
2:6–11	264	3.53.1–3	20 n. 28
4:2	18	10.48.5	135 n. 48
4:3	20 n. 28	13.57.1–3	256 n. 103
4:22	27, 29		
		Ephrem	219
Hebrews			
11:31	159	Eusebius, *Historia ecclesiastica*	
		7.32.4	26 n. 51
James			
2:25	159	Eusebius, *Praeparatio evangelica*	
5:3	210	9.27.1–37	192 n. 191
1 Peter		Isho'dad of Merv	219
1:6–7	210		
1:7	210	John Chrysostom, *Epistula ad Cyriacum*	
		Letter 125	10 n. 4
Revelation			
2:9	277 n. 7	John Chrysostom, *Expositiones in Psalmos*	
2:10	194 n. 196	Ps 113	10 n. 4
2:20	277 n. 7		
3:18	210 n. 17	John Chrysostom, *Homiliae in Acta apostolorum*	
3:20	16		
13:16–17	232	35	10 n. 4
14:18	247 n. 85	36	10 n. 4
17:4	135		
		John Chrysostom, *Homiliae in epistulam i ad Corinthios*	
Early Christian Writings			
		15.14	10 n.4, 12
Acts of Paul and Thecla			
1–4	156 n. 98	John Chrysostom, *Homiliae in Matthaeum*	
18	190, 260	73	10 n. 4, 11

Origen, *Against Celsus*		1452a30–32	49
2.34	256		
		Aristotle, *Rhetoric*	
Protevangelium of James		1356b8	46
10.2	134 n. 42	1356b10	47, 50
11.1	134	1367a27	137 n. 54
		1393b4	47
Greco-Roman Literature		1394b1–2	46
		1400b29	121
Aelius Theon, *On Syncrisis*			
10.112	102	Arrian, *Anabasis*	
10.112–113	103	1.11.1–8	150 n. 89
		2.18.1	168
Aeschylus, *Fragmenta*			
31	193 n. 195	Arrian, *Epicteti dissertationes*	
		2.9.2–5	255 n. 101
Aeschylus, *Septem contra Thebas*		2.9.19–21	255 n. 99
545	222 n. 38		
		Artapanus, *Moses*	
Anacreon, *Fragmenta*		23–24	192
136	127 n. 33		
		Athenaeus, *Deipnosophistae*	
Anonymous, *De Physiognomonia Liber*		12.515d	126
806b	55 n. 58	12.515e–f	129
		12.516a–b	127
Aphthonius, *Progymnasmata*		12.516b	128
31	102 n. 100	12.526a–d	130
		12.526f–527a	128 n.34
Appian, *Bella civilia*		12.545d	128 n. 34
4.137	257	12.547a	181
		13.573a–b	125 n. 25
Aristophanes, *Ranae*		15.686e–687a	135 n. 48
1385–1388	142	15.690b–c	127
		15.694e	205
Aristophanes, *Equites*			
165	185	Bacchylides, *Fragmenta*	
177–181	142	10	206
1258	142 n. 68		
		Choricius of Gaza, *Preliminary Talks*	
Aristotle, *Mechanics*		Decl. 3 [14]: The Lydians	129 n. 36
849b.85	142		
		Cicero, *De amicitia*	
Aristotle, *Poetics*		25.95	207
1452a1–10	49		
1452a21–29	49		

ANCIENT SOURCES INDEX

Cicero, *De officiis*
1.42.150   137 n. 56, 140 n. 61
1.42.151   139
3.10.45   195 n. 199

Cicero, *De natura deorum*
2.16.42   55

Cicero, *In Verrem*
2.4.26.58–59   133

Cicero, *Topica*
20.77   168 n. 132

Claudian, *Rape of Proserpine*
1.275   16

Demosthenes, *Philippica iii*
10   83 n. 59

Dio Chrysostom, *Tarsica Prior*
23   123 n. 21

Diodorus of Sicily, *The Library of History*
10.4.3–4   195 n. 199
12.20.2   150, 150 n. 91
12.21   133
15.74.2   177 n.149
17.16.3–4   150
31.9.2   191
32.10.2   146 n. 81

Euripides, *Bacchae*
234   193
257   184
353–354   193
440–449   193
455–458   193
461–463   121 n. 14
616–640   194

Euripides, *Iphigenia in Tauris*
1275   184

Euripides, *Medea*
516–519   206

Eustathius Thessalonicensis, *Commentarii ad Homeri Iliadem*
180, lines 16–18   127 n. 33

Hermogenes
18   102

Herodotus, *Histories*
1.50–52   184
1.53–54   184
1.77   176
1.79   130
1.93   123, 124
1.94   124, 143
1.136   143 n. 73
1.155   129, 143
2.141   145, 222, 172
2.164–167   222
3.22   135 n. 48
5.12–14   125
5.89   174 n. 141
7.10   208 n. 15
7.12   168
7.73–75   165 n. 123
7.145   174 n. 141
7.158   174 n. 142

Hippocrates, *Airs, Waters, Places*
12   55

Hippocrates, *Epidemics*
2.5.1   54
2.6.1   54

Hipponax, *Fragmenta*
92   127 n. 31

Homer, *Iliad*
14.231   249 n. 88

Homeric Hymns to Pythian Apollo
370   183 n. 166

Horace, *Carmina*
1.8	18, 19, 126, 131
1.13	18, 19, 126
1.25	18, 19, 126
3.9	18, 20, 126

Justinus, *Epitome historiarum Philippicarum*
1.711–13	129 n. 36

Juvenal, *Satire*
1.2.83	135
3.13–14	147 n. 84
3.290–300	147 n. 84
3.295	147
6.542–547	147 n. 84
14.173–189	133
14.198–201	182

Lucian, *Dialogi deorum*
15.2	126 n. 30

Lucian, *Toxaris*
30	192
30–31	195
31	190, 260
32	195
33	195

Lucretius, *De rerum natura*
5.1004–6	181

Macrobius, *Saturnalia*
2.5.9	119 n. 7

Martial, *Epigrams*
11.21	18, 126

Nicolaus of Damascus
Frag. 71	125

Nicolaus the Sophist, *Progymnasmata*
59–60	102 n. 100
60	102 n. 100

Ovid, *Metamorphoses*
1.94–96	181
8.631–636	118 n. 6
8.684–690	154 n. 96

P. Aelius Aristides, *To the Rhodians: Concerning Concord*
37–39	256 n. 103

Philostratus, *Vita Apollonii*
1.32	135 n. 48
5.32.2	128 n. 34
8.7.10	244 n. 84
8.7.23	255 n. 101
8.27.1	177 n.149
8.34	123
30	145 n. 78

Pindar, *Pythian Odes*
10.68	206

Plato, *Gorgias*
486d–e	206

Plato, *Leges*
4.704d–705a	139–40
5.747d–e	55

Pliny the Elder, *Naturalis historia*
7.57	15 n. 14
9.64	137 n. 55
9.65	135 n. 48
33.43	205

Plutarch, *Agesilaus*
17.3	177 n. 150
33.5	177 n. 149

Plutarch, *Aratus*
49.2	174 n. 141

Plutarch, *Artaxerxes*
14.3	177 n. 149
14.4	177 n. 149

… ANCIENT SOURCES INDEX … 311

Plutarch, *Cato Minor*
51.1   177 n. 149

Plutarch, *De Alexandri magni fortuna aut virtute*
328E   181

Plutarch, *De gloria Atheniensium*
347D   177 n. 149

Plutarch, *De Herodoti malignitate*
863D–E   135 n. 47

Plutarch, *Demetrius*
11.3   177 n. 150
17.5   177 n. 149

Plutarch, *Demosthenes*
22.2   177 n. 149

Plutarch, *How to Tell a Flatterer from a Friend*
49C–E   208

Plutarch, *Lucullus*
12.1–3   169

Plutarch, *Mulierum virtutes*
243B–C   102 n. 101

Plutarch, *Pericles*
29.1   174 n. 141
29.2   174 n. 141
29.3   174 n. 141

Plutarch, *Phocion*
16.6   177 n. 149
23.4.6   177 n. 149
23.4.11   177 n. 149

Plutarch, *Pompeius*
41.3   177 n. 147
66.3   177, 177 nn. 147 and 149

Plutarch, *Praecepta gerendae rei publicae*
799F   177 n. 150

Plutarch, *Questiones romanae et graecae*
270F   135 n. 48

Plutarch, *Regum et imperatorum apophthegmata*
184A   177 n. 149
188D   177 n. 149

Plutarch, *Sertorius*
11.1   177 n. 150
26.3   177 n. 149

Plutarch, *Table Talk*
646B   135 n. 48

Plutarch, *Themistocles*
30   167

Plutarch, *Vitae decem oratorum*
846E   177 n. 149

Polemo, *Physiognomy*
A11   131 n. 40
A13   131 n. 40

Polyaenus, *Strategums of War*
7.6.4   129 n. 36

Polybius, *Fragmenta*
21   168

Polybius, *The Histories*
2.51.1   174 n. 141
6.52.8–11   182
10.11.7   169
10.11.7–8   169
10.41.1–6   174

Quintilian, *Institutio oratoria*
2.15.25   141 n. 67

Seneca, *De beneficiis*		Virgil, *Aeneid*	
6.1–2	119 n. 7	4.191–194	128 n. 35
		4.215–217	128 n. 35
Seneca, *Epistulae morales*		4.262–263	128 n. 35
80.9	141 n. 67	4.266–267	128 n. 35
Strabo, *Geography*		Virgil, *Dirae*	
7.3.12	120	12	126 n. 27
13.4.4	119 n. 8		
13.4.5	119 n. 8	Virgil, *Georgics*	
13.4.7	125	1.489–490	257 n.104
13.4.12	119 n. 8		
		Virgil, *Lydia*	
Suetonius, *Divus Julius*		53	126 n. 27
32	164 n. 121		
32–33	168	Vitruvius, *On Architecture*	
		6.1.11	180
Theocritus, *Idylls*			
8.53–54	122	Xenophon, *Agesilaus*	
10.32	122	1.38	175 n. 143
Theognis		Xenophon, *Cyropaedia*	
117–124	204 n. 6	6.2.22	128 n. 34
415–418	208		
447–452	206	Xenophon, *De equitum magistro*	
		1.1–2	150 n. 89
Theophrastus, *Characteres*			
6.1–6	139	Xenophon, *Hellenica*	
		4.3.13–14	177 n. 150
Theophrastus, *De Lapidibus*		4.3.14	178
45	208		
47	208	Xenophon, *Memorabilia*	
7.46–47	205	2.1.22	57
Thucydides, *History of the Peloponnesian War*		Xenophon *Oeconomics*	
		7.22	146 n. 81
2.82.1	175 n. 143		
3.105.2	175 n. 143		
5.67.3	174 n. 141		
5.67.4	174 n. 141		
5.67.6	174 n. 141		
68.2	174 n. 141		
Valerius Flaccus, *Argonautica*			
4.369	16		

Modern Authors Index

Allen, Danielle S.   182, 186, 190, 261
Allen, O. Wesley   153 n. 94
Anderson, Janice Capel   130 n. 37
Arieti, James   135
Arterbury, Andrew E.   155, 158
Ascough, Richard S.   28–29
Astour, Michael C.   135
Aune, David E.   144, 247
Bal, Mieke   81 n. 49
Bang, Peter F.   140
Baring-Gould, Sabine   156 n. 99
Bauman, Richard A.   119 n. 7
Berenson, Jennifer K.   165
Bitzer, Lloyd F.   35, 277 n. 6
Bizzell, Patricia   37
Black, Robert Allen   2
Bloomquist, L. Gregory   6, 38–40, 44, 50, 52–54, 59–61, 63, 115, 163–64, 166–67, 173, 180–81, 188–89, 212, 260, 264 n. 120, 279
Bonz, Marianne Palmer   247
Born, Wolfgang   118, 137
Bradley, Mark   135 n. 48
Brooten, Bernadette J.   151 n. 92
Brown, John Pairman   207
Bruce, F. F.   100 n. 94, 107, 120 n. 9
Burke, Kenneth   41–42, 48–49
Burkert, Walter   141 n. 66
Burnett, Anne Pippin   154
Calvin, John   13–15, 95
Campbell, William Sanger   9 n. 1, 82 n. 53
Carey, Greg   275 n. 3
Caylus, Anne Claude Philippe   205 n. 8
Cohen, Shaye J. D.   172 n. 138

Crook, Zeba A.   229, 231
Culy, Martin M.   68 n. 9, 75 n. 38, 83 n. 58, 98 n. 87, 99 n. 88
D'Ambra, Eve   142–43
De Vries, Keith   128
Dover, Kenneth J.   185 n. 170
DuBois, Page   209, 261
Evans, Elizabeth C.   53, 56–58, 180
Fauconnier, Gilles   38, 60–62, 202–4, 233, 248
Fitzmyer, Joseph A.   65, 73 n. 27, 93 n. 71, 157 n. 102, 187–88, 240 n. 75
Gasque, W. Ward   10
Gaventa, Beverly Roberts   95
Geertz, Clifford   140
Géradon, Bernard de   44
Glancy, Jennifer A.   262
Gleason, Maud W.   56–57, 186 nn. 171–72, 232, 263
Graf, Fritz   145 n. 78, 171 n. 136
Grant, Robert M.   119 n. 8
Grant-Davie, Keith   35
Grotius, Hugo   14–17, 30, 63, 125 n. 24
Gruca-Macaulay, Alexandra   6, 9, 44, 277
Haenchen, Ernst   19–21, 65 n. 3, 97
Hamlyn, D. W.   47 n. 34
Hanson, Kenneth   243
Harrill, Albert J.   141
Hellerman, Joseph H.   167
Hemer, Colin J.   119
Herzberg, Bruce   37
Hester, J. David   6, 237
Hester, James D.   6, 39
Hillier, Richard   2

Horsley, G. H. R.   26–27, 120, 136
Hubbard, Margaret   126 n. 26
Isaac, Benjamin   54–56, 128, 130 n. 37, 181
Jacquier, Eugène   18–19
Johnson, Luke Timothy   3, 27
Kennedy, George A.   65–66, 76, 83 n. 59
Kratz, Reinhard   193 n. 192
Kurke, Leslie   124, 127, 141, 143 n. 73, 204 n. 6
Lausberg, Heinrich   70, 110 n. 113, 122
Lendon, J. E.   163, 178, 254
Levine, Lee I.   151 n. 92
Longenecker, Bruce W.   79
MacDonald, Dennis R.   5
Malina, Bruce J.   44–45, 56–58, 65 n. 3, 100, 105–6, 131 n. 39, 141, 144–45, 158, 159 n. 108, 187, 229, 231 n. 57, 233–34, 257
Marshall, Anthony J.   189 n. 181
Martin, Clarice J.   22
Mason, Hugh J.   235 n. 70
Matson, David Lertis   1–2, 30
Matthews, Shelly   1, 23–24, 120
McKay, Heather A.   148
Meeks, Wayne A.   1
Menirav, Joseph   140–41
Metzger, Bruce M.   93 n. 73, 107 n. 109
Meyer, Heinrich August Wilhelm   17–18
Miller, Carolyn R.   38–39
Miller, John B. Faulkenberry   9 n. 1, 94 n. 75, 164 n. 121
Moore, Stephen D.   130 n. 37
Morris, Ian   127
Moxnes, Halvor   1
Le Moyne, Pierre   16
Muilenburg, James   4, 65
Nestle, Wilhelm   193 n. 192
Neyrey, Jerome H.   56–57, 134, 138, 149, 187, 231 n. 57, 233–34, 257
Nisbet, Robin G. M.   126 n. 26
Noegel, Scott   179
O'Day, Gail R.   1, 21–22
Oakman, Douglas E.   243 nn.80–81
Olbrechts-Tyteca, Lucie   35–37, 43, 46–49, 51, 66, 71, 121 n. 17, 122, 197 n. 201, 199 n.203, 222–23, 229–30, 235
O'Toole, Robert T.   1
Otto, Walter F.   110 n. 113, 193 n. 194
Parker, Robert   149 n. 87
Parsons, Mikeal C.   65 n. 3, 68 n. 9, 75 n. 38, 78, 83 n. 58, 98 n. 87, 99 nn. 88, 90, 236–37, 247 n. 85, 261
Perelman, Chaïm   35–37, 43, 46–49, 51, 66, 71, 121 n. 17, 122, 197 n. 201, 199 n.203, 223 n. 40, 229–30, 235
Perrin, Bernadotte   102, 167
Perry, B. E.   184
Perry, Peter S.   7
Pervo, Richard I.   193 n. 192
Pilch, John J.   65 n. 3, 100 n. 91, 144–45, 158, 204 n. 7
Portefaix, Lilian   137
Quincey, J. H.   54
Rapske, Brian   182, 190–91
Rauh, Nicholas   141
Reimer, Ivoni Richter   15–16, 22–23, 261 n. 113
Reinhold, Meyer   26 n. 50, 118, 132
Renan, Ernest   20 n. 28
Reventlow, Henning Graf   14–15
Robbins, Vernon K.   6 n. 18, 33–36, 40–44, 48–49, 52, 62, 66 n. 5, 71–72, 82 n. 53, 115–16, 144, 210
Rosenfeld, Ben-Zion   140–41, 143, 160
Rubinelli, Sara   116
Sangster, Margaret E.   264 n. 121
Schurman, Anna Maria van   16
Seaford, Richard   192
Skinner, Matthew L.   191
Spawforth, Antony   131
Spencer, F. Scott   137
Staley, Jeffrey L.   1, 5 n. 14, 240
Sterck-Degueldre, Jean-Pierre   19 n. 25, 28, 136, 156 n. 99
Struck, Peter   212
Talbert, Charles H.   65 n. 3
Tannehill, Robert C.   3–4, 65 n. 3, 86
Turner, Mark   38, 60–62, 202–4, 233, 248

Van Stempvoort, Pieter A.   134
Wainwright, Elaine M.   275
Wallace, Daniel B.   69 n. 12, 83, 96, 99 n. 88, 265
Weaver, John B.   9 n. 1, 154, 193 nn. 192–193, n. 195
Weinreich, Otto   193 n. 192
Wikenhauser, Alfred   164 n. 121
Witherington, Ben, III   24–28, 145 n. 78
Zerubavel, Eviatar   62–63

Subject Index

Alexander the Great. *See* Macedonian man
antonomasia. *See* Lydia, name of
apocalyptic discourse, 146–47, 149, 164, 210, 239 n. 74, 252, 260 n. 108, 266–67, 277–80
Apollo. *See* mantics: Delphi and Apollo; mantics: Python and Apollo
argumentation. *See also* rhetoric; socio-rhetorical interpretation; *synkrisis*; *topos*
   deductive, 37, 46, 49–51
   enthymeme, 46
   inductive, 37, 46–50, 112, 222–23, 229
   qualitative. *See* inductive
   quantitative. *See* deductive
   rhetography, 46, 49–51, 66, 202
   rhetology, 46, 49–51
   rhetorical figure. *See* rhetoric
body-zone model. *See* sensory-aesthetic texture: definitions of
βοηθέω *boētheō*. *See* military discourse: calls for help and alliance
cognitive linguistics. *See* emergent structure; human-scale compression; *topos*: *topoi* and conceptual blending; *topos*: *topoi* and frames
collectivist personality, definition of, 56
Colonia Julia Augusta Philippensis. *See* Philippi
conceptual blending. *See topos*: *topoi* and conceptual blending
counterfactual. *See* rhetoric: use of the counterfactual in
Dionysus. *See* Euripides, *Bacchae*

disanalogy, 102, 203–4. *See also synkrisis*
dream-visions. *See* military discourse: dream-visions in
emergent structure, 62, 202, 211, 214, 216, 229, 278–79
emotion-fused thought. *See* sensory-aesthetic texture, definitions of: emotion-fused thought
enthymeme. *See* argumentation: enthymeme
εὐαγγέλιον, *euaggelion*. *See* military discourse: εὐαγγέλιον, *euaggelion*, role of
Euripides, *Bacchae*, 24, 52, 121 n. 14, 184, 193–94, 247 n. 85
exigence. *See* rhetoric: rhetorical situation
faith/fidelity, 165, 203, 209–10, 215, 229, 231 n. 57, 243 n. 81, 244–45, 266, 270, 276
   Lydia and, 12 n.7, 73, 79, 84, 96–99, 103, 108, 111–14, 156–57, 162, 227–29, 231, 233, 238–39, 259, 261, 264–65, 268–73
   Macedonian man and, 215, 216, 263, 266, 270
   Paul and Silas and, 109, 112, 203, 250–52, 259, 261–65, 272
   Philippian jailer and, 73, 88, 108–9, 267
frames in conceptual blending. *See* topos: topoi and frames
God-fearer. *See* worshiper of God
heart, 11, 44, 204–6, 215, 236–37, 242–44, 246, 248, 250, 253–55, 257–58, 265, 269–70, 278–79. *See also* faith/fidelity: Lydia and

heart (cont.)
  biblical, definition of, 35 n. 9, 225 n. 43
  emotion-fused thought and. See sensory-aesthetic texture: emotion-fused thought
  Mary, mother of Jesus and, 279–80
  opening of Lydia's heart by God, 10 n. 4, 14, 16–17, 33, 79, 84, 89, 91, 95–97, 112, 154–55, 221, 223–25, 227–28, 237–40, 261, 267, 271, 273, 279–80
historiography. See military discourse: historiography and
honor, 12, 19, 30, 57–58, 117, 131 n. 39, 180, 186–88, 242, 243 n. 80, 250, 262, 264, 266–67, 276, 279. See also hospitality: honor and
  hubris and, 103, 173, 185, 198
  shame and, 57–58, 131, 139, 142–43, 159–60, 162, 198, 226 n. 46, 250, 266–67
hospitality, 230, 232, 261 n. 113, 275–76
  honor and, 157–62, 197–98, 275–76
  Lydia the Hostess. See Lydia of Thyatira, commentary on
  piety and, 153–55
  women as hosts, 158–59, 162, 267
human-scale compression, 233, 246, 251–52, 266–67, 278. See also physiognomy
hypocrisy, 204–5, 208, 226. See also synkrisis: Lydian touchstone and
ideological texture. See rhetoric: rhetorical force
inclusio. See rhetoric: inclusio and
κύριος, kyrios, 68, 70, 73, 88, 90, 104, 106, 108–9, 163, 165, 225, 228, 234, 241, 243–44, 250–51, 260, 267–268. See also faith/fidelity; heart: opening of Lydia's heart by God
luxury. See Lydians, physiognomic stereotypes of: luxury and; purple: color symbolism of
Lydia, name of, 2, 6, 15, 18–21, 24–25, 27, 29, 31, 33, 63, 120, 126 n. 26, 217, 269. See also Lydians, physiognomic stereotypes of
  antonomasia and, 24, 121–22
  Lydian ethnicity and, 6, 15, 17–18, 25, 64, 116, 119–22, 269
  Lydias named in Greco-Roman literature, 18, 126–127, 131
Lydia of Thyatira. See also faith/fidelity: Lydia and; heart: opening of Lydia's heart by God; Lydia of Thyatira, commentary on; Lydia of Thyatira, omission of in commentary; Lydians, physiognomic stereotypes of; purpleseller
  as a textile worker, 15–17, 19, 21–22, 26–27, 29–30, 63, 118, 136–38
  wealth and, 1, 19–24, 27–31, 33, 118–19, 132, 138, 263, 273. See also Lydian kingdom: gold and, Lydians physiognomic stereotypes of: luxury and
Lydia of Thyatira, commentary on
  feminist, 21–24
  modern historical-critical, 17–21
  patristic, 10–13
  recent interpretations, 1–2, 24–30
  Reformation, 13–17
  topos of courtesan in, 7, 11–12, 18–19, 25, 27
Lydia of Thyatira, omission of in commentary, 2, 12–13, 13 n. 9, 219–21
Lydian kingdom
  geography of, 119 n. 8, 120–21
  gold and, 122–24, 129, 184 n. 169, 203, 205.
Lydians, physiognomic stereotypes of
  effeminacy and, 52, 128, 129–30, 131, 132, 143, 182, 193, 197
  innkeeping and, 160–61
  luxury and, 52, 123, 126–29, 130 n. 38, 131–32, 223–24, 161, 182, 197, 223
  "Lydian disease," 127–28, 130–31, 133, 161, 181, 187–88, 197, 203, 224–25, 239, 255, 272, 278

retail trade and, 124, 131, 138, 142 n. 71, 143–44
women and, 123–25, 127, 132, 161, 197, 228, 239, 267. *See also* Lydia, name of: Lydias named in Greco-Roman literature
Macedonian man, 13, 68–69, 72, 75–76, 78, 80–82, 84–85, 90–97, 99, 101, 110, 112–13, 117, 122 n. 20, 162, 166, 173–74, 176, 179–80, 198, 203, 211–16, 219–23, 225–27, 234–35, 237, 238 n. 73, 246, 249, 251–52, 254, 258, 260, 263, 265–66, 270–72, 277–78. *See also* faith/fidelity: Macedonian man and; military discourse: calls for help and alliance
Alexander the Great, 52, 150, 164 n. 121, 165–66, 168, 175–76, 181, 212, 223, 230, 278
mammon, 43, 46, 239, 243–45, 263, 274
mantics, 182–85
Delphi and Apollo, 146, 183–84, 234, 236
Python and Apollo, 183, 245
Python spirit slave owners/woman, 3, 5 n. 14, 13, 16, 18, 69 n. 11, 70, 74–78, 85–88, 90–92, 97–103, 105–7, 109–10, 112–13, 115, 117, 179–80, 182–83, 185–88, 198, 219–20, 235–36, 239–46, 248, 253, 255–56, 258–59, 261, 264, 272, 278
Mary, mother of Jesus. *See* heart: Mary, mother of Jesus and; purple: Mary, mother of Jesus and
merchants in antiquity. *See also* Lydians, physiognomic stereotypes of: retail trade and; purple-seller
bazaar economy, 140–41
physiognomic stereotypes of, 136–44, 206, 267
women as, 142–43
military discourse
calls for help and alliance, 162, 169–79, 198, 201–3, 211–17, 222–23, 226, 230, 246, 252, 254, 258, 263, 266, 270–72, 278
dream-visions in, 92–94, 167–73, 198, 211–15
εὐαγγέλιον, *euaggelion*, role of, 167, 169, 171–74, 177–79, 198, 202, 211, 214–15, 223, 225–26, 239–41, 263, 271, 275, 278
historiography and, 163, 165, 179, 277
Troas in, 165, 169, 198
warrior God, 163, 168–73, 211, 214–15, 246, 249, 252, 266
women and, 130 n. 37, 222, 238. *See also* Lydians, physiognomic stereotypes of: effeminacy and; Lydians, physiognomic stereotypes of: "Lydian disease"
παραβιάζομαι, *parabiazomai*, 17–18, 78, 84, 91, 155–57, 159, 231
παρακαλέω, *parakaleō* progression, 41, 69, 72–73, 75, 77–80, 83 n. 55, 85, 91, 94, 96, 110–11, 113, 117, 155, 156 n. 99, 170, 173–74, 176, 179, 202–3, 210–11, 214–16, 237, 239, 241, 246–47, 249, 251–52, 254–55, 258–59, 263, 265–66, 270. *See also* military discourse: calls for help and alliance
Philippi, 83, 145, 235, 256–257
physiognomy
cultural-social logic and, 7, 55–58, 98, 225, 228, 233–36, 261–62, 269–70, 273, 277
definition of, 53–54
ethnic stereotypes and, 54–56, 122, 189 n. 182, 236–37. *See also* Lydians, physiognomic stereotypes of; Romans, physiognomic stereotypes of
occupational stereotypes and, 54, 138. *See also* merchants in antiquity: physiognomic stereotypes of; prison: jailer, physiognomic stereotypes of
place of prayer, 70, 74–75, 77, 144

place of prayer (cont.)
  as space of territorial conflict, 146–49, 216
  synagogue and, 95, 144–45, 148, 152, 217
  women in, 14, 146, 151–52, 266–67
πορνεύω, *porneuō*. *See* Lydians, physiognomic stereotypes of: retail trade and; Lydians, physiognomic stereotypes of: women and
πορφυρόπωλις, *porphyropōlis*. *See* purple-seller
prison
  as space of testing, 194–98, 248–52, 261, 264
  conditions in, 188–92, 197–98, 248
  jailer, physiognomic stereotypes of, 189–91. *See also* faith/ fidelity: Philippian jailer and
  lictors, role of, 109, 189 n. 181, 248, 252
  prison escape scenes, 117, 192–96, 247, 251
  role of crowds in penal system, 182
progymnasmata. *See* rhetoric: *progymnasmata*
προσευχή, *proseuchē*. *See* place of prayer
purple
  color symbolism of
    as an element of deception, 135–36
    elite status of, 20–21, 30, 118, 132–34, 184 n. 169
    luxuria and element of corruption, 128, 130 n. 38, 132–33, 135, 152, 161, 209 n. 16, 219, 239, 267
  dye production of, 22, 26 n. 50, 118 n. 5
  Mary, mother of Jesus and, 134
purple-seller, 3, 10–12, 17, 25, 30, 63, 77, 84, 100, 112, 116, 118, 132, 137–38, 142, 144, 161–62, 197–98, 201, 218–19, 223–24, 227–28, 232, 245–46, 259, 264, 268–69, 272, 274. *See also* merchants in antiquity: physiognomic stereotypes of; purple: color symbolism of
purposeful action. *See* sensory-aesthetic texture, definitions of: purposeful action
Python. *See* mantics: Python and Apollo; mantics: Python spirit slave owners/ woman
rhetography. *See* argumentation
rhetology. *See* argumentation
rhetoric, 35–37. *See also* argumentation; sociorhetorical interpretation; *synkrisis*; *topos*
  communicative culture and, 4, 33–37
  inclusio and, 3–4, 124, 260, 270–72, 278. *See also* topos: topoi and frames
  presence, role of, 36–37, 43, 45, 71, 80
  progymnasmata and, 34–35, 102
  rhetorical figure, 5, 36, 80, 269, 276, 279
  rhetorical force, 7, 59–60, 164, 197, 204, 227, 270. *See also* emergent structure
  rhetorical situation, 35, 277
  traductio, 70
  use of the counterfactual in, 271, 278
rhetorical force. *See* rhetoric: rhetorical force
Romans, physiognomic stereotypes of, 52, 115, 147 n. 84, 180–82, 198, 253–58
sacred elements, rhetorical role of, 70, 113, 218–19, 239. *See also* κύριος, *kyrios*; place of prayer; θεός, *theos*
Sardis. *See* Lydian kingdom: geography of
self-expressive speech. *See* sensory-aesthetic texture, definitions of: self-expressive speech
sensory-aesthetic texture, definitions of
  body-zone model, 44–45
  emotion-fused thought, 44, 213–14
  purposeful action, 45
  self-expressive speech, 44–45
shame. *See* honor.

SUBJECT INDEX

sociorhetorical interpretation. *See also* argumentation; sensory-aesthetic texture, definitions of; *topos*
   background to, 33–34, 115–16
   features of, 5, 6 n. 18, 38–40, 62–63, 67
      cultural texture, 52
      historical intertexture 52
      logical progression, 48–49
      narrational texture, 43, 67
      oral-scribal texture, 52
      qualitative progression, 41–42
      repetitive and progressive terms, 40–41, 67–68, 71–72
      rhetorical unit, 42–43, 65–67, 76
      sacred texture, 52–53
      social texture, 52–53
stereotypes. *See* physiognomy
συμβιβάζω, *sumbibazō*, 70, 75, 213–14
synagogue. *See* place of prayer
synkrisis, 100, 102–3, 112–13, 202–3, 210
   Lydian touchstone and, 116, 202–10, 239–40, 246, 258–59, 261, 268, 270–72, 277–80
theophonic elements, absence of in Acts 16, 81, 87, 93, 94 n. 75, 104, 107, 173, 197, 211–14, 223, 235, 247–49, 267
θεός, *theos*, 70, 145, 149, 228. *See also* heart: opening of Lydia's heart by God; κύριος, *kyrios*
   as a monotheistic term, 145–146
   Most High God, 85, 98–99, 105–6, 185, 187, 241, 244
Thyatira. *See* Lydian kingdom: geography of
topos. *See also* argumentation; Lydia, name of: *antonomasia*; sociorhetorical interpretation
   definition of, 39–40
   rhetoric and, 6, 7, 37–41, 50 n. 43, 53, 59–63, 66, 115–17, 134, 154, 161–62, 197–98, 201, 233, 267
   topoi and conceptual blending, 60–62
   topoi and frames, 4, 61, 202
Troas. *See* military discourse: Troas in

we-group in Acts 16, 68, 81–85, 90–91, 93–95, 97–100, 112–13, 152–53, 155, 161, 163, 165, 167, 172, 177, 179, 188, 198, 203–4, 211–17, 220–21, 223, 225–27, 231–32, 234, 236, 238 n. 73, 239–42, 244–46, 254, 264, 270–71
we-passages in Acts, 68, 81 n. 52, 82 n. 53
women
   as hosts. *See* hospitality: women as hosts
   as merchants. *See* merchants in antiquity: women as
   in military discourse. *See* military discourse: women and
   in synagogues. *See* place of prayer: women in
   Lydian women. *See* Lydians, physiognomic stereotypes of: woman and
worshiper of God, 58, 117, 144–46, 151, 161, 204, 216–18, 227–32, 238–39, 241, 245, 254, 259, 268, 270, 273, 278

www.ingramcontent.com/pod-product-compliance
Lightning Source LLC
Chambersburg PA
CBHW021118300426
44113CB00006B/191